Good Housekeeping

OCTOBER 1932 — ONE SHILLING NETT

JESSIE WILLCOX SMITH

THE TECHNIQUE OF MARRIAGE
A New Series by Mary Borden

Martin Armstrong ~ Dame Ethel Smyth ~ Virginia Woolf
A.S.M. Hutchinson ~ Lady Violet Bonham Carter

Good Housekeeping

SEPTEMBER 1933
ONE SHILLING
NETT

MODERN GIRLS WANT TO WORK
by
Beatrice Kean Seymour

Pearl S. Buck
Lorna Rea
Clemence Dane
Lady Violet
Bonham Carter
Doris Peel

The Institute's Ninth Birthday

Good Housekeeping

MARCH 1934
ONE SHILLING NETT

Special Spring Household Number

NEW NOVEL by O. DOUGLAS

Joan Sutherland ~ Oliver Baldwin ~ Elizabeth Sprigge ~ Hugh de Selincourt

Good Housekeeping
Nash's Pall Mall Magazine

APRIL 1938
ONE SHILLING

EASTER FICTION NUMBER
★ *New Serial by* ALEC WAUGH

James Hilton • Beverley Nichols • Mary Roberts Rinehart
SPRING FASHION SUPPLEMENT IN COLOUR

THINGS MY MOTHER SHOULD HAVE TOLD ME

The Best of Good Housekeeping
1922-1940

A Prayer *for*
Womankind

By Grace
Noll Crowell

Illustrated   by   Marshall   Frantz

God, give each true good woman
Her own small house to keep—
No heart should ache with longing—
No hurt should go too deep—
Grant her age-old desire:
A house to love and sweep.

Give her a man beside her—
A kind man—and a true—
And let them work together
And love—a lifetime through,
And let her mother children
As gentle women do.

Give her a shelf for dishes,
And a shining box for bread,
A white cloth for her table,
And a white spread for her bed,
A shaded lamp at nightfall,
And a row of books much read.

God, let her work with laughter,
And let her rest with sleep—
No life can truly offer
A peace more sure and deep—
God, give each true good woman
Her own small house to keep.

THINGS MY MOTHER SHOULD HAVE TOLD ME

The Best of Good Housekeeping
1922-1940

COMPILED BY

BRIAN BRAITHWAITE

NOËLLE WALSH

EBURY PRESS
LONDON

First published by Ebury Press
an imprint of the Random Century Group
Random Century House
20 Vauxhall Bridge Road
London SW1V 2SA

British Library Cataloguing in Publication Data
Things my mother should have told me.
   I. Great Britain.   Household management, history
   I. Braithwaite, Brian   II. Walsh, Noelle   III. Series
   640.941

ISBN 0-85223-984-X

Printed and bound in Great Britain by Butler & Tanner Ltd.,
Frome and London

CONTENTS

6 Foreword

FOREWORD

EDITORIAL VIEWPOINT

When I was growing up, my mother used a top-loader washing machine which had to be laboriously filled from the kitchen taps and the clothes squeezed through the wringer before hanging out to dry. Doing my maths homework, I would turn to my mother for help with the geometry, only to be told she's never heard of Pythagoras's theory. I soon discovered there were lots of things my mother couldn't tell me. It wasn't long before I started questioning the things she *did* tell me. Telling me how to boost a dying fire back into life wasn't going to be of much use to me, I decided, since I would have central heating. Nor did I want to know how to hang clothes on the line without leaving a crease mark from the peg – I would have a tumble dryer. How to keep my tea towels white? Not when I'd just heard about these new wonders call dish washers.

Some time later when I started my own family, I'd wished I'd paid more attention to the things my mother told me. My world had changed and so had the world outside. With a new family, I no longer had the money to pay someone else to do the things I should have been able to do had I listened to my mother. Meanwhile, the world had gone green and I discovered that the things my mother was now telling me had always been green. A lifelong hater of waste, she'd been recycling, as had others of her generation, for decades before it became fashionable.

My respect for the ingenuity of past generations' mothers rose to even greater heights when I was compiling this book. I became engrossed in 'The Housekeeper's dictionary of facts' which were rich with household lore. The bonus was that unlike old wives tales you knew these 'nuggets of household wisdom' worked, because they'd all been tested by the Good Housekeeping Institute. Take, for example, this clever idea for preventing your glasses from steaming up when cooking in the kitchen (page 19) 'rub your glasses with soap and then polish them: you will find that the moisture does not rest on them!' There's a 'green' tip from 1924: 'Uses for old rubber hot water bottles' – 'If one is placed next to the cover of the underside of a small cushion, the latter can be used safely for kneeling on, even in damp weather' (page 29). They even found a use for old issues of Good Housekeeping! 'Keep one on hand in the kitchen for use under saucepans, roasting tins etc. It will make an excellent resting-pad and will often save cleaning. A leaf can always be torn off when the top becomes soiled.'

As well as the hundreds of invaluable household tips which this book contains, the features also give an insight into life for the housewife of the twenties and thirties. Some were fortunate enough to have servants and their problem was one of directing and organising their staff. For the majority, though, the servant days were over and the beginning of the tradition of women doing the housework began. As Rose Macaulay wrote in 1923 'Men have proved themselves far cleverer than women in shelving this onerous duty [housework]. A tradition has now too long been established that cooking and cleaning are woman's work. As these occupations are among the most tiresome which humanity has to endure, this tradition is very unfortunate for women!' Her remedy is radical but I'm sure effective

though I doubt whether many had the courage to take it up. 'The only solution of this problem, which I can suggest – and I almost hesitate to do so in these pages – is, Do not keep house. Let the house or flat, go unkept. Let it go to the devil and see what happens when it has gone there. At the worst, a house unkept cannot be so distressing as a life unlived.'

This book may be a piece of history, reflecting a way of life long past and gone. But the advice and information contained in the following pages are as up-to-date and useful today as they were 60 years ago. Read it – and you too may have something useful to pass on to your children.

NOËLLE WALSH

ADVERTISING VIEWPOINT

The main purpose of this book is to present all those fascinating pages of household advice and information taken from Good Housekeeping between 1922 and 1940. I thought it would be interesting to track those years with advertisements which would reflect the social and domestic life of the times including Mother's own lifestyle in and out of the home.

Hence it is not without interest to study her armoury of corsetry from Bon Ton and other fashions in the 1920's. And any Mother would have shown proper gratitude to be presented with her Hoover or Electrolux (even as a surprise Christmas present) and probably overjoyed by Miss Blick's miracles of dish and clothes washing on page 48. By 1936 she was even being offered a Mechanical Housemaid, a machine of breathtaking versatility, (page 162).

Motor cars came into Mother's life with the Ford ladies' saloon and later with a patronising pat on the head with synchromesh gears she was inspired to follow the stirring example of Diana Strickland, nothing less than a 1928 Indiana Jones, (page 82).

Mother's complexion and fragrance were never neglected by Good Housekeeping's advertisers, whether Poudre Nilde's Deauville raffishness or the heady promises of Beau Geste, the perfume of gay adventure with the intoxication of dangerous moments. And I doubt if Pompeian's claims would receive the seal of approval from today's Advertising Standard's Authority. And Mother donned her Yardley lavender (page 150) when Uncle came to town and had herself a ball… if indeed it really was an avuncular trip!

And Mother danced through the years and spun round the ballroom in 1925 with the confidence of 4711 Eau de Cologne, no less confident than fifteen years later when Evening in Paris found her in the arms of that dashing pilot officer. She might have slipped into Liberty's in 1938 for that beautiful evening gown in black net and taffeta which would have knocked her back (or Father) a cool 9½ guineas.

I like the advertisement on page 174 showing Mother in 1938 hustling her two teenagers through their scholarship cramming, stuffed as they were with Shredded Wheat. It is a sobering thought that if they survived grammar school, and indeed the war, those two earnest students would be old-age pensioners today.

It's always a treat to wallow in nostalgia. It is also good to see that Good Housekeeping's advertisers half a century ago were busy keeping Mother up to date in all things domestic, personal and social.

BRIAN BRAITHWAITE

THE
20's

THE SEVEN AGES OF WOMAN

Fifth Age
WOMANHOOD
The Third Partner

Jean Brownrigg occupied the undistinguished middle position in a somewhat large family, saddled with a country home and very little to keep it up with. The eldest sister managed most things available, including her harassed father and docile mother, and the two youngest sisters, being pretty and jolly, annexed any young men who ventured within the range of their violet-blue eyes. Jean acted as maid-of-all-work to the former and as chaperone to the latter.

Then came the War, and it brought Jean Opportunity as well as Sorrow. When a shattered and blood-stained world sat down to contemplate its wounds, Jean felt that to return to the former restricted monotonous existence was impossible, so she and a W.A.A.C. pal, having extracted the irreducible minimum of capital out of the least disapproving of their relatives and friends, decided to open a little restaurant in London. The minimum was so very irreducible that their choice of premises proved limited and discouraging, but eventually they found a basement which to the eye of faith had possibilities, and set to work to develop them. They were both practical, energetic, sensible girls, and the chorus of baleful prophecies of disaster and ruin which assailed them spurred them to endeavour as no amount of complacent encouragement could have done.

Fortunately, they had a stroke of luck straight away, for they found a partner who halved not only the work but the expenses ; who was cheerful, obedient, adaptable, and trustworthy ; who possessed all the qualifications of an ideal helper without any corresponding drawbacks. With the help of this partner, whom they called Mary Ann . . . . . .

But if you will visit the British Empire Gas Exhibit at Wembley and ask for the booklet, "The Seven Ages of Woman," you will see how this "Third Partner" did solve the problem.
E.M.W.

> This is the fifth of a series of articles appearing in this magazine, describing the uses of GAS throughout a woman's life. Living Pictures illustrating these sketches are one of the many attractive and interesting features of the British Empire Gas Exhibit in the centre of the Palace of Industry at Wembley.

THE BRITISH COMMERCIAL GAS ASSOCIATION
30 Grosvenor Gardens, Victoria, S.W.1

Telephone : VICTORIA 6700

Telegrams : GASUPREME, SOWEST, LONDON

The Housekeeper's Dictionary *of* Facts

Some Nuggets of Household Wisdom

Loose Covers and Blankets

Now is the time to make loose covers for upholstered furniture. It is surprising how much more comfort there is in the home that is dressed for summer. Smooth, cool, crisp furniture covers and thinner curtains are worth thought and labour in the spring, for they spell comfort in the summer. It is now the time to have the blankets washed and to store those not needed for summer use in cedar-chest, store-room, or bag. Reserve the thinnest for use during the summer months.

Bluing

We should always include those tints that now take the place of bluing for many coloured fabrics. The first housekeeper who discovered that blue tint added to the water would make her clothes a clearer white handed down the custom ; but to-day we use, in addition, many cold-water dyes, the pinks for flesh tones, blue for white, greys for grey, etc. Lingerie made in light coloured silks is vastly improved in appearance by occasional re-tinting with cold-water dyes.

Borax

This glistening white, crystalline salt is a mild alkali. In districts where hard water is common a jar of it placed in the bathroom will enable one to wash the hands in softer water.

Spring

Is the season for inspection and renewal. Scrutinise the house inside and out. Start a notebook and jot down as they occur to you all repairs, etc., needed. See the mowing-machine is in order, overhaul the gardening tools, and examine the outside safe and make sure its perforated zinc is sound, leaving no cracks or loophole to make easy the entrance of the objectionable and destructive fly.

A Novel Garnish

An attractive garnish for cold meats or salads may be made by rolling tightly several large lettuce leaves and keeping them in a cool place until needed. When ready to serve, cut the roll into half-inch pieces, and pretty, light green rosettes will be the result. These add greatly to the appearance of the dish.

Marketing

Lamb is in high favour this month, although it is less economical and nutritious than mature meat. Joints off small animals are best, and the flesh should be firm, clear, and of a delicate pinky tint, with plenty of firm white fat free from any yellowish shade. The kidney and its surrounding fat must be free from taint, discolouration, and flabbiness. If a forequarter is chosen, note that the neck veins are of a blue, not greenish tint—the latter denotes staleness. Like all young meat, lamb does not keep well, as it speedily sours ; also it needs thorough cooking, for under-cooked lamb is neither nice nor wholesome.

Burner

This needs no definition. Gas-bills and cookery are both affected by the burner deficiency of your gas-range or your oil-stove. Be sure that the burner is adjusted to produce a clear blue flame in the gas-stove. Be sure that oil-burners have daily care. It takes but a moment. First: don't cut the wicks ; instead wrap a piece of tissue paper about the forefinger and press down the burned carbon, making an even, smooth, compact wick surface. Brush off loose particles from wicks with a stiff lamp-brush to make them last a long time.

Salmon

Salmon is now in prime condition, and, if the markets are watched, can often be bought at reasonably low prices. The middle cut is the most expensive, the head and shoulders being the least costly. The latter part contains far more flesh than many imagine, and is well worth buying. Against the cost per lb. of this fish must be taken into account its high food-value, also that its firm consistency makes a small helping of it quite sufficient. Choose fish with small heads and tails in comparison to their size, large thick shoulders, silvery scales, and flesh of a rich, bright, yellowish red, with the flakes mingled with creamy-looking streaks.

Carbonate of Soda

Is used instead of the ordinary washing soda, which is a crude commercial form of the former. It is used for cooking purposes ; to soften water ; to counteract the harmful effects of acids ; to remove stains, as well as for many medicinal purposes.

Common Salt (sodium chloride)

Is of immense value in the household. In the laundry it prevents the dye in coloured articles from running or dissolving ; it removes freshly made fruit-stains ; cleanses handkerchiefs ; and, mixed with vinegar, or other acid, is a good scourer for copper and sink. It is essential in the kitchen and for health and remedial purposes.

Carbolic Acid

Is a valuable disinfectant, but a dangerous poison. Keep it always in a coloured bottle bearing a " poison " label and under lock and key.

Chemicals

Of various kinds remove stains, but weaken fabrics, so always first try less drastic methods, such as the use of sour milk, lemon and borax, or salt, and soaking in boiled milk or soft water.

Dishes

Can be washed or rinsed quickly and effectively, if a two and a half foot piece of garden rubber hose with a *spray* nozzle is used by screwing it on to the hot, or cold, tap at the sink. The force of the spray is far greater than the ordinary flow, and the water can easily be directed to specially flush any particular corners or crevices.

Easter Trees

Form a pretty decoration for the Easter table, as well as a novel and pleasing way of distributing the time-honoured egg. They are just tiny fir-trees hung with bright-coloured eggs, wee Easter hares and yellow, fluffy baby chicks.

Fuller's Earth

A greyish coloured clay, usually sold in powder form. Very useful for removing greasy dirt and stains when dry-cleaning materials, or from wood, etc. Specially refined, it makes safe and valuable dusting powder for toilet purposes.

Hot-water Bottles

Made of rubber are worth keeping even when old. They make excellent lining for fancy sponge-bags, or travelling-cases for nail- and tooth-brushes. The rubber is covered with coloured linen, or other pretty bits from the scrap-bag. Another use is to fashion them into finger-stalls to slip on when paring fruit and vegetables.

The Housekeeper's Dictionary *of* Facts

Things Worth Remembering

Asbestos Paper.—This can be a great help in baking. Food in the oven can be kept from browning too much by putting one or two sheets of asbestos paper over it, and there is no danger of it burning as ordinary paper does. If the bottom of the oven is too hot, a piece of asbestos paper can be slipped under the baking tin. Asbestos mats are also useful; they can be slipped under a saucepan on the top of the stove to reduce heat and prevent the contents burning.

An Easy Way to Clean Windows.—Rub them well with a soft rag or a pad of paper dipped in a little paraffin; then polish with a dry duster or chamois cloth. The windows will be beautifully clean, and the slight smell which clings to the glass helps to keep off the flies.

Instead of Toast.—Have you ever tried fried croûtons in place of toast when serving scrambled eggs or Welsh rabbit? Cut the bread in small dice, and fry or toast in the oven until brown and crisp. Croûtons give just the proper crunchy background for the other mixture, and they are the means of using up small pieces of dry bread.

To Clean Light Cloth Garments.—Fig dust is excellent if the material is only soiled on the surface. This is like meal in appearance, and can be bought at any corn-chandler's or household stores. Brush the garment first to remove all dust; then lay it on a sheet, sprinkle it with fig dust and rub it well in with the fingers. Wrap up in the sheet and let it remain some hours. Then brush off with a soft, clean brush and shake out.

To Cement Broken China.—Ornaments or other articles which do not require frequent washing, can often be mended very successfully with cement. The sooner this can be done after the breakage the better, before the edges get rubbed or further chipped. Prepare the cement by mixing plaster of Paris into a smooth, creamy paste with slightly beaten white of egg. Heat the broken pieces of china in the oven, making them as hot as the hand can bear. Apply the cement thinly to the two surfaces to be joined, press together, and rub off any surplus cement. Prop up the pieces to keep them in position, or apply an india-rubber band or binder until the cement is dry. Do not attempt to join too many pieces at once; rather join the fragments in pairs, and when dry fix them together.

Lacquered Brass should be rubbed frequently with a soft duster or chamois leather and, when necessary, washed with a good soap and water. Neither soda nor brass polish should be employed; the lacquer is only a kind of varnish and is easily removed with any strong treatment.

To Remove White Stains from Mahogany.—A little spirit of camphor is an excellent thing to use. Apply it very lightly with a clean soft rag—do not rub it in—then use a soft duster to polish. Stains caused by hot dishes being put on a table can be instantly removed by this simple method.

Care of a Thermos Flask.—To get the greatest efficiency out of a thermos flask, it ought to be tempered first by pouring cold or scalding hot water into it, according to what it has to be filled with. No vacuum bottle should be expected to increase heat or cold; its function is to maintain the temperature of the contents placed in it. After using the bottle, always wash it thoroughly, finish with a scalding rinse, and be sure it is dry before putting it away. Keep the cork out when not in use, and boil it occasionally in a baking-soda solution to keep it sweet. Never force the cork in, but work it in gently. The glass container can be replaced, should any accident happen to it.

Care of Soiled Linen.—This should never be allowed to accumulate, and in hot weather especially a weekly washing is most important. Meanwhile the soiled linen should be stored in a light basket or other ventilated receptacle, and if possible kept away from bedrooms. This is important from a hygienic point of view.

Meat.—When choosing meat its colour is an important factor. Good beef, freshly cut, is a rich deep red. Veal ranges from almost white to a dull pinkish hue, and lamb should be a delicate red. Pork is best when a pale brownish pink, or even nearly white, in young pigs; whilst mutton is a dull brick-red if freshly killed; if well hung—a great point in its favour—the cut surfaces are a blackish purple in colour. Veal and lamb, being young meat, have less flavour and nutriment, and are more difficult to digest than meat from mature animals. Also, they sour very rapidly. All meat, but beef especially, is nicest when well marbled with creamy-white fat, and all should have a firm, smooth, fine grain, or fibre. Both these signs are indications that the meat is likely to be tender—a matter of utmost importance. So also are the colour and texture of the bones. If these are reddish in colour, and comparatively soft and pliable, the joint is from a young animal. The opposite is the case if they are white, hard, and dense.

Ventilation.—During the heat of the day close windows in cellars, storerooms, or cupboards that are situated in a specially cool place, and open them at night. The reason for this is that during the day the atmosphere in them is so much cooler than that outside, that the moisture in the warm air coming in through an open window condenses on walls, metals, etc., producing rust and mildew. Never allow chimneys to be closed or blocked with screens in summer, and keep the dampers of the kitchener pulled out, even if the stove is disused, as the flues which they open act as valuable ventilators for the kitchen.

Navy Blue Serge.—Grease marks on the collar of a blue serge coat can be very successfully removed with eucalyptus. Brush the collar first to remove dust, and then apply the eucalyptus with a clean rag, rubbing it well in. Dry in the open air and the smell will soon disappear.

To Remake a Feather Pillow.—This need not be a messy job if it is done in the following manner. Make the new case of strong ticking and leave a ten-inch opening. Make an opening in the old case the same size, and then sew the two openings together. Now shake the feathers down into the new case, and run a tacking thread just below the opening. Unpick and remove the old cover, and then oversew the seam neatly.

If the ticking is not very close in texture, it is a good plan to rub over the inside of the case with beeswax before filling, as this will prevent the points of the feathers working through. If the feathers are soiled, the simplest way to wash them is to turn them into a large muslin bag and sew them up in the same way as above, and then to wash them in one or two soapy lathers, well rinse, and dry in the open air. This will make little or no mess and the feathers will be beautifully clean.

A Laundry Bag.—The most satisfactory laundry bag can be made from a yard of thirty-six-inch cretonne. Fold it lengthwise and shape it at the top to fit over a coat hanger. On the front side, cut a slit long enough to push the soiled clothes through, and bind it firmly. Then cut the back side of the bag longer, enough to enable you to turn it up at the bottom for a flap, which should be fastened on the front side with five large snap fasteners. With a bag made in this way, the bottom can be unsnapped and the laundry dropped out without removing the bag from the hook on the cupboard door.

To Wash Heavy Rag Rugs.—A simple way of washing heavy rag rugs is the following: Soak the rugs for five minutes in cold water, then spread them on a bare floor and sprinkle heavily with any good washing powder. Scrub the rags until they are clean with a clean broom dipped in hot water. Rinse thoroughly in clear water in the laundry tub and hang on the line to dry.

THE
20's

A PLEASANT REVIVAL *of an* OLD ART
Patchwork and Embroidery Lend Colour to Handkerchiefs

By Anne Orr

DAINTY handkerchiefs are an ever-welcome birthday gift to a woman, and when they boast a touch of handwork they are doubly acceptable. Here are several suggestions in handkerchiefs combining patchwork and embroidery. Patchwork, which for years was a lost art, now finds itself restored to former greatness. It is at times inserted in the linen by means of a hemstitch; at other times just whipped on, and the little flowers and leaves embroidered in a solid bullion, or rambler stitch. Several of the patterns would look very attractive embroidered on lingerie.

The handkerchief above and the two at left show patches whipped or hemstitched into the linen, while the flowers are solid-stitched in two shades of pink above, and in purple at the left. The leaves are green and the stems outlined

The grey basket is in solid and outline stitches; blue ribbon and green leaves in solid stitch; stems outlined, and flowers in French knots. Pink roses in wreath in bullion stitch, and in bouquet in French rose stitch

Hot iron transfers for five handkerchiefs above and one at top cost 4d., post free. Each group contains two sets of 6 patterns. Directions for embroidery enclosed

Two above and left. Grey vase and stems are outlined; blue, pink, lavender, and rose flowers are in rambler rose and French knot stitches; green leaves in lazy-daisy stitch

Hot iron transfers for five handkerchiefs above and one at left cost 4d., post free. Each group contains two sets of 6 patterns. Directions for embroidery enclosed. Address: Needlework, "Good Housekeeping," 1 Amen Corner, London, E.C.4

HINCHLIFFE of BOND STREET

GOWNS · MILLINERY · CORSETS · LINGERIE

SUMMER SALE

DURING THE MONTH OF JULY

EXCEPTIONAL BARGAINS

IN THE NEW TYPES AND FAVOURITE MODELS OF

BonTon CORSETS
TRADE MARK.

THE HIGHEST GRADE OF THE ROYAL WORCESTER MAKE

NOWHERE CAN YOU OBTAIN THESE CORSETS FOR LESS MONEY

Post Orders receive expert attention

YOU MAY SAFELY ORDER BY POST IF YOU CANNOT ATTEND PERSONALLY

All prices reduced during this month

Model 564. A beautiful model for average figure in pink broche, with all-round elastic top. Lacing below busk. Six hose supporters. Sizes 21—32.
Regular Price 16/11. SALE PRICE **13**/11

CORSETS AND CORSET BRASSIERES

Model 547. A splendid corset for the full figure. In white coutil. Low bust. Six hose supporters. Sizes 22—36.
Regular Price 21/-. SALE PRICE **16**/11

Model 1943. Semielastic Belt, in orchid colour, with panels of exquisite silk broche, back and front. Six hose supporters.
Regular Price 8 gns. SALE PRICE **4** Gns.

Model 208. Pink elastic, with fancy material sections and elastic panel back. Lacing below busk. Four hose supporters. Sizes 21—30.
Regular Price . 10/6. SALE PRICE **8**/11

Model 6007. Corset Brassiere Combination, No. 6007. Very chic, in pink Milanese silk, with elastic over hips and at back. Hook back. 32—42 bust. Regular Price 5 gns. SALE PRICE **3**½ Gns.

Model 1917. All-Silk elastic hip-confiner of the finest quality in flesh pink. Lacing below busk. Six hose supporters.
Regular Price 10 gns. SALE PRICE **5** Gns.

Model 444. A smart average figure corset in pink fancy material with satin stripe. All-round elastic top. Lightly boned. Four hose supporters. Sizes 21—32.
Regular Price 14/11. SALE PRICE **10**/11

HIP-CONFINERS AND FIGURE BELTS

Model 898. In white coutil. A comfortable shape for the full figure. Very low bust. Sizes 22—35.
Regular Price 29/11. SALE PRICE **21**/9

Hinchliffe of BOND STREET

HINCHLIFFE, LTD., 169 NEW BOND STREET
LONDON, W.1

The more facts about home management that the housekeeper stores in her mind the less time she will waste in the business of housekeeping

The experts who conduct the Home Management and Cookery Departments of "Good Housekeeping" have supplied these facts, so you may rely on them

The Housekeeper's Dictionary *of* Facts

Things Worth Remembering

Don'ts in Sea-bathing

(1) Don't bathe too soon after a meal.

(2) Don't bathe when over-heated or over-exhausted.

(3) Don't bathe before breakfast unless you are vigorous and strong. The best time is two or three hours after breakfast.

(4) Don't remain too long in the water, but leave it as soon as there is any feeling of chilliness.

(5) Don't attempt to go beyond your depth unless you can swim.

(6) Don't stand about and get chilled after bathing, but take some brisk exercise.

(7) Don't bathe at all if subject to attacks of faintness or giddiness.

(8) Don't bathe at all if the hands and feet remain numb after you leave the water.

To Enamel a Bath

First wash the bath thoroughly, using hot water, a little soda, soap, and a scrubbing-brush. Be careful to get rid of all grease, rinse with clean water, and dry. Rub down any rough surfaces with fine sandpaper and brush away the dust. Then with a good paint-brush apply bath enamel. This can be bought ready prepared and in several different colours—white, cream, flesh-coloured, or eau-de-nil. Allow the first coating of enamel to dry and smooth again with sandpaper if necessary. Then apply a second coating and dry as before. Some kinds of enamel will take one or two days to dry. When finished, fill the bath with cold water and allow this to remain for two days in order to harden the paint and take away the smell.

To Clean an Electric Toaster

Crumbs collect in the toaster each time it is used, and it is often found difficult to remove these from the framework. A flat paint-brush which can be purchased for a few pence will be found most handy for this purpose; it will remove all trace of crumbs very easily.

Fruit and Vegetables

To ripen fruit and vegetables place them on a wire cake-stand which is slightly raised from the surface of the table. As the air will completely surround the fruit or vegetable, there will not be the same need to keep turning them over, and there will be no bruises resulting from pressure on a hard, flat surface.

The Linen Cupboard

It is often a bother to know the size of certain sheets when they come from the laundry or are taken from the shelves of the linen cupboard. It is a good plan to mark them in such a way that it can be seen at a glance whether they are narrow, medium or wide. The narrow sheets might be left unmarked, the medium marked with one cross in red marking-cotton over the edge of the narrow hem, and the wide marked with two crosses in the same place. If space permits, the sheets might be kept in three different piles in the linen cupboard, and when others are returned from the laundry it can be seen at a glance to which pile they belong by the special marking.

Gummed Labels

If gummed labels stick together, lay a thin piece of paper over them and press with a warm iron. They will soon come apart easily and the gum will be intact. Spread out to dry. The same applies to stamps or jam-pot covers.

Measuring Butter

Half a cupful of butter is given in many recipes. The quickest way to arrive at this is to fill the measuring cup half full of water, and then to drop in the butter until the water rises to the top. Drain this off, and half a cupful of butter will remain. This takes far less time than to pack the butter down into the cup, it also saves butter, as none will be left sticking to the sides of the cup. Other fats can be measured in the same way.

The Correct Way to Wash Berries

There is always a best way of doing even the simplest things. If berries are washed the best way, rather than what may seem easiest, there is a great difference in their appearance and taste. Always put the berries into water; never turn water upon them, for it bruises, spoils their shape, and wastes their juices. Very carefully stir the berries about in the water with the finger-tips until all the sand has been dislodged, then lift the berries out on a square of absorbent cloth spread in the sun, if possible. In ten minutes the berries will be dry and ready to hull. The berries will look fresh and beautiful and will have lost none of their natural flavour.

Curtain Tabs

An economical device for saving the tops of curtains or portières is to sew on tabs about two inches long at regular intervals along the top. If these are sewn on the *inside* of the curtain and the furniture safety-pin passed through them (instead of through the material), the curtain is greatly saved from wear and tear.

Some Problems
of a
Woman's Life

by Rose Macaulay

Author of " Potterism," " Dangerous Ages," " What Not," etc. etc.

Often—alas! too often—there are no servants. Then some-one has got to do something about it, and is there any reason why it should be a woman rather than a man?

LIFE — any life — is full of problems. Already I have held forth in these pages on the problems of married persons and the problems of writers. And now for the problems appertaining in particular to women. Many writers are married; many writers are women; many women are married. So the three sets of problems overlap and coincide in the same life. But there is no reason why one should not, if one likes, separate and consider some of the problems incidental to belonging, as we nearly all must, to one of the two sexes commonly found upon this planet. There are such problems, though most problems have a wider application and present themselves impartially to those of both sexes. But not all. There are occasions when a problem arises for a woman merely because she is a woman. Such as washing the hair, for instance.

Let us consider, for example, jury-women. The learned judge is apt to turn kindly to the honest twelve and remark, " There are some (or there is one) unmarried women in the jury. They (or she) may retire before the hearing of this case." (There are also, probably, some unmarried men among the jury, but judges do not seem to think that these have minds capable of tarnish from anything they may hear. It is, for some odd reason, only women whom marriage is supposed to harden · from sensitiveness to insensibility. These things are a mystery.) So here is the problem. Is the unmarried jurywoman to retire at the judge's word, like a child ordered out of the room before a private conversation, and look a fool? Or is she to stay where she is, and be thought a hardened, insensible, and un-womanly creature? Or is she to raise a question about what marriage has to do with it and why marriage affects only one sex, and be thought insubordinate and over-inquiring? Or is she to de-

part, but with an explanation, remarking that she does not in the least object to hearing anything, but that she has business elsewhere and would rather attend to it, and be thought unworthy of the rights of a citizen? Or is she to pretend not to hear, and be thought deaf or half-witted? I offer no solution: I merely state the problem.

More serious and more frequent in the normal feminine life is the problem of what is called housekeeping. Minding the home. Running the house. This strange occupation has many names, but they all mean the same thing. Ordering meals. Telling the cook what to prepare; or, rather, being told by the cook what she intends to prepare. To those who do not housekeep, it seems as if this conversation with the cook was a trifle unnecessary. Be sure that the cook will prepare something to eat; it is her job, and you had much better leave her to it, instead of worrying her with ignorant suggestions or protests or idle chit-chat. " That will do very nicely," I have heard many of such dialogues end. Well, then, if it will do very nicely, why talk about it beforehand? For God's sake, let the cook cook, the housemaid housemaid, the laundress launder, the dustman remove his dust, without interference. There is no reason why all this interference should be one of the problems of a woman's life. Further, if someone has got to housekeep, there is no reason why it should be a woman rather than a man. But that is the convention.

Often—alas! too often—there are no servants. Then someone, of one sex or another, it does not matter which, has got to do something about it. Men have proved themselves far cleverer than women in shelving this onerous duty. A tradition has now for long been established that cooking and cleaning are woman's work. As these occupations are among the most tiresome which hu-

manity has to endure, this tradition is very unfortunate for women. But there it is; and the problem is how to get what is needful done as rapidly as possible, so that one can go and do something else, more lucrative, interesting, or amusing. There must be something to eat at stated intervals, and the house or the flat must be about as clean as the houses and flats of one's acquaintances. (This is not to say much, since no house or flat is ever very clean.)

It sounds simple, but actually to secure both these results will often be found to take the entire time. All the time there is. And that is so tragically little. None left over for reading, writing, walking, sitting in woods, playing games, making love, merely existing without effort. And ever at your back you hear Time's winged chariot hurrying near . . . and so the grave yawns, and at the end you will be able to say, not " I have warmed both hands before the fire of life," but " I have Kept House."

The only solution of this problem which I can suggest—and I almost hesitate to do so in these pages—is, Do *not* keep house. Let the house, or flat, go unkept. Let it go to the devil, and see what happens when it has gone there. At the worst, a house unkept cannot be so distressing as a life unlived.

What is commonly supposed to be another problem specifically feminine is that of Beauty, how to acquire it, or how to retain it when any. Mrs. Atherton, in a recent and rather entertaining novel, suggests one solution of this problem. Her heroine, at the age of sixty, has her ductless glands X-rayed, and is restored thereby to her marvellous beauty and youth of thirty years before. Here is indeed a solution of one of the most acute of female problems. Other solutions will be found (I expect) among the advertisement columns of this useful (Continued)

Some Problems of a Woman's Life

magazine; I have certainly seen them there in ,other numbers. For myself I have no remedy to offer for this distressing and almost universal complaint of Losing the Looks—except, grin and bear it. Consider also that men, too, suffer from it (though apparently less acutely), that life is at best a brief and perishing episode, that in the grave none are beautiful, and that any-how human beauty is an artificial conven-tion, varying from period to period of history, and from country to country. In certain parts of the globe blubber lips, flat noses, and woolly hair are all the rage. Who knows, then, but that at any moment withered faces or double chins may not come in? There is hope for all, and none need despair; and beauty, anyhow, is but skin deep. And so on and so forth; similar maxims of consolation will occur to all. Let us leave the subject and consider sartorial problems—those of them which belong peculiarly to women. The chief of these is, of course, how to dress well on expenditure insufficient for that purpose. And it may at once be admitted that this is impossible. You must either dress badly or spend more money than you wish to—in most cases more than you have got. It is a simple alternative, and every woman must make up her own mind which she intends to adopt. Many women adopt both. Another sartorial problem has always been how to reconcile a certain conformity to fashion with a certain comfort and grace. This problem is not so acute just now as it has often been in the past—in the days, for instance, of crinolines, bustles, tight waists, hobble skirts, long trains, and the other monstrosities of fashion which have come and gone. But it is always there; and if longer skirts—that most clumsy and unlovely of fashions—really come in, it will become acute. And it, too, is in-soluble. You cannot be at once graceful, comfortable, and in the mode. Probably you will be none of these things. Life is hard for women, as the saying goes.

One article is not enough in which to consider feminine problems at large. I turn the pages of a recent issue of this magazine, and problems of which I had not thought confront me on every page. How to clean chintzes. Yes, indeed. Why look lined and unlovely? Is your neck too fat? Is it too thin? How to prepare hearty meals of eggs. How to express your per-sonality by your scent; how to perfume the ears. Are you nearly bald? How to dress the kiddies, keep the home nice, make your husband comfortable, succeed in business or at the Bar, use your vote, choose a car . . . What a life is this into which we have been flung!

But it should console women to consider that, as a sex, they have fewer problems than they had some forty or fifty years ago. Not long since I was reading an *Observer* of the eighteen-eighties, and there was a leading article on the habits of the modern young woman, among which was mentioned with contumely the growing custom of demanding latch-keys to the front door of their homes. No explanation is given as to why this simple and labour-saving device is reprehensible for the femi-nine sex. But, if it was really unusual, life must have held for women a problem we do not have now—how to get in to their own houses without continually disturbing the maids at their work. In those far days the whole of life must have been, for women, a problem indeed.

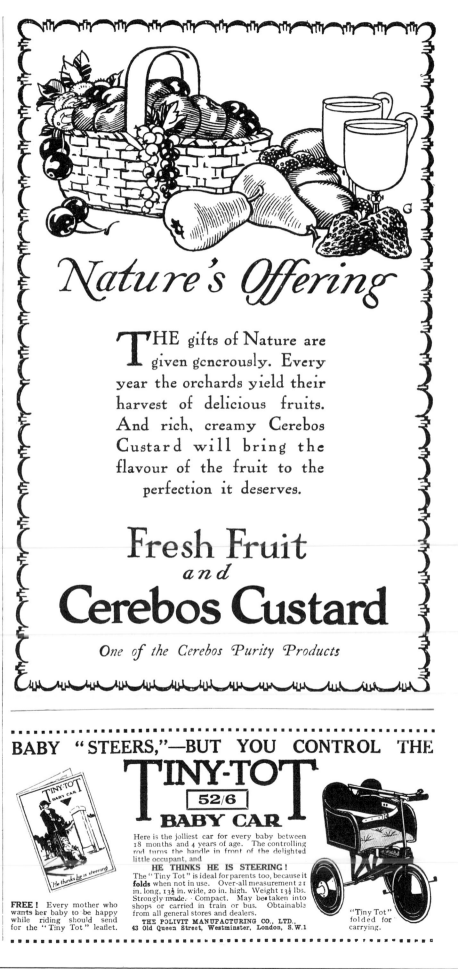

*Right and left her " smashes " dealing,
May displays " that Kruschen feeling ! "*

Well Taken !

On the tennis courts the victory is not always to the strongest, or even to the most skilful.

You cannot feel confident of winning your matches if you start handicapped by slackness and depression, if for any reason you are " out of sorts." Your eye and your hand do not then work in unison, you miss " sitters," you're tired before the game is halfway through.

Then you excuse yourself by saying, " Oh, I was off my game."

Being " off your game " is not an accidental state which comes and goes in some obscure, mysterious, uncontrollable way. It is all a matter of the working of your inner mechanism.

That's where Kruschen comes in.

Keep your blood pure, your liver and kidneys working regularly and efficiently, by taking your daily pinch of Kruschen Salts. All the waste matter that has been clogging your system—the effect of errors of diet, indigestion, overwork, worry and the like—is gently but surely expelled ; your eliminating organs are stimulated to a proper and habitual performance of their functions ; new, pure blood is sent coursing throughout your body, making you tingle with health in every fibre.

It costs you less than a farthing a day to maintain the healthy Kruschen habit. But it puts you and keeps you always " on your game "—and not only on the tennis courts. Is it not well worth it ?

Tasteless in Tea
Put as much in your breakfast cup as will lie on a sixpence. It's the little daily dose that does it.

Kruschen Salts

Good Health for a Farthing a Day

A 1s 9d. bottle of Kruschen Salts contains ninety-six doses—enough for three months—which means good health for less than a farthing a day. The dose prescribed for daily use is " as much as will lie on a sixpence," taken in the breakfast cup of tea. Every chemist sells Kruschen. Get a 1s. 9d. bottle to-day and start to-morrow.

For the *Home* Dressmaker

Four New Designs that Teach the Season's Lesson of Simplicity

AUGUST, the month of holidays, picnics, and garden parties, calls for light, gay dresses and smart summer frocks. The first frock (Fig. 12) has a delightfully Quakerish suggestion with its cross-over fichu effect, and a new idea is expressed in the tunic which, like the fichu, is detachable. The dress, of figured or dotted voile, is made on very straight lines, with a somewhat fuller tunic of white organdie attached to an organdie sash which, like the fichu and cuffs, is piped with a bias binding to match the predominating colour of the foundation. The frock can be of a solid colour throughout if desired, and would be pretty in that delectable shade of apple green which has that peculiarly refreshing quality of always looking cool. Any light summer fabric, such as voile or dotted muslin, could be adapted to this model.

This frock consists of a one-piece underdress, having one front and one back section, one sleeve, a tunic of two pieces with a seam down the centre back, and a fichu, cuff, and sash of plain material. If of white organdie and figured voile, this dress would cost about:

		s.	d.
3½ yds. of 36-inch figured voile at 2s. 6d. a yd.		8	9
2½ yds. of 44-inch plain white organdic at 2s. 11d. a yd.		7	4
1 yd. of plain voile for binding at 2s. 6d. a yd.		2	6
		18	7

Fig. 13 makes an extremely practical street or travelling costume for this time of the year, and has the virtue of engaging simplicity that white collar and cuffs always seem to impart. It could be made of crêpe marocain, linen, or stockinette, in navy blue or the deep brick red which is so attractive this season, with the vestee, collar, and cuffs of silk crêpe or linen. In one of the new sport fabrics it would make a delightful country frock.

This is a two-piece model, consisting of one front and one back blouse section, one sleeve, one vest and a two-piece skirt. Of crêpe marocain, it would cost about:

		£	s.	d.
4½ yds. of 40-inch crêpe marocain at 10s. 6d. a yd.		2	7	3
1 yd. of 45-inch linen at 3s. 11d. a yd.		0	3	11
		£2	11	2

Its companion frock (Fig. 14) could be made of French blue linen and stitched with a deeper blue thread. This consists of two fronts and one back section, one sleeve, and one collar. The dress fastens at the left side of the front, just inside the band, which is white like the cuffs. Made of linen it would cost about:

		s.	d.
4½ yds. of 45-inch linen at 3s. 11d. a yd.		17	7½
½ yd. of 45-inch linen at 3s. 11d. a yd.		1	11½
		19	7

The fourth dress (Fig. 15), is very simple and need not be expensive. The lace, which forms the collar, continues to below the bottom of the skirt, forming side panels, and the lace on the blouse, skirt, and sleeves is put on in wide, straight bands. It would be lovely made of pale-yellow chiffon or georgette combined with a cream-coloured lace, but any of the lighter shades would appear to advantage.

The over-dress is in one piece, with one front and one back section, sleeve, and side panels. Perforations on the pattern mark where the lace should be inserted, and the vestee and neck are bias bound with self material. It would cost about:

		£	s.	d.
2 yds. of 40-inch georgette at 8s. 11d. a yd.		0	17	10
5½ yds. of 18-inch silk lace at 7s. 11d. a yd.		2	3	6½
2½ yds. of 40-inch silk messaline at 4s. 11d. a yd.		0	12	3½
		£3	13	8

A well-cut pattern for any one of the dresses below may be obtained in sizes 36 or 40 (bust measurement) for 1s. Patterns cut specially to measure are 3s. 6d. each. Kindly state correct size and number of pattern required, and address, enclosing price of pattern, to Paper Pattern Dept., "Good Housekeeping," 1 Amen Corner, London, E C.4

Fig. 12   Fig. 13   Fig. 14   Fig. 15

A Quaker-like cross-over fichu and detachable panels of plain white organdie, bound in colour, are the chief points of interest in this dainty frock of gay, figured voile

(Right) A smart town or country costume, with a new vest and sleeve, could be made of crêpe marocain or one of the new sport materials, with demure white collar and cuffs

(Left) A delightful morning or walking costume is this slip-over model of French blue linen with stitchings of a darker blue

(Above) Lace is daily growing in favour and a creation of maize-coloured chiffon and cream lace would make a delightful informal dinner gown or garden-party frock

The Housekeeper's Dictionary of Facts

Things Worth Knowing

The Value of Rain-water

In districts where the water is very hard more use should be made of rain-water. If kept in a tank with a tight-fitting cover it does not get dirty, unless, of course, it is collected in a busy town, in which case it should be strained through two thicknesses of butter muslin before use. For washing flannels and woollen underwear rain-water and a little dissolved soap are invaluable. Washing blankets in rain-water in a dolly tub with a vacuum washer or wooden dolly is not a difficult task.

Grease-spots on Carpets

The usual method of removing grease-spots, by the use of petrol or benzine, is apt to leave white marks. Turpentine can be used instead, and does not leave the light patch. Moisten a small piece of cloth with turpentine and rub over the spots vigorously until no trace can be seen. Take a clean dry duster and rub hard so that all the turpentine is removed from the carpet, or the dust will stick.

How to Touch a Sleeping Child

It is often necessary to touch a sleeping child; to set an arm under the blanket, or change its position. The trouble attendant upon awakening it can be obviated by wearing a pair of soft woolly gloves. It is the touch of flesh that registers through a child's sensitive skin. With a small baby it is easy, and well worth while to keep a pair hanging on the cot ready for "changing time."

Iodine Stains on Blankets

Blankets often get stained with iodine during an illness. This stain can be removed successfully if treated in the following way. Dissolve a piece of washing soda about the size of a walnut in an eggcupful of boiling water. Stretch the stained part of the blanket over a basin or saucer and brush in the soda solution until the stain disappears. Then wash thoroughly in warm soapy water, taking care to remove all trace of soda, for if allowed to remain in woollen goods, it would cause them to shrink. Although this simple remedy rarely fails, a very old and persistent stain might require the use of thiosulphate of soda, known to photographers as hypo, instead of common washing soda.

The Advantage of a Basket Fire

In many modern houses, the fireplace recess is left, in readiness for the tenant to provide gas fires. Those who do not like gas for warming cannot do better than to buy a small basket grate. These are not expensive, and can be carried from room to room.

Repairing a Rubber Hot-Water Bag

If the weakness appears along the seam, a strip of fine unbleached linen can be fixed by sticking with a little solution of celluloid. Most of the waterproof lacquers sold for coating brasswork can be used as the adhesive. A small hole can be repaired with a rubber patch and solution in the same manner as a bicycle tyre is mended.

Cleaning Fur Collars

The back of the collar, which quickly becomes rubbed and soiled, can be cleaned with petrol or benzine. This should preferably be done out-of-doors, owing to the inflammability of the vapour. Place the collar on a flat surface, and apply the petrol with a small nail brush. Rub gently so that the spirit is well worked into the fur. Remove the soiled petrol by rubbing hard with a clean piece of flannel. Dry out-of-doors, and if very soiled repeat the process. A clothes-brush will quickly improve the appearance of the fur.

Waterproofing for Boots and Shoes

Clean the soles and welts of the boots and shoes of all mud and dust, well drying the soles. Warm about 2 oz. castor oil and apply before a fire; use a small brush, working the oil well into the welts and soles, and taking care not to touch the uppers. When the oil has soaked in, give two further applications and stand the boots and shoes for twenty-four hours in a warm place. A single coat applied every ten days will ensure a watertight sole during the most inclement weather. Do not treat suède-leather shoes in this way.

Uses for Common Salt

A little salt on a damp cloth quickly removes the brown stain that appears on egg-spoons. The brown particles on the edge of piedishes can be removed by scouring with salt. A heaped teaspoonful of salt dissolved in a glass of water makes an excellent gargle for a sore throat. After washing brushes, use a tablespoonful of salt in the last rinsing water, as this stiffens the bristles.

An Inexpensive Home-made Cordial

The following particulars will enable the most inexperienced easily and cheaply to prepare a cordial which is always acceptable, particularly during the winter season. Take 3 lb. of loaf sugar, ½ oz. of the essential oil (not essence) of peppermint, and add enough boiling water to make 2 quarts of syrup. Stir well, and when cold put into well-corked bottles. Should the cordial be required stronger or weaker, add water accordingly.

New Fenders From Old Ones

People sometimes have old black-and-brass or all-brass fenders on which the open metal-work around the top is either broken or the brass is worn off. If you have one, do not give it to the old-iron man, but take the open metal-work off. When this is done, there will most likely be holes showing where the top has been bolted on. You now need some cup-headed brass bolts, which can be bought at most ironmongers. Fix these in, either with nuts or, if there isn't room for nuts, with a little solder. These provide simple ornamentation, and you have an up-to-date fender which requires very little cleaning.

Cups That Cheer

Claret Cup: Put a lump of clean ice in a large jug or bowl and pour over it 1 bottle of claret. Add the strained juice of a lemon, a sprig of mint, a sprig of borage, and one or two slices of cucumber. A few fruits in season may also be added. Sweeten to taste with loaf sugar, which has been dissolved in boiling water and, just before serving, add two bottles of soda or seltzer water.

Cider Cup: Cut a lemon in thin slices and put it into a large jug. Pour over it two pints of cider, add sugar to taste and a sprig of borage. Stand for an hour at least, then strain and add two bottles of soda-water and some small pieces of ice. A small quantity of fruit cut in small pieces may also be added.

Orange Cup: Put a lump of ice into a large jug and strain over it a pint of orange-juice and the juice of 2 lemons. Sweeten with dissolved sugar, and fill up with plain water, or soda-water and plain water mixed. Add one or two glasses of sherry or vermouth, and a few thin slices of orange just before serving.

Damp Beds

No bed, that has not been in constant use, should be slept in without being thoroughly aired. In winter a fire should be put on in the bedroom, and all the bedding put in front of it and well toasted. In summer it will be sufficient to leave the bed open for a day or two to the sunshine. There is nothing more dangerous than a damp bed, and no linen or blanket should ever be used before making sure that it is absolutely dry.

Rest in the Kitchen

A high stool, or a high chair on castors that can be easily moved about, should be kept in every kitchen. It is wonderful how many jobs can be done when sitting down. The preparation of fruit and vegetables, the beating of cakes and eggs, the chopping of meat, suet, and parsley, etc., do not necessitate a standing position. It is often injurious to the health of a woman to stand all day long and, with a little forethought, about half her work might be done sitting.

The Housekeeper's Dictionary *of* Facts

Things You Should Remember

Some Cookery Hints

(1) When baking a custard, stand the dish containing it in a tin of cold water. This will prevent it curdling, as it will cook more gradually without forming whey.

(2) To make fried onions more tender, slice them very thinly, put them into a frying-pan with a little fat, and cover them with cold water. Boil quickly until the water has evaporated and then fry until brown.

(3) Instead of grating small pieces of dry cheese, put them through the mincing machine, using the small cutter. It is easier and quicker.

(4) Do not put fresh meat in the larder wrapped in paper, as paper absorbs the juice.

(5) Put a clean marble in the saucepan when heating milk or a milky substance. This will roll about, and is almost as good as stirring.

(6) One or two marshmallows added to a cup of coffee or chocolate will make a good substitute for whipped cream.

(7) When yolks of eggs are left over, cover them with cold water and they will keep quite fresh until the following day without a skin forming.

(8) To make coloured sugar, put some castor or granulated sugar on a plate or sheet of stiff paper and sprinkle a few drops of liquid colouring on the top. Work this in with a palette knife until an even tint is obtained. Leave to dry, and then keep in a covered jar or bottle.

To Relieve Earache

Take the small centre part or core from an onion that is cooked sufficiently to make it soft. Insert it in the ear as hot as can be borne: it ought to fit

in quite easily, and will be found wonderfully soothing.

Make Your Flowers Last

Drooping flowers may often be revived by plunging the stems into boiling water. When the water is cold, cut a small piece off the stems, and arrange the flowers in fresh cold water.

Even a fern can often be restored to freshness by standing the pot in a basin of very hot water and letting it remain until the water cools.

If a piece of camphor or charcoal is added to the water in which flowers stand, it will help to preserve their freshness. Salt is also good, especially for roses.

A drop or two of melted wax dropped into the calyx of tulips will keep them from opening too quickly.

Crème de Menthe Jellies

Put 1 lb. loaf sugar into a lined saucepan with 1½ pints of cold water and 1½ oz. of sheet gelatine cut in pieces. Melt slowly, then bring to the boil and boil for half hour, stirring frequently. Remove from the fire, add essence of peppermint to flavour, and colour a pretty green with vegetable colouring. Strain through muslin or a fine strainer. Wet a tin or dish with cold water and pour in the liquid at least 1 inch in depth. Leave to cool, then turn out and cut the jelly in equal-sized pieces. Roll them in sieved icing sugar and leave them for a short time to dry.

Eye-Glasses

If you are obliged to work in a steamy or moist atmosphere, rub your glasses with soap and then polish them: you will find that the moisture does not rest on them. This is a good tip for those who do cooking or laundry work.

Gilt Picture Frames

If the frames are of good quality, when cleaning dust them first with a soft brush or silk duster. Then with a small, fine sponge wash them gently with equal quantities of methylated spirits and water, and dry with a chamois leather. Onion water is also very good for restoring the colour of gilt frames, and it helps at the same time to keep off flies. Chop up 4 or 5 onions and boil them in about 1½ pints of water, adding enough powdered sulphur to give a golden tinge. Strain off the liquid, and when cold apply it to the gilt with a sponge or soft brush. Inferior gilding will not stand much cleaning. The frames should be simply dusted, and if necessary touched up with gold paint, which can be bought at any oil-shop.

Cooking for an Invalid

Be sure to carry out the doctor's orders regarding the food.

Simple methods of cooking are as a rule the best.

Seasonings should be used sparingly.

See that all food given is the best of its kind and not stale or tainted in any way.

Pay special attention to cleanliness in its preparation.

Never make large quantities of anything.

Serve everything as daintily as possible, and see that hot dishes are really hot, and cold ones really cold.

Vary the food as much as possible, even if it is only in the way of serving it.

Never ask a patient what he would like—let the meal come as a surprise.

Serve it punctually, at the time expected.

The Housekeeper's Dictionary *of* Facts

Things Worth Knowing

A Novel Clothes-line Post

To avoid the unsightly appearance of a permanent post in the garden to take the clothes-line, which may be required for a few hours only each week, a 10-foot length of wrought-iron pipe, one inch in diameter, may be used. This is inserted in a piece of pipe 1½ inches in diameter placed about 2 feet deep into the ground to form a socket. The post may be put away out of sight when not in use. The two lengths of pipe, 10 feet of 1 inch and 2 feet of 1½ inch, may be bought at any gas or hot-water engineer's shop, and by plugging the top of the long length with wood, a strong hook or ring can be driven in to which to attach the line. When digging the hole in the ground for the socket-piece, it should be kept as small as possible, the bottom of the pipe must rest on a piece of brick or stone, and other stones should be well rammed against the pipe as the hole is filled in, to prevent it working loose.

Glass Containers for Cereals

In a house not fitted with a modern kitchen cabinet, a very useful substitute for storing various food supplies may be improvised by using one shelf in a convenient position in the kitchen to hold 3-lb. glass jam jars for the various groceries, sugar, rice, etc. These will not require labels, and the amount of stock in hand being always on view should obviate the annoyance of running out of supplies unexpectedly. Flat - shaped potted - meat glasses make excellent stoppers for the jars, and the whole arrangement may be carried out for the trouble expended in saving sufficient jars.

A Use for Cotton-reels

Empty cotton-reels may be turned to good account as handles for the various boxes in which boot-brushes or other cleaning materials are kept and will facilitate their removal from shelves, where it is otherwise difficult to get them down with one hand. If the reels are cut in half, each end will make one handle which may be easily fixed to the box with an ordinary wood screw through the hole in the reel. If a stronger job is required, a small bolt can be passed through the half

reel and through a hole in the box end, and fitted with a nut inside the box, the handle will then take any reasonable strain which may be put upon it.

A Useful Writing-table

A folding card-table can be made into a very useful writing-table by the addition of a bookshelf for railway guides or other books of reference. A table with X-pattern legs is best, and by fixing two pieces of thin wood—about as long as the table is wide and joined together to form a trough—to triangular pieces at each end, a handy bookshelf is made which will rest securely in the V formed by the upper parts of the table legs. The weight of the books will keep the case in place, and if it is necessary to fold up the table, shelf and books can be taken out quite easily.

Mats for Polished Tables

Hot plates when used on polished dining tables always present a difficulty. Cork mats, as non-conductors of heat, are not very decorative and quickly soil, the rough surface readily absorbing any grease. Rubber crêpe mats, both washable and impervious to grease, are now obtainable for the table. They are provided with coarse net covers, in different shades, and look quite attractive on a dining table.

Peeling Oranges

When making a fruit compote or salad, try soaking the oranges first in boiling water to cover, letting them stand five minutes. You will find that the white pithy part will come off quite easily with the skin, and the orange is left clean for slicing.

Poached Eggs

When serving this dish to an invalid or convalescent, it is a good plan to cut the toast in small sections before placing the egg on the top. It will be much more easily eaten.

To Improve Apple Tart

Try sprinkling 2 or 3 tablespoonfuls of orange-juice over the apples. This gives a delicious flavour and is an immense improvement to apples that are inclined to be dry and tasteless.

When Storing Fine Linen

Linen that is not in constant use should be wrapped in something blue to preserve the colour and prevent it becoming yellow. Blue paper will do, or part of an old sheet that has been previously dipped in a deep blue water.

A Tip for Smokers

To keep cigars in a damp climate, buy half a pound or so of cheap tea, put it into a tin or wooden box and keep the cigars in this. They will remain dry and in good condition.

To Save Labour

When baking fish, line the baking tin or dish with a piece of strong, white paper, greased with a little oil or butter. Lay the fish with any accessories on the top of this, and you will find that it is easily removed when cooked. Also, when the paper is slipped out the tin or dish is left comparatively clean and can be easily washed without the usual scraping.

To Economise Gas

Use a gas radiator, which enables you to cook three saucepans on one burner. This can be had in a triangular form made of heavy steel which does not warp, and constructed in such a way as to conserve all the heat.

When using the gas griller, always place a kettle or saucepan of water on the top, this utilises the top heat as well as that underneath.

Use saucepans of a strong, light make, and broad and flat in shape. Be careful to keep them clean—outside as well as inside; sooty saucepans heat badly and require longer to boil.

When using the oven, try to arrange your cooking so as to fill all the shelves. It is a waste of gas to cook one dish only.

Do not boil a gallon of water if a pint will serve your purpose.

Do not turn a light so high that it blazes round the sides of a kettle or saucepan. Do not light a burner sooner than is necessary, and always turn it off directly you have finished with it. Turn the gas off from the main pipe when you have finished using the stove, and always at night.

The Housekeeper's Dictionary *of Facts*

Nuggets of Household Wisdom

THE
20's

Storing Woollens

Winter woollies that are not required during the summer months can be kept safe from moths, if they are packed in newspaper with a few pieces of camphor or naphtha in each packet. The printer's ink on the newspapers repels moth. Instead of closing the packages with pins, which readily tear out, it is an excellent plan to use gummed paper-package tape. This fastens very securely and leaves no holes through which the moths can enter.

To Raise a Kitchen Table

To overcome the difficulty of tables and benches that are too low for comfortable work, door stops can be fixed on the bottom of each leg. If bought to match the table leg in colour, they form a neat finish to the leg, the table stands as solidly as before, and it is three inches higher. This simple contrivance does away with much backaching, occasioned when cooking or ironing at a table too low for one's height.

When Hemstitching by Hand

When hemstitching, wrap a piece of coloured paper around the first finger of the left hand, sewing it on if necessary. Use this when doing the hemstitching; the fine threads are much more easily seen and eye strain is eliminated.

Cleaning the Gas Cooker

Gas cookers require to be overhauled from time to time to prevent an unpleasant smell when cooking. The top bars and burners are easily removed, and they should be well cleaned with a wire brush. If, however, food has boiled over and corroded the burner holes, they should be put in an old pail and boiled in water containing some caustic soda. Avoid getting any of the liquid on the hands; a pair of tongs can be used to remove the stove-parts from the solution when clean. The oven should be entirely dismantled and cleaned in the same way. First remove the grid shelves and browning sheet, then the crown plate and burners. The sides of many gas ovens are enamelled. If the burnt grease is difficult to remove, moisten it with a fairly strong solution of caustic soda, leave to soak for half an hour, then wash off with hot water.

Saving the Bathroom Towels

So that the bathroom towels should not be cut, when drying safety and other razor blades, a small towel or cloth should be hung near to the shaving mirror, for the use of the menfolk in the house. A small piece of chamois leather, taped and hung on the small nail, will be much appreciated for polishing the blades after drying them on the towel.

Care of Patent Floors

Floors made from sawdust and a mineral substance which petrifies after being laid a few days, require a plentiful supply of linseed oil when new, until a thoroughly good surface is obtained. The oil should be well worked in, and the surplus allowed to remain on the floor overnight. If coarse sawdust was used in making the floor, it may be necessary to rub down the floor with steel-wire balls. When a smooth surface has been obtained, patent floors only require polishing with one of the well-known and efficient floor polishes.

A Linen-cupboard Hint

An excellent arrangement which prevents the edges and folds of sheets, towels, and other household linen from becoming discoloured whilst stored in the linen cupboard, is to fix glazed linen or old glazed blinds at the top of each shelf as close to the back of the cupboard as possible. Allow sufficient material to cover the back, the shelf and contents. Small brass hooks can be screwed into the wooden battens, and rings attached to both sides of the linen. This ensures the cover remaining in position. The glazed surface repels dust and moisture.

To Remove a Thorn

If it has entered too deeply in the flesh to be pulled out, wrap up the part in wet boracic lint with oil silk over it. Leave it for some hours, and the thorn will be found on the surface.

To Waterproof Cloth

Put 1 gallon of rain water into a pail and add to it 1 oz. powdered alum and 1 oz. sugar of lead. Stir these about, let them settle, and then pour off the clear upper liquid. Put the material to be waterproofed into this and let it soak for 24 hours. Wring out, dry partially, and then mangle or press with a heavy iron. This treatment will not injure the material, and it will enable it to stand any amount of rain.

A Cooling Drink

There is nothing pleasanter nor more refreshing than barley water flavoured with lemon. Wash 4 tablespoonfuls of barley, put it into a saucepan and well cover with cold water. Bring this quickly to the boil, pour off the water and rinse the barley and saucepan. Put in one quart of fresh cold water and the thinly peeled rind of a lemon, bring to the boil and then simmer gently for at least one hour. Strain into a jug, add the juice of the lemon and sugar if desired. If too thick, more water may be added. Grape-fruit juice is also very delightful as a flavouring.

When Mayonnaise Curdles

Put another yolk of egg into an empty basin, and add the curdled sauce gradually to it, stirring all the time.

To Whiten the Hands

Shred down 6 oz. of brown Windsor soap, and put it into a jar with ½ gill of lemon-juice. Stand the jar in a saucepan of water and let the contents melt over a slow fire. Then cool slightly and add ⅓ gill of eau de Cologne. Stir occasionally whilst cooling. Keep the mixture in a jar and apply it to the hands after washing.

To Make Baking Powder

Weigh out 2 oz. tartaric acid, 2 oz. carbonate of soda, and 2 oz. rice-flour. Mix these together and pass them twice through a fine sieve. Store in a paper-lined tin, or in a glass jar with a stopper. Keep covered and in a dry place.

Fragrant Tea

A very delightful flavour can be given to tea by putting the thinly peeled rind of an orange into the tea caddy. Cover with the tea and close down for an hour at least. Stir the tea about before use. This is well worth trying.

When Mixing Mustard

Use a little milk and add a pinch of salt. The mustard will keep a better colour and not dry up so quickly as when made with water.

Blemishes on Wooden Furniture

To remove match marks on polished wood rub with a cut lemon, and then with a rag dipped in clean water. You will find that the mark has disappeared. Ink stains can be removed with a little oxalic acid. Be careful not to spread the acid over the wood, but apply it with a small brush or with the point of a feather. Wash off with warm water and polish in the usual way.

To Remove a Dent in Furniture

Make a pad with about six folds of thick brown paper, and soak it in water. Lay this on the injured part and apply a hot iron, pressing it on until the moisture has evaporated. Moisten the paper again, and repeat the process, if necessary, to raise the bruise level with the surface. Then polish.

When Buns are Stale

Dip them in a little milk and heat them gradually in the oven. Butter them while hot and they will be delicious.

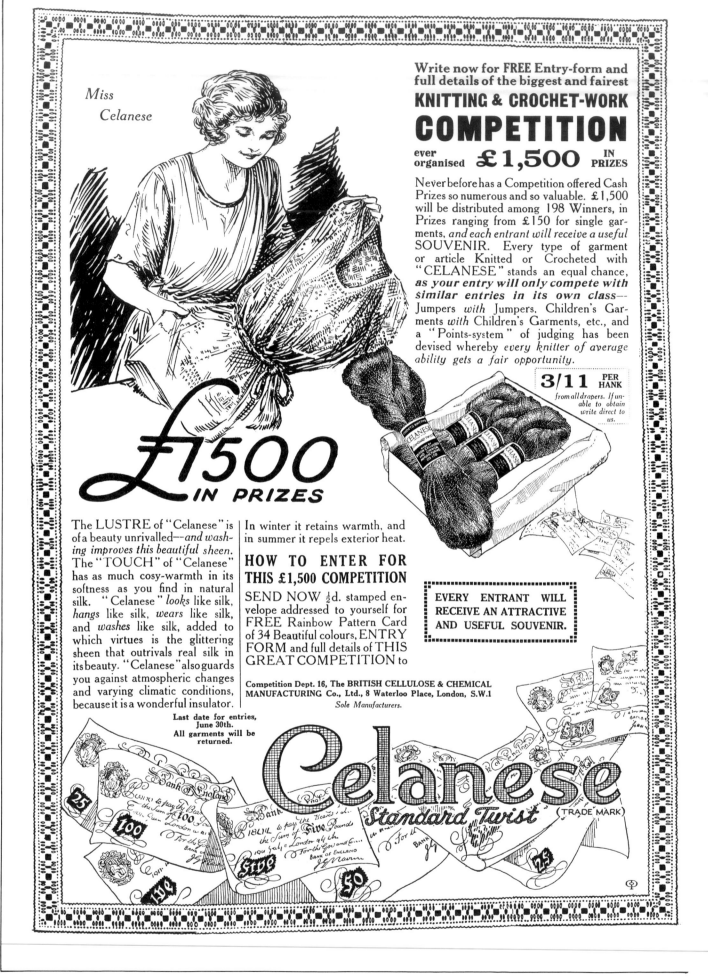

In learning the arts of housewifery in another woman's house the young professional domestic worker would gain invaluable knowledge for running a home of her own in the future

The *Professional* Home-Maker

Another View of Domestic Service

By Mrs. Alfred Sidgwick

Author of " The Severins," " Lamorna," " Below Stairs," etc. etc.

 CELEBRATED nurseryman told me that, when he employed unskilled labour, he sometimes had five pounds' worth of stuff destroyed in a quarter of an hour. This is nothing to the damage a rough, untrained female can do in a house in the time if she chooses. I once saw a housemaid dust a mantelpiece. It was in an old fashioned room and had a pair of very valuable vases with slender stems on either side of the clock. She snapped the stem of one. Three days later she snapped the other. That same afternoon she brought in a heavy lump of coal, dropped it and broke the bar of the grate. She was quite an ordinary housemaid.

If you put an unemployed factory girl into that room, she would break the clock, too, and the chairs. She would strew small coal on the carpet, thumb your paint and your cretonnes, scratch your silver, wash your glass in bacon fat, use her tea cloths for the boots, and give you notice because you were fidgety. That is why I feel lukewarm about the unemployed and the dole. At least I would rather they lived on the dole than came into my home. But I wish the money spent on doles could be spent instead on training schools. It is largely ignorance that keeps girls out of private houses.

The other day I heard a man say there was no servant difficulty. He is a wealthy bachelor living in a big northern manufacturing town where cinemas and young men abound. Cooks and housemaids fly to him. Another friend told me that when she advertised for a butler the street was full of them, applying. It is the "general" who commands the market, and after her the plain cook and the house-parlourmaid.

WHY don't women of all classes who want occupation combine to organise themselves into armies of domestic workers, wearing a chosen uniform and bound by certain rules? By this means the prevailing idea of the "inferiority" of the domestic worker would gradually disappear. Mrs. Alfred Sidgwick develops this scheme along practical lines in a very constructive article on the servant question

Their price is above rubies, and the heavily taxed middle-class householder finds it difficult to pay them, impossible to do without them, and almost impossible to get them. It is about time that he, or rather his womankind, faced the situation and solved it.

I have been interested in the servant's point of view for years, and I have never found that they mind work. Of course some dawdle and shirk, but I should say that most girls will carry on from morning till night in a way that commands my admiration. They are untiring. What they dislike about indoor service is loneliness, unkindness, the restriction of liberty, and the loss of social prestige: all drawbacks we should feel acutely ourselves. They would rather suffer privations in their own rough, badly found homes than exchange their birthright for the mess of pottage offered them in ours; and since affection and liberty are part of what they value, they are not to be blamed.

Otherwise, since working-class girls have their living to earn, they might do worse than help to make the homes of their country, and by learning the arts of housewifery prepare themselves to run a home well when they marry. Everyone knows that a man and wife who have been in service succeed in letting furnished rooms because they

understand how to cook, wait, and clean. In fact the wife by herself will know enough to make people comfortable. Now, I, being a democrat at heart, believe that the working man wants much what other men want when they marry: good cooking and as well-kept a house as he can afford; and he stands some chance of getting this if he marries a girl who has learned many things in a private house that she cannot learn in a factory. She has served her apprenticeship as a home-maker and he gets the benefit.

For this state of servitude only lasts a few years: after which a woman is in servitude to her husband while he probably serves the State or a private employer. I wish women of all classes would combine and organise armies of women wearing a uniform in which they took a pride, bound by a discipline of which they approved, and undertaking, with open eyes, the home-work both men and women need for their health and comfort. The mothers of families and the old should have the first claim on such service, and have it given when they could not pay for it: just as they now get medical help free in hospitals. For the chief objection to domestic service at present is the loss of social prestige attached to it, and that would be done away with if a better class took it up and if it became an ambitious, graded calling like that of soldier, sailor, or civil servant.

Over and over again girls have told me what a stigma there is on the business at present, and how it operates against them when it comes to courtship and marriage. "A man will dance with you, find out that you are a 'skivvy,' and never dance with you again," one very clever, *(Continued overleaf)*

The Professional Home-Maker

(Continued)

charming girl said to me. She was embittered because the swain of her fancy had deserted her for a farmer's loutish daughter who could neither reckon nor spell. The "skivvy" could do both admirably. She had a lovely figure, dressed well, was delicate with her needle, and had both brains and humour. But as a servant neither a tradesman nor a farmer would marry her, and in the end she took a species of small clerk "because he looked like a gentleman on Sundays."

So it is of no use for people to say solemnly in print that the work is honourable and that no loss of status should attach to it. At present a certain loss of status does attach to it, and you cannot change a fact by deploring it. You must alter the conditions, and in this case the chief stumbling-block is the question of companionship.

The truth is that we want work done in our houses, but we do not want companions. We greatly value the privacy of family life, and the thought of a "lady-help" is as oppressive as a nightmare. More and more, gentlefolks with small means are learning to do without servants. I know of a married couple who are building their house to this end: without a chimney. There will be no fuel used in it, and as it is in the country there will be little dust, and no grime. It will be warmed and lighted by electricity, and the cooking will be done by electricity, too. The installation and the process are both expensive at present, but not more expensive than one servant.

If people are content to live plainly, to be on the lookout for the best labour-saving appliances, and to make bonfires of the flummery that encumbers houses, they can help themselves as well as our kinsfolk overseas do. Before the war I heard of a woman who went to bed and cried because her maids walked out of the house suddenly. She was as helpless as one of those ants that die if slave ants do not feed them. I hope the type belongs to an older generation, soon extinct. Fortunately "helplessness" is not fashionable to-day. On the whole, modern women believe that when they undertake to run a home, it is their business to know, or at any rate to learn, how to do it. Housewifery is on the upgrade again, partly through the dearth of knowledgable servants: and because what you understand and practise yourself you can impart to others.

Women living in remote country places find that their best way is to take quite young girls and train them in household arts. Such girls are plastic and often apt. It is astonishing what a child of sixteen will learn in six months if the mistress or an older maid is patient at first and capable. To let a girl like that into your house is a very different thing from employing older ones who have been in factories. In short, there are two remedies for the present trouble, and they do not meet all cases, but they would relieve it. In the first place, if every woman who is

young, strong, and unoccupied would apply herself to the arts of the home and learn them thoroughly, she would be acquiring knowledge of great value wherever and however she chose to practise it. In many small households the work could be done by the women of the family without bearing hardly on any of them, as it is done overseas.

The idea of any necessary work being "menial" or "degrading" is so silly and out-of-date that it may be left to the "Reds," whose ideas are becoming more out-of-date every day. It is no more "degrading" to see that people in good health have clean rooms and well-cooked food than to wash and feed the sick. We can not turn ourselves into savages or animals, and to live in a civilised way makes some one busy all the time. Moreover, in most homes there are children to be reared and mothers of every station need help with them.

The war has shown us what our nation can do in the way of providing large numbers of women ready for any kind of work, paid and unpaid. It used to be said that women cannot organise and can not combine, and there is a real danger of the wrong women—the fussy, self-advertising ones—taking up a new movement. Perhaps it is one that is better not formed publicly, with noise, but should grow by degrees and almost unawares.

A great many girls of all classes must earn their bread nowadays, and if well-to-do people would employ several so that they were not lonely, their employees might find household work less trying and more varied than work in offices and factories. They should, in such cases, have pleasant rooms, reasonable liberty, and smart uniforms. The wisest woman I ever knew told me her maids went out for an hour or two whenever they pleased provided they left someone on duty, and that she never found the privilege abused. She thought it absurd that a grown-up woman should not take the air for an hour if she wished. I have gone on the same plan for years with the same results. You cannot have an eight-hour day in small households, but the work of any well-managed house is intermittent, with hours of very light duties or none at all.

So my remedy for the present trouble is not in any sense legislative. It is a trouble the women of the nation must face, consider, and settle. They must remove the prejudice against service by "serving" themselves and raise home-work to the social level of the typist, the shop assistant, and the factory girl. Servants of the home are in the truest sense of the phrase servants of the State, and the wit of woman should devise some way of getting this recognised. It may not be easy or swift to execute. It was not easy to replace the drunken Mrs. Gamp of sixty years ago by the trained nurse of to-day, but it was done: not by politicians, but, in the first place, by one determined woman and afterwards by her successors.

TWO VERY SUCCESSFUL AUTUMN STOCKINETTE FROCKS.

THE TREMENDOUS POPULARITY OF BROCHÉ KNITTED COATS & SKIRTS

We show here just one out of the great variety we hold in stock in all fittings. We can send you a selection on approval if you cannot call.

"GAINSBOROUGH"

Knitted Suit in broché wool effect, with convertible collar, cuffs, and hem of coat in brushed wool to tone; plain, straight-hanging skirt - - Colours: White, putty, grey, beige, almond and leather brown. **84/-**

Also plain knitted **Wool Cardigan Suits** from 19/6

"ELMA"

Wrap Coat in the new Autumn design, of all-wool Stockinette, brushed wool collar, cuffs and hem-band, floss-stitched design to match, wearable open or closed, convertible collar. Colours: Grey, tabac, almond green, white, putty, and beaver - **69/-**

The "Elma" Coat and "Rowan" Dress are stocked in shades to "go with" each other, and constitute a smart outdoor Suit.

"ROWAN"

A new Frock in Autumn-weight all-wool Stockinette, silk design to tone, neck-band and turn-back cuffs of artificial silk to match. Colours: White, lemon, fawn, beaver, tan, light grey, helio, saxe, tabac, and almond green **43/6**

"MIGNONETTE"

An exquisite design in all-wool Stockinette, with the pretty trimming of inset panels (so favoured just now) on skirt, ceinture and sleeves. The colours stocked include tabac/nigger, putty/nigger, saxe/white, grey/white, navy/white, navy/red, black/white, navy/lemon, and nigger/tan **47/6**

"Rowan"   *"Mignonette"*

"Gainsborough"

"Elma"

TWO DAINTY ARTIFICIAL SILK FROCKS.

WRITE FOR FREE COPY of **OUR CATALOGUES** from following Departments:

Ladies' Frocks and Wraps, Girls' School Outfits, Tiny Tots' Clothing, Boys' School Kit, Ladies' Jumpers, Underclothing, and Shoes.

"BEGONIA"

French Artificial Silk Jumper, lace stitch, scarf collar, low waist line with tie sash, long sleeves or three-quarter sleeves. Colours: White, grey, fawn, champagne, jade, and other shades. **18/9**

"DELPHINE"

Useful every-day style, with the new berthe collar, medium-low waist line, with beading design and tie sash; also with beads omitted from the skirt 4/6 less - - **50/-**

"GERALDINE"

Effective afternoon dress, all-round belt with loose panel effect on one side, charming bead design as sketch or similar; also with beads omitted from skirt 4/6 less - - - - **53/6**

Colours: Black, navy, cinnamon, nigger, tan, putty, copper, light & dark grey, and other colours.

"Delphine"   *"Geraldine"*

"Begonia"

The Housekeeper's Dictionary of Facts

Things Worth Remembering

When Boiling Potatoes

If you wish your potatoes to have a dry and mealy appearance, pour off every drop of water after cooking and shake the saucepan for a second or two in front of an open window. The potatoes will dry and fluff up immediately and no further steaming will be necessary.

A Delicious Lemon Syrup

Take a pound of fresh juicy lemons, wash them and peel off the yellow rind in very thin strips. Then remove all the white pith from the lemons (this is not used in the syrup), and cut the inner part into thin slices. Use a very sharp knife and take out as many of the seeds as possible. Put the yellow rind and lemon slices into a large jug or basin, add 3 lb. loaf sugar and 3 pints boiling water. In a small saucepan dissolve ¼ lb. citric acid crystals in 1 pint of boiling water, and when quite melted add to the other ingredients. Cover the syrup over and let it stand for two or three days, stirring occasionally, and pressing the lemon with the back of a wooden spoon. Strain through muslin, and bottle and cork tightly. Put one or two tablespoonfuls of this syrup into a tumbler and fill up with plain or aerated water.

A Tip About Mayonnaise

It is not generally known that the whites of the eggs can quite well be used up in the making of this sauce. When the sauce is quite finished, whip up the whites of the eggs to a very stiff froth and mix them in very lightly. They will make the mayonnaise of a nice creamy consistency, and there is no danger of them separating.

To Clean Mirrors

These should first be dusted, and the frames lightly wiped with a dry, clean cloth. Polish up the glass with a pad of soft newspaper, or if it requires more cleaning moisten a little fine whitening with methylated spirits, and rub this well over the glass with a soft rag, being careful not to touch the frame. Rub off again with a duster and polish with a chamois leather. If the frame is gilt, wipe it gently with a wet chamois leather and dry with a very soft duster—a piece of old silk is best. Onion water applied with a soft rag is excellent for reviving the colour of the gilt and keeping the flies away. Boil one or two onions in a pint of water until tender and reduced to a pulp. Then strain off the liquid, allow it to cool, and use as required.

To Keep Sauces Warm

Stand the saucepan containing them inside another pan of hot water, and cover the sauce with a lid to prevent a skin forming on the top. If the sauce is very thick, a little water may be run over the top.

Cleaning Electric Light Bulbs

To avoid unnecessary waste of electric current, by obscuring light, the lamps should be cleaned at least every six weeks. The risk of breakage is minimised if the light is switched on before cleaning, as the filament is stronger when incandescent. A damp wash-leather quickly removes all dirt and leaves the glass free from smears.

The Care of Irons

Irons that are put away in a cupboard or hung on hooks in the kitchen are very liable to rust. This happens more particularly to those heated over a gas flame, because of the quantity of water vapour always produced when coal gas burns. If a pad of white ironing wax is kept in a handy place, such as the drawer of the kitchen table, the iron, when partly cooled, can quickly be rubbed over it. A pad can be made at home by wrapping broken or odd pieces of candle inside a piece of clean muslin or old handkerchief.

Old Wash-leather Gloves

When these gloves are too worn to be of further use for wear, they can be utilised to make window polishing pads. Cut open the fingers, remove any buttons or press-stud fastenings, lay the gloves flat on the table, placing several on top of each other; six is a good number to use. Keep in position by machining or backstitching a small circle round the middle of the pad.

Pottery that is Porous

To overcome the difficulty often encountered of water percolating the base of vases, jars, and bowls made of pottery that is either unglazed or insufficiently glazed, paint the outer surface of the bottom, when dry, with some petrifying liquid, or apply two coats of any good enamel. To safeguard furniture from becoming marked by pots that may be slightly porous, cut two or three thicknesses of blotting paper the exact shape of the base of the vase; should a little moisture work through, the wood will not then be damaged.

Cleaning Brass Curtain Rods

Brass rods are more suitable for casement curtains than painted wood, for the rings slide more easily on metal and there is no risk of the rod sagging. The so-called brass rod in reality is iron cased with brass, and the latter quickly tarnishes from atmospheric moisture. To save constant cleaning, thoroughly well polish the rods, taking care that every trace of metal polish is removed, then apply a thin coat of clear shellac. This lacquer will last for quite a long time, thus saving both labour and time that would be spent in cleaning.

Papier Mâché Trays

Should be washed in warm soapy water and occasionally rubbed over with sweet oil. An excellent polished surface can be retained by the application of any good wax polish. This requires to be very well rubbed in, and then finished off with an old silk duster.

Patching Wall-paper

When a papered wall becomes damaged or soiled, the paper can be patched so that it is inconspicuous. First remove the dirty or torn paper by soaking it slightly with warm water. Cut out a piece of wall-paper somewhat larger than that which has been removed. Tear the edge so that it is irregular and jagged. If the patch is carefully pasted, the unevenness of the edge makes it hardly noticeable.

A Clothes-boiler Hint

To protect linen that has to be boiled in a rough or rusty boiler, a boiling-bag is excellent. Procure a child's ordinary wooden hoop with the circumference slightly larger than the top edge of boiler. Cut a circle of linen or calico approximately the same size as the bottom of the boiler, and a band of the same material of sufficient length to reach round the hoop. The band should be cut as deep as the boiler. Gather the lower edge of band into the circle; the top edge should then be attached to the hoop. This makes a rigid and very convenient lining for the boiler.

A Practical Pin-cushion

Fine sand enclosed in a strong case makes a cushion which is heavy enough to stay where it is placed and which keeps the pins and needles sharp and bright.

If bran is used for stuffing pincushions, it should be thoroughly well baked in the oven before being used, or it is likely to become sour and smell unpleasant after the cushion is made.

Essentials of Cupboard and Storeroom Care

CUPBOARD care, both routine and occasional, is an important part of home management. Fortunately architects are putting more and more cupboards into our homes. For instance, the linen cupboard is no longer a novelty, and even if you are without one its convenience and real economy can be enjoyed at small expense, if you will build a set of more or less shallow shelves depending on the space at your command. Then enclose them with doors. In this particular linen supply cupboard, deep drawers are placed under the shelves for storing supplies.

The upper shelf is the blanket shelf. Therefore, it is lined throughout, ceiling, walls, and shelf floor, with heavy sheets of white paper or glazed linen, which helps to keep moths away. As a further precaution one of the liquid insecticides is sprayed thoroughly over the blankets on the shelf. Use this treatment in winter once a month, or oftener if a flying moth gives warning of trouble. Blanket care in summer is more of a problem. They should be cleaned either by washing or dry cleaning and stored in cedar chests or trunks.

Every individual in a family should have his or her own cupboard or wardrobe, where they should be held responsible for the simple routine care of hanging up the garments and the orderly arrangement of shoes, hats, etc. Shoes need a word of mention because they are often the cause of an untidy appearance. Occasionally one finds a cupboard properly equipped with a shoe rack, but if you do not have one, any carpenter, at comparatively small cost, can build you a set of sloping shelves like the illustration. Kept on these shelves with

shoe trees in each pair, one can expect the longest possible period of service.

There is no better arrangement either for men's or women's garments than the pole suspended from the walls of the cupboard from which almost a limitless number of garment hangers may be hung. Be careful that this pole is changed in height in the children's cupboards, so that it becomes easy for them to learn the tidy habit of hanging up their own garments. Even a cupboard that is too shallow for the ordinary coat-hanger can be utilised if you will purchase children's small hangers. A coat-hanger does not have to reach so far into the shoulders of the garment in order to hang properly.

Men's clothes are far more difficult to care for and protect than the average woman's. Possibly because they are almost, if not quite, all wool, and also because an occasional grease spot often missed in cleaning offers the most attractive of meals to the moth. The following precautions have proved a real protection from moths: First, every cupboard has its monthly cleaning and final spraying with an insecticide. And, secondly, every cupboard is equipped with the moth-proof bags into which seasonal clothes are placed after being cleaned.

And that brings us to the question of storage. What shall we keep, what is it wise to dispose of? It used to be thrift to maintain "piece bags," to store a garment with little

possibility of another use. To-day all that is changed. Every garment, every blanket that is not worth the cost or the effort, or both, of thorough cleaning is not worth storing. It will prove too costly in its possible damage to other garments.

In preparing suits and overcoats, either send them to the tailor for his cleaning and pressing, or you may do the work at home. Work in a good light and use an ironing board with an old cover, because it will be stained and useless after this task. For cleaning use either petrol, benzene or benzoline; these substances are strong moth repellents.

Dip a stiff, short-bristled brush into the fluid and brush the entire garment with strong, even strokes. Of course, pay especial attention to all spots, also to the seams of the garment. As soon as each garment is completed, hang it in its protecting bag before the fumes have all passed off, and hang in sunlight.

Finally, just a word about the home that is really infested with moths. It is sometimes one's experience to purchase a house in which this pest is appallingly present, and it is not until a pest exterminator is called in that the house can be entirely rid of the pest. It is a good procedure, when going into a home that has been occupied by other people, to have this fumigating process done irrespective of the painting and redecorating that may be planned for. It must be done by skilled workers, but it does not require an undue time.

To protect furs from moth during the summer months, put them inside a bag made of glazed linen, with a good supply of naphtha. Close the open end of the bag by machining, using the finest stitch possible.

A convenient linen cupboard. Sloping shoe shelves are accessible. Protect unused garments in bags

THE SEVEN AGES OF WOMAN

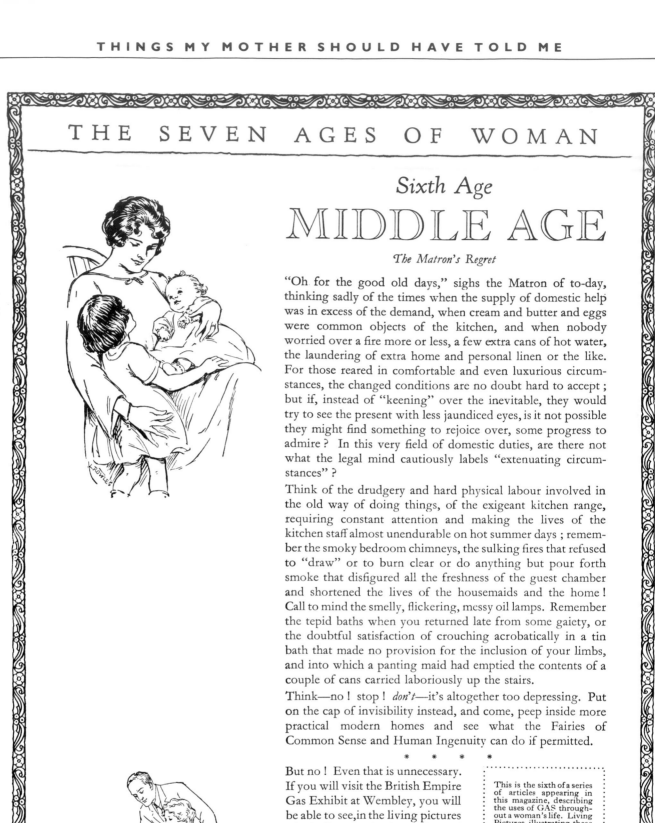

Sixth Age

MIDDLE AGE

The Matron's Regret

"Oh for the good old days," sighs the Matron of to-day, thinking sadly of the times when the supply of domestic help was in excess of the demand, when cream and butter and eggs were common objects of the kitchen, and when nobody worried over a fire more or less, a few extra cans of hot water, the laundering of extra home and personal linen or the like. For those reared in comfortable and even luxurious circumstances, the changed conditions are no doubt hard to accept ; but if, instead of "keening" over the inevitable, they would try to see the present with less jaundiced eyes, is it not possible they might find something to rejoice over, some progress to admire ? In this very field of domestic duties, are there not what the legal mind cautiously labels "extenuating circumstances" ?

Think of the drudgery and hard physical labour involved in the old way of doing things, of the exigeant kitchen range, requiring constant attention and making the lives of the kitchen staff almost unendurable on hot summer days ; remember the smoky bedroom chimneys, the sulking fires that refused to "draw" or to burn clear or do anything but pour forth smoke that disfigured all the freshness of the guest chamber and shortened the lives of the housemaids and the home ! Call to mind the smelly, flickering, messy oil lamps. Remember the tepid baths when you returned late from some gaiety, or the doubtful satisfaction of crouching acrobatically in a tin bath that made no provision for the inclusion of your limbs, and into which a panting maid had emptied the contents of a couple of cans carried laboriously up the stairs.

Think—no ! stop ! *don't*—it's altogether too depressing. Put on the cap of invisibility instead, and come, peep inside more practical modern homes and see what the Fairies of Common Sense and Human Ingenuity can do if permitted.

* * * *

But no ! Even that is unnecessary. If you will visit the British Empire Gas Exhibit at Wembley, you will be able to see, in the living pictures which illustrate the Seven Ages of Woman, what gas can do towards solving a woman's problems throughout her life from the cradle to the grave. E.M.W.

This is the sixth of a series of articles appearing in this magazine, describing the uses of GAS throughout a woman's life. Living Pictures illustrating these sketches are one of the many attractive and interesting features of the British Empire Gas Exhibit in the centre of the Palace of Industry at Wembley.

THE BRITISH COMMERCIAL GAS ASSOCIATION

30 Grosvenor Gardens, Victoria, S.W.1

Telephone : VICTORIA 6700

Telegrams : GASUPREME, SOWEST, LONDON

Keep a file in your kitchen of the—

Housekeeper's Dictionary *of Facts*

Beech Leaves for Decoration

Gather large sprays of the leaves in autumn when they are rich in colour. Place them between sheets of old newspapers, and press under rugs or carpets. The leaves will keep for weeks, and at Christmas time will be found most useful for decorative purposes.

A Table-cloth for Domestic Animals

A square of oil-cloth spread in a dog or cat's eating-place will often prevent a greasy floor. It is easily removed and cleaned.

A Use for Old Magazines

Keep one at hand in the kitchen for use under saucepans, roasting-tins, etc. It will make an excellent resting-pad, and will often save cleaning. A leaf can always be torn off when the top becomes soiled.

Instead of Eggs

Dissolve 1 tablespoonful golden syrup in ½ pint warm milk, and use this for mixing a cake when eggs are expensive. The result is excellent.

A Tip about Baked Potatoes

Allow the potatoes to lie in hot water for 15 minutes before baking. This not only improves the flavour, but reduces the time required for baking by one half. If crisp and brown potatoes are wanted, brush them over with melted butter or fat before putting them in the oven.

Grass Stains on White Material

These will yield to a dry application of soap and soda. Rub the stained part well with a piece of plain white soap. Then rub with powdered washing soda, and rinse immediately, when the stain will disappear.

When Cooking Macaroni

After 10 minutes' quick boiling, finish cooking in a double boiler. This will save the trouble of watching and stirring the macaroni.

Glazing Pastry without Eggs

To one tablespoonful of brown sugar add two tablespoonfuls of milk. Boil them together until the sugar is dissolved and then cool. Brush over the pastry with this before putting it in the oven, and it will produce a beautiful brown crust.

To Remove Glass Stoppers

Stoppers that are difficult to remove can easily be unfixed with glycerine, even if heat has failed. Paint the neck of the stopper with glycerine, leaving sufficient to penetrate between the neck and stopper. If this does not answer, insert the bottle so that the stopper is immersed in a small quantity of glycerine.

Improving a Sink-Tidy

Fix three cotton reels to the bottom of the sink-tidy with nails. This raises the receptacle from the sink, and prevents water and other waste liquids that are thrown down the sink from rinsing out the contents of the basket, and so keeps the sink much cleaner.

Brightening Linoleum

Light-coloured linoleums, whether plain or patterned, are apt to lose their bright appearance after being wax-polished for several years. By cleaning with turpentine or petrol, soiled wax is entirely removed and the colour revived. The cause of darkening is generally due to the use of soiled polishing cloths. It is essential to wash such cloths frequently.

Uses for Old Rubber Hot Water Bottles

Old bottles, that show signs of a leak and which cannot safely be used for their original purpose, come in handy when gardening. If one is placed next to the cover of the under-side of a small cushion, the latter can be used safely for kneeling upon, even in damp weather.

To Prevent Puddings Sticking

Puddings that are boiled in cloths are very liable to stick to the bottom of the saucepan. This can be prevented if one or two lids from golden syrup tins or a round pastry cutter is placed on the bottom of the pan.

Bass Brooms

When new, these should be soaked for twenty-four hours in cold water to prevent the fibres breaking. If, during use,

---

Devonshire Cream

Strain new, warm milk into a shallow pan 8 or 9 inches deep. Leave in a cool place until the cream has risen—12 hours in summer and 24 in winter. Then remove the pan to a stove and heat the milk slowly by steam or on the side of the range. The heating must be done very gradually, not less than ½ hour being allowed, and the temperature must not exceed 176° Fahr. When the process of scalding is completed, transfer the pan of milk to a cool place, or stand it in cold water. Natural cooling is best, as the cooked flavour which is wanted in Devonshire cream is then better retained. When quite cold, skim off the cream into tins or pots. One gallon of fairly rich milk should produce 1 lb. cream.

---

this treatment is repeated occasionally, the life of the broom is prolonged.

Improving the Kitchen Table

Space can be increased in the small kitchenette if a shelf is fitted. The position of this should be such that it can be reached by anyone working at the table without bending, and it must

be raised sufficiently from the floor to enable a broom to go underneath it for sweeping purposes. To save scrubbing, the shelf should be covered with light-coloured oil-cloth or, preferably, with patent enamelled iron.

Uses for Asbestos Board

It sometimes happens that small cakes and tarts are sufficiently cooked at the bottom before the tops are browned. If a piece of asbestos board is placed beneath the baking-sheet whilst the cakes are finishing, there is little risk of the bottoms becoming burnt. If fireproof pans and casseroles are placed on asbestos there is little chance of breakage.

How to Make Quince Marmalade

Wash and brush the quince and remove the blossom ends. Then cut them in pieces, removing the seeds, and throw them into a preserving-pan with cold water to cover. Allow the fruit to simmer slowly until reduced to a pulp; then rub through a hair-sieve.

Weigh the purée, and to each pound allow ¼ lb. sugar. Cook these together for twenty minutes, or until the marmalade will set, stirring frequently to prevent burning. Pour into pots and cover when cold.

How to Clear Soup Stock

White of egg slightly beaten, or raw beef finely chopped, may be used.

Remove all fat from the stock and put it into a saucepan, allowing the white and shell of one egg, or ¼ lb. lean beef, to each quart. Place on the stove and beat with a fine whisk until it reaches boiling-point; then remove whisk and let stock boil up once. Then place it at the side of the stove and keep it warm, without boiling, for ten minutes. Strain through a jelly cloth and re-heat as required.

When Preparing Fish for Boiling

When boiling fish in one piece, place the piece of fish on a plate before tying the cloth around it—thereby saving much trouble in removing the fish from the kettle, also preventing waste and unsightly food caused by the fish adhering to the cloth and breaking into small pieces.

When Sending Food Away

When packing a box of food to be sent by post, do not put each sort of food in a separate box to go in one big box, but wrap each package containing cakes, sandwiches, etc., separately, then run string round each package, through two holes in the side and two in the bottom of the large box. Then place sweets and fruit in the spaces which are left. Each article keeps its place and reaches its destination in perfect condition, with a great saving of postage.

THE
20's

Lustrous coils of transmuted sunshine

Sunshine poured into the forest, through the long and by-gone years. Fed on sap the leaves and branches, lived again in verdant green.

Thro' the ages dreamed the forest; lovely, lonesome, unexplored. **Then came Science with its magic: waved a wand and, lo—From the trees that once stood sturdy, 'gainst the tempest's cruel beat, came a wealth of lustrous fibres; shining, gleaming, dazzling, fair—**

SYLVAN
ARTIFICIAL SILK

Of all drapers and fancy repositories.

Manufactured by C. A. RICKARD LTD., Bradford

10,000 Beautiful Women

MRS. Hemming's skill has been exercised on far more than this: but among them, at least 10,000 have had rare natural beauty which did itself no justice until the crowning charm of a perfectly healthy skin revealed it.

Faces spoilt by powders and cosmetics, lined by neglect, dulled for want of the searching purification that "Cyclax" Beauty Preparations are alone able to give, are daily being restored to the health and beauty that is their birthright by Mrs. Hemming's discoveries.

It is worth while, if you live within reach, to consult her personally, and learn in a first thorough treatment (which costs only 12/6) how to give the skin the irresistible, magnetic charm of glowing health. Thereafter, ten minutes' pleasant self-care daily will preserve your beauty and smooth away the lines caused by neglect.

"CYCLAX" Beauty Preparations, sent post free, have full directions with them if you cannot come.

"CYCLAX" SKIN FOOD is the only cream which is bracing and nourishing. Prices **4/-** and **7/6**

"CYCLAX" SPECIAL LOTION clears the skin from all impurity and produces a flawless complexion. Prices **5/6** and **10/6**

"CYCLAX" BLENDED LOTION imparts a beautiful surface to the skin and is most nourishing and protective. Prices **4/6** and **8/6**

"CYCLAX" FACE POWDER is the finest face powder existent and is most beneficial to the skin. Price **6/6**

"Cyclax" (Mrs. Hemming)

13 & 14 (O) NEW BOND STREET, W.1 (Regent 2563)
58 (O) SOUTH MOLTON ST., W.1 (Mayfair 3972)
New York, Paris, Calcutta, Edinburgh, Liverpool, etc.
Write for a FREE complimentary copy of Mrs. Hemming's wonderful book, " The Cultivation and Preservation of Natural Beauty."

To "CYCLAX" (Mrs. Hemming)
13 & 14 (O) New Bond Street, W.1

I enclose.............please send me
"CYCLAX" Skin Food 4/-
"CYCLAX" Special Lotion 5/6
"CYCLAX" Blended Lotion......4/6
"CYCLAX" Face Powder 6/6

Name ....

Address ....

USE THIS FORM OR WRITE BY POST

A Lesson In Millinery

One Hat May Be Made of Five Different Fabrics and Trimmed in Six Different Ways

CHRISTMAS is a time at which our thoughts turn readily to new hats. If we are going to create a new hat ourselves, a wise choice would be a small model, with a narrow, rolling rim, which may be turned up in the front or back or on either side according to taste, and also which may be turned up or down all the way round as one prefers.

For this lesson we are going to centre our interest in the fabric hat, but a felt hat of the shape described could be bought and the various trimming suggestions we shall make be carried out on that equally well. There are a few fundamental rules, however, on which success depends : simplicity of design, quality of material, and neatness of work.

The lines of this little French hat recommend it as a model convertible for sports, street, or dress occasions, according to the trimming or fabric used. You may take your choice of velvet, faille, satin, or suède, depending on what use you expect to put it to. Ready-made frames may be purchased and covered at home, or the entire hat may be constructed.

First, collect the necessary materials and plan to work on a large, firm surface. The materials may be summed up as follows :

One yard of the fabric of which the hat is to be made; some thin or French lace-wire; milliner's canvas; light-weight, or tailor's, canvas, for the soft hat; either light-weight milliner's flannel or soft milliner's muslin with which to cover the frame. This tends to soften the finished effect. Milliners' needles and sundries, a reel of forty cotton, a reel of silk the colour of the hat, pins, scissors, and tape-measure.

The first step in making a hat is to obtain the correct head size. Loop the tape-measure around the head, low on the forehead and above the ears, just where your hat rests most comfortably.

Cut a piece of French lace-wire two inches longer than the actual measurement and overlap to required size, twisting ends securely together. Sew this to a bias strip of canvas one inch wide, which forms the headband or foundation to which the crown and brim are sewed as the work proceeds.

Next, pin the pattern of the brim to the canvas, centre-front of pattern to corner of canvas, outline both edges exactly in pencil, then draw a second line one inch above on the inside of the canvas. This extra part is afterwards snipped, turned up, and sewed to the foundation headband. Faille, satin, velvet, and all soft fabrics require this canvas foundation; suède does not, as it has sufficient body and thickness to hold the shape itself.

Cut a piece of the fabric from the

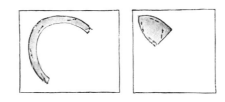

Brim pattern and sectional crown pattern placed on material for cutting

Tacking sections of crown together

The brim is joined in the back and is gently sloping

Sewing foundation and material together

canvas pattern, and as it is essential that the front be bias, be sure to place centre-front of pattern to corner of fabric just as in cutting the canvas. Cut two pieces exactly alike for the outside covering of your hat brim, and one piece of soft millinery flannel or muslin to lay between canvas and fabric. Next, place the two right sides of the fabric together, then the muslin, then the canvas, pin, tack them, and stitch on machine. Trim off any unevenness, turn on the right side, crush with fingers along the edge, but do not press. Before doing this last, however, overlap the ends of the fabric and canvas separately from one-quarter to one-half inch at the back, and seam by machine. Now the brim is complete.

Bias is again necessary for the crown sections, and although one pattern will do for all, as they are exactly alike, it is advisable to cut each section individually. Place pattern for each section cornerwise on material, cut and tack together, one at a time, till all six are done, then stitch by machine. Press the seams open on underside. Unlike the brim, the crown sections are unlined and simply placed over a blocked canvas foundation, which in turn is attached to the headband, to which you have previously joined the brim, and your hat is ready for the finishing touches.

The accompanying sketches suggest various methods of trimming which may be carried out in grosgrain ribbon, bands of felt, scarves of figured silk, or aigrettes. A faille hat with one of the three different bows of grosgrain ribbon would be suitable for sports. A felt or satin hat with scarf knotted as shown would make a more dressy hat. And a velvet hat with a cluster of aigrettes serves the purpose of the perfect afternoon hat. Varnished ribbon and narrow bands of leopard are other suggestions which can be successfully carried out. Patterns for this hat are 1s. each, and obtainable from Pattern Department, GOOD HOUSEKEEPING, 153 Queen Victoria Street, London, E.C.4.

Round the London Shops

Specially designed for motoring, golf, or country wear, this hat is light-weight, uncrushable, and is available in light or dark corduroy lined silk. Price 25s. 9d., post free

(Below) A special find is this attractive dinner frock in black or navy taffeta, excellent quality, with vest and trimming of rows of écru or white narrow lace. Price 42s., post free

(Below) For chilly days this medium weight, all-wool Botany stockinette dress has a cross-over effect, and is trimmed with fancy gallon in contrasting shades. Available in filbert/café, nigger/café, grey/white, willow/grey, café and white, navy/grey, and black/white. Price 43s. 6d., post free

Our Shopping Service

is designed to help those who are out of reach of the London shops. Any of the articles illustrated in these pages, or in the advertisement columns of this number of GOOD HOUSEKEEPING, we shall be happy to buy for you, without extra charge, on receipt of money order and your name and address. Money orders from the Colonies should include cost of postage and insurance. Cheques and money orders should be made payable to the National Magazine Co., Ltd. In the case of millinery, 1s. extra for the box should be enclosed. When ordering any article please give a choice of colours. When ordering a hat please state exact measurement (i.e. circumference of head) required

(Below) For young girls this is a most useful and becoming coat. Made of velours and trimmed with mole coney, it is lined to the waist. Available in fawn, navy, black, nigger, tan, mid grey, and almond; lengths 42, 45, 47 inches. Price for all sizes, 69s. 6d., post free

(Right) A specially recommended "step-in" cami-knicker in extra quality artificial silk in soft shades of mauve, pink, and ivory. Price 21s., post free

(Left) A Princess slip specially designed to wear under straight frocks. It is exceptionally well cut and made of artificial silk in brown, navy, covert, mole, rust, parma, ivory, and black. Price 19s. 11d., post free

This case of 6 pairs of fish knives and forks, electro-plated on nickel silver blades with round white ivorine handles, complete in leatherette case lined dark blue velvet, costs 14s. 9d., postage 6d.; without case, 12s. 6d., postage 4d.

A wristlet bracelet in heavy black moiré ribbon with best quality French paste initials and small ivorine ring for handkerchief. Any initial. Price 4s. 11d., post free

A charming new gauntlet glove, laced with contrasting braid in doeskin; in putty, beaver, or light grey. Price 6s. 6d. per pair, post free

(Right) For all kinds of jobs in the house, the studio, or the garden this attractive smock is useful. In tub fabrics, in a wide range of colours, price 17s. 11d.; in gingham, 21s. 9d.; in fadeless fabrics, 25s. 9d.; in holland, 29s. 9d.; in plain tussore, 42s.; in coloured, 50s. 6d. Post free

A novel and very smart semi-evening frock showing the new bare look at the neck. It is made of good quality crêpe de Chine with finely pleated vest and cuffs of silk georgette to tone. Available in almond, camel, grey, nut brown, navy, ivory, and black. Price 59s. 6d., post free

A sunray pleated satin bag with moiré top and antique paste knob fastening and nice fittings is available in black, nigger, and navy. Price 14s. 9d., postage 4d.

(Left) A very smart suit for early autumn in fine quality Botany suiting, made with black jumper coat, with scarf and pleated skirt in black and white with or without overcheck in mauve, apricot and blue or burnt orange. Price complete, 69s. 6d., post free

Useful good-looking house-frock of heavy weight non-ladder artificial silk stockinette with motifs of Oriental embroidery. Available in almond, tan, grey, saxe, brown, navy, and black. Special price, 32s. 6d., post free

For Country Readers

All letters, money orders, and cheques should be addressed to "Shopping Service," GOOD HOUSE-KEEPING, 153 Queen Victoria Street, London, E.C.4.

Returned Goods: If any reader desires to return goods purchased through the Shopping Service, the following rules must be observed. The goods, together with the reader's full name and address, and a reference to GOOD HOUSEKEEPING Shopping Service, should be returned to the shop. If goods are not returned in perfect condition the money cannot be refunded. Postage must be paid on goods that were correctly sent in the first instance. All correspondence regarding the goods, with all instructions concerning them, must be sent to "Shopping Service," GOOD HOUSEKEEPING, 153 Queen Victoria Street, London, E.C.4.

These stockings are recommended. The cashmere hose have strengthened soles, toes, and heels, and are specially spliced to resist strain of suspenders. Available in shades of grey, fawn, brown, or black. Sizes 8½, 9, 9½ inches. Price 3s. 6d., post free; 10 inch feet, 2d. per pair extra. The silk stockings are 12-strand pure silk with ravel stop to prevent seams and ladders. Available in mole, champagne, leather brown, putty, navy, grey, fawn, nude, evening shades, and black and white. Price 8s. 6d., post free

A wonderful new way to plan and make your own clothes

The Woman's Institute—the largest woman's school in the world —announces a New Course in Dressmaking and Designing which is so simple that any student can now learn at home in spare time to make every garment her heart desires.

Here, at last, is a wonderful new way of learning Dressmaking and Designing. It is easy and practical. You begin at once to make something pretty to wear, and proceed step by step until you can make every garment and hat you require—all exactly to your individual taste.

It doesn't matter where you live—it doesn't make a bit of difference how little you know about sewing. Any woman or girl who really tries can learn to plan and make her own and children's clothes in spare time at home. That is our promise to you.

Perhaps you think dressmaking difficult, or wonder why you do not have more confidence in your own ability to make becoming clothes.

Many women have felt just as you do. Yet it isn't because there is anything so terribly hard or mysterious about dressmaking—for their isn't—but simply because no one has ever shown you how.

There's a right way to make every stitch—every seam—every detail—a certain way to alter patterns—a certain way to cut the material—a certain way to do everything that the best dressmaker can do. Once you learn that way, it is really a joy to make all your own clothes, in the very latest style, for a half or a third of what they would cost you in the shops.

We say positively that this can be done, because in the last eight years the Woman's Institute has taught nearly 200,000 women and girls to plan and make their own clothes in spare time at home—the natural place to learn to sew.

Throughout these eight years and in serving so many thousands of

women, the constant purpose has been to simplify the plan of teaching, to add to its interest, to make it of even more practical helpfulness. To-day that aim has been attained in a new measure of educational achievement in the new Woman's Institute Course in Dressmaking and Designing.

Here are five distinctive features of this New Course:

You Start by Making Actual Garments. From the beginning much of the time spent on your course is devoted to the making of clothes to wear. Your very first instruction book shows you, step by step, how to make an attractive garment.

Materials Furnished Free. To make it easy for you to start at once and to help you save money on your clothes, materials for several garments are furnished to you without cost.

Reference Volumes. In addition to the practical lessons on dressmaking and designing, you receive three handsomely bound Reference Volumes—a complete library of dress information on Textiles, Sewing Materials, Colour Harmony, Care of Clothing, Renovating, Dyeing, Dry Cleaning, etc.

Personal Consultation Service. You receive the benefit of an unlimited personal service on individual problems of dress, affording intimate advice and help on the planning and making of appropriate, becoming clothes for yourself and others.

Fashion Service. Twice yearly —each Spring and Autumn—you receive an exclusive Fashion Service, containing 100 or more designs interpreting the season's correct mode, with complete detailed instructions for developing and making each garment shown.

In addition to the instruction in Dressmaking and Designing, the Woman's Institute teaches *Tailoring*, *Pattern Drafting*, and *Millinery* by the spare-time method. You can, through our training, soon acquire skill in making smart costumes and becoming hats, thereby saving much money.

The way is easy. Just send the coupon or a letter or postcard to the Woman's Institute, Dept. 1, 71 Kingsway, London, and you will receive the full story by return of post.

READ WHAT THESE LADIES SAY

Now Independent of Dressmakers

" I have from my six months' studies gained enough knowledge to make me independent of dressmakers for the rest of my life, and if necessary make my living by sewing should the need ever arise. The Dressmaking Course I am now studying will help very much ; indeed it is quite a mental tonic to me. It puts garment construction on a scientific basis and makes the study interesting and elevating."
(Miss) M. M., Edinburgh.

Better Dressed at Half Pre-War Cost

" I want to thank you for enabling me to be better dressed this year than I have been for five years past. My total outlay on clothes for the whole year will only be a little more than half my pre-war dress expenses. The clothes I have are certainly quite as attractive as any from the very good dressmaker I used to go to. I have just made two evening dresses at a cost of £7 the two, using the very best materials."
(Miss) V. T., St. Mawes, Cornwall.

A Comfortable Income, Earned Easily

" It is with a feeling mixed of gladness and sadness that I am sending in my last paper of the Woman's Institute Dressmaking Course—gladness because I have accomplished a big thing and sadness because I shall miss the pleasure I have always felt in the study and the knowledge gained and the joy of the work. But the work and the ever-increasing joy of it still goes on, for since I started in business I have had no lack of work, sometimes more than I can well handle. Up to the present I have worked single-handed in my home, and I find I can make a very comfortable £2 per week without interfering with my household or social duties. I am now going to start in earnest on the Millinery Course."
(Mrs.) P. A., Selly Hill, Birmingham.

USE THIS COUPON TO-DAY

The Housekeeper's Dictionary *of* Facts

Details That Simplify Housekeeping

THE
20's

To Keep Dress Linings from showing

It is often impossible to keep the lining of a dress from slipping and showing at the neck. When it cannot be tacked to the neck of the dress, try clasping the dress and lining together by sewing clip fasteners on the two shoulders. If these are sewed on properly, they are not noticeable, and the slipping and showing is prevented.

A New Use for the Soap Shaker

A soap shaker will be found invaluable when redipping fabrics with soap dye. Place the cake of soap dye in the soap shaker and shake it back and forth in the water as when using soap. In this way the hands are not stained, and an even distribution of colour is ensured.

Steel Wool for Suède Shoes

The finest steel wool is one of the best cleaners obtainable for suède shoes. Just brush the surface lightly with a small quantity of the steel wool, and the spots will disappear as if by magic.

To Save the Pockets on Dresses

Most women are apt to catch their pockets on door-knobs and other projections, often spoiling the appearance of an otherwise good dress or apron by a rent that no clever mender can conceal. To prevent this, rip the pocket down one inch on either side, finish it with a hem, and sew a fastener at the top. Then, when the pocket catches, the fastener loosens, and no rent is made.

For the New Baby

Crib blankets are expensive to buy. It will be found more economical to buy an all-wool blanket for a large bed and to cut it into four. These can be bound with inexpensive blue material or with cream satin ribbon. One of these could even be used as a pram rug by ornamenting it with a Peter Rabbit patch or some suitable embroidery.

Individual Towels and Face Cloths for Children

One is often confronted with the problem of keeping the bathroom neat without spending too much valuable time in performing the duty. Sometimes it seems a hopeless task with a number of children to throw towels down, and only one pair of hands to pick them up. Try giving the little ones towels and a face cloth of a special colour; they will like the idea of having these as their very own and will take a pride in putting them in their proper place. The appearance of the bathroom will be greatly improved as to neatness and the towels will not become so badly soiled. Another big advantage of this plan is that each child knows his own towel

by colour, and it is not necessary for him to learn to read a name that might have been put on towels of the same colouring, and used as a distinguishing mark.

To Straighten Needles

It often happens that while knitting, the needles become bent. By pouring hot water over them and straightening them immediately with your fingers, and then dipping the needles into cold water, the needles will be perfect once more.

A Hat-box Suggestion

If you have a light-coloured hat that must be kept in a hat-box that has to be taken down from a shelf each time, try slitting the front of a square hat-box, leaving it attached to the box at the bottom only. Then, when the hat is wanted, simply lift the cover with one finger, and let the front drop down, and behold your hat! This saves taking the box down, and it is an easy matter to put the panel back under the cover.

For the Baby Beginning to Feed Himself

When the baby is beginning to feed himself, you will find it saves sticky fingers to make his bread and butter into sandwiches, instead of merely spreading the bread.

Under-slips

Worn with one-piece dresses, will not hang below the dress, when the arm is raised, if snap-fasteners are sewed to the under-arm seams of the dress and slip. When the dress rises with the arm, the slip must come too.

Let the Children Paste Pictures

Tack a piece of white oilcloth on the wall where the kiddies can reach it easily. Let them cut out pictures and paste them on the oilcloth. When they get tired of the pictures, wash them off with a cloth and warm water. Then the picture-board is ready for another set of pictures. Perhaps they will cut out a picture of a barn and paste it near the top of the "board," and then all around it they may paste animals of all kinds, chickens, etc. Soon you will find them displaying much ingenuity in arranging different pictures.

Marking everyday Handkerchiefs

Use a piece of fairly stiff writing-paper, and write the initials on it in one continuous line. Then pin the paper to the centre of the handkerchief and stitch in the initials on the sewing machine, making the stitches as small as possible. Occasionally it is necessary to retrace part of an initial when stitching, as in the letter "C," but it is not noticeable.

For Baby's Bed

Often it is difficult to provide a bed for a young baby visitor. Put a flat pillow in a small drawer from a chest or bureau, cover it with a blanket, and you have a safe, comfortable bed. It can be put on two chairs near the mother's bed for convenience.

A New Use for Shaving Cream

An excellent soap for use in an office, or when travelling, is a tube of shaving cream. It takes but a small quantity to cleanse the hands thoroughly. It is sanitary, especially when one is called upon to lend soap, and is in a convenient form to carry.

A Tip for the Storeroom

How do you tell what stores you have in hand? Stand on a chair and count the jars of jam and pickles on the shelves each time, or have you a means of telling at a glance directly you open the store-room door? This is quite possible. Get a sheet of graph paper from any stationer, cut it in half and paste it on a piece of card. Now write down one side the names of the stores you have —Strawberry Jam, Red-currant Jelly, etc.; and put in the same line one vertical stroke for every jar, varying the size of the stroke according to the size of the pot. For instance, every 3-lb. pot could have a stroke three squares high, every 2-lb. pot a stroke two squares high, and so on. Pierce the card at one corner and attach a pencil on a string. As you use a jar of preserve or pickle, strike off its corresponding stroke on the chart with the pencil.

Care of Old Oak

On the recommendation of a cabinet-maker who specialises in the renovation of antique furniture, it was found that by melting old and disused wax gramophone records, and mixing with turpentine, a polish was obtained which produced an excellent surface and shine on the wood. To improve the appearance of oak furniture that has been neglected, apply the wax liberally, rub in well, and leave for a day or longer before polishing with a soft cloth.

Care of Entrance Doors

Fog, rain, and moisture impair the appearance of coloured painted doors, causing them to become dull and smeary. Wipe with a damp cloth and leather to remove the traces of soot and dust. When quite dry, rub in a little good furnishing oil, or any good wax polish thinned down with turpentine. Polish lightly with an old silk duster, when the door will look as though newly painted. Doors of white paint should be sponged with water and wiped dry with a leather.

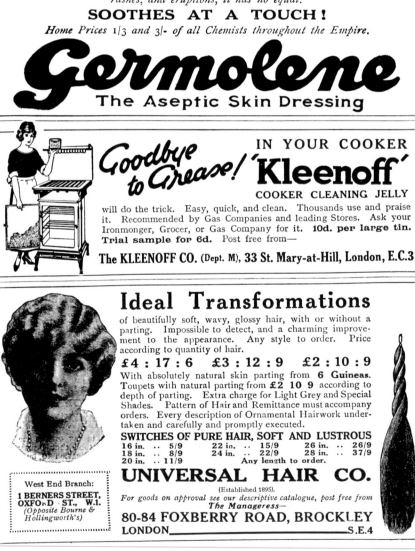

A Country House-wife's *Economies*

By Mabel Leigh

A WOMAN who takes a small country house for her family in the summer, or who lives in the country the year round, must possess more forethought in domestic matters than the town-dweller, whose supplies pour in upon her from every side as part of the day's routine. We are all more or less capable nowadays. The war made us so. This is as well, for to manage a house economically in these times is not easy. One thing is on our side. It is no longer derogatory, if it ever was so, to do one's own work. Rather the contrary. Nearly everyone is

---

To Wash a Sheepskin Rug

If the skin is soft when clean, washing will do it no harm. Shake the rug out-of-doors to get rid of all loose dust. Then take a bath large enough to hold the rug comfortably and half fill it with hot water. Make a lather with melted soap or soap flakes, and add a few drops of liquid ammonia. If the rug is very much soiled, a tablespoonful of paraffin may also be added. Squeeze the rug in this, working it up and down with the hands, or use a small vacuum washer. Repeat the process in a second soapy water if the rug is not clean. Then rinse in warm water until clear of dirty soapsuds, and finally dip it into clean soapy water in order to keep the skin soft. Squeeze the rug as dry as possible, shake out, and dry in a good draught or in the open air. Avoid too rapid drying as it hardens the skin, and while drying rub the rug occasionally to keep it soft and shapely.

---

in like case. We are in honourable company.

As we take a share in domestic work ourselves, it were surely well to teach our children, when they come home from school, to lend us a hand. It is kinder to prepare them at home, in this way, for the times that they will live to see. The boys who have been cooking at Eton, or sweeping out studies at Winchester as fags, will think it no hardship to be made, if not actively, at least negatively useful. Let them abstain from flinging their possessions down haphazard, or tracking in dirt. They might even be asked to polish brass taps —supposing we are foolish enough to have such things, instead of the new painted ones. The girls should make their own beds, and dust the rooms, or even be trained in cooking. There is no reason for rearing them as "beautiful and ineffectual

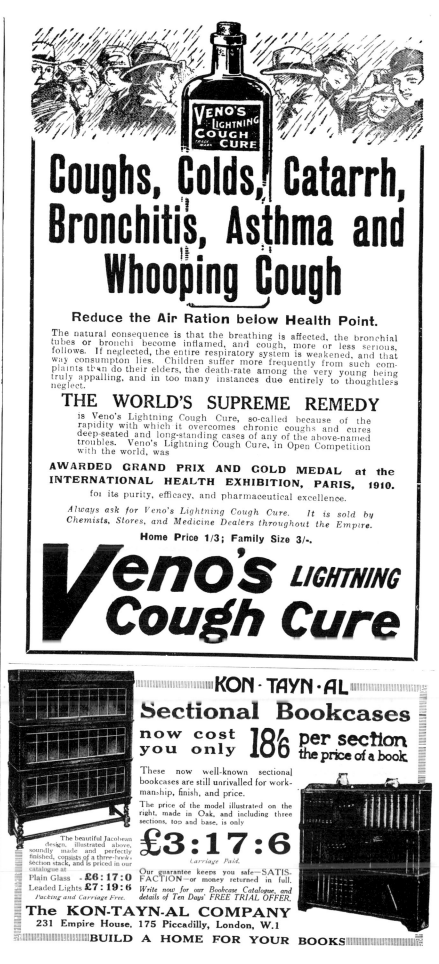

A Country Housewife's Economies

angels." An American writer has said: "The trouble in this country now lies in the fact that there are so few who want to do things with their hands, and so many who want to do things with their bulging brows."

We recommend a course of doing things with the hands for all alike. Servants are the chief source of expense nowadays, not only because of their high wages and keep, but of the somewhat luxurious standard they insist on maintaining. They require many costly utensils and appliances, and are not as careful of these, or of food and fuel, as their mistress is. Hence if we can save on the number of these assistants by doing something ourselves it will be the first economy. The second is that we must learn to execute small repairs about the house. Here the boys again might come in usefully. They can be taught to renew washers on taps, to mend fuses, make the bells ring, or even run the electric engine if we are fortunate enough to possess one.

After all, what difficulty is there in these things compared with those that gentlewomen used to undertake in olden times? They busied themselves in the still-room, making preserves, simples and cordials, medicines and cleaning materials. They spun linen and wove cloth, dyeing the wool for the latter with home-made dyes, much as the crofters' wives in Scotland do to-day. In a humbler sphere they added to these employments the plaiting of straw for horses' collars, stitching and stuffing sheep-skin bags for cart saddles, peeled rushes for wicks, and made candles. I fancy they were the better for all these various occupations. One does not hear of many whimsies among those women— the "vapours" came later—and they needed not to fear obesity, necessitating artificial and grotesque movements to reduce it.

If, in compliance with these precepts, the housewife takes on a share of the daily work, there are a few hints that may lighten her labour. Instead of the white mats, now used to save washing tablecloths, we have mats of bright-coloured linen, yellow, red, or blue, which keep clean longer, scalloped in white. A yellow check cloth for the tea-table, or the breakfast-tray, comes to us from Paris. Asbestos mats, placed under the linen ones to prevent the table from being scorched, used to be troublesome to clean. Now we cover them in dark-brown silk, run through with narrow elastic. The dressing-table and washstand mats are of coarse plaited straw, in bright colours, replacing the white ones which used to be always in the washtub. Tumblers, water-bottles, and glass jugs have been relegated to the shelf. They are too much trouble to clean. Instead we have the pretty cottage pottery, wide-necked, squat jugs and mugs in brilliant patterns. China can be got to match the cretonne curtains. These are not too light in colour, and the quilts, toilet covers, and chair covers are all made of the same material, which does not soil easily.

It is not necessary to go to the expense of a workman to put up brass rods and short curtains; we can make our own, and the blinds will not have that "sag" in the middle which is the fatal mark of the amateur. Lengths of cane or rounded stick can be obtained, painted the colour of the woodwork and cut to the desired size. Sharpened ends fit into hooks each side of the window. The curtains are run on rings. There is a new sort of short curtain made of oatmeal cloth, a loose-meshed fabric of pretty café-au-lait tint.

A Country Housewife's Economies

This is blanket-stitched round the edges in coloured wool. One single figure, a bright bird or flower, is worked on to the centre of each curtain in coarse wool. There is no fullness in such blinds; they hang straight.

To turn to the kitchen: there should be here one of the many new contrivances for producing hot water independently of the kitchen range. Hot water is a vital need in any household—but above all in the country, where baths may be called for at odd hours after sports or garden work. The work of the coal range or oil stove is thus lessened. Soup, or such casserole dishes as require simmering, can be left to complete the process in the new fireless cooker, a thing like a glorified thermos flask, which requires neither watching nor fire.

If there are children, it is cheaper to make jams and marmalades at home. We can make apple chutney out of quite poor apples, and home-made pickles are excellent. I found it a great help to make soda water at home in a special large siphon, using soda powders and seltzogene charges. At breakfast, stewed fruit should always be served and cereals cooked with raisins. Americans attach great importance to fruit in the dietary, but English people are apt to forgo it on account of its cost. In the country one seldom sees the finer sorts, and their cultivation is neglected except by professionals for the London market. Gone are the days when Sir William Temple grew oranges in England, and declared that an excellent bitter cordial could be made of them, "most useful against the

plague." He was right. They still serve against the modern plague, influenza. Dried fruits, such as prunes, apricots, and peaches, are not dear; stewed in a casserole they are excellent to serve with meat, or as a sweet. Till required for cooking they must be kept in glass jars in the store-room.

All these things, and many more, should

Handsome Covers

in cloth gilt, for binding the fourth six numbers of GOOD HOUSEKEEPING — which will be completed with next month's number—may be obtained from all booksellers and newsagents for 2s. 6d. each, or 2s. 10d., post free, from GOOD HOUSEKEEPING, 1 Amen Corner, London, E.C.4

be written down in the woman's Household Book. From these lists she compiles her store orders, month by month and year by year. Here, too, are the tradesmen's addresses, and the names of the char-ladies who might be called upon for help on occasions. There is the catalogue of homely remedies, kept in the medicine cupboard in

case of illness or accident. Such lists are duplicated on cards inside the door of the cupboard, and a card hangs outside on which are printed directions for cases of emergencies. In the country one cannot count on getting a doctor the moment he is wanted. We all know the good wife's herbal and need not repeat this list. But in the store cupboard it must be remembered to keep a tin or two of the usual patent foods, arrowroot, pearl barley, chicken jelly in tins, and meat extract, in case of illness.

In the household book is the linen, plate, glass, china, and wine list. New purchases are added under their date, and cost subjoined. This enables us to see at a glance the rise or fall of prices. A kind of diary is kept at the end in which is stated the year the cretonnes were renewed, what kind of labour-saving device we found a failure, and why we don't buy So-and-so's patent what's-its-name any more. The best of such a book is that, leaving it behind, the tired housewife can escape for a holiday, knowing that her substitute will have a sure guide in running the house. She cannot flounder far when constantly pulled up by a notebook whose finger serenely points to the solution of every difficulty.

Lamb, who, like most men, approved of the domestic female, and who never lived to see the Jazz one, said of a woman: "She happily missed all that train of female garniture which passeth by the name of accomplishments." Despite him, we contend that it *is* an accomplishment, and a great one, successfully and economically to run a modern house in such a world as ours is to-day.

Fig. 1. With a firm, rotary motion, work outwards, downwards, and backwards, pushing the flesh to the centre of the back

Fig. 2. Work with rotary motions around the excess fat

Fig. 1

Fig. 2

Health and Beauty

Restoring the Contour of the Neck and the Shoulders

By Nora Mullane

PERSONS who suffer from an excess of fat, or a prominence of muscle at the back of the neck, and others who have become round-shouldered, will be glad to know that there is a way of counteracting these defects, and a comparatively easy one. To accomplish this the person must be in earnest, must persevere in the treatment until the desired result is obtained, and then continue the treatment to prevent a recurrence of the condition.

When you first realise that your neckline is broken, that your back is no longer flat, it is time to begin treatments. If you begin at once, you will have no difficulty in counteracting the defects and regaining control of the muscles. Fat accumulates where there is very little muscular effort, and the reverse condition will work it off. The success of your efforts will depend upon the use and activity of the muscles, and the systematic and regular application of the remedy.

A neck massage and pressure will wear away that little prominence at the back of the neck; the shoulder exercise will restore the tone and flexibility of the muscles, making them capable of responding to the will; while the wand exercise establishes a correct carriage.

The shoulders are the most difficult portion of the body to relax. It is perhaps because we are made conscious of them as children by being so often reminded to " sit up straight," "stand up straight, or hold your shoulders back," with the result that later they either look too stiff, or droop forward, which causes the backward curve, and, in time, round shoulders. It will require patience and perseverance to restore contour and correct carriage. But do not be discouraged; it can be done. Young people under thirty years will have no difficulty in restoring youthful lines, if they are in earnest. Older persons will improve their appearance to such an extent that it will pay to make the effort.

In all cases, the degree of force and the right amount of exercise are quite important and must be decided by the person exercising, until the muscles are accustomed to be stimulated. It is better for beginners not to repeat movements the given number of times. Do each one of them two or three times and work up gradually to ten. There are persons who are in such a hurry to see improvement that they overdo. The part

of the body not used to exercise becomes a little sore. Do not come to the conclusion that you cannot take exercise, but miss a day or two and begin again.

Always wash the neck with warm water and soap, and dry it thoroughly before treatment. Rub a small amount of pure cold cream on the hands and neck so as to lubricate the skin and prevent irritation. Then work in front of a mirror.

Position: Sit upright on a stool, or chair.

First—Place the right hand on the right side of the neck and lift the left hand on the left side, the fingers facing backward. Hold the fingers close together, and with a firm, rotary motion work outward, downward and backward, pushing the flesh to the centre of the back, until you can raise the muscle from the normal point of attachment, as in figure 1. *Do not try to accomplish this at the first sitting.*

Second—Work with rotary motions around the excess fat, as in figure 2.

Third—Stroke the muscles outward from the centre to the shoulders as in figure 3. Do not work on the spinal column. Repeat five to ten times.

Fourth—Tip the head backward, then forward.

Fifth—Draw the chin far in. This is excellent for the muscles at the back of the neck. Do it slowly at first. Repeat three times.

Sixth—Turn the head one way as far as possible and then in the opposite direction. Repeat five times.

Walking with the Wand.—For this purpose a round stick is sufficient. The stick should be passed across the back through the arms. The arms are bent upward and pressed firmly back and close to the sides, the body being held as upright as possible. Walk round the room for five minutes or longer.

This exercise, while it assists in strengthening the shoulders and back muscles, is principally to form the habit of correct carriage, and to correct slight defects and faulty habits.

Shoulder Exercises

First—Relax the shoulders and let them droop; then bring them back to a normal position. Let them droop five times. Then raise the shoulders to the normal height and bring them forward, rounding the back, then backward, expanding the chest. Repeat five times.

Fig. 3

Stroke the muscles outward from centre of shoulders

In the dressing-room of any woman's club, it is the middle-aged women who block the looking-glass

L. Allen Harker

On—

The Modern Middle-Aged Woman

As Seen by the Modern Girl

Illustration by Bert Thomas

MUCH adverse criticism has been hurled at the shingled head of the Modern Girl, and it seems only fair that she, in her turn, should have her say as to her elders. Therefore I have for the last three months been busily collecting opinions from various representative and youthful sources. It is always salutary, even if somewhat disillusioning, to see ourselves " as others see us," yet I must, at the outset, like those editors who publish correspondence in their magazines, declare " that I disclaim all responsibilty alike for the opinions themselves and the manner of their expression."

So far as is possible, I use the young people's own words.

"I'm devoted to Mum," Kitty said. " She's clever and kind and awfully capable, but I do wish she wouldn't everlastingly hold up the past to admiration, and disparage the present. We can't get the past back. It's gone. And she ought not to expect us to thrill with admiration over a set of circumstances we never have experienced. What strikes me as comic, too, is that aunts and people when they reminiscence, give each other away like anything, and they seem to have been every bit as giddy as they say we are, only they had to be slyer about it. Besides, if we do run about by ourselves, we have to, for there's no one to take us. Our mothers are, quite rightly, far too busy over their own committees and things to run round after us. And nobody nowadays has enough servants to

send out maids to take or fetch girls either from classes or private houses. Please make no mistake; I get on with my people perfectly. I'm quite awfully fond of them, but I do get a bit tired of the ' glorious past ' stunt. It's the glorious future that interests me."

Gwen has quite another bone to pick with the older generation.

" Servants," she complains, " have become a regular Moloch with my people, and they sacrifice us and our happiness to the servants all day long. We mustn't do this, and we mustn't do that, because it ' will upset the servants.' It's always Connie's afternoon out, or Ruby's evening, or Doris's half-day when we want to have our friends. We can't have any jollification ever in the house, because it would be ' too much ' for the other two, and there never seems to be more than two in at the same time. I wish to goodness they'd all go out together, then we could do what we like. But as it is, everything of a cheery, hospitable nature is vetoed. I don't believe they'd mind a bit really if we did have an occasional beano; but the elders have got it into their heads that they would, and as they're not over-fond of a lot of extra people themselves, we're obliged to go out for any fun we want, because we never are allowed to have it at home. Talk about ' the restaurant habit,' why, one's *driven* to restaurants and nightclubs by one's own people. If you happen to be away and it's spring-cleaning, you can't come home, because it would

' upset their routine.' If you've been out for a long day motoring, you can't have a meal an hour late, at least not without reproachful glances and murmurs as to ' the servants,' and every mouthful you eat chokes you. I've come to the conclusion that in my family—and there are plenty like it—the children's comfort counts for nothing compared to that of ' the servants.' I'm sick of hearing about them. I'm perfectly ready to lend a hand and help, and I do want to be able to ask my own friends to the house sometimes; but it seems to me that it isn't my home any more. My people are decent as they can be in every other way, and my mother is kind as kind; but we do come a bad second after the servants, and we think we ought to come first. We don't grudge the servants their constant outings and their good times, but we do grudge, and bitterly, the fact that their convenience and their comfort seems to have ousted us from any sort of consideration. And that's why such lots of us would rather live in the horridest little flat with another girl, *where we can have our friends whenever we like,* than in the loveliest great house where we're in thrall to ' the servants.' "

Dolly is more tolerant, but is a little bored because her mother, who was in the van of the suffrage movement, thinks that present-day girls are not grateful enough to the pioneers who won for them the privileges they accept so easily as rights.

" Why should   *(Continued)*

we be grateful?" she asked. "They wanted the vote for themselves. They *wanted* to be doctors and lawyers and chemists and cabinet-ministers, and they got their desire. Why should we be grateful to them because we, too, can be all these things. You might as well ask us to express enthusiastic gratitude about Magna Charta or the repeal of the Corn Laws. They seem to forget this—that when they were so frightfully keen on careers and votes and things they were older than we are. And most of them had had their fun. It's natural between nineteen and twenty-three to want to play about a bit, and those of us who had the misfortune to be about seventeen when the war broke out had none of that sort of fun. It's coming back now, but it was absolutely stamped out for many of us during five long years. Nothing can give us back those years, and we simply can't pump up gratitude for so much solid food and no savouries. No doubt the women who are middle-aged now made a splendid fight for their rights, and *enjoyed fighting*, but they can't expect us to go on admiring them and thanking them when it's all been over such ages ago, and the Great War came in between.

"When they all rub it into me how lucky I am to have so many 'careers' open to me, I sometimes think it must have been rather jolly to have lived in times when one 'came out' at eighteen and wasn't expected to care about anything useful till one was married. Nowadays one can't even be good at games without some elder suggesting that one should train for a games mistress. Girls get no rest if their people are intelligent and keen. I'm awfully proud of my parents, but I wish they weren't quite so anxious about my future."

Christabel, with quite respectable brains and a pretty face, is nevertheless "no good at exams.," yet she, curiously enough, has a good word to say for the scholastic profession. "If I wanted sympathy and understanding," she said, "when I'd got into a very bad mess, I'd far sooner go to my old headmistress than to any of my people. A first-class headmistress has had enormous experience of girls, and can see all round a situation far better than most mothers, who nearly always see everything from the purely personal point of view, and that view is so often limited by the blocking opinions of a host of relations. A wise headmistress can detach a girl from her surroundings, realise the girl, and judge how circumstances affect her. A great schoolmistress is often one of the most tolerant of human beings because she has seen such a tremendous lot of human folly. Most middle-aged women are not tolerant where girls are

concerned. I don't for a moment believe they hate us, as certain novelists would make out, but they do see our defects with the most powerful magnifying glass. For example, the question of make-up—how they shriek at us for using it; and yet if you go into the dressing-room of any woman's club, it's the middle-aged women who block the looking-glass and stay there an unconscionable time using lip-stick, powder, rouge, and the whole bag of tricks —and then they call us 'painted minxes.'"

Lucy thinks that the "middle-aged woman would be less catty if only she would become middle-aged a little sooner. People remain young quite excessively long now, and there's no doubt that the daughters of pretty, attractive, and exceedingly youthful-looking mothers have rather a dull time. Where the mother, admirably turned out, holds every gathering by her wit and charm, what chance has a girl? Girls need a little help, that only older women who don't mind being older women can give them. It's quite the rule now to hear a girl compared unfavourably with her mother. There ought to be no possibility of such comparison. Mothers are not always generous, and as for the undatable spinster who has made a place for herself, the mere girl hasn't a chance in competition with her. It's true we may have more liberty than girls had in the past, but we have to find our fun for ourselves. Nobody arranges parties for us, as one reads they were arranged for young people in the nineteenth century. And if we are as selfish as our critics make out, they are selfish too. They are so much absorbed by 'causes' and by their own affairs, that they care very little, really, what sort of women we are going to be.

"Yet, though they may not believe it, girls *are* grateful when older women are interested. The woman who will listen, who is gentle in her judgments and not 'down on' one, who wants one to be good and charming, and yet to have some fun, can have immense influence just because she is middle-aged. So many of them seem to have forgotten what it feels like to be young—looks have nothing to do with it. You may have grown-up children, and look five-and-twenty, and do everything better than they do, and yet be æons of ages old in your heart."

I must testify that there was no rancour in any of the criticisms. Upon the whole they were much more generous to their elders than their elders are to them, and in none of the girls I interviewed did I find the pained bewilderment of the young actress, in Clemence Dane's most poignant story *Wandering Stars*, who exclaims, "Why are old women always catty to a girl?"

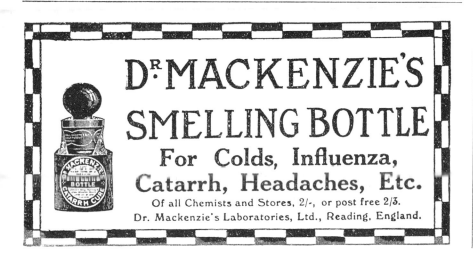
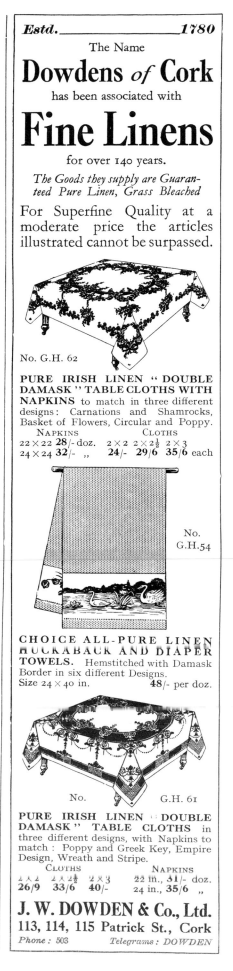

The Housekeeper's Dictionary of Facts

Things Worth Remembering

THE
20's

Ginger-Ale Jelly

When making a packet jelly, try using ginger ale instead of water. Dissolve the jelly in a small quantity of water, then make up the quantity of liquid with ginger ale. When served with whipped cream, the jelly has just a little pleasing sting in it, but not enough for anyone to guess how it has been made.

A Substitute for a Hot-water Bottle

When the family hot-water bottle springs a leak and one is needed in an emergency, try the following. Place an old magazine in the oven until thoroughly heated, then wrap it in a piece of soft flannel. It makes a good substitute, being light and pliable, and retaining its heat for a long time. To heat the magazine quickly, open it in a number of places, and roll some of the leaves to hold it open.

Rainy Days made Easier

It is a well-known fact that all children enjoy most the things that are kept for special occasions. You will find that rainy days are looked forward to, if there is a rainy day scrap-book. Have in a convenient place a box or basket where all bright pictures, magazine covers, even labels from fruit tins, can be put. Have ready also a scrap-book, scissors, and paste, but allow no one to work unless the rain appears. You will find that the children will love their play, and the rainy days will become a pleasure, instead of a problem.

Scraps for Little Seamstresses

Many little girls have their first needlework lessons in sewing for their dolls under their mother's supervision. In order to make such work interesting, it is a good plan to go through one's own scrap-basket at frequent intervals and to put aside bits of lace, embroidery, or ribbon, etc.—anything in fact that can be made use of in the dressing of a doll. The interest taken in the sewing after such an acquisition of new material is out of all proportion to the time and trouble it has cost.

A Child's Privilege

It is not every mother who recognises the wisdom of providing for each child some definite place where his own belongings may be kept. If each child can have his own room, that, of course, is ideal. The next best thing is to have some one article of furniture, a cupboard, chest of drawers, or set of shelves, as the child's very own. The right of absolute ownership invests the child with a dignity which is worth much trouble to secure, and begets within him a sense of the obligation which he owes to society of looking after his own things—and in time of making his own way in the world.

Home-made Soap Flakes

If you live where it is impossible to buy laundry soap in flake form, buy bars of soap and run them through the mincing machine. The drier the soap the easier it is to mince; but in any case it is easier than shaving it down with a knife. The soap will be in a form which will readily dissolve, and it can be kept in readiness for washing-day.

A New Use for Picture Wire

Instead of using twine or any kind of string for hanging up brooms, mops, brushes, and all kinds of kitchen utensils, use ordinary picture wire as a substitute. It will wear indefinitely, and being stiff will catch on hooks more easily than string.

The Secret of Success

in cookery, as every clever housewife knows, lies in providing plenty of variety. Introduce a new dish often, and let it be carefully prepared. The Cookery Section of GOOD HOUSEKEEPING will make this easy. All the dishes described in these pages, each month, have first been thoroughly tested in the Model Kitchen by the Director of Cookery. You can depend upon them absolutely.

When Travelling

When packing your travelling-case for a night on the train or boat, put in a tube of good shaving soap instead of the usual cake of soap. Besides not having a wet cake of soap to repack, you will find that the shaving soap lathers and cleanses so much better if the water is hard.

A Sand Pin-cushion

This is practical in many ways. Make a small bag of double cloth (so that the sand will not sift through) on the sewing-machine, and fill it with fine dry sand until it is plump and hard. Then sew it shut and cover it with some pretty material. This kind of pin-cushion is heavy enough not to fall about easily, and the sand keeps the pins and needles sharp and shiny.

A Hint for the Work-box

Transfer patterns for embroidery or other needlework may be kept indefinitely by the following device, which is a distinct advantage when one's favourite design is out-of-date and unobtainable in the shops. Take the used transfer, lay it on a piece of drawing paper, and place a piece of carbon paper between, the copying side towards the drawing paper. Trace over the pattern with a sharply pointed, hard pencil. This will give a clear reprint. When you wish to use the pattern again, take a copy on tracing paper, and with the aid of carbon paper transfer it to the material.

Washing Pillows

Given a bright, windy day, it is quite possible to wash pillows without first removing the feathers. Prepare plenty of warm, soapy water, adding a teaspoonful of turpentine to a gallon of water. Wash the pillows by kneading and squeezing, or with a suction washer, until no more dirt comes from them. Rinse in plenty of warm, soft water, and hang to dry in a windy spot in the garden. The pillows can be suspended to a clothes-line or tree by tying one corner of the tick with string. Shake from time to time whilst drying to prevent the feathers becoming matted.

A Use for a Bicycle Pump

Housewives who do not possess a vacuum cleaner will find a bicycle pump very handy for getting rid of dust from behind radiators, and in other cracks and corners. After using the pump, wipe the dust up with a slightly oily duster.

To Remove Stains from Brown Shoes

If oil is inadvertently allowed to come into contact with brown shoes, an ugly stain appears. This may generally be removed by cleaning carefully with petrol, rubbing the spot with a circular movement. If this fails after repeated treatment, cover the stain with rubber solution, leave it on until all the naphtha has evaporated, and then remove it. The appearance of shabby brown brogues can often be improved by cleaning thoroughly with turpentine, using a nail-brush for the cracks.

Only £3.14.0 down and you have the Hoover

Give Your Work To The HOOVER

Winter housecleaning's apt to bring a little shudder of discontent to almost every housewife. A spotlessly clean home is her pride, but doesn't it too often entail cruelly hard work *unless* she makes the beating*, sweeping, suction cleaning Hoover her electrical, tireless servant? Then her housecleaning becomes almost effortless. For in its easy, gliding motion the Hoover dustlessly dislodges even the most deeply embedded grit. And the Hoover Dusting Tools—for curtains, upholstery and difficult corners of the room—are just as easy and simple to use. Your local Authorised Hoover Dealer will demonstrate the Hoover to you on your own carpets, free of charge or obligation.

The HOOVER

REG. TRADE MARK

It BEATS . . . as it Sweeps . . . as it Cleans

*To Prove Carpets Need Beating:** Turn over a corner of a carpet ; with the handle of an ordinary table knife, or something about that weight, give the back of the carpet 15 to 25 sharp taps, and watch the dirt dance out from the pile depths on to a piece of paper ; feel the destructive character of this grit. *This is the dirt your present cleaning methods have missed and that beating has dislodged.* Correct use of the Hoover causes the embedded dirt to be *vibrated* to the surface by the rapid, gentle *beating* of the Hoover brush, as powerful suction *lifts* the carpet from the floor and draws all the beaten-out, swept-up dirt into the dust-tight bag.

HOOVER LTD., 229-233 REGENT STREET, LONDON, W.1, and at Birmingham, Manchester, Leicester, Leeds and Glasgow

REFRESHING GRACE AND BEAUTY.

In the full glare of the ball-room beauty reveals itself to the most critical eye, and, like all beautiful things, feminine charm hangs upon a slender thread.

A consistent daily use of " *4711* " in the bath or toilet water helps to keep the complexion and skin in such wonderful condition that beauty and daintiness are maintained at very little trouble and so little cost.

Of all Dealers in High Class Perfumes, 2/6, 4 9, 8/9, 14/-, 15/-, 30/- & 56/- per bottle

Companion Aids to Beauty Preservation :

"4711" Bath Salts	"4711" Vanishing Cream	"4711" Soap
1/6 & 2/6 per bottle	1/- & 2/- each	2/- Box of 3
"4711" Cold Cream	For Men Folk	
1/6 & 2/6 per pot	"4711" Shaving Stick in aluminium case 1/3	

No. *4711* Eau de Cologne

By Hazel Hunkins

Keep a Budget

By doing this you will be able to keep expenditure in the right proportion, and so make the most of your income

GRANDMOTHER, bless her serene heart, kept carefully what she called "household accounts"; I, more fortunate perhaps, keep a "budget."

There is a world of difference between the two.

A whole world of difference, I repeat, though thousands of women don't realise it. When the word "budget" is mentioned, they shudder, for it calls up a picture of grandmother's laborious, meticulous Victorian "accounts" in which every penny spent was carefully put down, partly to satisfy grandfather that she was not squandering the household funds, and partly—let us be frank—as an end in itself, for the mild pleasure of doing it. The modern housewife, especially she who runs an establishment that is understaffed, has not time or inclination for "book-keeping"—sufficient unto the day are the bills thereof. When you say "budget" to her, it sounds like bondage, the irksome accounting of every penny.

Well, that is wrong. I, who am a devotee of the budget system, will not keep "penny accounts." I find my system is the gateway to greater liberty. My budget is merely my device for so apportioning my income that it puts me in possession of what I really want, instead of what I would otherwise choose out of impulse or through passing extravagance. This involves minor denials, but it is the beginning of permanent satisfaction. Grandmother's laborious system of accounts, be it noted, had no such end in view.

Those home-makers who are harassed each week by the fact that the income doesn't cover their necessities, will find revealed through the budget system just what items are too high. One home-maker I know was struggling along trying to meet the bills as they came, and growing each month more and more depressed over that ever increasing deficit. Her impulse had been merely to watch more carefully leaks in the kitchen and to cut down on goods consumed. She was given a model working budget, and then worked out one for herself, based on the family income.

Much to her surprise, she discovered that their rent and gas bills were both entirely out of proportion to their income and style of living. She let her spare room to decrease her own rent, and put a shilling check meter on the kitchen stove to reduce the gas bills. The next time I saw her, the strained look had quite left her face; those two items, it seems, had made all the difference in meeting the current bills each week! It is not always, however, as easy as that.

In making your first budget, start in some such fashion as this. Under heading FOOD put down what you pay week by week not only for such items as bread, fish, green-groceries, provisions, meat, and dairy products (eggs, butter, and milk), but also put down meals taken regularly outside of the home, such as school lunches and the man's lunch in the city. If your budget is to be worth anything, the item FOOD as well as every other item must be inclusive.

Then comes SHELTER, which may be rent including rates, or it may be the cost of ownership. Perhaps the home-maker does not pay this item, but it has its influence on the other expenditures and she should know the amount. The item CLOTHING should include all the clothing bought by any member of the family, except perhaps those little extravagances which are bought out of personal money.

Then comes OPERATING COSTS, which loom so large these days. That item includes, naturally, gas, electricity, coal, telephone, laundry, wages (all wages, both of living-in and occasional servants), and all household supplies. Regarding this last item, it is quite misleading to classify necessities like soap, cleaning powders, polish for floors, silver, etc., brushes, brooms, floor-cloths, etc., under FOOD, as one is inclined to do, since they usually come from the same place as the groceries. It is really worth a little trouble to separate these things from the food bill. I save myself that trouble by ordering all such things from a different shop, so that the respective totals automatically come in separate each week.

Other items in the family expenditure are not so definitely one thing or another and may be shifted to suit your personal choice of classification. Personally, I have grouped expenses in the following way. HEALTH includes doctor's and all chemist's bills, and a lump sum for the holidays. Under PLEASURE one would include small trips, theatres, parties, perhaps the upkeep of a motor, and that most important fixed sum which each member of the family receives for his or her own, to save or squander with no questions asked, no accounting to be done. It is obvious that the distinctions between these items is a matter of personal choice. Who is to say but yourself whether membership in a swimming club is for health or for pleasure?

REHABILITATION includes any item requiring a builder, like carpentering, papering, etc., and also new house-furnishing and furniture. No budget is complete without a SAVINGS item, covering direct savings, if any, deposited in bank or post office, as well as investments and insurance. Even though the home-maker does not handle that department of the family income, she should know about it, and as far as possible it should have a definite relation to the other items. Under

(Continued overleaf)

THE
20's

THE
20's

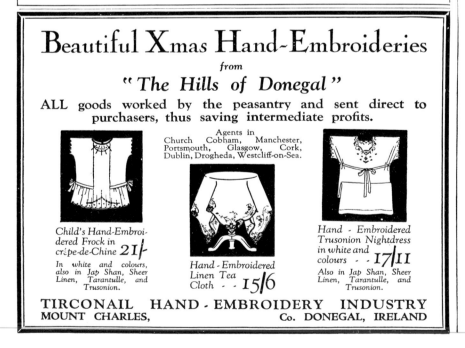
Keep a Budget

EDUCATION I include not only school fees but also books, magazines, and papers that come regularly, and library memberships.

EMERGENCIES is an item seldom occurring in typical budgets, but it is a useful, indeed a necessary, heading. You must allow for the unexpected because, as has been sapiently observed, the unexpected always happens.

You can subdivide your budget until the thing becomes a nightmare or you can make the headings so inclusive they do not mean much. The happy medium is the thing to strive for.

When you have done this for several weeks, examine the totals. Notice what your average expenditures are for the various items—food, shelter, clothing, health, education, etc. Of your weekly, monthly, or yearly income note what percentage goes for rent, what percentage for food, for clothing, etc., in the same period. Now at last, and perhaps for the first time, you face facts, the economic facts of your household.

Some percentages will seem fairly reasonable; some will strike your common sense at once as being far too large. From this basis you can frame your ideal budget, a simple guide for yourself in the expenditures which you control. Ultimately, I might almost say inevitably, by sheer contagion and the persuasive power of facts, it will become a guide to the entire family disbursements.

But don't start too elaborately or you may arouse unnecessary opposition. Some member may demur, "Our expenditures will not tally with your well-oiled system until our family suddenly becomes ideal." The pessimist will point out the exigencies that will arise and rend it to bits. He is right in part; your budget cannot be too tidy, too dogmatic, or that is what will happen.

Above all, don't let your budget appear a feminist device for depriving *pater-familias* of his masculine prerogatives; don't make *him* feel that you want him to "account for every penny" ! All you need from him at the start is his weekly estimate for lunches. The rest—his other personal expenditures—can be lumped as his private money under the family item PLEASURE, for which no further accounting is necessary.

And now a further caution. Don't make your budget a list of receipted bills. It is not that. You may be in arrears to the grocer, the milkman, or your builder; never mind, put down your weekly expenditures regardless of when they are paid and keep them within the total you have set. At certain times you may have to send substantial cheques to a schoolmaster or your landlord; these should be the sums accumulated each week of the fifty-two for which the family purse has made itself liable. Then you do not have those periodic scrambles to meet those large bills that come due seldom. In other words, your budget is your record of current expenses, even though they are in arrears of payment or are merely accumulating towards a payment.

Your first gain from your budget will be a bird's-eye view of your expenditures; for the first time you will see "where the money goes." You can then begin to direct your expenditures more intelligently. Your second gain will be equally concrete, consisting of the definite saving of time and money you can affect by planning ahead and buying in quantity.

For example, you can determine the quantity of certain supplies you will use over a period of weeks or months and order that much ahead. You can save money by buying a season's or a month's supply of tinned goods—meat, fish, soups, fruits, jams, and marmalade—and if you have adequate storage receptacles, a supply of rice. beans, tapioca, etc.

The money saved by this method, however, can be easily lost. Every worker is more careless in the handling of supplies when there is an apparent *cornucopia,* and leakages are likely to develop which quite offset the original saving. But if you guard against this tendency by a weekly allotment or some other economy check, you can still enjoy the advantages of quantity buying.

Not only is there frequently a saving of money by buying in this way, but there is also a saving of time and trouble. I know many households where every tradesman calls every morning for orders and the servants' morning duties are continually interrupted by calls at the kitchen door. This is waste every way you look at it. You can save a great deal of it by having a weekly delivery of your requirements of such things as sugar, butter, bacon, margarine, tea, coffee, etc.

In the winter, when our selection of vegetables is mostly limited to root vegetables, you can save time by ordering a week's supply of carrots, turnips, swedes, Spanish onions, apples, and oranges. Arrange to have all these deliveries on the same day, then the rest of the week there are only perishable vegetables and fruit, meat, fish, and bread to be delivered daily.

From my budget, I noted one year how many eggs we used during the season when new-laid eggs on the market were from three shillings to four shillings a dozen. The next year I preserved as many eggs in water-glass as we would be likely to use during that period. I paid 1s. 3d. a dozen to a poulterer in the country for from five to eight dozen a week during April and May. That winter as soon as eggs reached three shillings, I began to use the preserved ones. In this way I effected a saving of several pounds, and found that my own preserved eggs were as good as, if not better than, the "new-laid" on the market.

Each home-maker will discover her own way of saving after she has seen her budget in operation and has studied its possibilities. The main thing is the elimination of "hand-to-mouth" management, and the recovery of control over one's·time, energy, and money, that we may get out of life those things we really value.

THE
20's

The Housekeeper's Dictionary *of* Facts

From the file at Good Housekeeping Institute

THE
20's

When Troubled with Flies

Although often difficult to account for, certain houses are troubled with a pest of flies in the late summer and early autumn. To overcome this trial, the use of fish net of medium mesh is recommended. This should be stretched tightly over those windows which are constantly kept open and also over the entrance doors. The net is easy to fit over the windows, for it may be stretched on ordinary white hat elastic, the ends of which are provided with loops, and these should be attached to four hooks screwed into the woodwork. Spiral expanding curtain rods, which can be bought quite cheaply, may also be used. The net is a little more difficult to arrange over the doors; two or three overlapping pieces are required, and it is advisable to weight the bottom so that they keep in position when a breeze is blowing. This arrangement has been found efficient by a reader, whose house is surrounded by farmyards, and who previously had always been pestered with flies.

Care of Garden Furniture

Unpainted garden furniture should be preserved against winter rains by rubbing in a liberal amount of linseed oil: after about a week has elapsed a second dressing should be applied. The same treatment also preserves and prevents unpainted wooden doorsteps from cracking and wearing unduly.

Paint Cleaning Hint

When cleaning paint great difficulty is often experienced in removing dust from the cracks, ledges and frames of windows, bannisters, etc. An ordinary small enamel paint brush, which decorators call a "sash tool," is excellent for this purpose. First wet the paint with soapy water, apply soap to the brush, and work out the dirt with the bristles. Afterwards, rinse and dry in the usual way. Needless to say, only an old brush should be used for this purpose.

When Cooking Cakes

The colour of plain fruit cakes can be improved by the addition of a small quantity of cocoa essence. About half a tablespoonful to one pound of flour answers this purpose, but is insufficient to impart a chocolate flavour to the cake.

Renovating Kitchen Tins

Kitchen tins, or metal articles such as a housemaid's box, can be renovated by painting them with Brunswick black thinned with turpentine. This gives the tins a bronze colour, which is quite attractive in appearance and preferred by some housewives to black paint.

Cleaning Discoloured Marble

If badly stained, the judicious use of lemon-juice will remove stains and discolorations from marble. It must be remembered, however, that lemon-juice, being an acid, will impair the surface if allowed to remain in contact with it for very long or if applied too frequently. It should only be used, therefore, after rubbing the stained part with a paste made of soap and whiting has proved ineffectual. Friction soap cleansers should not be used for polished marble as they roughen the surface, and in consequence the marble soils more readily. After the use of lemon-juice, all trace should be removed by thorough rinsing with warm water and drying. When dry, the rubbing in of a very little salad oil, followed by vigorous polishing with a soft duster, improves the appearance of the marble, giving it a gloss. Oil, however, should not be applied to other than a smooth surface, for it is practically

POT POURRI

ANYONE who has rose leaves in plenty can make this fragrant mixture. Collect the rose leaves and dry in the sun—a shelf in a greenhouse is a good drying place as there is no chance of the petals being blown about by the wind. Then collect equal quantities of such sweet-smelling spices, etc., as musk, lavender, cloves, orris root, vanilla pod, storax, and grated lemon-peel. These should all be pounded together or crushed as finely as possible. Fill a basin or suitable jar with alternate layers of dried rose leaves, powdered spices, and bay salt. To draw out the full fragrance of the rose leaves, the mixture should be stirred or shaken fairly frequently.

impossible to remove every trace of it from cracks.

Shredding Soap

When making dissolved soap or soap flakes, the quickest method of shredding is to utilise the ordinary vegetable grater. This divides the soap into fine particles, which dissolve very readily. To ensure the complete removal of soap from the grater, place it in the washing-up bowl and pour boiling water over it. This removes all trace of soap and also lathers the water for washing up. The flakes may be dried and stored in a tin ready for use.

A Jam Making Hint

Difficulty is sometimes experienced in getting jams of all kinds to set. This is generally due to one of two reasons; either by using over-ripe fruit (the choice of slightly under-ripe fruit for jam is therefore advised) or by the fact that the fruit is not cooked sufficiently before the addition of the sugar. When making plum jam, cut the plums in halves, stone them, put into a preserving pan and slowly draw out the juice; then simmer until the fruit is thoroughly cooked. Add the sugar, which should previously have been warmed in the oven, and boil until the jam sets. After the fruit and sugar have been boiled together for 10 minutes, it is advisable to test the jam for setting by pouring a small quantity on to a plate. When cold it should be quite firm.

Fresh Lemon Peel

Knives and forks that have been used for fish should be rubbed with the rind of a fresh lemon after washing. It will be found that no flavour or smell of fish will then remain.

When Washing Brushes

Prepare warm soapy water such as is used for woollens. For toilet brushes, the addition of a tablespoonful of borax to two quarts of water softens it and helps in the removal of grease. Household brushes, such as those used for boots, blackleading stoves, etc., are generally very greasy, so that the use of a small amount of washing soda is generally necessary to facilitate cleansing. Wash by dipping the bristles up and down in the soapy lather, afterwards rinsing thoroughly in warm water to remove the soap. Then rinse in cold water to harden the bristles, shake and hang out of doors to dry. Brushes with flat backs, such as hair brushes, should be stood on their backs to dry, after as much moisture as possible has been shaken from them.

To Weigh Golden Syrup

When making gingerbread or puddings containing golden syrup, it is advisable to weigh or measure the syrup accurately. If the scale-pan is well floured, the syrup may be poured into it and weighed without soiling the pan.

Home-Made Polish

One gill turpentine, one gill linseed oil, ¼ gill methylated spirit, ¼ gill vinegar, mixed together and shaken well before use, make a most efficient polish for furniture and all kinds of leather work, papier mâché, and leather trunks. This mixture should be applied sparingly with a soft rag, and the furniture then polished with an old silk duster.

The Housekeeper's Dictionary *of* Facts

Recommended by "Good Housekeeping" Institute

Protecting the House From Mice

The use of efficient mouse-traps is not the only means of exterminating this pest. The utmost care should be taken to prevent the entry of field mice. Damaged ventilating gratings should be renewed or covered with fine mesh wire netting, and any other possible means of entry looked for. Mice often come into the house by means of small holes in the larder or in cupboards, particularly those under the stairs. Holes too large to be repaired easily with cement should first be filled with corks and then cemented. Worn linoleum or floorboards should be repaired or renewed.

Conditions are made unpleasant for mice if cayenne pepper is sprinkled on shelves and near food. Special precautions should be taken that no food is left uncovered, and in houses that tend to be overrun with mice all foods should be stored in tin or wood containers, not in sacks or bags.

To Untie Knots

Place the knot on a table and gently hammer with a wooden article for a second or two, reversing the knot as you do so. Then insert the closed points of a small pair of scissors, gradually open them, and the knot will come untied.

A Light Yorkshire Pudding

Mix the necessary flour, eggs, salt, and a small quantity of milk to a very thick, smooth paste, and then add the remainder of the milk made very hot in a saucepan. Bake the puddings, if possible, in fairly small round tins, and you will find they will puff up to the top of the tins and be delightfully crisp and light. By mixing in this manner less eggs are required.

Mending With Sealing-Wax

Sealing-wax can be used satisfactorily for effecting small repairs in enamel basins, jugs, etc., not used to contain hot liquids. By the following simple method tiny holes can be mended and the vessel given a new lease of life: Get a stick of sealing-wax the colour of the vessel to be repaired, cleanse and thoroughly dry the part to be made good, and apply the sealing-wax, melted, over the worn surface, pressing down firmly and neatly. Any leakage will be effectively stopped.

Boiling Cracked Eggs

Cracked eggs can be boiled without the loss of any of the egg if the following method is adopted: Add a tablespoonful of salt to the water in which the egg is boiled, rub the crack well with common salt, and put the egg at once into the fast-boiling salt water. The white of the egg will not ooze out nor the crack become larger.

Some Uses for Glycerine

A mixture of two parts glycerine and one part lemon-juice makes an excellent cleansing lotion for the skin. Apply it sparingly, and rub well into the hands. Glycerine may also be used for loosening round glass stoppers in bottles when they cannot be removed by any other means. Apply it with a paint brush around the top of the stopper. It will gradually soak between the two surfaces and facilitate the removal of the stopper. If this is very persistent, the bottle should be inverted and placed in a small egg-cup or jar of glycerine and left for several days. Patent leather shoes may also be cleaned with glycerine. Rub it well into the leather and polish with a soft cloth.

A Nursery Suggestion For Dull Days

The making of jigsaw puzzles is a fascinating amusement for dark days in the nursery. Select a pretty picture

A Lasting Joy—

That is the test which thoughtful donors apply when sifting through their list of possible Christmas gifts. The Christmas number of GOOD HOUSEKEEPING, *with specially augmented Cookery, Household, Furnishing, and Shopping Service Sections, reaches the high-water mark of practical, literary, and artistic excellence, and will be hailed with delight by every reader. All the year round the magazine reacts to the pulse of women's interests and activities, and caters for miscellaneous moods as well. Therefore one of the most appreciated gifts you can possibly make to your friends at home or abroad is a year's subscription to*

Good Housekeeping

and paste it on to a fairly thick piece of smooth cardboard. When quite dry, cut the picture into many pieces of different sizes and shapes, and shake these up in a box before trying to fit them together.

A Substitute For Ice.

It is often necessary to cool jellies, blancmanges, etc., quickly, and when ice is not available the mould or basin may be stood in water containing equal parts of common salt and washing soda in solution. Sufficient should be added so that just a little is left undissolved. Other chemicals which make a good freezing mixture are ammonium nitrate and washing soda, in equal parts.

Washing a Heavy Artificial Silk Jumper

Artificial silk jumpers require care in laundering to prevent undue stretching. If tacked flat on to a towel before being washed, a jumper will not lose its shape. When dry, it should be pressed with a warm iron before it is untacked from the towel.

A Portable Kitchen Range

A portable or self-setting range is so called because it requires no brick-setting. It is merely connected to the chimney by a short length of smoke-pipe. This pipe should pass at least one foot through the sheet iron register-plate which closes in the bottom of the chimney. A range should not, if possible, be placed directly opposite an outer door. This causes the fire to burn too rapidly, wasting fuel and burning away the fire-bricks. As sheet iron wears out after two or three years' use, it is advisable when buying a range to have one that is fitted with a cast-iron back and ends. It is also advisable to have the smoke-pipe of cast iron. This should be fitted with a loose door on the front to admit the flue brush.

A removable oven which can easily be renewed without removing the range for repairs is a distinct advantage.

Etceteras for Convenience

Other features which add to the convenience of a stove are a lifting fire, which also effects economy in fuel, and a pedal opener to the oven door, so that the latter can easily be opened with the foot, leaving both hands free to put the dish in the oven. A plate-rack is also very useful. It is often not supplied with the range, but may be obtained for a small extra charge. A side boiler fitted with a draw-off tap is not recommended in a range of this type, unless it is kept automatically supplied with water by a ball valve. A boiler of this kind holds very little water and has to be constantly filled by hand.

Getting the Best Results

If a false bottom is used, the space between the real bottom and the grating must be kept clear of ashes, or the fire will become clogged.

Fire-bricks should be renewed before they are burnt through or the ironwork will be burnt away as well, making much more expensive and extensive repairs necessary.

Before using a range for the first time, examine it to become thoroughly acquainted with the direction of the flues and the position of the soot or flue-cleaning doors. These doors must all be closed while the range is working. Clean the flues thoroughly at regular intervals, at least once a week when the fire is used daily. If there is a back boiler, the boiler flue must be cleaned every day.

"Come in the Evening, or
Come in the Morning,
Come When Expected, or
Come Without Warning"

Samplers are in such demand that Anne Orr has designed the one at right in black and full colours. Centre is in silhouette and border in colours. Hot-Iron Pattern No. 5404, 1s. 2d., post free, has silhouette, motto, and border and directions for making this sampler in cross-stitch

To purchase patterns or directions for designs on this page send stamps or postal order to Anne Orr, "Good Housekeeping," 153 Queen Victoria Street, London, E.C.4, stating exactly what you require

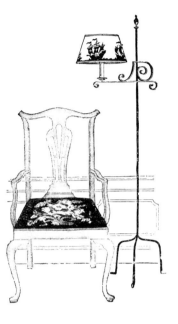

NEEDLEWORK

Smart Designs Suggest Varied

Uses for the Home

By Anne Orr

The charming 16th century ship design on sconce shield above, bridge lamp at extreme right, and table lamp in centre are painted in silhouette on parchment paper. Hot-Iron Pattern No. 5405, 1s. 2d., post free, includes several sizes and designs of ships with full directions for painting parchment paper

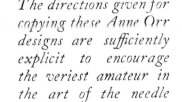

The directions given for copying these Anne Orr designs are sufficiently explicit to encourage the veriest amateur in the art of the needle

A near tapestry chair seat is shown above and the detail of the design below. It is called near tapestry, because it is worked on tapestry cloth or heavy upholstery wool material, which eliminates the necessity of working a background, but the effect is like real tapestry. Printed Pamphlet No. 5402, 1s. 2d., post free, includes working pattern and directions

The pillow above is made of heavy black satin with a 5-inch band of tapestry in the centre, worked in lovely shades of rose, brown, blue, and green. A scallop in the pattern is followed with a blue satin cord, and the band is edged with blue and rose-coloured cords. Printed Pamphlet No. 5401, 1s. 2d., post free, includes working pattern and directions for making this pillow and also some other tapestry bands

At left is a fancy rug, to be used over a plain, one-tone rug in a young girl's room. Worked with heavy wools—the design in bright colours and background in black— it is quaint and charming. Done in petit point stitch on black satin, this design makes a lovely picture for the wall. Printed Pamphlet No. 5403, 1s. 2d., post free, includes pattern and directions for rug and picture

THE
20's

He: Did you gamble at Deauville?

She: Everybody does—I almost lost my . . . *Poudre Nildé.*

He: A very apt way of saying that you almost lost that from which you would be parted last.

The girl who knows always carries Poudre Nildé with her everywhere. The sifter in the box enables her to powder with discrimination. The fine fragrant powder gives an ever even and fresh complexion.

There's a Poudre Nildé tint to suit every complexion: rachel, naturelle, blanche, rose, basanée, indienne.

POUDRE NILDÉ

In the sifter box, hand-bag size, with puff - **1/-** | In the new large box for the dressing-table (*without sifter or puff*) **1/6**

Rouge Invisible Nildé :—Rouge in powder form in the sifter box with puff, especially prepared for the discreet woman. The sifter box absolutely prevents too much being taken —the delicate colouring cannot be detected. Three shades : *brune, blonde, orange* **1/6**

Nildé preparations are on sale at all good chemists, coiffeurs and stores.

If you have any difficulty in obtaining, write to :—

Nildé (Paris) Agency, Ltd., 296 Regent Street, London, W. 1.

Poudre Nildé at Deauville

Hands That Rule Their Worlds

By Nell Clare Splitstone

Part I. Women's Hands in Industry

THE other day I called on a friend who has an adorable baby girl, and the infant did that inimitably comic stunt of gazing with wonder at the uncertain movements of its own tiny hands.

"I hope she'll always be as interested in using her hands as she is now," laughed the mother. "But I'm not worrying about that, for her hands are like her Grandmother Brown's and hers are almost never idle."

After I went home I kept thinking about women's hands, and I saw an endless variety of them—small hands, large hands; stiff hands, supple hands; cold hands, warm hands, weak hands, strong hands; incompetent hands, trained hands; practical hands, artistic hands; hands that make things, hands that break things.

Then there floated into my dream of hands the memory that someone once said a beautiful thing about "the hand that rocks the cradle," and I couldn't resist the temptation to add, "—and the hand that's *in* the cradle rules the hand that rocks the cradle and the hand that buys the cradle."

As time goes on those baby hands find other worlds to conquer—mud-pie worlds that are not to be won by grip alone, but by the deep desire to make the very best mud pies.

All too soon the chubby mud-pie hands, now grown slim and strong, have to grapple with the great industrial world, or the business and professional world, or the world of home-making. How shall they train to conquer?

Once day, as I was driving in the country, I stopped to chat with a woman who is a successful farmer in her own right, and I asked her if she believed it possible for the average farm woman to keep her hands from becoming "rough and calloused with honest toil."

I pass on her reply to the women whose hands are exposed to many hardships:

"My hands are my most valuable tools," she said, "and I never let them get rusty. Never shall I forget that day in my childhood when I 'borrowed' my father's best saw, and left it in the orchard, where it got rusty. When father discovered it, I got my first real lesson in the care of good tools. I got the idea

then, and applied it to my hands as well as to the bright steel tools in my father's workshop.

"One thing I have learned is that we should never use our finest tools for our coarsest work. I never subject my hands to undue hardships, such as doing by hand what I could do as well by the use of tools. I do much of the work on my farm myself. But I manage to keep my hands presentable. Any woman can do as much if she cares to take the trouble.

"Then I have schooled myself in the use of gloves. Most women hate them. They like the freedom of going bare-handed. So do I, but I find that bare-hand freedom for women in industry means bondage in the form of tan, blisters, callouses, stains, roughness, broken nails, and hangnails. I don't think it's worth the price, so I wear gloves—long-wristed ones that protect my wrists as well as my hands.

"The gloves I wear are of different kinds—light canvas ones for general work with tools; light leather ones for rough and greasy jobs; old kid ones with the fingers cut off for berry-picking and other fine finger-work.

"To guard against the grime and roughness resulting from contact with the soil, before beginning such work I rub a little tallow or mild white soap over my fingers and work a bit of it in around the nails. This aids greatly in the wash-up afterwards. Stains from vegetables, weeds and fruits I can usually remove by rubbing my hands with a cut lemon or tomato.

"After my day's work I wash my hands thoroughly, remove all stains, and massage my hands gently for a few minutes with olive oil or plain dairy cream, always massaging from the fingertips upwards. Then I wipe off any excess grease, apply a cooling astringent lotion, and have hands that can go where they will, and be at ease. It's some trouble, naturally; but she who rules must first obey.

"One of the best cleansers and whiteners that I have found is a mixture of cornmeal and buttermilk, two simple things that we always have on hand on our farm. My hands always feel so grateful for a good washing with this mixture."

THE
20's

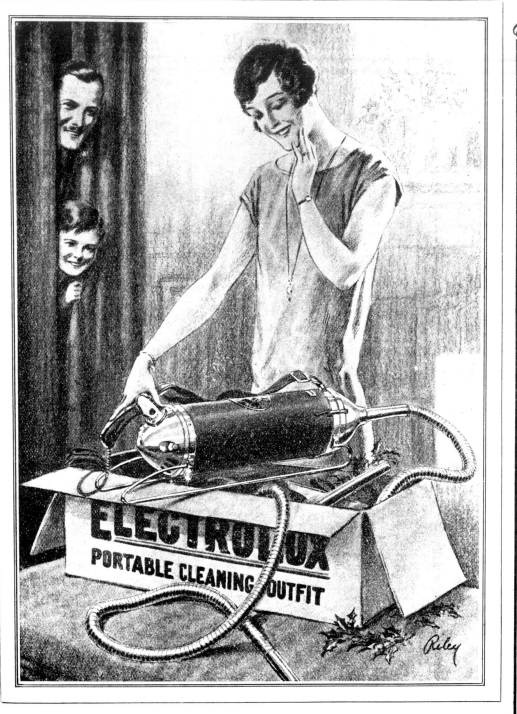

Present pleasure and future freedom

You confer the "freedom of the house" upon your wife when you give her an Electrolux. Such a gift this Xmas will lighten all her future by cutting out the drudgery of cleaning and by brightening her home. Electrolux possesses important features which other cleaners lack, such as the protected dustbag, filter pad and sleigh runners. These and many others are clearly described in the Electrolux Booklet. Write for a copy and details of Price Reductions or call at our Showrooms and see an Electrolux demonstration.

Electrolux
The New Cleanness

More Reliable Hints from Good Housekeeping Institute

The Housekeeper's Dictionary of Facts

A Home-made Clothes Sprinkler

A quick and effective means of sprinkling clothes evenly is to dip a clean clothes-brush into water contained in a soup plate, and then shake it over the clothes.

Marble-topped Washstands

Many people possess a discarded marble-topped washstand. The marble slab, if removed, can be fixed to the side of a lavatory basin, where it makes an excellent shelf and is particularly easy to keep clean. If the washstand is in good condition but is no longer required to serve its original purpose, the marble top can frequently be replaced by a wooden one, and the washstand thus converted into a dressing-table.

Cleaning Neglected Kitchen Tins

An excellent scouring paste for cleaning neglected tins can be made by mixing together equal proportions of pumice powder, soap powder, and whiting.

Keeping Curtain Fittings in Good Condition.

Metal curtain fittings of all descriptions should be rubbed periodically with a cloth slightly moistened with sweet oil. This will allow the rings, which may also be treated in similar manner, to run freely and prevent them jamming.

To Soften Boots

To render boots that have been out of use soft and pliable, wash them in warm water, and afterwards well rub castor-oil into the leather. They will not polish well until they have been in use, and the heat of the foot has caused the oil to be thoroughly absorbed by the leather.

To Destroy Moths in Carpets

Carpets that have been stored away should be periodically examined, and if any traces of moth are found, a damp huckaback towel should be placed over the affected part, and well ironed with a very hot iron until dry. This will destroy moth eggs and maggots.

Making Putty for Household Uses

One often needs putty for various purposes in the home. It is very easy to make the quantity desired by mixing some unslaked lime in hot glue. If coloured putty is needed, the colour desired should be mixed with some dry whiting, and then both added to the lime and glue.

Mending China and Glass

Cement for repairing glass and china can be made at home, and will save many bills for repairs. Articles, too, that would not justify the money required to have them riveted can be made serviceable again. Mix together 3 oz. of gum sandrac, 3 oz. white shellac and one gill of methylated spirit. This mixture will not leave any black marks.

Drying Umbrellas

When wet, umbrellas should be stood ferrule upwards over a sink or any other suitable place. This prevents the ironwork rusting, since the water does not run into the framework of the umbrella. When all moisture has drained away, the umbrella should be left open until dry.

Removing the Smell of Fish from Cooking Utensils

The smell of fish is particularly obstinate to remove from cooking utensils. These should be washed as soon as possible after use in lukewarm water to which two tablespoonfuls of salt have been added. If they are then rinsed well in clean water and dried no smell should remain.

Cleaning Upholstered Furniture

Remove as much dust as possible by the aid of a vacuum cleaner or gentle beating and brushing. Use hot bran to remove more obstinate dirt. This should be well rubbed into the fabric with a clean brush or with a soft pad made of an old white cloth. When all possible dirt has been removed by this means, brush off all trace of bran and clean any spots, sponging either with

IF YOU WANT

to win fresh laurels by your cookery, make a point of buying " Good Housekeeping Menu and Recipe Book " and " Invalid Cookery Book." Both books contain a wide selection of attractive and reliable recipes, and are now on sale, price 2s. 6d. each, or all stationers and bookstalls, or, 2s. 9½d. post free, from Good Housekeeping Institute, 49 Wellington Street, London, W.C. 2

water or with a petrol brush. Spots of a greasy nature will require petrol or some other grease solvent, those of a sticky nature will be removed by careful sponging with soap and water.

To Launder a Sunshade

Cretonne sunshades or even those of silk, provided the fabric is not rotten, can be cleaned successfully with soap and water. Open the sunshade and have ready a basin of warm soapy water, a piece of hard soap and a soft nail-brush. Moisten the sunshade, and commencing at the centre and gradually working down to the edge, use the nail-brush, on which a little hard soap should be rubbed, to clean specially dirty parts.

Mincing Machines

Parts of a mincing machine are very liable to be lost. To obviate this, make a bag from heavy crash or holland 12 in. wide by 18 in. long (or according to the size of your particular machine). Finish the top with a hem and draw-string. After the mincer has been washed and dried, put all parts into the bag and hang or place in the kitchen dresser. If a thin strip of wood be placed under the mincing machine, the table is not damaged or marked in any way when the machine is used.

Fixing Rubber Heels

When one essays to save cobbler's bills by fixing rubber heels to boots or shoes at home, it is often found that the screw of a former rubber heel has worn the hole in the leather too large to accommodate the new-comer comfortably. This defect is easily remedied by hammering a small plug of wood (even a match-stick will answer the purpose sometimes) into the hole, and then forcing the new screw into the fibres of the wood.

Removing Iron Mould

If neither salts of lemon nor oxalic acid are available rust stains can be removed by soaking them in an extract of rhubarb. Cut the rhubarb into small pieces; put into a saucepan, well cover with water and boil for 10 to 15 minutes. Strain off the solution and soak the stained part in the hot liquid. It may be necessary to repeat the process once or twice.

To Separate two Tumblers

When two tumblers become fixed one inside the other, pour cold water into the inner glass and stand the outer one in warm water. In this manner the inner glass contracts and the outer one expands, so that they are easily separated.

Care of Vacuum Flasks

It is a wise plan not to mix milk with tea or coffee that is to be kept in a vacuum flask. A special flask or other container should be used for the milk, and the cork should afterwards be washed in hot water and placed in an airy spot. The flask itself should be washed with soapy water, rinsed several times and allowed to drain. If a flask is to contain a hot liquid, first rinse with boiling water; if cold, rinse first with cold water.

To Prevent Rugs Slipping on a Polished Floor

It is often difficult to keep rugs from slipping on a polished floor, whether parquet, wood, or linoleum. It is an excellent plan to attach small portions of crêpe rubber to the corners of rugs of a light or medium weight. For heavier rugs or small carpets strips of rubber can be sewn across their length and width, the number necessary being determined by the size and weight of the rugs or carpets.

The Ladies' Saloon
£190

Here's the very car for a lady—cool when it's hot and cosy when it's cold. The easiest car in the world to drive, good-looking and always comfortable.

It's the Ford Tudor Saloon — costing only £190.

Its bodywork is of the very latest type of construction — all steel — ensuring lightness with strength, freedom from rattles. Seats have been lowered and more comfortably upholstered, steering pillar more conveniently raked.

Just try the cosy comfort of this Ford Tudor Saloon at your Authorised Ford Dealer's. Then ask yourself if you can find anywhere such truly luxurious motoring at £190.

FORD MOTOR CO. (ENGLAND) LTD.,
TRAFFORD PARK, MANCHESTER

The Housekeeper's Dictionary *of* Facts

More Labour-Saving Discoveries from Good Housekeeping Institute

When Covering Jars

To prevent the bother of tying down when covering jars, it is an excellent and labour-saving plan to use elastic bands instead of string. These bands however, must be of good quality rubber, as cheap, thin ones are apt to perish. The special advantage of this method is that once a jar has been opened the top may be easily replaced and the jar kept tightly covered.

To Tint an Alabaster Globe

A dye of the required shade should be tied in a piece of rag and moistened with a little boiling water. This should then be used to rub over the inside of the globe until it is evenly covered.

To Move Heavy Boxes

Heavy boxes can be moved easily by one person, without dragging over the floor, if a rolling pin is placed under one end of the box and the box then pushed over it. The process should be repeated until the box is in the desired position.

An Emergency Sleeve-board

An old cricket bat makes a splendid emergency sleeve-board if it is covered with a piece of old blanket and a piece of sheeting.

Mending a Tea-pot Handle

Fix the broken parts of the tea-pot handle in position, and wind some adhesive tape tightly round the fracture. The edges of the tape should overlap on the underside of the handle, where the join will not be noticed, while a little daub of paint the same colour as the tea-pot will hide the "bandage." Stand aside for two days after mending to allow the adhesive tape to set properly: the tea-pot can then be washed in hot water as usual.

Hints on Colour-washing

The following hints may be found helpful by housewives who are doing colour-washing for the first time. When whitewashing a ceiling always stand with your back to the light; you will then be able to see much better what you have done, and there is little risk of leaving spaces or going over the same ground twice. During the colour-washing process, close the windows and doors to prevent uneven drying, which produces a dark or patchy effect. When the work is finished the doors and windows may be opened to allow the room to dry. A bathing cap will be found an excellent headcovering when whitewashing ceilings as it can be pulled well down over the hair and the whitewash removed afterwards by sponging.

Walnut Stains

When pickling walnuts it is almost impossible to prevent the fingers becoming badly stained. This discoloration can be readily removed, however, by washing the fingers in a cupful of cold water, in which the skins of several walnut kernels have been placed.

A Laundry Hint

A peg apron is very handy for use on washing day as it prevents stooping and backache. It can easily be made from a piece of any suitable material such as cretonne or holland, 22 by 36 inches. Cut off 4 inches from the length and make a short band. Hem the sides and bottom, then fix the band in position, also tapes to tie. Turn up 12 inches from the bottom to form a pocket and stitch the sides. If desired the pocket may be stitched in the middle to make two divisions.

A Home-made Scouring Powder

An excellent and inexpensive scouring

HOLIDAY HINTS

The day before you set off for the seaside or country—

Grease all bright steelwork—such as fenders, fire-irons, and ordinary steel knives—to prevent rusting.

Turn off the gas, electric current, and water before leaving the house.

Thoroughly clean all sinks and lavatory basins and remember to pour a little disinfectant down each drain.

Dispose of all perishable foodstuffs. Cereals and non-perishable foods should be stored in air-tight tins so that mice and other pests will not be encouraged.

If the house is to be left entirely unattended all house plants should be placed in a shady part of the garden.

Cancel delivery of the daily papers and give notice to tradesmen that supplies will not be required.

Cover delicate upholstered furniture and carpets with dust-sheets in preference to drawing the blinds and curtains.

powder can be made by mixing together 1 lb. powdered pumice, 1 lb. powdered whiting and 1 lb. soap powder.

When Trussing Fowls

Housewives who have to truss fowls frequently, will find that a pair of medium-sized secateurs is a very useful implement. The wing tips and leg-bones can be neatly cut exactly where required, and the base of the neck, always an awkward problem even when a sharp knife is used, can be snipped through cleanly without any trouble or exertion. The best secateurs are those with narrow blades.

To Keep the Nails Clean

Before doing any rough or dirty housework it is a good plan to fill the nails with soap. This prevents any dirt getting right into the skin under the nails, and the soap can easily be scrubbed out after the work is done.

Making a Window Mop.

To clean windows easily and quickly a fairly long-handled mop is invaluable. To make this at home, take a brush handle, or similar stick, from 20 to 30 inches long, and on the end of this securely nail slantwise a stout piece of wood about 6 inches long and sufficiently thick to enable pieces of wash leather to be attached. Small pieces of leather are best for this purpose. Fix two or three at a time with a small tack in the corners until the surface and edges of the stout piece of wood are completely covered. The shape ensures easy cleaning of corners: first wash the glass with the mop fairly wet, then squeeze with the hand and polish. No duster or other polisher is required.

Washing Feather Pillows

When feather pillows require washing they should be emptied from the ticking case into a muslin bag rather larger than the case. The bag must be sewn up tightly and put into a large bathful of warm, soapy water. The use of a vacuum washer simplifies the washing process considerably, but if one is not available the feathers can be cleaned quite satisfactorily by squeezing the bag and contents under water. Continue washing, if necessary using two or three waters, until no more dirt comes from the feathers, then rinse thoroughly in warm water. Squeeze as much water as possible from the feathers and hang the bag to dry in an airy position. The washing of pillows should not be undertaken unless the weather conditions are ideal for drying.

Bleaching Clothes

The months of July and August are generally the best for bleaching linen, as exposure to brilliant sunshine is the natural method. Garments or table linen which have become a bad colour through careless laundering may be bleached by spreading in the sunshine for several hours. If necessary the process should be repeated on successive days. First wash and boil the clothes in the ordinary way, and spread them on the grass without rinsing. As bleaching takes place much more rapidly in the presence of moisture, directly the garments are dry they should be moistened with clean water.

The Average Husband—

As the Average Wife Knows Him

By Dell Leigh

THE average husband is a complex mass of contradictions—particularly to his wife.

Although she understands his character intuitively and thoroughly for all practical purposes of the smooth-running machine of home life, and acts accordingly without ever drawing attention to her prowess in this direction, she is at the same time continually faced abruptly with enigmas about him which she fails entirely, and not unnaturally, to grasp. And when she sits down to think about him, which she does very frequently without his knowing it, a host of his mysterious peccadilloes flood her mind.

Her chief perplexity is, of course, his attitude about other women in relation to herself. He is immediately attracted, as a moth to a candle, by the propinquity of the scarlet-lipped, liquid-face-powdered, short-skirted, cocktail-drinking woman, to whom he refers pleasurably as "a fascinating woman, by Jove!" But the moment his wife, faint but pursuing, lifts a red lip-stick to her mouth, or her skirts another inch towards her knees, he is vociferously and scathingly indignant. "Great Scot, my dear girl," he says, "you don't suppose I am going out with you like that, do you? Be reasonable, for heaven's sake!" It is useless to point out to him that a week ago he openly admired Mrs. Maladroit in the same garb and embellishments. His curt answer will be that what Mrs. Maladroit does is "a totally different thing"—he is not going to have his wife doing it.

Her clothes generally are a source of perpetual anxiety and *bouleversements* to the woman who owns an average husband. A considerable amount of thought and planning ("far more than he deserves!") is devoted to pleasing her mysterious mate in this respect, seldom with complete success. She will save up for the very latest creation in French hats, for example, which half a dozen women have said, and their husbands have inferred, suit her perfectly. When timorously she parades before him in it, awaiting breathlessly the verdict, he condemns it with a gesture as the most awful thing he has ever seen her in.

Conversely, in one of those careless, hopeless moments (he stampeding in the hall) when she crams hurriedly over her hair an old brown felt, shapeless and obsolete, that she bought for a few shillings many seasons ago, he points a staccato finger at her and says: "A—h! there you are; best hat you ever had in your life; can't think why you don't wear it more often."

He will point out a woman at a dance club wearing a frock which he describes as "perfectly topping," deploring the fact that his wife did not get one of that sort instead of the grotesque thing she bought the other day. It is pointed out to him meekly that the frock he is rather rudely staring at across the room may look very well on that particular type of young woman, but for *her* it is entirely unsuitable both as to colour and line. To which, quite unconvinced, he replies: "Don't see why: jolly nice I call it," and relapses into a moody silence.

In the matter of other people's food, too, he is most peculiar. At a small dinner party in the flat of some intimate friends he will consume everything with tremendous relish, saying: "Why is it, dear, we can't get food like this at home?" Whereas his wife knows perfectly well that it is only Canterbury lamb they have been eating, and that the cheese is a cheap Canadian, as against the best Southdown mutton and pure Gorgonzola he invariably has at his own table, where they both feed infinitely better than here.

She is given a grain of comfort, however, occasionally when she hears quite by chance that her virtues have been extolled by him to others. She very rarely hears these at first hand. She would give a great deal sometimes if she could. If a discussion crops up upon the errors and omissions of wives when she is present with him, he generally maintains a slightly embarrassed silence, punctuated here and there with a rather grudging admission that she is "not so bad, take her all round."

But his loyalty to her when absent is quite touching. Other people hear that *his* wife is a marvel at most things. Whatever errors of other women may be under micro-

The Average Husband

scopic dissection she is immune from the stigma of any of them; other women may be guilty of so and so, but his wife—certainly not. He volunteers ecstatic information about her capabilities and personality to some other woman, who is frankly bored and incredulous; though to his men friends he maintains a stolid proprietorial silence about her. Indeed, more often than not, in the company of men only, the average husband's attitude seems to be contained in a desire to conceal the fact that he has a wife at all; just as he does not speak unduly about his super-tax: it is rather bad form, and very boring for the other fellows.

The longer a man is married the more dual seems to become his personality. His wife is bewildered to find, for instance, that he is regarded by his friends as a born organiser; as a great man to have at hand on the crowded platform of a railway terminus; as an expert at getting a taxi after the theatre; as the prevailing spirit of gaiety at every party. Her experience of him on such trying occasions is distinctly unfavourable. She has a vivid recollection of last year's summer holidays when she, the nurse, three children and a heap of luggage, struggled through the maelstrom at Paddington because Edward "could not

get away from the office," but came down the next day, when the settling into the seaside lodgings had been coped with by her. She has also a poignant mental picture of him in the vestibules of theatres, struggling peevishly into his coat and saying: "Not the slightest good careering about for a cab here: much better walk a little way"—though a slight drizzle of rain is falling, and she has got a new frock on.

The trouble about the average husband, indeed about most married men, is that "the wife" becomes a habit, like shaving in the morning. She is there, or thereabouts, and is an accepted fact, an institution, like the safe in the office, and the chiming of the church bell on Sundays. Not the average man but nine hundred and ninety-nine out of every thousand married men, when the glamour of the matter has died down, entirely forget, if some of them ever knew, or troubled to think about it, that the term of endearment, the tender look, the soft touch, the compliment, the praise, is to most women as the breath of life, when it comes from their man—they desire nothing more. In fact, their aspirations in this respect may be summed up in the quotation:

"Oh, the little more, and how much it is!
And the little less, and what worlds
away!"

But then, of course, the average husband does not read poetry. He does not understand it. That is a woman's job—don't you know!

A Straight-from-the-Shoulder Talk on

Discontented Wives

By Dr. Cecil Webb-Johnson

THE poet sings somewhere of "divine discontent"; and in some cases it is a positive duty to be discontented. The contented person never does anything or gets anywhere; and in some people a contented nature is but an indication of slackness, inertia, and lack of energy and ambition. The great reformers, inventors, discoverers, and explorers were all discontented people—discontented with the world as they found it. If Napoleon had been contented to be like thousands of other efficient and diligent Army officers, he would never have crowned himself Emperor in the Cathedral of Notre Dame, and become master of Europe.

There is, however, discontent and discontent. One is the noble quality which urges men and women on to try to leave the world better than they found it —the "divine discontent" of which the poet wrote. The other is petty, sordid, and ignoble; and, so far from being divine, seems to have a directly opposite origin. This is the discontent with circumstances and surroundings which affects so many modern women, and is concerned solely with material things. The woman who is discontented with her home, with her clothes, with her circumstances generally is now a far more familiar figure in the world than in bygone days. How she would have shocked our mothers! Not so very many years ago it was thought "wicked" to be discontented with one's lot. To-day the very opposite obtains, and many women deem it the sign of a proper spirit to be dissatisfied and grumbling, and spend their days in envying other and luckier women their possessions. For it will be observed that it is always possessions—material things—that are the subject of discontent. The discontented wife does not say, "I wish I had a happy disposition like Norah's." No; she says, "I wish I had a sable coat like Norah's."

It is always luxuries that the discontented wife craves for; and it is a sign of the times that the modern woman has lost all sense of proportion. In place of "cutting her coat according to her cloth," she is desirous of everything that she sees other women enjoying, regardless of the fact that the other women's social and financial position may be far superior to hers. An old-fashioned proverb, or fable, told us of the fate of the earthen pots which endeavoured to swim in the same stream as the brass pots; but, like many other old-fashioned things, it is totally forgotten now. The suburban bank-manager's wife wishes to have as good a time, and wear as fine clothes, as the wife of the merchant prince. All sense of values is lost, and women wish to be on a level as regards clothes, amusements, and holidays with the wives of men with ten times the income of their husbands. The wife of some struggling City man reads in her morning picture-paper that the Duchess of Chicago and Mrs. Sangazure have been dancing at the Upper Ten Club, and immediately

In March

GOOD HOUSEKEEPING

STEPHEN LEACOCK

HUGH WALPOLE

E. M. DELAFIELD

ELINOR MORDAUNT

ELLEN GLASGOW

J. E. BUCKROSE

GENE STRATTON-PORTER

wants to go and dance at that expensive resort as well. It is in vain for the wretched husband to point out that he cannot afford the night life, that the people who dance and sup in this costly fashion are in the enjoyment of a much larger income than his. The invariable, cold-blooded answer is, "Other women can do it; why can't I?"

It is beyond contradiction that this is the attitude of many wives of to-day: an intense and bitter envy of people who are luckier, or a sullen discontent with their own lot in life. What, then, is the explanation of this position? It is so different from the attitude of women of the earlier part of this century, when a "treat" was a thing to be eagerly anticipated and happily discussed afterwards—not an essential part of the day's routine. Modern women take everything for granted, and demand a life of hectic pleasure—so-called—as their right and just due. This attitude, one may venture to say, is an aftermath of the Great War. During that period, London was filled with idle women, whose idea of helping their country in her hour of agony took the form of what they euphemistically called "cheering up the boys on leave." This cheering-up process involved being taken about (and paid for) by the said "boys" to as many restaurants, theatres, music-halls, and night-clubs as could be crammed into the time. London in war-time was feverish. There seemed to be rivers of money about; everybody was spending recklessly, in the true "let us eat and drink, for to-morrow we die" spirit; all the theatres, the West End restaurants, and the dancing-clubs did a roaring trade. This kind of excitement blazed up at the finish into Armistice Night—and then, the awakening came!

Unfortunately many women cannot be persuaded that that hectic period is now at an end. The habit of reckless pleasure-seeking, regardless of all consequences—moral, social, and financial—has become too strong. They do not wish to forgo their enjoyments, in spite of the fact that circumstances are entirely changed. The reckless young officer, with plenty of money in the pockets of his khaki and a limitless thirst for excitement and pleasure (so-called), has now given place to the hard-working business man, with hair going a little grey at the temples. The discontented wife, however, cannot recognise this. She cannot forget the glorious days of the war-period.

It is not only recollections of the war-period's febrile nights and days that make the modern wife so very discontented with her lot. The whole standard of living has changed; the luxuries of yesterday are the necessities of to-day. The ordinary middle-class wife was content to go out for the evening now and then; to-day she is inclined to demand a dance, a theatre, or a restaurant dinner every week. There is a constant craving for change, for amusement, for excitement at any cost. This has an effect on the nerves which cannot fail to be disastrous in the long run. Late hours, constant excitement, and an atmosphere of alcohol and tobacco combine to act with toxic effect upon the nervous system. The effect is soon seen in the lined and weary face, the constant headaches, and the uncertainty and irritability of temper which mark the woman who is "fond of life," as the sardonic phrase goes.

"MISS VIOLA
IN THE POND."

An amusing incident in the life of a very charming lady revealed by

LADY TREE, O.B.E.

This portrait sketch of Lady Tree was drawn by the Duchess of Rutland about the time when this incident took place.

THE following story was told to me by Lady Tree. Its rich humour is characteristic of one of the most charming personalities of our time. During the lifetime of Sir Herbert Beerbohm Tree, Lady Tree's charm and talent made an admirable support for his great career. That same charm and talent still keeps Lady Tree in the forefront of famous personages to-day.

"When I was a small child (oh! what ages ago!) there was a soothing balm for aches and bruises called 'Pomade Divine,' only to be found in the best nurseries. When I myself acquired a nursery, I wanted to call in my old friend 'Pomade Divine.' But I found that a mother is but herself a child under the iron rule of nurse. And I was soon made to know that there existed but one remedy for all the little aches and pains of childhood : *Pond's.* After that, bottles of *Pond's Extract* were kept always at hand."

"One day, my five year old Viola came to grief on the gravel of our three acre Hampstead garden. Her knees were badly grazed, and I rushed to the house shouting, 'Miss Viola—pond—quick, quick!' Six maids rose as one man crying, 'Miss Viola's in the pond. Help! help!' and they all rushed madly from the house. 'No, no,' I cried, vainly

trying to stem the torrent, 'Extract, Extract.' 'We'll extract her mum, alright, if so be she is still alive,' cheerfully cried the gardener, dashing off with a ladder and rope. I was left alone to find my precious bottle of *Pond's Extract,* and soothe little Viola. When the would-be rescuers returned they persisted in regarding the incident as a merciful escape of Viola, and added one more to the laurels of *Pond's Extract.*"

"Our adored child blossomed into an adorable girl and our trust in *Pond's* led to the introduction of a new kind of *Pond's* into her life : first *Pond's Vanishing Cream* and subsequently *Pond's Cold Cream.* Viola is much loved and much admired for many things, and not the least, for her fresh fairness of face and her delicate gracious hands. The consistent use of *Pond's Two Creams,* I am sure, has been of very great service in preserving this deli-

EVERY SKIN NEEDS THESE TWO CREAMS, USED BY COUNTLESS THOUSANDS OF WOMEN TO MAKE AND KEEP THEIR COMPLEXIONS EXQUISITE.

cacy ; and I would strongly recommend every girl to follow this method. Freshness is, I think, the special distinctive attraction of the English girl—a *natural* freshness."

"Sometimes when I look back," continued Lady Tree, "it seems to me our girls grow more lovely. The modern girl has many critics among the old generation I know, but I am not one of them. I think it is delightful to see them as they move about our cities, alert and athletic, with clear healthy complexions. I think much of this must be due to *Pond's Two Creams,* and I am pleased to hear so many of my young friends speak enthusiastically of them. I think they are so much better than all those elaborate so-called beauty parlours which some women seem to think so necessary to their existence."

Maud Tree

Special Sample Offer.

Pond's Extract Co. (Dept. 831), 103 St. John Street, E.C.1, will send for 2d. in stamps for postage and packing a sample tube of both Creams, sufficient to prove their beneficial effect. All chemists and stores sell Pond's Cold Cream and Pond's Vanishing Cream, in handsome opal jars, price 1/3 and 2/6, and in tubes, price 7½d. (for handbag) and 1/- : Pond's Cold Cream also in extra large jars 5/- and in extra large tubes 2/6.

Household Lore from Good Housekeeping Institute

The Housekeeper's Dictionary of Facts

When Making Curtains

When making curtains of large-meshed filet net, it is advisable to place a strip of brown paper, about 3 inches wide, along the hem before machining. This will prevent the material gathering up during the process of machining. When the stitching is completed, the paper can easily be torn away close to the perforations caused by the needle.

To Dry Wellington Boots

Long rubber Wellington boots, so necessary for children on stormy days, very often get soaked inside. To dry them quickly, procure some bran, warm it in an iron shovel, and pour it into the boots. When this is cold, warm it again and repeat the process until all the moisture has been absorbed and the boots are thoroughly dry. Needless to say, the bran should not be allowed to get very hot.

Extended Use of Enamel-ware

Enamel trays similar to those used in butchers' shops will be found most serviceable in the house, as, apart from its utility, this high-grade enamel-ware imparts a tone of cleanly efficiency to a kitchen. Whilst pre-eminently suitable for keeping meat fresh, a fair-sized tray of this kind is handy when trussing poultry, filleting fish, or preparing steak. In the pantry it is convenient for such items as bacon, butter, lard, and margarine, all of which can be placed on it and thus be transported with a minimum of effort. A container of this substance is also suitable in the nursery for holding baby's bottles, milk, etc.

Hot Flannels for the Sick Room

Place the flannels round a stone hot-water bottle, which will heat them rapidly and prevent the tedious business of wringing them out of hot water.

To Remove the Smell of Paint

Slice up sufficient onions to cover a dinner plate, and place in the room for 24 hours. The onions must then be destroyed, as they are poisonous if used for food.

Mending Linoleum

Grind up some old corks very finely and mix with liquid glue. Put this mixture in the holes, smoothing the surface carefully, and, when set quite hard, rub over with glass paper, colouring with paint or stain to match the linoleum. The repair, if carefully done, will hardly show.

Strong Linen Labels

Unworn parts of old stiff linen cuffs and collars, cut neatly and pierced to allow of string being passed through, make excellent labels for use on parcels.

Nursery Friezes

A gay frieze to be hung just out of reach of mischievous fingers by means of drawing-pins can be made from strips of black, shiny paper 13 inches by 45 inches, if on each strip four pictures from the covers of GOOD HOUSEKEEPING are pasted. The lighter-coloured pictures give the best results, and the strips look more attractive if they do not touch each other, as the unbroken black band is too overwhelming.

Cleaning Brown Shoes

Brown shoes that have become neglected, or on which a too liberal amount of polish has been used, may be cleaned efficiently with a mixture of 2 parts turpentine to 1 part water. Put the shoes on trees, moisten a cloth in the mixture, and rub the shoes evenly all over. Allow them to dry whilst still on the trees: the next day polish with a liberal amount of any light-coloured shoe cream. Use a nail brush to remove grease and dirt from brogue shoes.

Do YOU Know?

Housekeeping can be made both pleasant and interesting by using practical and efficient labour-saving equipment. Good Housekeeping Institute is always investigating new methods of work and the relative values of all types of domestic appliances, including gas or coke water heaters, washing machines, cooking stoves, and labour-savers of every kind. Each appliance is carefully tested by our staff of experts before receiving our Certificate and Seal of Approval. As usual the Institute will be represented at the Ideal Home Exhibition to be held next month at Olympia.

To Remove Glass Stoppers

If stoppers cannot be removed, apply glycerine, either by painting it round the top of the stopper or by placing the stopper and neck of the bottle in an eggcupful of glycerine. It may be necessary to leave the bottle in this position for several hours, or even for a day or two, if it has become very firmly fixed. The glycerine works its way between the ground glass stopper and the neck of the bottle and so facilitates removal.

Cretonne Cuttings

Very attractive book covers can be made from pieces of cretonne left over from the making of curtains and chair covers. Make them in several different sizes. As heat readily damages the binding of books, a cover of this kind serves a very useful purpose when reading by the fire.

To Make a Strong Paste

An especially strong paste can be made by substituting rice-water for ordinary water when making a flour-and-water paste, as the starch in the rice-water makes the paste more adhesive.

A Home-made Crawling-Rug

If two pieces of double-knit Turkish towelling, 36 inches wide, in brown or some other serviceable colour, are joined together and the edges bound with carpet binding, a strong yet soft crawling-rug is made. This is easy to wash and will be found suitable for use in baby's playing-pen, etc. Tapes should be sewn to the four corners.

A Frill for the Mantelpiece

When hanging a frill from an oak mantelpiece, the best method is to insert a small screw-eye underneath the shelf, at either end, and possibly one in the middle, through which the frill may be hung on a thin brass rod of approximately $\frac{1}{2}$ inch in diameter. The ends of the rod should be fixed through the screw-eyes, and the frill will then hang under the oak shelf without obscuring the wood in any way.

To Remedy a Clogged Pipe

When water in a bath, etc., refuses to run away as quickly as it should, owing to an obstruction in the pipe, this can be frequently be remedied at home if a 6-feet length of spiral wire is worked down the pipe. When withdrawn, this will bring away the accumulation of soap, etc., which generally forms the obstruction.

A Use for Old Stockings

When woollen stockings are beyond wearing, wash and dry them, cut off the feet, draw one leg over the other, and then fold over and tack down the sides. You then have a splendid polisher for stoves, floors, or bright articles.

Shrunken Blankets

Stitch a wide strip of unbleached calico to the sides or ends of the blanket. The depth of calico depends entirely upon how much additional length or width is required. The calico is then used for the " tuck in " and the warmth obtainable from the blanket is in no way diminished.

PROBLEMS of the
Middle-Aged
WOMAN

Illustrations by A. K. Macdonald

Married women, whatever their age, used to wear caps. . . . Nowadays grandmothers kick up their heels in night-clubs. . . .

WE have travelled a long way from the days when married women, whatever their age, wore caps—you can see them in du Maurier's drawings in *Punch* of the 'seventies and 'eighties—and when the "frisky matron" was a phenomenon to be regarded with more curiosity than approval. Nowadays grandmothers kick up their heels in night-clubs and dress in knee-length modes, shingle their hair, drink cocktails, and generally conduct themselves as if time had stood still. While it is true that we are living longer as well as faster—thanks to more enlightened ideas on hygiene—still, Nature will not be denied. Nature, the wise old mother, did not intend a woman of forty-eight to behave like a girl of eighteen; and disregard of this fundamental fact will lead to disaster.

It is comparatively easy for a young woman to throw off the effects of a succession of late suppers, with rich and stimulating food. The modern girl takes abundant exercise, and her organs are, as a rule, actively functioning in a satisfactory manner, and in this way a large quantity of food can be disposed of without much harm being done—*always provided that excess is not habitual.* Occasionally the over-charged system is relieved by a " sick headache " —or what our mothers called a bilious attack—and this, though intensely disagreeable and humiliating at the time, is Nature's safeguard.

The woman between forty and sixty is in a very different category. The functional activity has already begun to " slow up," if one may speak colloquially. There is less power of assimilating and digesting food, on account of changes in the alimentary canal and the secreting glands. Unfortunately, it is at this very time that women are apt to take an exaggerated interest in the " pleasures of the table." The flagging appetite demands artificial stimulation, the cook is taxed to provide rich and savoury foods, and this in turn leads to overeating. In middle life, the relief of a sick headache is often denied by Nature. Instead, the excess of food goes to the formation of fat, or to tissue which clogs the internal organs. Often the excess material causes disease of the liver, or brings on gout or rheumatism.

The regulation of the diet is therefore the first consideration. Believing, as I do, that if only people could be persuaded to eat sensibly, ninety-nine per cent. of illnesses would be prevented, I am inclined to lay stress on this, remembering the Japanese proverb which says, " All diseases enter by the mouth."

In middle age, therefore, the intake of food must be diminished. The continual and heavy waste that goes on in a young girl actively engaged in work or exercise has no longer to be repaired. Occasionally one hears a woman exclaim, " Oh, I am not as young as I was; I need more support." She means that she intends to " support " herself by burdening her degenerating digestive processes with more food than they were called upon to tackle at their healthiest and most active period! The utter fatuity of this view needs no demonstrating. One might as well say, " This horse is old and failing; his shaky old legs will scarcely bear him along the road. Let us therefore pile upon him a bigger load than if he were young and strong."

Unfortunately, this error, gigantic as it is, is widespread; which is why one often sees a middle-aged woman working her way doggedly through an enormous meal which a healthy young woman athlete could hardly tackle. The mistaken notion that, as one grows older, one needs to be " supported " by larger quantities of food, has caused much needless suffering and cut short many a life. A little observation only is needed to show the falsity of this idea. One always finds that elderly people who enjoy extraordinarily good health for their time of life are strictly moderate in their eating and drinking.

Moderation in the matter of animal food is especially to be observed by the woman no longer young. In the immature, animal food may be a necessity, as it helps to build up the constitution and repair the waste which is constantly going on. With the mature woman, especially when approaching middle life, meat is not required so urgently. Dishes containing flesh meat should only be taken at one meal of the day—preferably at the evening dinner. Long menus, containing heavy and elaborate dishes, should be avoided by the middle-aged; and unfortunately, it is precisely at this time of life that they make their greatest appeal! However, the practice of self-denial is good for the soul, or so we are told, and it is indubitably good for the body. Of course, a good deal depends on the personal idiosyncrasy. Some constitutions are better suited by small meals at fairly short intervals, while others flourish best when some time elapses between each meal.

Caution in the use of alcoholic beverages is especially wise at this time. All opinion is agreed that in the middle period of life, when regrets for lost youth invade the mind, and the pleasures of early life can be nothing but memories, the temporary comfort of alcohol makes a special appeal. Care must be taken that a habit is not formed. It has been observed in innumerable cases that the alcoholic habit appears in middle-aged women, who as girls and young matrons scarcely knew the taste of dis-

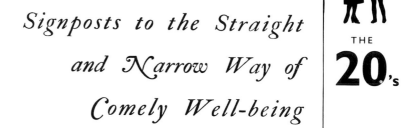

By Dr. Cecil Webb-Johnson

Signposts to the Straight and Narrow Way of Comely Well-being

few moments in the bedroom, both night and morning. The corsets should be discarded, as they interfere with the movements of the chest and the abdomen.

While a certain amount of exercise is absolutely necessary, moderation should be practised in this as in all things. It is a saddening sight to see a woman with grown-up sons and daughters floundering about a tennis-court in a desperate but vain attempt to keep up with the younger generation. It may be far from palatable, but the unpleasant truth must be faced that the middle-aged heart and the middle-aged blood-vessels are no longer in a condition to bear the strain of violent exercise. Golf is not so trying for the woman who is " getting on "; but it might be as well to record that a woman golfer dropped dead upon the links some time ago.

tilled or fermented beverages. This may seem a harsh saying, and happily it does not apply to millions of cases; but there are exceptions, and no good can be done by blinking the facts.

In middle life the digestion should be carefully watched, for the organs tend to lose their tone in time; and this may give rise to unpleasant symptoms unless the appropriate measures are taken. The woman no longer young, however, will probably escape these ills if she takes for her motto: " Moderation in all things."

Exercise is necessary at all ages; but the woman of middle age tends to fall into one of two extremes. She either becomes extremely slack and lazy, or, on the other hand, she continues to practise games and sports with desperate energy, in order to show the world that she is not so middle-aged, after all. Both these courses should be avoided; for each has its peculiar dangers. The perils that beset the armchair woman need no stressing. Obesity creeps upon her; she becomes shapeless; while the very real dangers (of apoplexy, etc.) which obesity brings in its train menace her health and even life itself! However much of an effort it may be, she should *force* herself to take a certain amount of open-air exercise every day. It is no use relying on what the Victorians, with unconscious humour, called " carriage exercise "; that is no exercise at all. In fact, the woman who wishes to keep fit in middle age should do some walking every day. It is no doubt a great temptation to avail oneself of the handy omnibus and the convenient taxi-cab; but a determination to *walk* to the shops instead of being carried there will be rewarded by improved health and looks.

Gardening is another pleasant and

healthful occupation, in which the woman no longer young will find not only interest but improved looks and well-being. For one thing, it keeps a person out in the open air and sunlight —both health-giving—and the various little tasks to be found among the flower-beds and the shrubs and rose-bushes insensibly provide the body with needed exercise. It is not suggested that a woman unused to manual toil should actually take a spade and dig; there are many others ways in a garden of benefiting both body and mind. Some women have a turn for carpentry; this occupies the mind and gently exercises the body, but it is not often carried on in the open-air, which is a disadvantage.

The benefits of fresh air and sunshine are impossible to over-estimate. The blood is oxygenated when a person exercises under the blue canopy of the sky, the nervous system is toned up, the functions of the skin are stimulated, and, almost the most important thing of all, the resistance to infection is improved. Disease holds sway in darksome corners of the town where fresh air and sunlight seldom penetrate; the same holds good of the human body. Busy professional women, who are precluded from open-air exercise to a great extent, may obtain much benefit from deep breathing. This can be practised for a

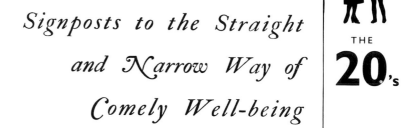

Gardening is another pleasant and healthful occupation

The Housekeeper's Dictionary of Facts

Recent Household and Cooking Economies discovered in the Institute

Fireproof Glassware

While the ovenproof glass which is manufactured into so many attractive dishes to-day is made of a special heat-resisting glass, it will not withstand direct contact with a hot open flame. Glass cracks when it expands unevenly, and this is apt to happen if a glass utensil is put over a direct heat, just as sometimes happens when boiling jelly is poured into a cool jelly glass. A thin asbestos mat should be placed between the bottom of a glass percolator, etc., and the open gas flame or electrical heating unit.

To Remove Tomato Skins

When there are only a few tomatoes to be peeled, and they are firm and not over-ripe, instead of scalding them put one tomato at a time on a sharp fork and hold over a gas flame. Turn it rapidly so that all the surface is heated and when the skin splits it may easily be peeled.

To Preserve Cut Lemons

A cut lemon will keep for several days if a piece of wax or parchment paper is pressed firmly over the cut end. A half-orange or grapefruit may be kept over-night in the same way. A cut onion, cabbage, or half a cucumber will also keep fresh and crisp if carefully wrapped in wax or parchment paper before putting in the larder or refrigerator.

Sock and Stocking Hints

In most large families the socks and stockings of each member are given a distinguishing mark, but it will also be found helpful when each person has several pairs either very much or absolutely alike, to make on these an additional distinguishing mark. This can be, say, a small cross, an upright line, or a square dot, and either the same mark can be done in various fast coloured embroidery cottons or different marks in the same colour. If the socks belong to small children the mark should be embroidered on the foot where it will not show. This system will be found of great help when trying to match up a large basket of socks and stockings.

To Keep Written Recipes Clean

In using cards or papers from a recipe file, clip a paper fastener over the edge and hang on a nail in the wall or shelf before you. The cards will then remain clean and will also be available for easy reference while in use.

Cleaning the Ovens of Oil Stoves

Many people experience difficulty in keeping the interior of oil stove ovens clean, particularly those provided with a corrugated tinned metal lining. The oven should always be wiped out with soap and water after use, particularly if meat has been roasted. If very neglected it should be scoured with a fine abrasive, though this treatment should not be repeated more than is absolutely

THE INSTITUTE SHOPPING GUIDE

Extract from letter received from a leading firm of electricians and ironmongers.

"*I beg to acknowledge your letter, enclosing Application for Test Form, which has been completed and is returned herewith. I am fully aware of its aims as I am a reader of " Good Housekeeping " and think the object a most commendable one. May I give you one instance of its advantages both to purchaser and retailer ? A lady recently purchased nearly £50 worth of goods from me. She brought your list of kitchen equipment and household appliances, to which she referred quite frequently and found very useful. I ordered one or two special lines I had not in stock and there again found your list with the manufacturers' names most useful.*"

Our LATEST LIST OF APPROVED APPLIANCES for 1927–1928, containing 430 pieces of equipment which have received our Seal of Approval, will be sent free by the Director, Good Housekeeping Institute, 49 Wellington Street, Strand, London, W.C., on receipt of stamped, addressed envelope.

necessary, as it would in time wear off the tinning on the metal and rust would ensue. The exterior of the ovens should be washed with soap and water when necessary and then polished with a thin furniture cream. If the door is provided with a glass panel occasional washing and polishing with a dry cloth will be found sufficient.

When Washing Up

A cheap glass salt pourer, filled with silver polish powder or whiting, kept on the shelf over the kitchen sink, is useful. It takes very little trouble to shake a little powder on a spoon discoloured with egg, or on a tarnished silver knife or fork, and is most efficacious.

Canned Asparagus

If cans containing asparagus tips are opened from the bottom instead of the top, the tender tips will not be broken when the asparagus is removed from the can.

Old Silk Stockings

Ordinary silk stockings, no longer fit for wear, will be found useful for stuffing out the toes of the soft kid shoes which are so fashionable just now. Ordinary shoe trees are generally found unsatisfactory for this purpose, and screwed up paper forms into hard balls, but silk stockings will keep the shoes exactly the right shape.

Kitchen Time-Savers

A methodical cook has an overhead shelf to her worktable from which to hang pots and other utensils. Standing at her table she then has all tools within reach and would not think of storing them away in cupboards and drawers, for time would not permit her to collect them at rush hours.

Storing Cooking Utensils

The kitchen cabinet has proved to thousands of housekeepers the great convenience of having supplies and utensils stored at the worktable within easy reach, instead of in the pantry or a distant cupboard. Many housekeepers now endeavouring to conserve energy still further, are extending this convenient arrangement to cutlery and other household appliances in daily use. They are hanging these utensils where they are first needed, some at the range and others at the sink, instead of storing them away in a cupboard. Utensils which are used less frequently are stored in a cupboard or on high shelves, pots and pan covers on the wall or shelf above the range.

Mildew Stains

To remove mildew or other obstinate stains from linen dissolve ½ lb. of washing soda in a pint of boiling water, add ¼ lb. of chloride of lime to 1 quart of cold water and allow to stand for several hours. Strain the latter through fine muslin into the soda solution to prevent any undissolved lime getting into the bleaching solution. As the solution is strong, it should always be diluted four or five times before use with cold water, and all traces thoroughly rinsed away afterwards. It should never be used on silk or wool, or on coloured things.

THE
20's

Keeping a Youthful Skin

By William Allen Pusey

WHAT can be done to keep the complexion of youth? This problem of how the youthful qualities of the skin may be maintained is an interesting one. The skin is a living tissue, and like all other living structures, it shows the effects of age. First, it loses its youthful qualities of colour and softness. It tends in some cases to become florid and in others to become yellowish. It ceases to be tensely drawn over the underlying structures, and in places wrinkles occur in it. Old-age freckles may appear long before a woman is willing to admit that she is becoming old, and later, flat, warty irregularities may come on the surface.

It is an interesting fact that these changes are chiefly confined to the exposed parts—the hands and the face. And there are much stronger reasons than this fact for the opinion that these changes are largely the result of chronic irritation of the skin from exposure to wind and weather. Indeed, the chief irritant that produces these chronic changes, after years of effect, is sunlight.

The most important thing that the woman can do who wants to keep her skin youthful as long as possible is to *avoid excessive exposure to sunlight*. This does not mean foregoing the advantages of outdoors—which no sensible person would advise—but it does suggest that she must shun excessive exposure to sunlight if she wishes to avoid the premature changes in the skin that indicate old age. Going bareheaded constantly in summer is a reckless practice; the face should be shaded by a hat or sunshade. A thick layer of powder, either pink or brunette, is a good protection for the face.

It is curious that while almost all women are anxious to keep the delicate colour and texture which characterise the skin of youth, and will go to great trouble and expense for all sorts of beauty treatments, they place little importance on the fundamental need—protection from wind and sun. Incidentally, the best thing for preventing to some extent the wrinkles of increasing years is to keep from getting too thin.

When one gets thinner than usual, the fat under the skin, which gives the rounded contour to the body, disappears. When this happens, the skin gets loose and wrinkles exactly as an over-size garment does. In old age this layer of subcutaneous fat in part disappears spontaneously, and this is the cause of the wrinkling of old age.

The fat in the skin, as in the rest of the body, is in the form of living fat cells. It is developed and nourished from within, and therefore the way to feed the skin is the way the rest of the body is fed, through the digestive tract.

Plastic operations, when employed to improve faces that are practically normal, are inadvisable. They are justifiable only for the relief of actual deformities. They should never be undertaken except upon the judgment of a medical man who has standing in the profession in the community in which he practises.

Small defects, such as brown spots and warts, which occur in old age or prematurely as they often do, can readily be removed.

In my last article I described the sort of care necessary to keep the normal skin in good condition, and by keeping it in good condition, one does much of what can be done to keep it youthful. The person who has good health and who does not become too thin has a good chance of preserving a youthful appearance beyond the average, if good care is taken of the complexion. This care, to recall what I have already said, means chiefly that the skin should be kept clean and free from infections, and also protected from irritations, and not unduly exposed to the harsh effects of sun, wind, and weather.

THE TOILET OF THE SHOES

LIGHT-COLOURED SHOES are still as fashionable as ever. They owe their long life to Meltonian White Cream – so say the people who ought to know. It certainly does preserve their beauty of complexion and turns them out day after day as spick and span as ever.

Use Meltonian Cream sparingly – it is really the most economical of leather dressings. Use it for your shoe's sake.

Dumpijar 9d. *Handitube 6d.*
Traveltube 1/-

Meltonian
CREAM *for* GOOD SHOES
Made in White, Black and two shades of Brown

E. BROWN & SON LTD., CRICKLEWOOD, N.W.2

Tested Hints for

The Housekeeper's Dictionary of Facts

To Make Bath Salts

Home-made bath salts are always a much appreciated present. In order to make attractive looking salts it is essential to choose well-shaped and glassy soda crystals, or if specially good ones are desired, borax crystals may be used. The latter, however, are considerably more expensive. The crystals may be coloured in two ways.

First Method.—Dissolve a spirit dye, such as metanil yellow or eosine, in pure alcohol or directly in eau-de-Cologne, lavender water, or some other scent dissolved in spirit. Only a very small amount of dye is required, and in most cases it is quite sufficient to use .25 per cent. If scent is not used for dissolving the dye, a small amount of some essential oil, such as violet or lavender, should be added. The mixture should then be sprayed on to the crystals by a scent spray, whilst the crystals are turned frequently with a spoon.

Second and Cheaper Method.—A cheaper way of making bath salts is by dissolving any good cold water dye in water and adding about one dessertspoonful of glycerine to one pint of liquid. This should be sprayed over the crystals. The dyed crystals then need scenting by adding a few drops of some essential oil. In this case the crystals may need drying for a short time and should be spread out on a tray. They should not, however, be left for long as they tend to lose water, and the outside becomes powdery in appearance.

Carving the Turkey Economically

Turkeys vary considerably in size. Small ones may be carved in the same way as a large fowl, but with larger ones adopt the following method:

The bird should be placed with the tail on the left-hand side of the carver. The fork should be placed firmly in the bird and the leg and wing removed by cutting through sinews with the point of the knife. Serve a slice of leg and a slice of breast on each plate. The bird should then be turned round and the other side carved in the same way. A small piece of liver and forcemeat should be served with each portion.

Hints when Marking Linen

The labelling of linen is not easy because of the porosity of the fibres which tends to cause blurring of the letters. If a fine pen is used, however, with not too much ink, and the fabric stretched, the difficulties are minimised.

A Household System of Labelling

When labels of different shapes are used for marking jars and bottles in different cupboards it is easy to see at a glance where a particular container belongs.

Square or rectangular labels are suggested for the storerooms, while for the contents of the household medicine chest diamond-shaped labels might be used.

A ruled border can be added if it is desired to direct special attention to a particular jar. Large

Electric kettles and saucepans which use all the heat generated are certainly the most economical means of heating small quantities of water electrically. The nickel-plated copper kettle above boils 2 quarts of water in 14 minutes and consumes approximately $\frac{1}{4}$ unit. The saucepan takes 11 minutes to boil $1\frac{1}{2}$ pints of milk or water

store tins and jars should, of course, have large labels printed with block capitals, while smaller jars require small labels. For very small jars and bottles a label fixed at a slope gives more room for the description.

A Tidy Store Cupboard

The following hints on the labels themselves may prove useful. The printing should be done in waterproof ink, and on good paper. The adhesive should be strong so that there is no trouble from the labels coming off or from their refusing to stick readily.

An Excellent Gum

An excellent gum for this purpose is made from gelatine and acetic acid. A solution of gelatine is made of the consistency of ordinary gum and a few drops of glacial acetic acid added.

The label should be slightly damped before applying the gum and pressed firmly into position, using a clean cloth.

Waterproof Labels

Waterproof and dampproof labels are obviously very useful for such things as luggage, parcels, and particularly in the garden. The waterproofing is easily done by dissolving a small amount of candle-wax in carbon tetrachloride and applying the solution to the label after it has been printed.

The Care of Oxidised Silver and Copper

Silver and copper articles with an oxidised finish are frequently ruined by careless cleaning. The "oxidisation" is only on the surface and is easily spoilt. Metal polish and abrasive cleansers should on no account be used, for they wear the surface to such an extent that the only remedy is to send the article away to be re-oxidised. Metals with oxidised and other special finishes of a similar type should be kept in good condition by daily dusting and occasional rubbing over with a slightly oily rag.

In the Mirror

In Belgium, many windows have a mirror, sometimes two, placed outside at an angle so as to give anybody sitting inside a view of happenings up or down the street. The mirror can be placed inside, with nearly the same effect, and by changing the angle occasionally the outlook can be varied. Mirrors can often be utilised in this way to inform the housewife inside whether to take a jug for milk or a basket for vegetables, so saving another journey.

Invalids, too, would often be tremendously grateful if their beds were placed near the window, with a mirror at an angle so that they could watch what is happening down the street as they lie in their beds.

A Home-Made Tray

Small trays can readily be made at home from old picture frames. The frames selected should be plain and strongly made. A small piece of cretonne, having a suitable design, should then be cut and stretched tightly over the plywood backing, the edges being carefully neatened. A sheet of plate glass should be placed over this and the frame itself placed in position, and firmly fixed to the backing. Two small brass handles should be procured and screwed one on either side of the frame. These trays may be made most decorative by a judicious choice of pattern and frames, and can be used for a variety of purposes.

Make them marvel at your prettiness this summer!

If only I could afford it! How many times have you said this to yourself! Of lovely things that almost took your breath away with their loveliness. Of smart little frocks that looked as if they'd been made for you. We know just as you do that however attractive your face and figure, you must have the proper clothes to set them off. We know, too, the difficulty of doing justice to your appearance—if you've only a little money. And that's why we have brought out for you these wonderful free Duro books.

None of the sixty designs—created for you by an expert designer from Paris—will *look* cheap or home made. Every one is made of cool silky Duro fabrics, woven and coloured expressly for you. Yet you can buy these fadeless washable fabrics, at prices ranging from only 1/6 a yard. Doesn't matter, either, if like lots of other girls we know—you haven't heaps of time to spare! For we have had all the Duro designs specially cut to the marvellously simple Kut-Eezi patterns.

Sit down and write for the Duro books to-day—and see what surprises we can plan together. Chic, boyish little frocks that look as if they'd cost a fortune. Smooth dainty lingerie to make any frock look at its very best. A whole wardrobe of gay delightful things that will be a joy to wear! Don't even let out the secret to your friends—for a bit. Make them green with envy—*first!* And then tell them how you wrote for the Duro Books to-day.

DO WHAT MAISIE DID. Send for the FREE DURO Dress & Lingerie books, to Burgess, Ledward & Co. Ltd., Dept. 2, 22 Dickinson St. Manchester

'And I only earn £2 a week'

SAYS MAISIE

'My dressmaking used to be a sort of family joke. When the dress was finished and I'd got a permanent wave in my forehead from worry, all they said was, "You made that yourself didn't you dear?" But that was before I got my Duro books. The very first frock I made with a Duro Kut-Eezi pattern was a darling little suit in bois-de-rose. You know, that frock simply made itself. I knew it was a real success. Because the girls at the office all asked me where I bought that heavenly dress.'

The Housekeeper's Dictionary of Facts

Saves Your Time, Your Money, and Your Energy

A Curtain Hint

Casement curtains are frequently used as blinds, and when the windows are open they often tend to blow about. This difficulty can be overcome by sewing a pair of small press-studs about half-way down the curtain.

To Renovate Iron Fire-Grates

Many people possess inartistic iron fire-grates, often showing a large expanse of the metal, but many do not know that it is possible to obtain metallic paints which give a pleasant shade of bronze, gold, etc. These are applied directly on to the iron surface, which should be previously cleaned and freed from rust, and will often effect a tremendous improvement in the general appearance of the room.

A Decorating Hint

A problem which frequently confronts readers is that of applying wallpaper to a surface which has been previously treated with a petrifying liquid to correct dampness, for it is often found then that the wallpaper does not adhere satisfactorily. It is exceedingly difficult, if not impossible, to remove such a preparation when this is no longer required, and those wishing to hang wallpaper under such conditions are advised to apply a coat of white lead oil paint well thinned with turpentine over the petrifying liquid. This provides a " key " to which the paperhanger's paste will adhere.

Grapefruit

When serving grapefruit see that the fruit is carefully freed from the skin as otherwise it is very awkward to eat. It is in fact frequently refused at table solely on this account.

Method of Preparation

Clean the outside skin thoroughly, cut the grapefruit in halves and free the flesh of the fruit from the white pith. To do this a special grapefruit knife with a curved blade may be used. This enables the flesh to be freed more easily from the sides and the bottom of the skin without risk of piercing the skin, which must, of course, be kept intact if the fruit is to be served in it. Be sure that the flesh is freed from the centre skin also. Add sugar and one teaspoonful of maraschino or other liqueur to each half and top with a cocktail cherry. Grapefruit is now frequently served out of the skin in tall glasses, and many people consider it more enjoyable in this manner, as the skins frequently have ugly bruises and stains on them.

Removing Grease from Lizard Shoes

Greasy marks can usually be removed from lizard and other light-coloured leather shoes by gently rubbing with a cloth dipped in carbon tetrachloride. Although excellent for occasional use, however, this solvent should not be applied too frequently as it tends to remove not only any polish used, but also the natural grease present in the leather.

The Last Two Cookery Demonstrations of the Present Course

Will be held at Good Housekeeping Institute, 49 Wellington Street, Strand, W.C.2, on Wednesdays, July 6th and 13th, at 3 p.m., sharp. Tickets, price 1/6 each, should be obtained beforehand from the Director, who will also be pleased to supply full details. The subjects are :—

July 6th, at 3 p.m.

The Theory and Practice of
JAM MAKING AND FRUIT BOTTLING

July 13th, at 3 p.m.

FROZEN DELIGHTS
Ices in Variety, Iced Puddings, etc.

Before Staining and Polishing Floors

It is essential that the surface should be even, and sometimes hand rubbing with sand-paper is not effectual. In such cases it is useful to know that there is a firm which undertakes electric sand-papering of floors at a small cost. A floor having a very bad surface can often be rendered absolutely smooth by this method.

Gingerbread

When making gingerbread do not let the syrup get too hot as it toughens the cake. Keep the oven temperature very steady, and do not allow it to go above 340° F. as the large proportion of syrup tends to make the cake burn easily.

Luminous Door Numbers

It is often impossible to see the number of a house clearly, when there is no illumination. In badly lighted streets luminous door numbers will be found a great blessing.

Treating a Shiny Coat

The shiny appearance of an old coat can often be successfully removed by rubbing gently either with a piece of very fine glass-paper or a wire brush. Great care should, of course, be taken not to rub too hard, or the fabric will be damaged.

Boiled Custard

When making custard with cornflour, allow the minimum time for cooking after adding the eggs, because the slight acidity of the yolks of eggs acts on the starch of the cornflour and tends to produce a thin custard. For the same reason use the custard as soon as possible after cooking.

To Clean Light-Coloured Furs

White furs, which are only slightly soiled, can often be cleaned successfully by rubbing gently with a little warm magnesia. After treatment, the fur should be shaken vigorously in the open air in order to remove all traces of the powder. Rubbing with a cloth or nail brush dipped in a little carbon tetrachloride is generally successful with other light furs. Special care should be taken that there is not sufficient spirit to penetrate to the skin of the fur, as it tends to render it stiff and hard.

Old Linoleum

The surface of painted linoleum frequently wears off long before the linoleum itself is really worn out. It is then an excellent plan to paint it over with a good make of floor paint. Such an application being only a surface one, however, it is advisable to place rugs in the centre of the room or in other places where there is much wear and tear.

Baking in a Gas Oven

When baking in a gas oven, do not use baking trays that fill the whole oven space as they act as browning sheets and throw the heat down into the oven. Have enough space round the baking trays to allow the heat to circulate over the top of the cakes.

Carlton Salad

Skin and core a large ripe pear and cut it into wedge-shaped pieces. Place a few on a crisp lettuce leaf and add half a dozen black or white grapes, skinned, seeded and cut in two. In the centre place a slice of skinned tomato and over it all sprinkle some chopped parsley. Serve with mayonnaise.

Ruby Salad

Cut a good-sized beetroot into slices, not too thin. Over this lay thin slices of Spanish onions. On the top of this place a few slices of banana and over the whole sprinkle chopped parsley. Serve with a French dressing or with a mixture of French dressing and mayonnaise.

Grandmother "went bathing"

—girls like Molly go in to swim!

MOLLY is a real Miss 1927. If her grandmother, complete with flapping, head-to-toe bathing costume, could see her fly down the beach, take a header into a man-high breaker and strike out with a long, powerful side-stroke for the raft, grandmother would have delicately swooned away. No swift "Australian crawl"—no neat, healthy, freedom-giving swimming suit for Grandma! That's why very few young ladies of the early "seventies" could swim very much better than the average brick. Girls like Molly know better. They may not embroider with quite the patient cunning, but by reason of better health, greater "pep" and endurance they're twice as self-reliant—and need neither smelling-salts nor an ever-ready masculine arm to swoon into.

But why, you say, girls "like Molly"? Who's Molly? Well, she's just a bachelor-girl who depends entirely upon herself for her "keep"—she's got a pretty responsible job in a big shipping firm and it needs a "live wire" to look after it. Molly knows that perfect physical fitness means everything, and to achieve that she must have plenty of fresh air, plenty of exercise, plenty of sleep—and the right kind of food. That *last* item most of all.

For, to be healthy, energetic and vigorous, your body must be supplied with certain vital elements. Only the right kind of food can supply those elements.

Do you know the Grape-Nuts secret? It's this! Grape-Nuts supplies the body with those essential elements it *must* have—in a very *easily digestible* form.

Grape-Nuts is a crisp food, which you will like to chew. Ask your dentist how important it is that the teeth and gums be properly exercised. The crispness of Grape-Nuts promotes good teeth, tending to prevent cavities and toothache.

Grape-Nuts is a most delicious food, with a rich, natural, nut-like flavour. Get a package from your grocer to-day and try Grape-Nuts with milk or cream for tomorrow's breakfast. Or post the coupon below and we will send you *two* sample packages of Grape-Nuts free—enough for two breakfasts, and "A Book of Better Breakfasts," by Mrs. D. D. Cottington-Taylor, A.R.S.I., the famous Health and Cooking expert. It contains delightful menus which will help you to form the habit of more healthful breakfasts. Send it now!

Grape=Nuts

—Do you know the Grape Nuts Secret?

THE

20's

Swimming for Beauty

By
Margaret
Crawford
Steffens

SWIM for beauty, for health, or for pleasure—you are bound to get all three if you do it well. Swimming is the best exercise in the world for grace and poise. It stimulates the circulation, and good circulation is the basis for all good complexions. The fresh air and sunshine bring health to the body and buoyancy to the spirit. The exercise helps to keep the hips slim and the abdomen flat. While the arms make their graceful but vigorous motions, the chin is lifted in such a way that its double is discouraged, and as for that roll at the back of the neck—it simply melts away. The arms, the neck, the shoulders are all benefited.

But there are certain rites you must observe if you wish to use swimming as a beauty exercise, because while it is a friend to the figure, it is apt to be a foe to the skin.

It is pleasant to play for hours in the water until you are weary; it gives you a feeling of warmth and deep contentment to lie in the hot sun on the beach and get thoroughly tanned, but it is foolish! It means that you will go around all the summer with a dry peeling skin, and will spend the winter trying one bleach after another to whiten your neck and shoulders. Be wise, and don't get deeply sunburned.

The water robs the skin of much of the natural oil, leaving it dry and sensitive. The sun continues the process. To avoid this, try the simple precaution of applying cold cream to the exposed skin before going out into the sun and water. Apply it lavishly and rub it in well. You will find it impervious to cold water, and if you simply cannot resist the temptation to linger in the waves, it will do much to keep your skin in a good normal condition.

After swimming, a cleansing bath is necessary. This is especially true when you bathe in beaches near manufacturing plants or in harbours where the water is apt to be contaminated somewhat by the refuse from ships, or in muddy lakes and rivers. Treat the skin tenderly when you dry it after the bath. A rough rub is not good for a burned or too dry skin. Now apply over the whole surface a light film of cold cream or of your favourite foundation cream or lotion, and dust with a talcum powder.

The lips quickly show the ill effects of too much exposure to sun or water. A good lip salve used before and after swimming will keep the lips smooth and soft. The nails and the cuticle around them often become dry and brittle, and need to be treated with cream frequently.

If your eyes smart from salt water or from disinfectants used in pools, bathe them with absorbent cotton saturated with a solution of boric acid. Many persons who feel uncertain about the purity of the waters in which they swim like to spray the throat and nose with an antiseptic after swimming.

There are many styles of bathing caps, but there is none which will keep the hair really dry. The plain, round skull caps are probably the most efficient, but they will admit some water. Chamois skins, and other devices, solve the problem for some, but are apt to cause a headache.

When water seeps in, the natural oil of the hair is washed out, and the hair is left stiff and sticky. Dry the wet hair along the base of the head thoroughly with a towel, and then apply a good hair tonic with a bit of absorbent cotton. Much of the dirt will be removed by the cotton. Follow this with a brisk massage and your hair will feel soft and silky again.

If you swim every day, you will probably have to shampoo oftener than you would otherwise. If you find your hair becoming too dry, use a good oily tonic to keep it healthy.

Don't forget that as you tan you may need a slightly darker shade of face powder. White powder on a sunburned complexion makes the skin look rough.

These simple precautions take little time. They become a part of the routine of dressing, a matter of habit. Yet they save you from becoming the kind of girl who looks so queer in a shimmery summer evening frock—the girl whose attempt to get a nut-brown tan has resulted in a red nose and a peeling skin. Don't be a modern foolish virgin! Remember the oil for the lamp of beauty. Save your complexion in summer and you'll save worry in winter.

To every Woman who, of her own volition, or of
is an intimate appeal in this

Illustrations by
Stella Steyn

The

The happiest women are those whose activities are connected with home and children and a man

A woman alone, a man alone, seem to me to be just half-creatures until the other half joins up

I WRITE as a converted sinner, at the age of thirty-seven. Until about three years ago, I was convinced that a woman could get along quite well without a man, and went seeking in political and religious activities of all sorts the happiness that always seemed to elude. I made friendships, too, most of which brought great pain and disillusionment. What is more—and what is very instructive in these so-called equality times when women are supposed to have equal chances with men in the labour market—I found myself very often badly underpaid for work, or given the left-over jobs that men who were my fellow workers would not do.

I know now that physically, mentally, spiritually, economically and socially a woman needs a man, and that without him, except in the most extraordinary cases, she will struggle along, fighting things inside herself and outside, perhaps becoming embittered and cynical, possibly becoming violently revolutionary and "queer" simply because she is blaming Life in general for her own unattached condition.

I don't think anyone has ever satisfactorily explained that mysterious "lostness," that ghostly homesickness that afflicts most women—and men, too—from the time when they become conscious of themselves as individuals until the time when they realise themselves in someone else. It isn't "sex" entirely—it is something much deeper than that, if by "sex" you mean the attraction that draws two people together, usually physically rather than spiritually.

I believe that there is a deep urge towards union between men and women, but that the union has to be complete to be satisfying and that the reason why a marriage based on physical attraction, or a marriage of purely intellectual kinship, so often fails, is because union in the strict sense is never achieved. We are the products of two sexes, inheriting very largely the characteristics of both. A woman alone, a man alone, seem to me to be just half-creatures, always feeling an ache of emptiness and lostness until the other half joins up with them. Perhaps a bi-sexual creature is the ultimate aim of nature, but in a union between a man and a woman who are complementary we have this aim realised, and then we find that very rare thing, perfect happiness without any of what we call "sex antagonism;" perfect comradeship with absolute confidence.

It is necessary to strike the personal note to prove my thesis. I come of a rather savagely independent people—so independent that at eighteen I ran away from the charity of relatives and came to London with less than £1 in the world. I married almost immediately a man who was not a very strong character, and although I married him I very adequately "did without" him. I earned my own living and his, and supported my children when they arrived. I never called on him for comradeship because I realised superficially very quickly that he had none to give, and it never occurred to the independent creature I was then that I ought to have tried to rouse friendliness in him; when troubles came, in my pride I shouldered them without even mentioning them to him. When, being very young, I used to feel an almost overmastering desire for love-making and romance, I crushed it down sternly, horrified at the very idea of admitting, even to myself, that I longed for even such a small physical manifestation of love as a kiss or a caress.

There, I think, I was like many women. We are too proud —or it may be too mean-spirited —to let a man see how much he is needed; a man frankly admits his need of the woman he loves and proceeds to win her. A woman usually bestows herself with an air, not admitting to her man that her need is as great as his. A "feminist" woman will usually torture herself rather than yield to her longing for a man's love, which she feels degrades her by making her realise her incompleteness. I

necessity, is flying the brave flag of independence there
frank pronouncement about—

Unattached Woman

By Leonora Eyles

Physically, mentally, spiritually, economically and socially a woman needs a man

Socially, a woman without a man is at a grave disadvantage. Socially, a bad husband is better than no husband

prided myself on making no demands whatever upon him, thinking that thus we should have perfect equality. The result was that in the end he came to hate me and after eleven years of great unhappiness, he begged me to divorce him and let him go to a woman who "really loved him." I know now that if I had ever let him know how much I needed him if I had ever insisted on his taking a share of the financial burden, the end of the story would have been very different.

After the divorce I found some curious things. I found, first, that socially a woman without a man is at a grave disadvantage. Socially a bad husband is better than no husband. Even in the most sordid sense this is so. Landlords look askance at a woman with children who wants to take a house; tradespeople don't like us. My married women friends whose husbands are earning no more than I am, and who are not spending so much with a tradesman, get much more courtesy than I have had, and as for credit——!

I know married women whose housekeeping bills run on from three to six months and whose dressmakers' bills mount up to the hundreds; they receive unctuous politeness from their trades-

men, while I, who am a scrupulous payer, get "Kindly remit" on a bill which is only a week late.

A really laughable thing happened to me when I was hiring a household fitment recently. A form had to be filled in and I put a dash opposite "Husband's name." The clerk pointed out the omission. I said, "I have no husband." "Oh, you're a widow," he announced. "No, I'm not. My husband is divorced." He looked doubtful, took the form away, consulted two other clerks and came back. "You'd better put *widow*," he said, "I don't think the firm would like it if you put *divorced*." The financial transaction involved was 5s. 6d. a quarter for hire of the article and I was wearing obviously expensive clothes. But that is typical. In shops I have noticed during the past two years, when I have frequently had a man with me, how assistants rush to be attentive and how, in the past, I have been cynically kept waiting. I am now in the fortunate position of being solicited by tradesmen who merely *served* me before!

In my work, too, I have found much the same thing. Some of the firms for whom I work have known that, with three children to support, I am by no means well off. I was told once by a sub-editor that her editor deliberately marked ten guineas off the agreed price of a series of articles. "Oh, she'll take it! She's always hard up," was the remark, and I did take it because I needed the money for school fees.

Twice I have worked on staffs with men who were quite kind and friendly, indeed so kind and friendly that I was given all the difficult interviews, all the jobs that meant standing about in the rain for hours, or missing meals, or getting up abnormally early and going to bed abnormally late—and I was paid considerably below standard rates.

Yet with these same people now, when they want an article from me, it is: "I wonder if you'd be so awfully kind?" when they put a really pleasant and easy job on to me, and the pay is doubled.

*There's a man, not
a machine, behind
this business*

Mrs. EVERYMAN

'About the furniture-can I arrange terms without my husband, Mr. Drage?'

Mr. Drage : Of course you can. Men can't always get away, and ladies so often make a better bargain.

Mrs. Everyman : That's an encouragement to me, Mr. Drage, because I want to take advantage of your 50 Pay-Way terms.

Mr. Drage : And you're very welcome. Your order comes to £120, you need only pay 48s. now, this being the first of 50 monthly instalments.

Mrs. Everyman : How delightfully simple and convenient. I'll pay 48s. now and I want the furniture sent home on Thursday, if that is all right.

Mr. Drage : You can rely on that, Mrs. Everyman. Drages always keep a promise.

Mrs. Everyman : My husband said that you would need references.

Mr. Drage : Sometimes husbands are wrong. At least my wife tells me so. It is my strict rule that we never ask for or take up references.

Mrs. Everyman : It's very pleasant to be trusted in this way. Are there any extra charges for the 50 months' credit ?

Mr. Drage : Not a penny will be added to our plain marked prices. £120 is all you pay and here is your Drage Protection.

Mrs. Everyman : What is that, Mr. Drage ?

Mr. Drage : A written agreement giving you the right, in case sickness or unemployment prevent you from going on paying, to keep all you have paid for less an agreed reasonable deduction for use and cartage.

Mrs. Everyman : That's most thoughtful of you, Mr. Drage.

Mr. Drage : I've built up this business by thinking first of my customers. Another protection is a Free Fire and Life Policy which the Eagle Star and British Dominions Insurance Company will send you.

Mrs. Everyman : You've been charming to me, Mr. Drage, but so has everyone here. I never spent such a pleasant afternoon shopping in my life, and your terms are just wonderful.

DRAGES
(DRAGE'S LIMITED)

HIGH HOLBORN · LONDON · WC1

Next door to HOLBORN TUBE STN. 'Phone: Holborn 3655
OPEN FROM 9 a.m. to 6.30 p.m. CLOSE THURSDAYS *at* 1 p.m.
OPEN ON SATURDAYS TILL 6.30

COUPON Please send me free and post free the New Drage Book and full particulars of your 50 pay-way "No Deposit" System for approved accounts.

NAME ....

ADDRESS...

G.H.9. ....

Cut out and post in unsealed envelope with ½d. stamp to Drages Limited, 230 High Holborn, London, W.C.1.

Kitchen Economies to Add to

The Housekeeper's Dictionary of Facts

What to do with Bones

Better use could be made in the average kitchen of bones which are frequently thrown away, for they are rich in mineral matter, also containing gelatine and other good material. If boiled slowly for a long period, much of this goodness is extracted, therefore the use of a stockpot is strongly recommended in small and large kitchens. Garden enthusiasts may also be willing to dry and pulverise the bones after they come from the stockpot, as they possess a decided value as a phosphatic manure.

Two Ways with Bread Crusts

Do not throw away bread crusts for they can be softened and made quite palatable if soaked in hot milk. Actually, bread and milk made with crusts instead of the inner part of bread is as easily digested by invalids as the uncrusted portion. If preferred, bread crusts can be put in the oven until they are thoroughly browned and perfectly dry right through, when they should be crushed with a rolling pin and stored in an airtight tin. Brown crusts are useful for serving with game and for coating certain foods, such as rissoles, before frying.

Grading Fat

Many people do not care for very fat food and leave a large proportion on their plates if it is served to them. Housewives should bear this carefully in mind, as it is sheer waste serving fat if it is not going to be eaten. A great deal can be removed from the meat before serving, and in institutions where a considerabe amount of cooking is done, it should be divided into two grades, the coarser outer fat, which is generally rather dark in colour, and the finer inner fat, which is pale in colour and very mild in flavour, such as that situated on the undercut of joints of beef. Both grades should be melted separately, the coarser type being reserved for dripping and for basting, while the finer can be clarified and used to replace butter, margarine and lard for many cooking purposes.

Simple Soap Making

The grease that sets on the surface of soup, stocks, etc., when cold, can be clarified, or if preferred, this and other coarse forms of fat may be melted or boiled with a small quantity of caustic soda to form a coarse soap for kitchen use. If, on the contrary, caustic potash be employed for the boiling of this grease, a good soft soap is formed. The housewife who saves her fat, will therefore find her soap bill is appreciably reduced.

Coarse Soap from Oddments of Fat

Weigh out 1 lb. fat into an old double saucepan. Dissolve 2½ oz. caustic soda in 1 quart water and add to the melted fat, stirring well. Heat the mixture, stirring from time to time until saponification is complete. Continue heating until a little of the mixture gives a clear soapy solution when added to hot water. When cold, form into tablets of convenient size.

Kitchen Waste for Fowls

The outer leaves of green vegetables, the parings of potatoes and artichokes, the scrapings of root vegetables, such as carrots and parsnips, the crowns of beetroot and so on, can all be turned to advantage. Little effort is required to mix them together and put them through a chopping machine in a fresh wet state. When well mixed they can be dusted over with "sharps" or other farinaceous material.

When Boiling a Cauliflower

To prevent the unsightly discoloration of cauliflower, add about half a cupful of milk to the water in which it is to be boiled.

Renovating a Blind

When blinds become torn and faded at the base, they can be reversed, the lower part being attached to the roller. If long enough some of the faded and torn portion can be cut off before they are reversed.

To Keep Lettuce Fresh

In hot weather, lettuces have a tendency to become wilted. This can be prevented by washing the lettuce and allowing it to remain in the water until crisp and firm. If not required immediately, it should then be enclosed in either a clean, wet tea cloth or wet paper which will keep it crisp and fresh. Long immersion of green vegetables in water causes loss of soluble mineral salts.

To Mend a Knife

Knife blades and their handles which have become separated can be rejoined by filling the hole in the handle with resin, heating the rod attached to the end of the blade and while hot inserting in the resin.

A Window Cleaning Hint

A quick and efficient way of cleaning windows is to rub them over with a pad of tissue paper. If very dirty, wash them with warm water containing a little ammonia, allow to dry and polish with tissue paper.

When Steeping Clothes

If some soap solution is put in the water in which white cotton and linen clothes are steeped it will help to loosen the dirt and greatly minimise the labour of washing.

Charcoal as the Housewife's Aid

A saucer or bag of charcoal in the larder will absorb smells that arise from certain foods, and prevent the odour being taken up by other articles. It is well known how readily milk and butter will assimilate almost any strong smell, but a dish of charcoal placed near will act as a preventive. Gases prejudicial to health—which are most frequently produced by putrefaction changes—are absorbed by it.

Filtering Water

Water supplies for household purposes are now too closely watched by the authorities for danger to arise, although there are times, especially in summer, when the water is not obtained from the usual sources. On such occasions the water must be above reproach and fortunately there are now filters to be had capable of making almost any water quite safe. Such filters have long been used by explorers and on board ship where the water is drawn from tanks, and their price is within the reach of all. If only a small delivery of pure water is desired, the filter costs about one pound. The old-fashioned charcoal or sand filters are not much use. They remove suspended matter but they seldom remove germs. In fact, under certain conditions, they may even favour germ development.

Water may also be sterilised by boiling for some time, but such water cannot be stored for long in this condition since dust particles in the air are germ carriers. There are also chemical means of sterilising drinking water. Chlorine is used by some authorities, ozone by others, and for small scale sterilisation tablets may be bought that liberate small amounts of iodine when placed in the water.

To Renovate Shabby Linoleum

The surface of a painted type of linoleum usually wears off long before the linoleum itself is really badly worn. Such a floor covering can, however, be renovated by treating with a good make of floor paint. Before applying this, all soil and wax polish should be removed by scrubbing with hot soda water and the paint then applied with a fairly large paint brush. Such an application is, of course, only a surface one and where there is much traffic mats should be laid down.

Cosmetics from the Garden

By Eleanour Sinclair Rohde

FOR real goodness there is nothing better than the cosmetics which our grandmothers made from their own gardens. The fragrant petals of roses, cowslips, elder, etc., are rich in highly concentrated essences, which are most beneficial, and it is only we foolish moderns who neglect them.

Rose Water

Rose water made from scented roses, especially from the deliciously fragrant cabbage or damask roses, has a very whitening and softening effect on the skin, and this "sweet water" was commonly freshly made every day during the rose season. It is a very simple process, and there is no necessity to use freshly blown roses, as those which are just about to drop serve quite as well.

Cover 2 lb. of rose petals (they must be from scented roses) with cold soft water and bring slowly to the boil. Allow to simmer for a few minutes and then strain. To increase the scent, a few drops of oil of geranium may be added. A little jug of freshly-made rose water to wash in is a delicate attention to pay an honoured guest.

Rose Cream

Rose cream is one of the best face creams and it will keep at least a year.

Melt 2 lb. of the best fresh lard (salted lard is useless) in a large basin placed over a saucepan of boiling water. When the fat is melted, put in 2 lb. of scented rose petals, preferably red roses, and mix well in. Allow this fat to remain over the saucepan of boiling water all day, stirring frequently. Then pass through a sieve. Next day melt the fat as before and add another pound of fresh rose petals. This process should be repeated three or four times. When strained through a sieve for the last time, pour the fat into small pots and cover with paper and tie down. If liked add 2 drachms of oil of geranium.

Elder Flower Water and Cream

Elder flower water has long been famed for its effect on the skin and it is particularly good for sunburn. When picking the elder flowers, care should be taken not to let more of the pollen fly off than you can help. Elder flower water is made in exactly the same way as rose water and it is so fragrant that there is no necessity to add any scent. Elder cream made in the same way as the rose cream is wonderful for chapped hands and like the rose cream it will keep at least a year.

Quince Lotion

Our grandmothers also had great faith in quince blossoms for whitening the skin. Quince lotion is made thus:

Put half a peck of quince blossoms in a pan, cover with cold water and simmer for an hour. Cut two cucumbers into thin slices, chop finely, put into the saucepan with the quince blossom and boil five minutes. Strain through muslin and, when the water is quite cold, pour into bottles and tie down. To use the lotion, smear it on the face and hands and leave for fifteen minutes before washing.

Quince juice from the fresh fruit and freshly cut slices of cucumber rubbed on the skin act like a charm against sunburn.

Water scented with lavender flowers and leaves has, of course, been popular from Roman times. To make the water very fragrant simmer the lavender flowers and leaves in it for quite fifteen minutes.

For skins which require feeding, almond oil is very beneficial.

Almond Cream

Almond cream is one of the best of the home-made complexion creams, and unlike the elder and rose creams it can be used during the day as it is not at all greasy.

To make it take 5 oz. of almond oil, ½ oz. of white wax, 1½ oz. of spermaceti and a pinch of boracic powder. Put the white wax and the spermaceti in a saucepan and melt them. When melted add the almond oil and the pinch of boracic powder, take the saucepan off the fire and stir till cold. Then put into pots.

Rosemary Hair Lotion

Of the home-made hair tonics there is nothing to equal rosemary, and this lotion is very quickly and easily made. Rose-

Cosmetics from the Garden

mary being evergreen, the lotion can be made at any time of the year.

To make it, take a few sprigs of rosemary and cut up finely. Put into half a pint of cold water and bring to the boil. Then simmer for about ten minutes and leave to get cold. Rub the scalp all over with a small piece of linen dipped in this water. Larger quantities for washing the hair can be made, using the same proportions of rosemary and water. In order to make rosemary tonic which will keep through the winter, crushed camphor may be added, but camphor has a drying effect on the hair.

Spanish women, who are so famed for the beauty of their hair, use these simple home-made hair washes. Sage and peppermint water (made in the same way as the rosemary tonic, allowing, however, a good large handful of fresh sage and peppermint to half a pint of water) is very commonly used in the south of Spain but, unlike rosemary, it cannot be universally recommended as it has a darkening effect on the hair.

Camomile hair shampoos are fashionable at present so why not dry and use the camomile flowers from your own garden as your grandmothers did? The flowers should be dried, *not* by spreading them out on a table, but on a large wire sieve so that the air can circulate above and beneath. This is one of the secrets in drying flowers successfully whether for cosmetics or pot-pourris.

Our Health Questionnaire

QUESTIONS concerning health will be answered in this column each month by a fully qualified medical man. Prescriptional advice cannot be given. Letters should be addressed Doctor, Good Housekeeping, 153 Queen Victoria Street, London, E.C.4, and must in every case bear the full name and address of the sender

Is there any fear of infection from tuberculosis for my little boy who comes into contact with a friend who was in a sanatorium and gets returns of the disease from time to time?

(Mrs. C. S.)

There is always a slight risk of infection in such cases, but in this instance I should imagine it was very small, otherwise the patient would not be allowed out.

Answer to E. N. C., Red Hill.

I should think that as his doctors have told him that he can eat what he likes, any easily digested foods free from all grittiness would be indicated. A course of cod-liver oil and extract of malt may help towards regaining his former strength.

Answer to Worryer, N.W.2.

From what you say I do not think any slight operation would help matters much. No, there is no ground to suppose that your condition will tend to make you fat.

My mother, aged 62, suffers very much from pain in both hands. At times the fingers are stiff and swollen with no feeling in them. The pain often causes sleeplessness. Do you think electric massage would help?

(Mrs. J. M. N., Strawberry Hill.)

Owing to the age and the rheumatic tendency I doubt if very much benefit can be looked for from electric massage. It may help slightly. General constitutional treatment is probably necessary. Get your doctor to give her a thorough examination, particularly with regard to the condition of the blood and urine.

Answer to N. S. D., Newport.

Everything possible seems to have been undertaken for the child, and I should certainly continue as you are doing. Later on she may put on more weight; such a condition is not uncommon at her age. A change of air might help if this is possible.

Answer to Mrs. M. F., Wembley.

It is difficult to overcome these peculiar symptoms which are so characteristic of your condition. Fresh air night and day, adequate rest and moderate exercise, are all most essential; and strict attention should be paid to the condition of the bowels. Sometimes a mixture of potassium bromide, ammoniated tincture of valerian and tincture of Indian hemp is found helpful in such cases.

Answer to A. A.

If you are married, the answer to your question is " No."

Answer to I. M. S., St. Ives.

From your letter I should imagine your doctor was perfectly right and there is nothing for you to worry about. You probably need a tonic and sedative mixture. Why not try a course of extract of malt and cod-liver oil for a few months? It would help you, I feel sure.

Answer to C. H., Wilts.

Your weight is below normal for your height. Cod-liver oil and extract of malt will help you. Discontinue cigarette smoking altogether if you can. It won't do your chest any good if you keep irritating the condition with smoke. I daresay an examination by a specialist would be useful as you say. A patch on one lung, such as you describe, is bound to take a considerable time to mend, and you will require to lead a very careful and regular life indeed to effect a cure of your condition.

Answer to " J."

So far as I know, nothing with safety. Some try using a solution of nitrate of silver, but I don't recommend it.

I should be obliged if you would give me particulars of diet to avoid flatulence. There is no pain.

(Mrs. E. R., London, S.W.)

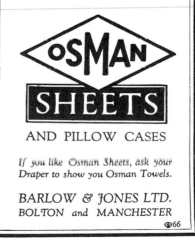
THE
20's

BEAU GESTE

the perfume of gay adventure

THE creators of Les Parfums de Molinelle count this their greatest achievement—the intoxication of dangerous moments—the promise of a glance—the insouciance of a light intrigue—captured in a perfume, Beau Geste.

This is more than a perfume—it is an adventure, a compeer of Molinelle's "ENGLISH ROSES" and Molinelle's "NO. 27"—for the first of these is pure rose-loveliness, and the second so subtle that it can only be numbered, not named. "BEAU GESTE" has the candour of the one, the allure of the other.

All three Parfums de Molinelle are offered in octagonal flagons of crystal, stoppered with a delicate crystal cameo engraved by hand. The silk-lined Molinelle coffrets have two doors, so that your perfume may stand enshrined beside your mirror.

In four sizes, priced at Three, Five, Nine and Fifteen Pounds, and there is an Introductory Size at Fifteen Shillings.

THERE ARE, OF COURSE, CREAMS AND POWDERS
TO BLEND WITH EACH PARFUM DE MOLINELLE

Crème de Beauté	5/6	9/6
Poudres	7/6	12/6

Sole Concessionaires:
MOLINELLE LTD., 10 St. Alban's Place, Haymarket, S.W.1

You will find Parfums de Molinelle at the following exclusive Houses :—

Asprey, Bond Street, W.1

Marshall & Snellgrove, Oxford Street, W.1

Bagley & Son, 8 Park Street, Minehead

J. Bury, Ltd., 5 St. Ann Street, Manchester

Taylor's Drug Co., Ltd., 4 Exchange Street, St. Anne's Square, Manchester

A. Fasnacht, 15 North Parade; Bradford

Grace & Hardy, 29 Montpelier Parade, Harrogate

E. B. Kendall & Sons, 6 Coney Street, York

Marjorie Dimsdale, Barton Chambers, Leeds

Gordon Hotel, Southbourne, Bournemouth

Hints Approved by Good Housekeeping Institute

The Housekeeper's Dictionary *of* Facts

When Making Marmalade

When a machine is not available for cutting up the oranges the labour is made much easier if the pulp is first removed and the skins then boiled for a short time. This softens them considerably so that they can be cut much more easily and quickly. The water used for the boiling should of course be saved and used later when boiling the pulp, etc.

When a considerable amount of marmalade is to be made, however, the purchase of a small cutter is well worth while. Various cutters have now been tested at the Institute, their prices ranging from 9s. 9d. to £2 2s. These have all been proved efficient labour-savers, and full particulars will be given to any interested reader who cares to apply to the Institute.

New Uses for Steel-wool

Fine steel-wool has innumerable uses in the household, its more familiar ones being for cleaning and polishing aluminium and parquet floors. In the Institute it has also been found excellent for cleaning windows without the use of water and with a minimum of effort. Needless to say, the very finest grade of wool should be used for this purpose.

Everyone who has used an oven thermometer knows how difficult it is to remove all traces of burnt-on food, fat, etc. After cleaning as far as possible with hot soda water, rubbing with fine steel-wool will usually remove all or most of the stains.

Where a considerable amount of the wool is used it is best to purchase it by the pound. The cost of course varies according to the fineness, the least expensive costing 1s. 4d. the half-pound packet.

To Keep Salt Dry

Trouble with salt-pourers is often experienced, especially in damp weather, or by the sea, on account of the tendency of the salt to absorb moisture and so cake. This may be obviated to a large extent if the pourers are placed in a closed tin of suitable size immediately after each meal.

This protects the pourer from the atmosphere, and if a piece of quicklime is also placed in an old cup or saucer and kept in the tin, no difficulty should be experienced in shaking out the salt even in the dampest weather, provided the quicklime is renewed at intervals.

When Laundering Shantung or Tussore Silk

These materials are woven from silk threads obtained from the cocoon of wild silkworms. In the process of manufacture they do not undergo boiling off or de-gumming as in the case of silks produced by cultivated varieties of silkworms. The result is that the natural gum remains, and consequently when ironing, shantung materials give the best results if allowed to dry completely first. To obtain good results it

Lecture Demonstrations at Good Housekeeping Institute

A course of Cookery Lectures is now being held on Wednesdays at 3 p.m. at Good Housekeeping Institute, 49 Wellington Street, Strand, W.C.2. The course includes instruction in the making of puddings, bread, cakes, pastry, réchauffé dishes, etc.

Full particulars of lectures, practice classes and fees for the course can be obtained from the Director.

is also important not to use too hot an iron. The result of ironing damp or of using too hot an iron is usually that the material becomes stiff and papery in appearance.

Worn and Discoloured Evening Shoes

Satin shoes can be re-dyed at home with very little trouble provided a good make of spirit dye is available. Before applying the dye, the shoes should be thoroughly freed from all traces of grease, etc., by rubbing well with a cloth dipped in petrol or other grease solvent. As petrol is highly inflammable this should not, of course, be done in a room in which there is a fire or naked light. When quite clean, the dye should be applied by means of a small soft brush. Tarnished silver or brocade shoes can be cleaned by rubbing well with a special powder. This can be obtained at many of the leading shops, but if readers experience difficulty either in obtaining a suitable dye or powder, we shall be pleased to supply the names of makes which have been used at the Institute with very successful results.

To Remove Rust Marks from Linoleum

Especially in the kitchen, where the iron legs of a gas or other stove may stand on the linoleum, rust marks frequently appear. These can, however, be readily removed by placing a few crystals of oxalic acid, or salts of lemon, immediately over the stain and pouring boiling water over. The stains will usually disappear almost instantaneously. After use it is important to rinse away all traces of the chemicals, both of which should be used with the utmost care as they are very poisonous.

An Attractive Way of Serving Left-over Sandwiches

It is often difficult to know what to do with left-over sandwiches. If toasted on both sides, under a grill or toaster, however, and served hot, they will be appreciated either for tea or supper.

A Home-made Polisher for Silver and Glass, etc.

An excellent home-made polisher can be made with a small bag measuring 3 or 4 inches by 6 or 8 inches and filled with finely powdered whiting. The bag should then be machine-stitched across the opening.

When using this pad a certain amount of the powder passes through the material and it therefore proves most efficient for cleaning silver, glass, aluminium, etc.

A Use for Old Tin Lids

The lid of a disused tin makes an ideal cover for an opened jar of jam. Keep a variety of sizes handy, enamel them to facilitate washing and also to protect them from rust, and you will have an adequate supply of covers for all requirements.

When Steaming Vegetables

One of the disadvantages of steaming vegetables is that they invariably become a poor colour. This can be prevented altogether, if after washing in the ordinary way they are given a final rinse in boiling water containing a little soda.

To Remove Tomato Skins

When there are only a few tomatoes to be peeled, instead of scalding them, put one tomato at a time on a fork and hold over a gas flame. Turn it rapidly so that all the surface is heated. When the skin splits, the tomato may easily be peeled.

DIANA STRICKLAND AND HER STAR

A 7,000-mile exploration through widest and wildest Africa.

Mrs. Strickland spent a year in traversing Africa on a Star, from Dakar on the West Coast to Massaua on the Red Sea. The drivers of a French car who attempted but a section of her journey were decorated by the French Government, though their car broke down utterly.

Her Star had a purely standard touring chassis. Beyond grinding in the valves once no repairs were effected, and, outside plugs and tyres, no renewals whatever.

Her mechanic returned sick early in the journey, and her other companion died of blackwater fever. Mrs. Strickland finished alone, in many instances driving for hundreds of miles across country in the rocky desert and bush, guided by her compass, fording rivers, and digging the car out of mud and sand.

Almost immediately upon her return, without inspection or repair, her Star, weighing 1½-tons with chassis and body, put up a 52 m.p.h. lap at Brooklands.

Both woman and car have established an absolutely unique reputation for hardihood.

The Star Motor Co., Ltd., Wolverhampton.
London Depot : 24, Long Acre, W.C.2.

By J. E. Buckrose

The Revolt of the Grandmothers

Within the last decade an amazing change has taken place in the attitude of women towards age. The grandmother of sixty—so charming, bless her!—in her smart gowns, with her shingled hair like a silver helmet, and her slim ankles uncovered half-way to the knee, does not consider herself withdrawn from life, but takes her part gallantly and gaily in it, infusing into her contacts and surroundings all the mellow charm of her experience

Drawing by L. G. Illingworth

WE are always hearing about the revolt of youth. Every newspaper mentions it either directly or indirectly at least once a week. No Sunday goes by, but in some pulpit in this land it is alluded to. The subject crops up in political speeches, in learned addresses, in municipal after-dinner speeches. It is, indeed, the King Charles's head of modern civilisation, which we can no more leave out than could poor Uncle Dick refrain from putting his fixed idea into the memorial. A City Father will open a bazaar with an allusion to short skirts—not because he wants to, but because he can't help it. The young must be spoken of, if only to condemn.

And all this has had a very queer result indeed. It has caused us to miss seeing a far more startling revolution. I mean, of course, the revolt of the grandmothers.

For so far as I know, there is no recorded instance in the whole of history where such a complete change has taken place in the attitude of women towards age, in so short a space of time. There is no need to seek further proof of this than the memory of any living person over forty. All such have in their minds a recollection of an entirely extinct species.

Another place where they may be observed is on the stage, and that in the most modern plays, for it seems to have escaped the notice of even the most intuitive and observant dramatists that the old maids and decrepidly doddering grandmothers of sixty whom they portray are not real people at all. They are only ghosts of prehistoric creatures no longer alive in the ordinary haunts of man, though perhaps to be found lingering on in remote spots here and there, like the great auk and the golden eagle.

But they do not belong to our everyday life any more. Then why does no fat alderman at prize-giving suddenly interest his comatose hearers by " going for " the ladies in the front rows of his audience? Because they *have* had the temerity to change in mental outlook in a far more startling fashion than the girls and boys.

Think of it! The grandmother of that alderman at the age of sixty had no alternative but to behave herself according to the then accepted code governing the behaviour of grandmothers, while she constantly reminded herself and was reminded that " her time was growing short." If, to her misfortune, she were given to forgetting this insecurity of tenure, she was thought a skittish old thing, who must be treated with constant douches of cold water.

No matter if the other attributes of this condition of mind made her a cheerful companion who was greatly beloved: the manner, outlook, and beyond all, the dress of youth, on the person of sixty, was such a subject for ridicule that this sartorial impropriety had its proper and general label of scorn: " an old ewe dressed lamb fashion." Public opinion was such that that charming grandmother now actually just under the alderman's nose, with her shingled hair like a silver helmet, and her slim ankles uncovered modestly only half way to the knee, would undoubtedly once have been considered mad, as well as disreputable.

If, in addition to this, she had happened to say she intended to go with a male friend to dine and dance—well, what would have ensued then, can scarcely be imagined. Only it is safe to say that

it would have beaten all the dramatic scenes of the revolting daughter hollow.

A strange feature of all this, however, is that the revolting children have been so taken up with their own revolt, that they scarcely seem to have noticed what was happening. Indeed, how should they?—for it was taking place during the engrossing development of their own point of view.

And of course, like the alderman and the playwright and the author, they were blinded to what they saw by their knowledge of what for years had been seen; and what therefore with the conservatism inherent in the human race —they expected to go on seeing.

But though they may not have realised the almost incredible revolution in the lives of older women of to-day as compared with those of a couple of generations ago, they are, I think, beginning to be unconsciously very much aware of the *effect* of this change.

Those mothers between fifty and sixty who used to feel that fun, at any rate, was over for them, made a reposeful background for turbulent youth. For youth is so, even if confined in boned bodices with behaviour to match. And the mother who is young and gay and full of her own interests is a delightful companion . . . but she is not a background. And the unpalatable truth is, that a background is what the vivid, self-engrossed girl of to-day really wants.

Inexpensive

for Christ

Right: evening dress in pure silk chiffon taffeta showing the new semi - circular skirt edged with heavy gold lace. Available in nil/gold lace, saxe/ gold lace, lemon/gold lace, and black/oxi-dised lace. In S.W. and W. sizes. Price 59s. 6d. Post free U.K.

Below, left: a very useful under - coat frock in printed arti-ficial silk and plain navy silk and wool marocain. The jumper bodice is of the fancy marocain printed in beige, brick and navy; the skirt, pleated in front, is of the navy silk and wool marocain. In navy only, in S.W. and W. sizes. Price 29s. 11d. Post free U.K.

Left: this is a very smart semi-evening frock in rich quality chiffon taffeta, be-comingly made with a tight-fitting corsage. The full skirt is bordered with gold tinsel and black galon and finished with a band of double silk net. In black only. In S.W. and W. sizes. Price 69s. 6d. Post free U.K.

Left: tweed stockinette, a pleasing new all-wool material, in a mosaic pattern, makes this cosy house frock with collar and cuffs of plain stockinette; the skirt is finely machine pleated. Available in predominating shades of beige/ brown, beige/almond, fawn/blue, and fawn. In S.W. and W. sizes. Price 35s. 9d. Post free U.K.

Immediate right: attractive evening gown in a pretty tinsel-stripe satin and silk net. The skirt is cut full in sections of net and satin mounted on an underdress of ninon to match. The tight-fitting bodice is composed entirely of striped satin. Available in two tones of prim-rose and gold, two tones of jade and silver. In S.W. and W. sizes. Price 3½ gns. Post free U.K.

Right: useful and well-made evening gown in the new fashionable printed velsa. Made with a semi-circular skirt and scalloped hem with rouleaux to tone. Available in silver ground with saxe and cherry flower; salmon ground with darker tone and saxe flower; champagne with jade and cherry flower. In S.W. and W. sizes. Price 49s. 6d. Post free U.K.

Left: smart and practical after-noon frock in silk and wool crêpe marocain. The attrac-tively tucked bodice is finished with double collar of beige georgette edged with rouleaux of marocain. Available in navy, Lido blue, almond, mushroom, Chanel red, cedar and black. In S.W. and W. sizes. Price 29s. 11d. Post free U.K.

Right: afternoon gown in heavy quality art silk crêpe de Chine; bodice has two box pleats con-tinued down skirt and finished with two nar-row belts and buckles. Sizes 40, 42, 44 inches. Black, navy, beige, rose, grey and cocoa. Price 39s. 6d. Post free U.K.

Centre of group on right: wool delaine frock printed in neat design and made with the new full skirt. The neck, cuffs and simu-lated pockets are in wool crêpe to match the print. In S.W. and W. sizes. Available in black/red/beige. Price 35s. 9d. Post free U.K.

Conditions of

Our Shopping Service is designed to help London Shops. Any of the articles illus advertisement columns of this number of happy to buy for you, without extra charge, name and address. Money orders from postage and insurance. Readers in Irish meet the Customs charges on dutiable and cheques should be addressed to "Shop ING, 153 Queen Victoria Street, London, a choice of colours. Articles are in stock If any reader desires to return goods pur vice, the articles, together with the reader's ence to GOOD HOUSEKEEPING Shopping shop. If goods are not returned in perfect funded. Postage must be paid on goods instance. All correspondence and instruc sent to "Shopping Service," GOOD HOUSE-London,

Dance Frocks
mas Parties

Left: pretty evening frock in all silk satin. Skirt made with three flounces and well-cut plain bodice. Available in shades of light and dark rose, light and dark saxe, green or black. Sizes, length 40 in., hips 40 in.; length 42 in., hips 42 in. Price 35s. 9d. Post free U.K.

Right: a very special bargain is this good-looking beaded frock. It is elaborately worked in silver lined bugle beads; the waistline is outlined with a design worked in beads. Available in ivory, lemon, nil, salmon, plumbago, Lido blue, and black, also in Chanel red. In S.W. and W. sizes. Price 29s. 11d. Post free U.K.

Right: charming evening gown in two colours in peach and green taffeta, with gold lace yoke to bodice. Made with the new circular skirt on which the green is introduced, and finished at waist with loop of the two colours. Also available in other suitable contrasts. In S.W. only. Price 3½ gns. Post free U.K.

Left: evening frock of taffeta trimmed with wide flounces. A sash of self material is finished at the side with diamanté buckle and large bow. Bodice with rosette on shoulder. Sizes, length 40 in., hips 40 in.; length 42 in., hips 42 in. Price 52s. 6d. Post free U.K. Outsizes to measure 4s. 6d. extra

Above, left: charming evening gown in all silk georgette. The skirt is made with handkerchief petals over an underdress of self material. The bodice is finished with a handmade flower of the georgette. Available in ivory, coral, eau de nil, lemon, hyacinth, blue and black. Price 3½ gns. Post free U.K.

Above: graceful evening gown for full figure in a heavy quality artificial crêpe de Chine. The bodice has a round neck and is gathered on the shoulders, and the skirt has a deep box pleat in the centre front with a drapery at either side giving an apron effect; the panels are edged with oriental scalloped embroidery to tone. Posy to match on shoulder. In sizes 46 and 48 fittings. Available in Lido, saxe, almond, grey, and black. Price 49s. 6d. Post free U.K.

Purchase

those who are out of reach of the trated in these pages, or in the GOOD HOUSEKEEPING, we shall be on receipt of money order and your the Colonies should include cost of Free State must be prepared to goods. All letters, money orders, ping Service," GOOD HOUSEKEEP-E.C.4. Where possible please give size except where otherwise stated. chased through the Shopping Ser-full name and address, and a refer-Service, should be returned to the condition the money cannot be re-that were correctly sent in the first tions concerning the goods must be KEEPING, 153 Queen Victoria Street, E.C.4

Graceful coatee suitable for bridge or after-dinner wear in black broché velvet banded and trimmed with plain chiffon velvet. The bottom of the coat is shaped and trimmed with a silk fringe; lined throughout silk. Price 69s. 6d. Post free U.K.

Left: good-looking coat frock showing the latest fashion in the details of bolero effect, new circular skirt and gauntlet cuffs; looks well in a cocoa shade of wool crêpe de Chine with a fancy vest, collar and cuffs to tone. Also available in beige, navy, green, and wine with collar, cuffs and vest to tone. Sizes S.W. and W. Price 3 gns. Post free U.K.

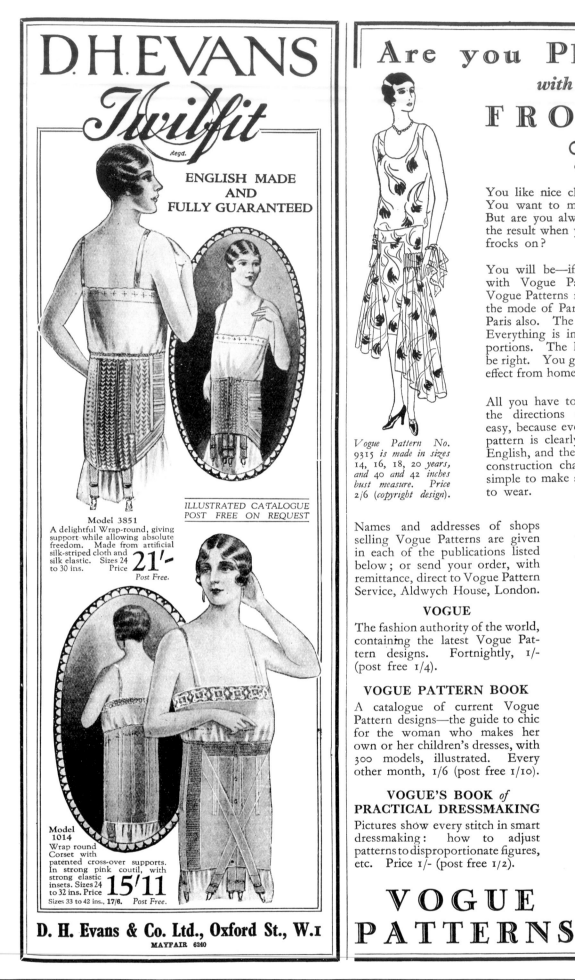
Are you Pleased
with your
FROCKS
?

You like nice clothes, of course.
You want to make nice clothes.
But are you always satisfied with
the result when you put your new
frocks on?

You will be—if you make them
with Vogue Patterns. Because
Vogue Patterns represent not only
the mode of Paris, but the *cut* of
Paris also. The lines are accurate.
Everything is in the correct proportions. The hang and fit *must*
be right. You get the professional
effect from home dressmaking!

All you have to do is to follow
the directions exactly. This is
easy, because every piece of every
pattern is clearly marked in plain
English, and there is a marvellous
construction chart. They are as
simple to make as they are smart
to wear.

*Vogue Pattern No.
9315 is made in sizes
14, 16, 18, 20 years,
and 40 and 42 inches
bust measure. Price
2/6 (copyright design).*

Names and addresses of shops
selling Vogue Patterns are given
in each of the publications listed
below; or send your order, with
remittance, direct to Vogue Pattern
Service, Aldwych House, London.

VOGUE
The fashion authority of the world,
containing the latest Vogue Pattern designs. Fortnightly, 1/-
(post free 1/4).

VOGUE PATTERN BOOK
A catalogue of current Vogue
Pattern designs—the guide to chic
for the woman who makes her
own or her children's dresses, with
300 models, illustrated. Every
other month, 1/6 (post free 1/10).

VOGUE'S BOOK *of*
PRACTICAL DRESSMAKING
Pictures show every stitch in smart
dressmaking: how to adjust
patterns to disproportionate figures,
etc. Price 1/- (post free 1/2).

*(Below) Vogue Pattern
No. 9321: Sizes 14,
16, 18, 20 years, and
40 and 42 inches bust.
2.s.6d.(copyright design).*

VOGUE
PATTERNS

The Housekeeper's Dictionary of Facts

Compiled in Good Housekeeping Institute

THE
20's

Using up Cake Crumbs

Stale cake crumbs can be used for making gingerbread and cheese cakes. Any favourite recipe can be taken but the proportion of crumbs depends on their quality; for example, those from sponge cakes, which contain no fat, can be regarded as flour and used in the same way, except that twice as many crumbs as flour are required. When using crumbs from rich mixtures such as Genoese sponge or Madeira, a smaller proportion of butter and sugar than given in the ingredients would be necessary as the crumbs already contain a fairly large proportion of these two commodities.

Stale Bread

This can be used for making *Thrifty Pudding* as follows :— Take ½ oz. cocoa, 3 oz. suet, 5 oz. sugar, 4 oz. cherries, currants, or sultanas, 1 egg, 1 lb. scraps of bread, and custard. Soak the bread, squeeze out surplus water, and whisk with a fork. Chop the suet finely, cut the fruit in half, mix all the dry ingredients together and stir in the beaten egg. Pour into a well-greased mould and steam for 2 hours. Serve with custard.

Kitchen Towels

Paper towels or kitchen paper kept near the kitchen sink prove both labour- and time-saving. The towels may be used for cleaning the sink, scraping refuse from plates and knives, and for drying the hands. Much of the unpleasantness of washing dish cloths and badly soiled kitchen towels will thus be saved.

To Remove Creases from Dresses and Coats

When dresses and coats are much creased after having been packed away, place them on hangers in the bathroom. Turn on the hot water and the steam will draw out all the creases, leaving the garments fresh again.

To Clean Lacquer

Lacquer articles are, as a rule, kept in good condition by daily dusting. In the case of trays, etc., which are apt to become slightly greasy, occasional washing with a cloth wrung out in warm, soapy water is required. After drying, the articles should be polished with any good make of furniture cream. Washing soda should be avoided.

A FURTHER COURSE OF COOKERY LECTURES

Will be given at Good Housekeeping Institute, 49 Wellington Street, Strand, W.C.2, on Wednesdays, beginning January 18th, 1928, at 3 p.m. Particulars of practice classes and fees for the course can be obtained from The Director

January 18th at 3 p.m.
HOT PUDDINGS.—*Canary, Cabinet, Viennoise, Apple*

January 25th at 3 p.m.
MARMALADES.—*Grapefruit, Orange, Lemon, Apple Ginger*

February 1st at 3 p.m.
YEAST MIXTURES.—*White Bread, Wholemeal Bread, Milk Bread, Doughnuts*

February 8th at 3 p.m.
FRYING AND GRILLING.—*Shallow Frying, Steak and Onions, Cod Steaks, Pancakes, Mixed Grill*

February 15th at 3 p.m.
ROUGH PUFF PASTRY.—*Veal and Ham Pie, Eccles Cakes, Sausage Rolls, Bakewell Tart*

February 22nd at 3 p.m.
SPONGE MIXTURES.—*Sponge Sandwich, Swiss Roll, Angel Cake, Genoese Pastry*

February 29th at 3 p.m.
DEEP FRYING.—*Fritters, Cheese Aigrettes, Fish Cakes, Fish in Batter*

March 7th at 3 p.m.
MILK DISHES.—*Milk Puddings, Junket, Danish Sponge, Chocolate Sponge, Milk Jelly, Baked and Boiled Custards*

March 14th at 3 p.m.
CAKE MAKING.—*Rich Plum Cake, Madeira Cake, Cherry Cake, Lunch Cake, Queen Cakes*

March 21st at 3 p.m.
FISH DISHES.—*Baked Stuffed Haddock, Baked Cod, Casserole of Fish, Sole à la Maître d'Hôtel, Fried Fillets of Plaice*

March 28th at 3 p.m.
RECHAUFFE DISHES.—*Kedgeree, Mince, Toad-in-the-Hole, Thrifty Pudding, Bread and Butter Pudding, Potato Scones*

April 4th at 3 p.m.
SHORTBREADS AND BISCUITS.—*Easter Biscuits, Shortbread, Jumbles, Almond Fingers, Macaroons, Shrewsbury Biscuits*

To Polish Ivory

When ivory articles become discoloured, they can be polished by rubbing with a mixture of gilder's whiting and water, followed by treatment with a mixture of olive oil and methylated spirit. To complete renovation they should be polished with a dry cloth.

A Delicious Nougat

1 lb. honey or golden syrup (white honey if possible)
4 oz. cherries (unchopped)
4 whites of egg
1 lb. blanched almonds (unchopped)
4 oz. blanched pistachios (unchopped)
1 lb. hazel nuts (skinned, unchopped)

For the syrup

1 lb. loaf sugar
Vanilla pod
1½ gills water

Put the honey into a copper pan and melt over a pan of water. Add the stiffly beaten whites and stir well over a pan of gently boiling water until the mixture will form a hard ball. Avoid overheating the copper pan and stir continually to hasten the reducing. (This will take about 1½ hours.) Meanwhile, line a tin with rice paper and moisten the edges with water to make the side strips stick. When the honey mixture is nearly ready, heat the sugar, water and vanilla pod, removing the pod when the syrup is nearly cooked. Cook to " small crack," 290°-300°F. Heat the fruit and nuts on a tray in the oven, pour the sugar mixture on to the honey by degrees and heat. Then add the prepared fruits, turn on to marble well sprinkled with icing sugar, press well to make it compact. Press into the tin, cover with rice paper, put a weight on it, and stand for 24 hours. When cold cut with a sharp hot knife.

To Stain Cork Carpet

When this floor covering is of a light colour cleaning difficulties are often reduced by staining it a darker shade, afterwards applying linseed oil and finally wax polishing. Either a water stain, such as Vandyke brown, or an oil stain, such as Brunswick black, diluted with turpentine, can be used, the latter giving slightly better results. When the carpet is sufficiently dark and is quite dry, linseed oil should be rubbed on with a cloth or nail brush. In ten days or so after the oil has oxidised, a further application should be made, and finally after another ten days to a fortnight wax polish applied. A good deal will be absorbed at first, but after one or two applications a more sparing amount will suffice. The cork carpet will then bear a fairly close resemblance to linoleum.

Come out of the kitchen!

and leave all the cooking to the **Parkinson** "NEW SUBURBIA" Gas Cooker.

Cooking requires no close attention because of the automatic oven heat control. In addition, it has the unique feature of having two flues and one burner in the oven itself. The top flue allows condensation moisture to escape, then closes automatically, after which the heat circulates all round the oven. Thus you get much more heat from much less gas consumption.

Ask for a demonstration at your local Gas Showrooms, but make sure you are shown the **Parkinson** "NEW SUBURBIA" Gas Cooker.

Descriptive Booklet "G" gladly sent upon request.

IT DOES ALL THE COOKING WHILE YOU SHOP OR PLAY

THE PARKINSON 'NEW SUBURBIA' GAS COOKER

THE PARKINSON STOVE CO., LTD., Stechford, BIRMINGHAM
London Showrooms : 8 & 10 Grosvenor Gardens, S.W.1. *And at* Glasgow, Manchester, Belfast, Dublin

Readers' Problems Answered through

The Housekeeper's Dictionary of Facts

Cleaning a Porcelain Sink

(1) Would you be kind enough to recommend a powder which would clean my porcelain sink without scratching it? (2) Eighteen months ago we moved to our present address from a large house. All this time the inlaid linoleum from a room has remained in two rolls. Is it likely to deteriorate in any way?

(N.7.)

I think you should find that you are able to keep your sink in good condition by daily washing with hot soda water. This will remove all traces of grease, while it should be rubbed over occasionally with a non-abrasive soap powder, or with a cloth dipped either in turpentine or paraffin. All cleansers of an abrasive nature should be avoided as their continued use impairs the surface.

The Storage of Linoleum

With regard to storing linoleum, this should be rolled up with the pattern outside, for preference on a strawboard tube not less than 6 in. in diameter. Should one of these tubes not be available, however, then care should be taken to start with as wide a diameter as is possible for the first turn, and to stand it on end to ensure that the roll is not crushed. If the linoleum should be stored in a cold room, when it is taken out it should be stood in a temperature of not less than 60° F. for at least twenty-four hours before being rolled out. Although linoleum can be stored satisfactorily for a limited period by following the above directions, storing for any considerable length of time should be avoided.

Keeping Meringue Tops Crisp

(1) Could you give me a few hints on the successful making of meringue tops for puddings such as Apple Snow? I find that if the pudding has been made in the morning, the meringue which was crisp when taken out of the oven, has become soft and sticky by the evening. (2) Could you give me a recipe for a simple sauce for masking either a cold fowl or turkey, together with directions for using same?

(Cricklewood.)

I am afraid there is no satisfactory way of keeping the meringue on the top of a pudding crisp when it is made with one white of egg and a small quantity of sugar. If the pudding has to be made several hours before it is required the making of the meringue should be delayed. The pudding should be put into the oven to warm through and then the meringue put on about 10 minutes before it is served. The reason that the meringue becomes soft is due

to the fact that steam from the pudding escapes whilst it is cooked, and causes the meringue to become sticky.

Coating Cold Foods

I am enclosing a recipe for an economical Chaudfroid Sauce, the foundation of which is a good white sauce. After it has been prepared, strained, and the aspic added, it should be suffi-

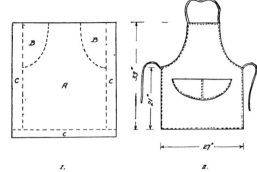

I.   *II.*

An Apron for the Handyman

The illustration above is a suggestion for making a handyman's or fitter's apron out of one square yard of material.

Fig. I shows the way in which the material is cut out, and Fig. II represents the finished article.

The main front of the apron is made of the part marked "A." The two pieces "B" are sewn together and form one or two (as desired) capacious pockets. The three remaining strips "C" go to form the loop which is slipped over the head and the two streamers which fasten behind. A few guide dimensions are given.

ciently thick to coat the back of the spoon before being poured over the chicken. Whilst being coated the chicken should be placed on a cake tray or meat stand. The success of coating cold foods depends largely on the consistency of the sauce. If it is not sufficiently set, or the quantity of aspic too small, it will not cover the meat.

Economical Chaudfroid Sauce

1 pint milk	2 oz. butter
A stick of celery	12 peppercorns
Mace	½ gill cream
1½ oz. flour	4 sheets leaf gelatine
½ gill aspic jelly	
1 small carrot	1 dessertspoonful
Shallot	lemon juice

Cut up the vegetables, and put them with the seasoning and milk into a saucepan. Bring to the boil and simmer gently for an hour. Melt the butter, stir in the flour, strain the liquid from the vegetables, and add to the blended flour and milk, whisking meanwhile to prevent lumps forming. Continue to cook for 10 minutes.

To ½ pint of this sauce when cold, add the gelatine, dissolved in the aspic jelly, the lemon juice and cream. Re-warm the sauce, pass through muslin,

stir until it is sufficiently cold and thick for coating the chicken.

Dyeing an Eiderdown

Will you kindly tell me how I can change the colours on a new eiderdown I have had given me? It is blue with a panel in the centre with figures and flowers coloured a vivid pink. As my room is blue and yellow, can I change the pink to yellow? Would crayons do it?

(Margate.)

Since receiving your letter we have purchased some of the crayons to which you refer and carried out various experiments with these. Although I consider that they undoubtedly are excellent for many purposes I hardly think you would find them particularly convenient for colouring your eiderdown, the disadvantage being that it would be necessary to unpick it, as after using the crayons it is necessary to press the material between blotting paper, using a hot iron.

I am wondering, however, provided the area you are thinking of treating is comparatively small, whether you might not possibly think of using a spirit dye, which I think would be satisfactory for the purpose.

New Curtain Fabrics

The window of my room is a square bay with leaded lights, and there is a window seat. The wallpaper is plain mauve and the fireplace has mauve tiles. Is artificial silk too thin for curtains?

(A. M.)

You do not tell me whether your windows are overlooked from the road, but if this is the case I would suggest you have short curtains of filet net in addition to long ones. Short curtains can be hung by means of small diameter brass-cased rods and thimble brackets. If the windows are not overlooked, curtains of the casement type, hung either with or without a valance or pelmet, could suitably be used.

With regard to artificial silk for curtains, this is now very extensively used and is made in a very large variety of weights. One of the most popular fabrics is repp, either self-coloured, shot, or with softly-blended stripes. Taffeta is another widely-used material, of which there is an almost unlimited range sold by various retailers under different names. If you choose a lightweight material the curtains could, should you desire it, be lined with linen, casement cloth, or sateen, in a neutral shade, or in one to match the curtains.

With plain mauve walls a soft green or dull gold fabric would look well. I hesitate to mention others as I do not know the colour of your carpet.

A Beauty Secret from Spain

By a Correspondent

*T*HESE *are some interesting pages from a letter which came to me one day last month from a friend on holiday abroad.*

"To-day the Calle de Alcala looked as gay as Bond Street on a Spring morning; it makes me feel quite home-sick—especially at tea-time! Over here we have five o'clock tea at half-past six, and then it's one of the strangest concoctions you ever tasted. Tea's one of the things you miss in Madrid. I went to see Artigas's new show last night, and on to the Ritz for supper afterwards. It was so crowded with smart people dining and dancing that there simply wasn't a table to be had. I've never seen such a collection of frocks and jewels, so many lovely women. Heaps of well-dressed English and Americans, but I thought the Spanish women looked loveliest of all, in their glowing, swirling 'mantones de manila' that somehow seemed to eclipse the prettiest frocks in the room.

"And then who should I run into but my old friend Senorita de Toledo, looking incredibly lovely and beautifully dressed as usual. She's one of the smartest Spanish women in Madrid. I joined her at her table, and between dances we talked about the things we'd been doing, and how deserted Madrid will be when the hot weather's come and everybody has rushed off to the coast. She's the real Southern type of beauty—tall, dark-eyed and dark-haired, with the exquisite creamy complexion you only see in Spain; the kind that makes the average outdoor Englishwoman sigh with envy every time she looks at it, and wonder how it must have been acquired.

THE SIMPLER WAY TO SKIN LOVELINESS

"I couldn't help saying something about this to Senorita de Toledo. She looked blankly surprised for a moment, and then laughed. 'You'd be sur-

prised yourself if you could see how little time and energy I waste on *my* complexion,' she said. 'Why, I never have a moment. I just take care of my skin the way most women do over here—by using the natural oils of our country. Our grandmothers—and their grandmothers before them—used pure olive oil, made from these,' and she held up a crystal dish of olives, 'and they perfumed it with an essence that they distilled themselves from rare wild flowers. Of course, it's different now; we get these natural ingredients blended in a soap. But the recipe's the same, and it is as effective now as it ever was.

"'But you English are funny—you and your complexions. *Either you neglect them entirely, or you are always rushing to the other extreme.* Listen,' and she leant forward across the little table, 'I'll tell you of the best Beauty treatment you can possibly have—and you can give it to yourself at home, every night and morning if you wish. This is what I do.

TRY THIS TEST.

"'I wash my hands carefully in warm water and this soap I was telling you about—Gal. At first the lather comes light and bubbly, but as you work it between your fingers you'll feel it thicken till it's as firm and fluffy as whipped cream. When it is firm enough to cling to my fingers I rub it into my skin like this'—she demonstrated with delicate white fingers—'as though it were a cream. Afterwards I rinse it away with warm water gradually cooled till it is icy. You'll be surprised to see how effectively it soothes and cleanses your skin, how wonderfully soft and fragrant it feels all day afterwards. Be sure to get the lather just fluffy enough. It only takes a minute, and the daily massage keeps your hands very smooth

and soft—just feel.' She laid a white hand on mine. 'Nearly all the women I know use Gal Toilet Soap this way. Simple, isn't it? But the best things often are.'

"She danced away, and I went home soon after. What she told me had given me something to think about, for it occurred to me that this simple Spanish way of cleansing the skin would come as a tremendous boon to thousands of Englishwomen who wish to preserve their natural beauty without resort to complicated and expensive methods. I do not know whether Gal is yet obtainable in England; but I have written down all I can remember of Senorita de Toledo's story, hoping that women at home will get some value out of hearing about a way to skin loveliness that is so simple and solves so many problems."—K. A.

. . . .

Readers will be glad to hear that Gal Toilet Soap is obtainable in England. You will find you can get it from all high-class departmental stores, chemists and hairdressers—easily recognisable anywhere by its dainty packing of sunshine yellow. In the case of an unusually sensitive skin, the use of *any* soap on the face is, of course, only to be undertaken with considerable caution. But for all ordinary purposes Gal Toilet Soap can be used quite confidently, even where other soaps might prove unwise, for its pure natural oils are so specially soothing and beneficial.

It is only a shilling a tablet, or two-and-nine for a box of three—a price that is surprisingly low for its class; but one single trial will convince you why it has been recognised in one of the most fastidious countries as a sheer necessity to beauty. If you should find any difficulty in getting Gal in your district, send a postcard to Perfumeria Gal (London) Ltd., Dept. 416H, 76 Strand, W.C.2. They will be glad to put you in touch with your most convenient source of supply.

Advertisement

Health and Beauty

White Hair

By Ruth Murrin

THE prettiest hair in the world is the pure gold given to many children and a few lucky grown-ups. Next to that undoubtedly is the silvery white that goes with wisdom, experience, and maturity. They are the loveliest, and they are the hardest to care for. The golden head worries constantly about the darkening that comes to tarnish her bright locks; the older woman must be always on the watch against anything that will discolour or dim the soft, shining whiteness of her hair.

She must spend a double effort to keep it from becoming thin and sparse; she must care for it so well that it will not look coarse and harsh; she must shampoo it often and with special precaution so that it will never have the ugly yellowish hue one so often sees. A coiffure of white hair, well cared for, fine, and abundant, is always beautiful in itself and makes a becoming frame for the mature face. By contrast the skin looks rosier and younger and the eyes brighter than they would if the hair were a youthful black, brown, or red.

The thickness and beauty of hair at all ages are largely influenced by health. Illness, fear, worry, and prolonged grief or overwork all are apt to show promptly in the condition of the hair. Falling hair, premature greying, and the loss of life and lustre are usually the result of physical or emotional disturbances. It is easy to see why this is so. The hair, like all the other structures of the body, is nourished and kept healthy through the blood stream. Anything that impairs the quality of the blood is soon evident in the hair. Consequently, the woman who has vigorous health, and who has cultivated poise and a philosophic mind, is apt to have nice hair.

But the care of the scalp and hair makes a great difference, and the older one grows, the more painstaking one should be. A few minutes of vigorous brushing twice a day, until you feel a glow, not only cleans and polishes the hair but livens the circulation of the scalp. Brushing is the simplest and the sanest hair tonic I know. Grey or white hair usually is most becoming when it is waved or curled softly about the face, and it is a pity that heat has such a disastrous tendency to give it a yellow tinge. If you have a permanent wave, choose only an operator who you know has been successful with white hair.

A well-known specialist recommends the following method: If you must curl your hair with an iron, wrap the shaft of the iron with yellow—not white—tissue paper, twisting the free ends so that they will stay in place. Use a low degree of heat and take time to do the curling. Then open the iron just far enough to slip off the paper, twist the ends together, and leave for a few minutes. If this method is carefully practised, there is no danger of turning the hair yellow.

White hair, like blonde, must be shampooed often to keep its silver quality. Use a good liquid shampoo, or make one by flaking half a cake of soap into a pint of hot water, letting this simmer until melted. With this wash the hair twice. Rinse thoroughly, using a bath spray so that you can keep water playing on each spot until you are sure every bit of soap is gone.

Put a few drops of French blueing in the final rinse to make the hair brilliantly white. Do not dry in the bright sun, but using warmed towels, rub it well, then lift it up strand by strand and let the air absorb the moisture.

If you need a tonic, use one which has no tendency to darken the colour.

THE
20's

Make Cupid a Caller

HE is waiting round the corner of life there—ready to bring you joy and happiness the like of which you have never known. Don't let Cupid pass you by—welcome him with your freshness and beauty. Love never fails to follow beauty.

You, to-day, can make such a difference in yourself by the aid of Pompeian that never again will you need to envy other women. Pompeian Beauty Preparations in-stantly develop your good features —make them radiantly attractive —make an ordinary face pretty, a pretty face lovely. Thousands of beautiful women you admire use Pompeian and treasure it as their best and most certain friend. Take Pompeian home with you to-day. See yourself for the first time as Nature intended you to be seen — fresh, attractive, a feminine personality—a woman that men must love.

New Prices

Pompeian Beauty Powder - - 1/9	Pompeian Bloom - - - - - 2/-
Shades : Naturelle, Rachel, Rosée, White, and Nude	Tones: Light, Medium, Dark, Orange, and Oriental
Pompeian Compact - - - - 1/6	Pompeian Day Cream - - - 1/3
Pompeian Lipstick - - - - - 1/3	Pompeian Night Cream - - - 1/3

pompeian
Beauty Preparations

The Pompeian Laboratories, 21, Eagle Street, London, W.C.1.

Please send me a free sample of Pompeian Powder and valuable advice on beauty by Madame Jeannette de Cordet, the famous Pompeian Specialist.

Name...

Address..

(66) June.

The Housekeeper's Dictionary *of* Facts

Salt and its Uses

Rock salt, our principal source of household salt, occurs as a deposit in numerous parts of the world. Authorities give the richest deposits of rock salt in the world as occuring near Iletz Zaschtchiti, in the province of Orenburg, South East Russia. In England, our principal sources of supply are in Cheshire, Nantwich, Droitwich and Northwich.

Dietetic Value

Sodium chloride, like the other chlorides, is a form of chlorine combined with a metal, in this case sodium. Common salt is found in the various tissues of the body and also in the blood. If salt is missing from the food, the body draws upon its reserves and when supplied with more, at once makes good the deficit. Serious harm is done by depriving the tissues of their normal amount of saline. Without salt we could not exist and the body would not function in a normal manner. The amount of salt to be used by the individual is best ascertained by his or her own particular taste. The household uses for salt are too varied and well known to be enumerated here. It may be mentioned, however, that salt is an important ingredient of most freezing mixtures; about 1 lb. of coarse or freezing salt to about 9 or 10 lbs. of ice is the usual amount to use for freezing ice cream. etc.

Hydropathic

Salt and water, or rock salt and soda solution will be found very beneficial for some foot troubles. In the waters of the various Spas, common salt plays an important part. Some of these mineral waters may not, however, contain as much mineral matter as ordinary drinking water, for it is the combination rather than the quantity of the salts which makes them of such great value.

Among the remedial mineral waters, those containing sodium chloride are found particularly effective in cases of rheumatism, dyspepsia, hysteria and some cases of bronchial trouble.

The largest constituent in the Kissenger mineral springs is said to be sodium chloride, as much as 55.088 grains to the pint being found, with various other salts in smaller proportion.

In Marienbad water the amount is much lower, being the

TWELVE COOKERY DEMONSTRATIONS

To be held on Wednesdays at 3.0 p.m. at Good Housekeeping Institute, 49, Wellington Street, W.C.2

SEPTEMBER 25th

THE PLANNING AND COOKING OF AN ATTRACTIVE WELL-BALANCED MEAL.—A discussion of the food value of each dish. Brussels Sprout Purée. Stuffed Rabbit, Gravy, Potatoes, Spinach. Apple Meringue Pudding, Custard

OCTOBER 2nd

THE ART OF COOKING VEGETABLES.—The food value of vegetables. Importance in the daily diet. Conservative methods of cooking, steaming and boiling. Aubergine Farcies, Duchess Potatoes, Curried Spinach, Choufleur Piquant, Tomatoes stuffed with Asparagus, Sea-Kale, Braised Spanish Onions, Vegetable Hot Pot

OCTOBER 9th

THE PLANNING AND COOKING OF SAVOURY OR SUPPER DISHES SUITABLE FOR TWO OR MORE PEOPLE.—Special attention paid to the choice and quantity of food purchased. Reference to the food value of various dishes. Curried Prawns, Scotch Eggs, Soused Mackerel, Bœufs, Darioles of Eggs, Brawn

OCTOBER 16th

PASTRY MAKING, including the making of Hot Water Crust, Short Crust Pastry, Rough Puff and Puff Pastry. Large and small Pork Pies, Cornish Pasties, Veal and Ham Pie, Oyster Patty Cases, Cream Horn Cases and Butterflies

OCTOBER 23rd

CASSEROLE COOKERY.—The various makes of Fireproof Glass and China Ware will be discussed. Liver and Bean Hot Pot, Casserole of Fish, Salmi of Game, Sea Pie, Hotch Potch

OCTOBER 30th

DISHES SUITABLE FOR A DINNER PARTY.— Fried Whiting. Fillets of Sole Colbert, Fish Flan, Vol-au-Vent of Veal, Tournedos à la Pompadour, Charlotte Russe, Jubilee Cream

NOVEMBER 6th
FRYING

NOVEMBER 13th
ICING AND DECORATION OF CAKES

NOVEMBER 20th
COLD DISHES FOR WHEN YOU ENTERTAIN

NOVEMBER 27th
DISCUSSION ON THE FOOD VALUE OF EGGS AND CHEESE AND THEIR USE IN VEGETARIAN DISHES

DECEMBER 4th
FROZEN DELIGHTS

DECEMBER 11th
PREPARING THE LIGHTER FARE FOR CHRISTMAS

The fee for the Course of Twelve Lessons is £2 2s. For further particulars application should be made to The Director, 49, Wellington Street, Strand, W.C.2, enclosing a stamped, addressed envelope

second largest quantity at 16.30 grains to the pint, with sodium sulphate or Glauber's Salts at 47.55 grains. Mineral-containing waters can be made by artificial means, and though not so efficacious as the natural ones they are found to be very useful.

In Switzerland the water is often found to be lacking in iodine, an essential constituent of all natural waters. As a direct result, thyroid complaints are very common.

Medicinal Uses

Saline, that is salt in solution, is much used in hospitals and similar institutions for various medicinal and other purposes.

In many cases of sore throat, a salt-and-water gargle will prove beneficial and it may also be used as an occasional dentifrice, while a saline eye-bath is sometimes recommended for strengthening and clearing the eyes.

Fragrant Bed Linen

Country housewives know of many wild plants that may be gathered in the early summer and laid between the folds of bed linen, the most fragrant of which are the Melilot, Yellow Lady's Bedstraw, Wild Thyme and Sweet Woodruff.

The Melilot is known by its pale yellow flowers on dainty spires, perhaps forty to fifty on a spire, set close together, and all hanging in rows from the same side of the stem. The plant contains a substance known as "coumarin," which has a very sweet and strong aroma. Yellow Lady's Bedstraw has a sweet and refreshing perfume, a mixture of almond and honey, and may be found along hedgerows and on sunny banks. The Wild Thyme is found on high hill pastures where the air is pure and strong. Its little purple-pink flowers are particularly fragrant and it is one of the flowers that help to make Heather Honey so delicious. Its flowers should be gathered on a warm day when the sun is on them, dried and put into little muslin bags.

Sweet Woodruff with its dainty white flowers grows in shady woods or on mossy banks by the roadside under the shade of trees. It has a sweetness of its own and may be used alone or along with lavender. Besides giving fragrance to linen it is also said to keep moths away from cupboards.

With All Her W

By Mrs. Belloc Lowndes

Illustration by Steven Spurrier, R.O.I.

THE problem implied in the title I have chosen has become acute of late years owing to the number of wealthy families who were bereft of elder and other sons during the world war. Owing to those terrible four years our country, with regard to certain strata of society, contains many more rich young women than, say, was the case in 1913. That being so, I should like to begin by dealing with the problem of the wealthy woman or girl who, longing for romance to be added to all the other gifts the good fairies have lavished on her, is thinking of choosing a penniless man as mate. To such a one I would say: " Force yourself to remember, and sometimes to ponder, the ugly double word, ' fortune-hunter.' "

We are all apt at certain moments of our lives to regard ourselves as happy exceptions to the general rule. The woman who is already the fortunate possessor of a large income, and who falls in love with a good-looking, delightful, impecunious lover, naturally supposes her case to be more or less unique. Other rich spinsters or widows may make fools of themselves, other heiresses may be the prey of idle men looking out for rich wives, but *she* is being loved for herself alone, and what is more, who can doubt that all those around her recognise that happy fact?

Now the rich girl or widow who is engaged, or thinking of becoming engaged, to a poor man, will be wise to face the fact, and that without feeling unduly sensitive, that not only many of the people who know her, but even many of whom she has never heard, but who are acquainted with her name and financial circumstances, believe she is making a mistake. Some of them, maybe, know a good deal about her *fiancé*, and if he is an idler, though they may think him a very lucky man, they feel, in their hearts, a certain contempt for him.

This, I need hardly say, is very much less the case if the bride-elect happens to be startlingly beautiful, popular, or delightful in other ways. However, I am not now thinking of the outstanding exceptions, but of the quite ordinary woman who, whatever may be the words of the marriage service, knows quite well that were she to tell the truth, it would be she, not her bridegroom, who would utter the words, " With all my worldly goods I thee endow."

I was once staying in a famous seaside hotel, and going down the corridor one morning, I heard the following dialogue between a smart-looking valet, the ideal gentleman's gentleman of comedy, and a pretty chambermaid. Obviously speaking of his master, the valet observed, " *He's* got nothing. She's got all the 'oof. He hadn't a penny to bless himself with till three days ago! I did laugh when I heard him say, ' With all my worldly goods I thee endow.' But though it's all lovey-dovey now, she'll teach him his place soon enough——"

A few minutes later I saw the bridal couple of whom those cruel, vulgar, spiteful words had been uttered, sitting in the hotel lounge, and very soon I felt that the valet had rightly summed up the situation.

The young wife was not unattractive: but she looked a delicate girl; and she had evidently been very much spoilt. Every few minutes she made her husband get up from his chair and do something for her satisfaction or pleasure.

Twice he had to go up in the lift to their rooms to get her a scarf. The first scarf he brought down was not the scarf she wanted to wear, so she made him go and get another. Then she made him ring for a glass of water. After that she asked him to go off to the smoking room to get her an illustrated paper. When at last, not having had five minutes' complete peace, he got up and said he thought he would go and stretch his legs a bit, she at once exclaimed, in a disappointed tone, " But we're going motoring, darling, this afternoon! Surely, you don't want to go out in the bitter cold wind *now*? "

With a heavy sigh, and it must be admitted, a rather sulky look, again he sat down.

The next time—and it was very soon —that she sent him on an errand, I longed to go up to her and say, " My dear young lady, at the risk of surprising you, and of hurting your feelings, I feel I ought to tell you that very soon that good-looking, kindly husband of yours will almost hate you."

The rich wife should remember that, human nature being what it is, the average decent man who falls madly in love with a penniless girl and, who having married her, feels vaguely disappointed, does tell himself that it is up to him to make their marriage a success. Not so does the man feel who has married a wealthy wife.

I feel convinced that had the young couple of whose start in life I caught a glimpse, been just an ordinary honeymoon pair, even on the third day of their married life, and however fond her husband lover was of her, there would have come a moment when he would have said, " Don't send me upstairs again, darling! This is the fourth time you've made me do some-

orldly Goods SHE HIM Endows

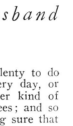

Reflections on the Thorny Path which Besets a Rich Woman who marries a Poor Husband

The poor husband and the rich wife start off on the Great Adventure heavily handicapped, and it needs great courage and tact from both to make a success of their marriage

working life? Surely he will always find plenty to do worth doing, without going to an office every day, or even, say, taking up farming, or some other kind of country work?" He, naturally, heartily agrees; and so the two start out, happy and confident, feeling sure that they will live happily ever after.

The average young man is generally "a good chap." When what must surely appear the stupendous luck of marrying a very rich, as well as a nice, girl comes his way, no doubt he swears most solemnly, not only at the altar, but to that inner self to whom no man ever lies, that he will be faithful, true, and loving, to the woman who has given him not only herself, but a vast fortune as well. Also he generally feels, quite honestly, that he will find plenty to do without taking the bread out of some penniless fellow's mouth by doing paid work.

But what follows in the vast majority of cases? That life flows happily for the first two or three years almost goes without saying. But, after that, and sometimes a good deal sooner, to the deep surprise and painful disappointment of the wife, things begin to go just a little wrong. For one thing, the husband, by then, has become quite used to having plenty of money to spend, and is now an entirely idle, pleasure-seeking man.

To his gratified surprise, he finds that all sorts of men and women—especially women—begin to make him feel what a splendid chap he is, and that his wife, though no doubt nice in her own way, is rather a drag on his wheel.

My second piece of advice is, I think, important, and one as to which the bride-elect may have to fight hard her trustees *(Continued overleaf)*

thing for you in twenty minutes!" And I also believe that, had their fortunes been equal, when she complained at the thought of his going out, he would have exclaimed, "But I must get my proper exercise; I shall be ill if I don't!" This poor young man felt— one saw it in the expression of his face —that his foolish, selfish bride had, in a way, bought the right to torment him, as she had transformed him from a poor, into a rich, man.

A girl who is old enough to make up her mind to choose a husband—and what more important choice can a woman make in life?—is certainly old enough to have her own way with regard to the disposal of her own property. My strong advice to any rich

girl contracting marriage with a poor man is that she insist on two things. The first, and I consider it the most important, is that her husband should either keep the job in which he is employed, or acquire one *which will mean real work*. It will be well for her, and for him too, even if he does not believe it, that he should be a working, and not an idle, husband.

This, however, may be, and probably is, a counsel of perfection.

When two young people set out on the voyage of life in a splendid argosy apparently laden with everything that makes life worth living, the woman, if generous and largehearted, generally says to herself, "Why should I make my darling take up the grind of a

Decoration by Edgar Spenceley

An Acre in Sussex

By
Kathleen M. Barrow

Take what you like out of my life to-day,
Deny me luxury and princely fare,
And priceless furniture and pictures rare,
Hours of music, evenings at the play,
A social round that's gayer than the gay,
And months of travel following the sun,
With a long life before these joys are done!
Take all of these!

But give me just that little piece of land
Perched on a wind-swept heath, that, as you gaze,
Melts at the last in a soft purple haze
Meeting the sky. Here shall my cottage stand.
For here, where clouds sail low like swans in flight,
Where the first lark is dazed with sheer delight,
And little eager flowers live their span,
Long thoughts and strange may come to mortal man
Give me my acre—take all else besides!

With All Her Worldly Goods she Him Endows

(Continued)

and her solicitors—all wealthy women generally have both. It is that she make a definite settlement on her husband from the day of their marriage, and one, I should add, free from humiliating conditions.

Now with regard to this important and delicate matter, there is a type of woman—I am sorry to say that though she is lovable, she is generally also foolish—who, in the first generous ardour of her love, proposes to endow her bridegroom with, say, half her worldly wealth. If she has twenty thousand a year, she wishes to settle on him ten thousand a year, and so on. Such an arrangement seems to me unwise, and likely to lead to trouble, from every point of view. What she should do, in my opinion, is to make up her mind as to what will make the man whose name she will share independent of her bounty, especially with regard to the kind of things that every man worthy of the name would hate to have to ask his wife to pay for him.

It is hard enough for a woman to have to go to her husband every week, every month, or even every year, and ask him for money. But it is much harder for a man to have to do so, because of age-long custom. Nearly every sympathetic-natured person who is intimate with a couple where the woman "has all the money," as the saying is, at some time receives the bitter confidence of how hateful the husband finds it to be entirely dependent on his wife, and that however generous and kind she may be.

With many masculine natures the sudden possession of wealth goes to the brain like wine. When a man who has had nothing, or only a small earned income, suddenly feels it is open to him to spend a great deal of money, he is apt to behave not only foolishly, but recklessly.

Unfortunately, or it may be fortunately, the very rich woman, even if she be quite young, has generally learnt more or less how to manage money; and she, therefore, feels a certain contempt for a man who does not know how to do so. It is humiliating for a husband to have to confess to his wife that he has made a fool of himself, and that even though there is no secret as to how he did it, and even if she, *at the time,* appeared quite willing that he should buy, say, all sorts of marvellous things for his own personal use.

Life, after all, is a balanced ration for the immense majority of human beings. The woman born to great wealth is, *ipso facto,* a fortunate woman—not as fortunate as many people think her to be, but still a very fortunate woman. Many of the terrible cares which assail, at times, most of us, will never assail her. She will never, for instance, have the agony of seeing someone she loves under-doctored and under-nursed in a bad illness. She will never be in the position to say honestly "I cannot afford it," over

some matter of supreme importance to herself or to one she loves.

Even so, the position of the wife who has all the money is likely always to remain a difficult one, far less difficult, of course, if the husband goes on working, and if the two in time become the parents of what we must now call an old-fashioned family. In such a happy case as that—the man working, the wife by now mother of half a dozen boys and girls—often the couple in time entirely forget that the lady is the richer of the two! In fact the more normal, the more commonplace their married life, the happier such a pair are likely to be.

But in these days the very rich woman who marries a poor man, is tempted to spend her life and her money in a very different way to what her grandmother, or even her mother, would have done under the same circumstances. Neither husband nor wife wants to settle down to what they regard as dull domestic life. They may buy a big estate; the bride may already be the possessor of a beautiful old country house; but their new estate, or the bride's delightful old house, as likely as not, will only see the fortunate couple for three or four months out of each year. The rest of the time they will be in London, or on the Riviera, or, even travelling farther afield, engaged in visiting India, America, or South Africa.

Let us, however suppose that the two have the sense to start a normal life in their own country? If the man becomes, and remains, an idler, the woman should teach herself to behave as if he, rather than she, is the possessor of the big income which makes their way of life possible. It grates on the ear to hear a rich wife talk incessantly, as most of us have done, of "*my* house," "*my* horses," "*my* car," "*my* baby." Oddly enough, yet perhaps naturally enough, too, it is almost always the woman with money who talks in that way. The average wife talks of "our car," "our house," though no doubt she still says with good reason "my baby." But the woman of vast wealth is apt, even if unconsciously, to blurt out the truth, though she would probably agree in theory that, as the French well put it, "all truth is not good to tell."

It is always wise, even I would say it is almost the supremely important thing in life, to look at things as they are, not as one wishes them to be, or as other people are apt to tell one they are.

Curiously few people, nowadays, seem to realise, or are even willing to admit, the undoubted fact that money is power. With money a certain type of man may hope to fulfil his highest and most honourable ambitions. Penniless, alas! he is almost bound to fail. Happy indeed is the woman who feels that owing, at any rate in a measure, to her fortune, her husband will be able to attain the goal he had set his heart on winning.

THE **20**'s

The Gordian

of

Domestic SE

*What is the "Open Sesame" to its un
this article is convinced that the vexed
can be solved mainly by the house
thoughtful organisation and the mo*

Illustrations by W.

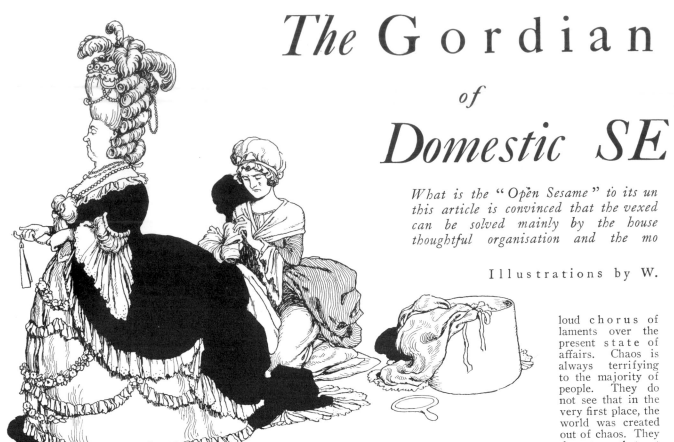

loud chorus of laments over the present state of affairs. Chaos is always terrifying to the majority of people. They do not see that in the very first place, the world was created out of chaos. They do not see that out of the present chaos is being built slowly but steadily a new civilisation that will be quite as definitely formed and quite as stable as the one which has just crumbled about us.

Meantime we of the present generation have to suffer for it. We are less fortunate than our predecessors on the one hand and our descendants on the other. We are paying bills for both of them. If we are genuine humanitarians, we shall not mind giving credit to our grandchildren; but we may be forgiven for grumbling about the debt which was run up for us by our grandmothers. It is such an unreasonably large one!

Our grandmothers got all the plums of domestic service without paying for them. They had willing servants by the dozen for practically nothing at all. The fact is, they kept servants very much as the Romans kept slaves. The only difference was that first, the classical slave was on the whole better housed and fed, and second, that he was occasionally fed to the lions or the crocodiles. In all other respects the human status of the nineteenth-century British servant and the first-century Roman slave was very much the same. English literature of the past century

THE servant problem is one of the most difficult that confronts the present generation. It is no new one, of course. Even in ancient Greece it was a stock joke in the theatre that when two or three women were gathered together, sooner or later the incompetence and ingratitude of servants would come up for enthusiastic discussion. Heaven forbid that I should seem to hold with Karl Marx and his dogma of the inevitable class war, but between mistress and servant with rare exceptions there has been enmity, either overt or latent, since the beginning of time.

In many ways, however, the problem has never been so acute as it is at the moment. Without taking too seriously the lamentations of the Victorian dowagers of Mayfair and Kensington, we may still admit that this difficulty is perhaps the most urgent that the modern woman has to face.

I am not thinking of the rich woman. In her case the traditional servile hierarchy of the great house can still be kept up with its elaborate ritual and division of labour. I am thinking rather of the general run of the middle classes, people who, in a family of two children, keep a cook and a nurse and consider themselves, as indeed they are, hopelessly understaffed. I have also in mind a class that is essentially modern and rapidly increasing, a most important class because it is forward-looking and is giving the cue to oncoming generations. This is the small but vigorous group of professional or semi-professional women who are also wives and

mothers. Theirs is the hardest case of all; for them the servant problem raises issues that are sometimes all but tragic.

Why has this latent trouble broken out in such violent form in our generation? It is largely because we are living in a period of transition. Transition is of course inevitable to development of any kind. Periods in history do not shift rapidly and completely like stage scenery; there is always between one period and another an interval of years during which the old is breaking down and the new gradually building up. Such a period of readjustment and transition from one established kind of life to another is always trying for the people who happen to be living in it.

To-day the firmly constructed civilisation of the nineteenth century has fallen to pieces, and the next era has not yet taken shape. Everything is in a state of flux and instability. There is no counting on anything as fixed and permanent. We are living in a kind of chaos. That is why there is such a

Knot

RVICE

*ravelling? The writer of
problem of domestic service
wife herself by means of
st up-to-date equipment*

Heath Robinson

By Constance
Eaton

is full of scenes that betray the callous and brutal way in which servants were treated. From lady's maid to kitchen slavey they were considered as belonging to a lower order of creation. They were supposed to exist for the sole function of brushing our hair, or cooking our food, or carrying bath water up endless dark flights of stairs, or laying our fires, or polishing our boots. That they had any hair of their own to brush, or appetite of their own to satisfy, or baths or boots of their own to attend to, never entered the superbly selfish calculations of our grandmothers.

It was only in line with the great humanitarian development which has recently inflamed the imagination of the world that there should be a social protest against this inhuman way of regarding servants. If we look deep enough, we can see that the status of the servant is going through the same process of change as the status of women in general, only very much more slowly. No more dramatic or radical difference could be imagined by the Utopian dreamer than that between the woman of 1850 and the woman of 1930. From being the social, economic, and legal slave of man she has become practically his social, economic, and legal equal. Woman in industry is also a very different creature from the economic serf of the middle of the past century.

The same big, impersonal forces which have brought about this change in the position of woman are also working, but more slowly and blindly, on the position of the servant class. The servant has been too near home to rouse philanthropic interest; we see first the wrongs of those who are at a distance from us. Many a Victorian mistress wept tears of pity over the poor heathen in foreign lands while under her own roof

some unfortunate little kitchenmaid was being stunted for life by overwork and undernourishment.

In what way will these forces that are so deeply modifying our lives affect the status of the servant? All sorts of predictions have been made about this question, from the most hopelessly conservative to the most rabidly radical. I have heard some so-called " advanced thinkers " declare that the solution will be reached only by the abolishment of the servant class altogether.

This is utter nonsense. As well say the marriage question will solve itself only by the abolishment of marriage. If we are to become a world of robots, of machine-made and machine-souled men, then we shall need no servant beyond the

machine. But if, as presumably the case will be, we continue to remain human, then there will always be human servants so long as the race survives. Hewers of wood and drawers of water I am afraid there always will have to be.

There is just as wide variety in the human kingdom as in the kingdom of plants or of beasts. The difference between one human being and another is as marked as that between sunflower and violet; tiger and mole. Our natures are all different, and our chief joy as individuals comes from expressing that difference. Self-expression for the bold and daring means adventure and danger; for the timid it means safety and sticking close to home; for the proud it means the mastery of others; for the servile it means hero-worship and service. We must not lose sight of this important fact, that the human being whose nature it is to obey receives just as much pleasure from obeying and serving as the person born to command receives from giving orders.

There is no getting away from the fact that those who serve will always be with us.

W·HEATH ROBINSON

"IF ONLY I'D WAITED TILL I'D TRIED THE HOOVER!"

Don't be rushed or persuaded into buying a vacuum cleaner. Insist on a chance of comparing the different makes one with another. Try them all! Watch them closely!

You'll find that when the Hoover is gliding over a carpet, the carpet is being agitated very rapidly up and down. Look closely and you'll see the trodden-in dirt (the *gritty* dirt that is the cause of wear in carpets) come dancing to the surface. Once loosened, suction can draw it away— but suction alone, however strong, cannot dislodge it from the bottom of the pile. Only Agitation can do that! Only the Hoover!

Don't take our word for these things. See the Hoover working along with as many others as you wish. *Then* judge!

Remember, the Hoover can now be bought for less than many an ordinary suction cleaner. For further particulars write to Hoover Ltd., Dept. A, 1, Hanover St., Regent St., W.1. Authorised dealers in every town.

By Appointment Manufacturers of electric suction sweepers to H.M. The King.

A British Empire Product

The HOOVER
It BEATS ... as it Sweeps as it Cleans

The Housekeeper's Dictionary *of* Facts

Take Care of Your Piano.

Sometimes little things go wrong with the piano for which it is not worth summoning a tuner, but which are nevertheless annoying.

If one or more of the notes has a rasping echo when played, examine the surrounding furniture in the room. Often the cause is a loose nut in the coal-scuttle, or part of the clock, etc. If the hooks on the music stand are loose, they may cause the notes to jar.

Discoloured ivories may be cleaned with a rag dipped in methylated spirits, but it should only be used very sparingly.

A squeaking pedal may be remedied with the application of boot-polish. Remove the front panel of the piano (if it is an upright one), and work the pedal, to locate the sound of the friction. It will be seen that the long wooden strip of the pedal is fastened to the outside part with a nut and bolt. Lift up the wooden strip and apply the boot-polish plentifully over the bolt, and over the wood nearest it. The pedal should not squeak after this, but if it does, cover all the touching parts with grease.

It is a good plan to use a vacuum cleaner to draw the dust from the strings which are behind the pedal panel. Examine these strings to find and remove any obstructing particles of dust or hairs.

Don'ts for Piano Owners.

Don't leave the keyboard lid open after playing. The ivories will quickly fade, and the dust will enter the crevices between each note.

Don't put ornaments on the top of the piano as they will cause vibration.

Don't leave the piano key in the space provided inside the piano. It will not only cause vibration, but may easily fall into the works.

Don't leave the frame lid open, or the dust will enter. It is not necessary to open this lid at all, except in a large hall where more sound volume is needed.

Don't place your piano near the fire, or near a window, as both heat and damp have bad effects on the strings.

A Precaution for Frosty Weather.

Particularly when having a house wired, it is well worth incurring the very slightly extra cost involved for arranging to have a point in the loft in the vicinity of the water cistern and pipes. During spells of cold and frosty weather it is then possible to connect a small electric heater, which as a rule effectively prevents pipes freezing and possibly bursting.

DEMONSTRATIONS AT THE INSTITUTE

A course of lecture demonstrations is at present being given at Good Housekeeping Institute on Wednesday afternoons at 3 p.m. Special attention will be paid to the food and health value of the various dishes demonstrated. The inclusive fee for the next five lectures is 17s. 6d., or individual lectures can be attended at a cost of 3/6 each.

FEBRUARY 5th

CONVALESCENT AND INVALID DIET.—Advice on catering for convalescents and invalids. Suggestions for dishes for a meatless diet. The use of Irish Moss for making jellies, creams, savouries, etc. Bran muffins, Cakes, Sugarless jams and marmalades will be discussed and dishes demonstrated.

FEBRUARY 12th

THE FOOD VALUE OF MILK AND EGGS AND MEANS OF INCORPORATING THEM IN THE DIET.—Soufflé Praline, Chocolate Soufflé, Savoury Kidney Soufflé, Milanaise Soufflé, Plain Omelette and Omelette Soufflé.

FEBRUARY 19th

SUGGESTIONS FOR USING WHOLEMEAL AND HEALTH FOODS IN CAKES, PUDDINGS, SAVOURY DISHES, ETC.—Flap jacks, Wholemeal gingerbread, Swiss Roll, Malt Bread, Koumiss, Baked Orange Soufflé.

FEBRUARY 26th

CONSERVATIVE COOKING OF VEGETABLES.— The uses of pressure, waterless and other patent cookers will be discussed. Demonstration of Savoury Haricot Bean Soup, Grapefruit Marmalade, Prune Whip, Princess Pudding, and, IN WATERLESS COOKER, Haricot Mutton, Canary Pudding, Steamed Potatoes, Steamed Carrots.

MARCH 5th

SUGGESTIONS FOR EMERGENCY DISHES.— Tinned fruits, packet jellies, etc., also, saving of labour and fuel by cooking vegetables, potatoes and meat in one dish. Trifle Russelle, Sausage and Tomato Pie, Peaches in Jelly, Pineapple Cream, Crab Soup, Lancashire Hot Pot

Further information can be obtained by writing to the Director, Good Housekeeping Institute, 49 Wellington Street, Strand, W.C.2, enclosing a stamped, addressed envelope.

Stains on Rubber Mats.

Although rubber can usually be cleaned satisfactorily by washing with soap and water, badly soiled or greasy mats, etc., can be cleaned more rapidly and with considerably less effort by rubbing with a cloth dipped in turpentine. This method of cleaning is therefore especially useful for doormats and other articles which are likely to get very dirty.

To make Lampshades

It is quite possible to make attractive lampshades at home at comparatively little cost. The silk, parchment or other material is as a rule fitted to a wire framework, but sheet metal and wood are occasionally used. Suitable frames costing from a few pence to, at the most, a few shillings can be purchased, or they can be made to one's own requirements by a wire-worker. It is, however, by no means a difficult job to make a suitable frame at home, provided one is familiar with the processes of soldering. The method to be followed is fully described in the article entitled "Simple Household Repairs," which appears on page 47 of this issue. For frame-making all the equipment required consists of a soldering outfit, a file, a wire-cutter or hacksaw, flat-nosed and round-nosed pliers, and brass wire of suitable and workable thickness.

In the case of shade-frames designed for ordinary pendant use, a $1\frac{1}{2}$-inch hole for the lamp-holder must be provided in the middle of the frame. Table and floor standards have shade-carriers which require a larger hole, and preferably a more rigid support for the gallery over the lamp.

To provide a basis of attachment for the main covering, the skeleton wires of the frame must be wound as tightly as possible with a one-inch strip of material cut on the cross and doubled, care being taken to hide raw edges during the course of winding. Each section of the shade should be covered with double material cut slightly larger than required, and it should first of all be secured lightly in a few places, then, using one needle on each side of the shade, and keeping the material as taut as possible, the two opposite sides stitched in position. The other sides of the same section should then be attached to the frame in the same way, and the work repeated until the frame is completely covered.

It should then be trimmed, and joins covered with narrow beading or braid, cut into strips of suitable length. In the case of side strips, it is sufficient to secure at either end, pulling the braid as taut as possible. The shades should then be given any final ornaments, such as hanging beads, fringes, etc., and should be carefully examined and any slight distortion judiciously corrected.

A simpler form of shade consisting of a hanging flounce surrounding the lamp is very attractive. For this, a 12-inch band, either square or circular in shape, will be required. Three link chains, a ceiling-plate, and a plain silk flounce, preferably lined with white or other pale colour, will also be needed. The flounce can, if desired, have a fringe of beads.

Farewell now to politics! Mrs. Hilton Philipson looks forward to spending many long and happy days with her daughter and two small boys

Even on the busiest day

Mrs. Hilton Philipson orders one of her children's favourites for lunch — they particularly like "Playtime Pudding" — always made with these raisins

BELOVED of London audiences as Mabel Russell — then, after the war, one of the first women M.P's. Now she has retired from politics, and the London stage welcomes her back.

And always — her main pleasure and interest is her own children. Even when the days are busiest, Mrs. Hilton Philipson finds time to plan for her household — delightful days and amusements, enchanting meals.

Like so many modern mothers — she insists on having Sun-Maids for all raisin dishes. She finds children just can't resist their rich flavour in the simple cakes and puddings. And then — there's no preparing to be done. In her busy home there's no time to be wasted on old-fashioned methods of cleaning and picking when delicious Sun-Maids are there, ready to use straight from the packet!

Try Sun-Maids too! The special table grapes from which they come give them the sweetest, richest flavour imaginable. Exclusive methods of selecting, cleaning and packing make them uniformly delicious.

Make Robin and Ann Hilton Philipson's favourite "Playtime Pudding" with them — your family will enjoy it as much as they do! Send too for the Sun-Maid Recipe Booklet — giving you 100 recipes

including the favourite ones of other famous children!

Let your children eat Sun-Maids out of the packet. There is no better sweetmeat for them! Dept. G.13, Sun-Maid Raisin Growers, 59 Eastcheap, London, E.C.3.

PLAYTIME PUDDING

Well grease a plain pudding basin and decorate it generously with Sun-Maid Seeded Muscat Raisins. Sieve half a pound of flour into a clean dry basin and to it add half a teaspoonful of salt, a teaspoonful of baking powder, four ounces of shredded beef suet, four ounces of fine bread crumbs, the grated rind of a small lemon and four ounces of Seedless Sun-Maid Raisins. With a beaten egg and a little milk — about a gill according to the kind of flour used — make these ingredients into a smooth, rather firm dough. Put it carefully into the prepared basin, twist a piece of greased paper on top and steam steadily for four hours. Turn out and serve with white sauce or custard. This quantity is sufficient for five or six people.

The Housekeeper's Dictionary *of* Facts

The Homely Herring

Many people cook fresh herrings in the same way that they cook plaice or soles, i.e. coated with egg and breadcrumbs and fried in fat. If you are one of those people, try the following method:

Cut off the heads and clean and wash the fish thoroughly. Now take a large packing needle and thin string and pass through the tails. Hang the fish outdoors to dry (or in the larder if the weather should be wet), for four or five hours.

Use no fat for cooking, but cover the pan with a good sprinkling of coarse salt and fry the herrings until brown. Do not be afraid that they will stick; if sufficiently dry they never do.

How to dispose of Broken Glass

People who live in the country often find it difficult to dispose of broken glass. Broken china may be used to repair the path or may be buried in the garden, but broken glass cannot be treated in this way. Have you ever thought of putting it on the fire? Everyone knows that glass will not burn, but when put on a fairly hot fire it will melt down into a lump or sort of clinker which can be thrown out anywhere in the garden with perfect safety.

Old Pots and Pans

The disposal of old pots and pans which accumulate in country houses and are very unsightly is another problem.

If a piece of spare ground is available, dig a trench about 2 ft. deep and place in it such rubbish as comes to hand. Then cover the tins, etc., with ashes and either finish (1) by putting back the earth that you have dug out and sowing grass seed, in which primrose roots may be planted, to make a gay corner in spring, or (2) by building up a rockery. Place any old stones, bricks, and bits of masonry in disorderly heaps on your mound of ashes, throw the earth over the top and plant little rock plants here and there.

How to soften Butter

The following hint for softening hard butter will be found useful when cutting bread and butter or sandwiches of the wafer variety.

Cut up the butter into small pieces, boil a few tablespoonfuls of milk and pour into the butter. Mash all together and pour away any surplus liquid. By this method, butter can be softened in two minutes without becoming oily.

To remove Marks caused by Heat from a Polished Table

The renovation of a polished table or other wood surface which has been impaired by some form of heat or by the spilling of spirit such as eau-de-Cologne or whiskey is a subject on

The Ideal Home Exhibition

Probably many of our readers are planning to spend at least a day at the Ideal Home Exhibition, which is a unique opportunity for men and women who are interested in the science of home management to add to their knowledge. · This year ten acres of ground are covered by exhibits and sections are devoted to Domestic Appliances, Housing, Heating and Lighting, Decoration and Sanitation, Food and Cookery, Furnishing, Gardens, etc.

Those who require new household equipment will find domestic appliances manufactured by different firms grouped together, enabling their efficiency to be easily compared. Many of the appliances will be found to bear the Good Housekeeping Seal of Approval, signifying that they have undergone a three months' practical test at the Institute, and have proved to be satisfactory.

Eight houses and bungalows have been erected, and the United Women's Homes Association are showing two compact and attractive flats for the bachelor woman. An exhibit entitled the " Room in the Roof " shows how an attic can be transformed into a living-room, sitting-room or playroom. There is a series of nurseries of different lands, including Holland, Hungary, France, and Lapland, and a set of kitchens as they appear in different parts of the Empire.

The Heating and Lighting section is of special interest on account of a competition which was held recently to encourage the application of modern art to electric light fittings. The results are shown in an attractively lighted lounge, bedroom, and dining-room, which form a Pavilion of Light.

The gardens this year have been laid out according to the designs of four well-known artists. There is a most interesting handicraft section, and keen housewives are sure to be interested by the exhibition of food and cookery, especially in its connection with Empire produce.

which our advice is frequently sought. Alcohol in any form dissolves the shellac that is deposited on the surface of wood when French polished, and heat actually alters its character, making it dull and of a milky appearance. If the damage is not too extensive the table need not be re-polished, but judicious and careful treatment with a very sparing amount of methylated spirit will improve its condition.

Make a small pad of cotton wool or other soft white cotton material, pour a few drops of methylated spirit on to the material and cover with a piece of old muslin. Then rub the pad over the damaged part of the wood, pressing heavily and working with a figure-of-eight movement. The spirit will slowly work its way through the muslin and soften the French polish around the damaged portion and the rubbing will work it into the part from which the polish has been removed. It may, of course, be necessary to add more methylated spirit, but on no account must it be applied direct to the wood or at all liberally.

A Suggestion for the Bathroom

The well-equipped bathroom has a profusion of towels, but the occasional guest or visitor (such as a doctor making a professional call) may not be able to decide on the towel to use. There may be several clean ones or all those to be seen may be in use. At least one towel rail should be definitely allocated to the guest, and in this event it is a good plan to have a small ivorine tablet engraved with the word GUEST and mounted over the special rail. Of course, there should always be at least one or two clean towels on the rail.

Family Bathroom Belongings

If you have any difficulty in getting each member of the family to remember which is his own towel, face-flannel, or toothbrush, it is a good plan to give a colour to each person and see that his belongings all show it. The towel and flannel can have a stripe or border of the colour, and the toothbrush a coloured handle. The guest-towels, etc., might then be plain white.

To Repair a Coal Bucket

When a coal scuttle or bucket develops a small hole it can often be repaired successfully by pasting strong, coarse calico over the damaged part. If, as is usually the case, it is the bottom of the bucket which is affected, two pieces of calico rather larger than the base of the bucket should be cut out and one pasted on the outside and the other on the inside.

If the hole is fairly large, or if the bottom of the bucket is thin and worn, it should be repaired with a rather stronger material such as linoleum or oil cloth, which should be firmly glued in position.

Like a lovely night in June

Night after night last winter, when it was time to retire, you braced yourself to face the ordeal of leaving the comfortable fireside for the freezing air of the bedroom.

"Here goes," you said, and hastily dropped off your warm things to don chilly night attire and slip between icy sheets.

This year ensure a never varying summer temperature by means of 'Unity' Electric Heaters.

Tubes of steel, just 2 inches in diameter, fastened to the skirting boards, will give an atmosphere like a lovely night in June.

**UNITY
Electric Heating**

Write to-day for a beautifully illustrated folder, "Heating the Home." It gives you prices and full particulars of this very inexpensive yet most efficient heating system.

YOUNG, OSMOND & YOUNG LTD

**47 VICTORIA STREET, WESTMINSTER
LONDON, S.W.1**

This shows the unobtrusive "Unity," fixed to the skirting board

Ogden's

104

H E A L T H & B E A U T Y

T H E   F I R S T   W R I N K L E

by
Ruth Murrin

RECENTLY I have been reading a tiny but interesting book with the provocative title, *Charm by Choice*. The chapter that interested me most was the last one, enumerating signs of age. Not wrinkles, grey hair, fading colour—these had been dealt with more or less in earlier chapters—but what the author considers far more significant signs that youth is passing. There were six of them, and all of them were mental: self-satisfaction, the conviction that one's own ways are the best and only ways; loss of interest in the affairs of others, particularly in affairs of national or world-wide importance, unless they are calamitous; increased enjoyment of material things such as food, money, possessions, and material comfort; inability to accept new customs because the old ways are best; prejudice, the unreasoning dislike or disapproval of unaccustomed things; and bitterness, the habit of thinking, "What have I done to deserve this?"

They do sound frightfully middle-aged, don't they, much more so than a few little lines at the corners of the eyes!

Why does it seem to make such a difference—that first time when, facing a strong light, a woman notices unmistakable crow's-feet? Lines and wrinkles are etched into faces by life. In the fine tracings under a mother's eyes there is a record of the anxious, wakeful hours she spent watching over a sick child. Laughter leaves its mark in the deepening of the arcs from nose to mouth. Worry and joy, work and play, all stamp their hieroglyphics on our faces, but we resent it. We prefer to tell how full our lives have been in some other way, because to every woman in the world the first real wrinkle says, "You're growing old."

I wish one did not hear so many women asking how to remove wrinkles already there. It is so much easier to prevent them than it is to remove them. One of the first things to remember about preventing them is that one should not get too thin or lose flesh too rapidly. Wrinkles are caused by the disappearance of the tissues under-

neath the skin which had given the contour a round, firm appearance. The craze for slenderness causes many a girl to look lined and worn long before she has to.

Next in importance, in keeping the face smooth and unlined, is the care of the skin itself. A dry skin easily develops many fine lines. It should be kept soft with creams and stimulated by nightly patting and massage to bring the blood up into the tissues. An oily skin needs quickening and stimulation, and creams and astringents will do this. Every girl in her teens should learn how to cleanse her skin perfectly, and how to keep it smooth and free from roughness. As a rule, a good cold cream, a bland soap, and a skin lotion are all she needs to keep her skin in good condition. In the twenties, she will probably need other special helps, additional creams, a good tonic or astringent, a powder base. Daily, regular care with good preparations will help put off the evil day of wrinkles almost indefinitely.

So much for prevention! Now, if lines have already come, can anything be done? I do not believe that wrinkles can be removed absolutely except by removing the cause. If one is thinner than she should be, she can fill out the lines only by putting on a little weight. If lines around the eyes are caused by late hours, by extreme fatigue, by reading for hours in a bad light, by driving continually in strong sunshine, the way to get rid of them entirely is to stop doing the things that cause them. A nap in the afternoon for the busy homemaker, or a half-hour's rest in darkness and quiet before dinner for the business woman, is one of the best cures for premature wrinkles.

I do not know of any way of fattening tissues except by eating more food, but I do think creams and oils help. The patting and massage are refreshing and bring the blood to the surface to do its good work. The creams soften the skin and make even deep lines much less noticeable. A lined face should wear a film of oil or cream every night, smoothed over the skin after the removal of cleansing cream.

The beauty book published by Good Housekeeping at 6d. net, or 7½d. post free, contains full directions for care of the hair, skin, figure, etc. Write for the "Primer of Personal Loveliness" to 153 Queen Victoria Street, E.C.4

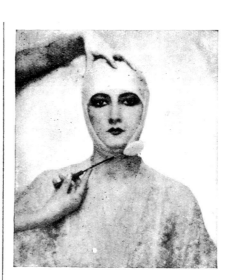

Elizabeth Arden is in Personal Touch with You

Through every one of her Preparations and Treatments

WHENEVER you use one of Elizabeth Arden's Preparations for the care of the skin you are secure in the knowledge that the Preparation was personally planned by Miss Arden and first used by her

When you follow Miss Arden's instructions for the care of your skin at home you know that each carefully planned move and rhythmic count came into being under the witchery of Miss Arden's own touch. Every cream and lotion, every treatment is the result of Elizabeth Arden's personal enthusiasm, an enthusiasm that today is as real and eager in the service of loveliness as ever, demanding and securing perfection for you

Elizabeth Arden's Venetian Toilet Preparations are on sale at the smartest shops in all cities of the world

Venetian Cleansing Cream. Melts into the pores, rids them of dust and impurities, leaves skin soft and receptive 4/6, 8/6, 12/6

Venetian Ardena Skin Tonic. Tones, firms, and whitens the skin. Use with and after Cleansing Cream 3/6, 8/6, 15/6

Ardena Velva Cream. A delicate cream for sensitive skins. Recommended for a full face, as it smooths and softens the skin without fattening 4/6, 8/6, 12/6

Venetian Orange Skin Food. Keeps the skin full and firm, rounds out wrinkles, lines and hollows 4/6, 7/6, 12/6.

ELIZABETH ARDEN
691 Fifth Avenue New York
ELIZABETH ARDEN LTD
LONDON
25 OLD BOND STREET W1
Telephone: Gerrard 0870
PARIS BERLIN   MADRID ROME
(Copyright Reserved)

105

Holidays
are Embroidery days

Make those idle hours worth pounds to you. Put just a few little skeins of thread in your holiday luggage and come back with such lovely things, such expensive looking things.

All the glorious hues of Fashion's Rainbow are waiting for you in Clark's Embroidery Threads. However hard wear you want, Clark's can supply an exquisitely tinted thread to give it. Take Clark's "Anchor" Stranded Cotton,

for instance—perfect for everything you make to wash and wear. Looks just like silk—costs much less, washes like a rag, can even be boiled and the colour will not run. Over two hundred shades to choose from.

Whatever your needlework requirements, embroidery thread, every kind of fancy sewing or crochet cotton, artificial silk, you make sure of the newest shades, the fastest colours, assured quality if you look for the famous names of Clark and Coats.

Clark's
Threads, Embroideries & Cottons

CLARK & CO. LTD. and J. & P. COATS LTD. PAISLEY   C 107

The Housekeeper's Dictionary *of* Facts

Restoring a Toilet Mirror

Difficulty is often experienced in keeping a swing dressing-table glass in position. When this is the case, the usual practice is to try wedging it or propping it up with a hairbrush, a comb, or anything that comes handy. The trouble can, however, be remedied fairly easily.

The metal fittings that hold the mirror-frame to the two standards between which it swings consist of an iron stud or ball fixing that fits in a brass hinged socket clip, tightened by a thumbscrew. A turn of the two screws should tighten the grip on the stud ball to keep the mirror in any position it is put, but with long neglect the screws get stiff and may need a pair of pliers to turn them. If the clips can be screwed quite close without getting a grip, it is probable that the socket parts are worn. A simple remedy for this is to put small bits of sheet brass or tin about ⅜ in. square in the sockets to make up for what has worn away. "Movements" that are tarnished should be taken off, cleaned and re-lacquered to preserve them. Broken movements should be replaced by new ones without delay, for if neglected the mirror is likely to fall out and get smashed.

Renovating an old Wooden Mirror-frame

There are very many old-fashioned looking-glasses in use, which after long service have got out of condition and shabby, but with a little trouble can be restored satisfactorily. A polished mahogany stand, faded by the strong sun through the window, should be treated as follows.

The thin wood backing should be taken off to get rid of any accumulation of dust and the glass removed and carefully cleaned, taking care not to injure the quicksilver back. The wood standards or uprights can be removed by unscrewing the two wood nuts under the base.

Then the wood work should be cleaned and renovated by lightly scraping off the old damaged polish. The surface should be smoothed with No. 1 grade glass-paper. When brushed free from dust, a little linseed oil rubbed into the wood restores the colour. After a rest of a few hours or longer it should be rubbed with a dry cloth, previous to a treatment with a French polish, applied lightly and quickly by means of a camel-hair polish brush in a warm atmosphere.

In about an hour's time it is ready for stroking over with polish applied on a pad of wadding in a piece of soft cotton rag, thus imparting an even moisture which dries off leaving a hard finish.

The Work of French Polishing

Readers who have had no experience of French polishing may like to have detailed directions, for although the polishing of large surfaces such as table tops is work one would hardly recommend an amateur to attempt, the

---

GOOD HOUSEKEEPING TESTED APPLIANCE SERVICE

Appliances which have been subjected to stringent and detailed tests at the Institute and have successfully gained our Certificate and Seal of Approval now number over 700. A list of these will be sent to any reader interested and any specialised help required on the choice of suitable equipment gladly given if desired.

The appliances tested include : bathroom and lavatory equipment, bed-warmers, carpet sweepers, china and glass, cleaning equipment, cooking appliances, cooking stoves, cooking utensils, curtain fittings, cutting and sharpening equipment, fires and heating stoves, freezers, household appliances, household fittings, household furniture, independent boilers, kettles, kitchen equipment, kitchen furniture, lamps and lighting fittings, laundry equipment, mattresses, nursery equipment, refrigerators, rubber appliances, table equipment, vacuum cleaners, wall and floor treatments, water heaters and water softeners.

In order to save readers trouble in obtaining our Tested Appliances we have appointed about 180 Ironmonger Agents in all parts of the country. A list of these is published on page 175. Any of the agents will be pleased to obtain any of the appliances on the list if the selected article does not actually happen to be in stock.

---

renovation of small articles such as mirror-frames may be attempted successfully.

If the work is to be satisfactory it is of the utmost importance that it be done in a warm, dry atmosphere, for dampness causes the polish to become cloudy before the rubbing process is begun. The article to be treated must be warm and dry and should have been kept in a warm room long enough to acquire its temperature before commencing to polish. The temperature of the room should, if possible, be nearly 70° F.

The polishing pad or rubber is made by covering a small piece of wadding or cotton wool with a soft cotton or linen cloth and twisting it round so that the pad formed has somewhat the shape of an egg. Most amateurs will probably find a prepared French polish most convenient to use, but if it is desired to make one's own, 2 oz. of best shellac should be dissolved in 1 pint methylated spirit and suitable colouring added.

After the preliminary rubbing down with No. 1 glass-paper (the fine grade referred to above) the polish should be shaken up in order to distribute the colour pigments evenly and a little then applied to the rubber by a brush. The pad should be rubbed lightly in a cir-

cular movement over the surface to be polished, rubbing continuously and evenly and applying more polish to the rubber as this is required. Care must be taken, however, not to apply too much at a time and so render the pad really wet. After treating the entire surface, the work should be begun over again, reversing the circular motion and increasing the size of the movements. Half an hour or so after the surface has been rubbed three or four times in succession in the above way, the wood should be smoothed with a piece of very fine and worn glass-paper and the polishing treatment repeated.

The Care of Tiles

Letters are frequently received at the Institute asking for advice on the care and treatment of tiled floors, tiled mantle surrounds, walls, etc. Dwellers in new houses often complain of the difficulty of removing the whitish marks which are apt to disfigure floors and other tiles. Scrubbing with soap and water or other cleansing preparation naturally is not effective as the marks are due to traces of cement left by the builders. They are, however, comparatively easily removed by treating with hydrochloric acid or, as it is often popularly called, spirits of salts. As it is extremely poisonous this needs to be used with the utmost care, and one must be very particular to rinse away all traces afterwards with plenty of fresh water. Only one or two tiles at a time should be treated and it is important to avoid the acid getting in contact with the cement fixing the tiles in position, as it will act on this and thus tend to loosen them.

In order to keep floor tiles in good condition with the minimum of effort, the most satisfactory treatment, after cleaning thoroughly and removing any cement marks, is to apply a prepared wax floor polish or a mixture of beeswax and turpentine. This fills up the pores so that the tiles do not mark or stain easily and they should only require to be washed very occasionally provided care is taken to wipe up spilled liquids, etc., as soon as possible. A fresh application of polish should be made weekly or fortnightly, but as with linoleum or other floor coverings, sparing applications only are required.

Fire-place and other highly glazed tiles can be given an excellent "shine" by rubbing up with a velvet shoe pad or an old piece of velveteen kept for the purpose.

When such tiles do not tone with the general colour scheme of the room, they can be treated with one of the cellulose enamels now on the market. These give an attractive finish with very little trouble, but naturally hearth tiles which have been enamelled must be protected from hot ashes, cinders, etc. Glazed hearth tiles can also be painted with an ordinary type of paint or enamel, but before doing this it is necessary to apply a special coat of metallium, a preparation which forms a key for the paint or enamel to be used over it.

CHANTAL   MOLYNEUX

WEDNESDAY

WEDNESDAY.—A summery day on the golf links and my game at its best—sufficient compensation for the enforced wearing of an old last-year's suit when green jersey allied with white or beige seems to be the smart choice of the moment! I much admired the clothes worn by the players ahead of us—a jersey ensemble of green striped with white, and a beige sports dress with scarf and pleats of green worn with a short green jacket

MIRANDE   MIRANDE

THURSDAY

THURSDAY.—The sun called me again into the open and I walked this morning in the Bois. Innumerable smart trotteurs, of course, a simple one of flecked brown lainage attracting my covetous eye, accompanied by another with black and white shepherd's plaid coat and black skirt (again that combination of two materials!)

FRIDAY.—Being the gala dinner night at Ciro's we arranged a party for some English friends at present stopping in Paris. The two daughters of the family had been buying evening frocks from Chanel, and looked exquisite, the dark one in tucked and pleated white chiffon, her sister in flowing pale mauve organdie

SATURDAY.—At last a day in which to rest! I shall relax comfortably at home to-night in soothingly pretty pyjamas of printed crêpe de Chine and peacefully plan events and clothes for the coming week

CHANEL   **FRIDAY**   CHANEL

JANE REGNY   SATURDAY

SEVEN DAYS OF PARIS CLOTHES

Pages from the Fashion Diary
of a smart Parisienne

MOLYNEUX

SUNDAY

SUNDAY.—The day being sunny and warm, I laid aside the dark silk ensemble with tunic of white georgette which I had intended to wear to the races and put on instead my new Molyneux gown of beige lace and chiffon. The admiration of Georges seems to have amply justified my choice of clothes!

CHANEL   LOUISEBOULANGER

MONDAY

JENNY   GOUPY   TUESDAY

MONDAY.—Lunching at the Ritz, one could not fail to notice the popularity of the suit, either of silk or wool, for day wear. I remarked especially on a black satin model worn with a tucked blouse, and an alliance of plaid and plain wool fabric, at once useful and chic

TUESDAY.—My birthday. Marie and Francois met Georges and me for dinner and theatre. I wore lace and satin, with discreet little cape sleeves, and Marie looked ravishing in a youthful chiffon velvet wrap with tiered frills. I am tempted to forget my age from now on!

HE BRINGS GOOD TIDINGS
welcome him

HE is the visible sign of "Singer Service." He shows how you can take the work out of needlework. No longer will you have to spend hours of drudgery over piles of mending and darning. No longer need you "make do" with last year's wardrobe. The Singer man shows how a length of fabric can be transformed into a "straight from Paris" frock at a fraction of the cost of a ready-made garment. How easily the Singer attachments enable you to darn, mend and achieve Fashion's most intricate stitchery effects. Picot edging, tucks, ruffles, flounces and gatherings will be as easy as A.B.C. He will explain, too, how a Singer can be bought out of income. Welcome him!

SINGER SEWING SERVICE
created to solve your sewing difficulties

Singer Sewing Machine Company Ltd., Singer Building, City Road, London, EC.1.   Shops in every town.

The Housekeeper's Dictionary *of* Facts

THE

30's

To Remove Ink Stains from Leather

UNFORTUNATELY drops of ink are sometimes spilt either on a leather chair or a leather-covered blotter; and prove exceedingly difficult, if not impossible to remove by ordinary methods. They can, however, usually be eliminated, provided they are fairly fresh, by treatment with a solution of tin chloride, using a proportion of about ¼ ounce to ½ pint water. A drop or so of the solution should be applied immediately over the stain by means of a glass rod or fountain pen filler, and afterwards removed by mopping up either with a soft cloth or a piece of cotton wool. In the case of an obstinate stain, it is often found that one application of the chemical is not sufficient, but that further treatment is necessary. With a little patience most ink stains can be removed in the above way, but care must always be taken to rinse away all traces with warm water, afterwards drying and polishing the leather with a reliable furniture cream.

Insulate Your Hot Water Pipes

Most people do not realise the very considerable amount of heat which is wasted, especially in houses where the hot water pipes are long, because of the lack of insulation. In some cases, however, what has previously been an unsatisfactory and inefficient hot water supply, has been considerably improved by insulating the pipes, and possibly the hot water cylinder. In connection with this, readers may be glad to know that ready-made wraps convenient for lagging pipes are supplied by various firms, the prices for which range from 3d. per foot.

A New Make of Tubing for Gas Lighting

A new make of gas tubing for lamps and other appliances, having many unique features, has lately been placed on the market. The makers claim this to be non-porous and it may even be pierced without causing leakage. It is seamless and can be tied in knots or trodden on without damage.

A Useful Appliance for Moving Pianos, etc.

Many people tend to overstrain themselves at times when it is necessary or desirable to move the piano about, possibly from one part of the room to another, or from one room to another. It is therefore useful to know that special rollers are supplied at comparatively low costs which render this operation simple and easy.

Stair Carpet Holders

Especially when furnishing and equipping, more and more people are realising the advantage of fitting stair carpet holders or clips rather than rods. The great advantage of these holders is that as well as being neat in appearance, since they are fixed at the side of the

---

LECTURE DEMONSTRATIONS

The following demonstrations will be given at the Good Housekeeping Institute on Wednesday afternoons, commencing at 3 o'clock.

NOVEMBER 4TH
Supper and Savoury Dishes.
Blanquette d'Œufs, Cheese Charlotte, Lobster Cutlets, Calves' Liver with Mushrooms, Nut Kromeskies.

NOVEMBER 11TH
Sweetmaking and the Principles of Sugar Boiling.
Barcelona Toffee, Nougat, Chocolate Caramels, Honey Fudge, Turkish Delight.

NOVEMBER 18TH
The Making and Icing of Christmas and Seasonable Cakes.
Genoa Cake, Pound Cake, Nursery Cake, Almond Cake, Dundee Cake, Walnut Layer Cake.

NOVEMBER 25TH
The Icing and Decorating of Christmas Cakes.
Almond Icing, Royal Icing, Fondant Icing, American Icing.
Piping and Decorating.
Sugar Flower Making.

DECEMBER 2ND
The Making of Chocolates— various centres, including Fondant, Liqueur, Almond Brittle and Opera Creams, will be made and the secrets of success when dipping will be discussed.

DECEMBER 9TH
Catering for a Dinner and Dance.
Dinner :
Hors d'œuvre Variés
Consommé Printanière
Filet de Sole Bercy
Dindonneau de Norfolk farci aux Marrons
Pommes Frites
Choux de Bruxelles
Mince Pies
Pouding de Noël
Mandarine Blidah

For further particulars regarding fees, etc., readers are invited to write to Good Housekeeping Institute, 49 Wellington Street, Strand, W.C.2, enclosing a stamped addressed envelope for the reply

---

carpet, they cannot become kicked or scratched, as often happens in the case of rods. A further advantage is that the carpet underneath can be readily cleaned or brushed without the necessity of completely removing the fittings as is necessary with stair rods. In the case of one well-known make, the holders slide out sideways to release the carpet and after cleaning they can be as readily slid back into position. These holders add rather than detract from the artistic look of the staircase and can be purchased for as little as 6d. per pair, either in oxidised copper or brass, or rather heavier models for from 10½d. upwards.

A Reader's Enquiries

Will you kindly give me your advice on the following points:

I stained a small leather suitcase brown, after cleaning it thoroughly, with some shoe dye, and when I took it out in damp weather, the case became cloudy and whitish. What could I do to it?

How can I remove lime deposit in a porcelain bath, where the taps have dripped? We have tried many things without success.

M. J., Epsom.

In reply to your letter, without knowing the particular dye used for your suitcase, we are afraid we are unable to say why the results have not been satisfactory. If the case is in good condition, and you think it is worth the expense, we suggest that you take it to a reliable leather merchant, and have it re-stained professionally. On the other hand, if you prefer to do the work yourself, as much as possible of the existing stain should be removed, rubbing over first with a cloth soaked in warm water and soap. After this, to obtain a uniform colour, methylated spirit should be smeared over the surface. While still damp, a spirit stain should be applied by means of the spreader usually provided, with a circular movement, working it in evenly.

With regard to the lime deposit in your bath, rub first of all with a cloth dipped in hot vinegar solution, which you may find removes the marks successfully. On the other hand, if more drastic treatment is required, a dilute solution of hydrochloric acid or spirits of salts could be used. This is a very corrosive poison and should be used with the greatest care and only applied immediately over the marks, otherwise you may find that the enamel of the bath is damaged. After use, all traces should be rinsed away very thoroughly.

NOTE TO READERS

The Institute is always ready to answer any questions dealing with household or cookery matters, and the Staff is glad to receive from readers any new solutions of domestic difficulties they have come across themselves. Should these be published, a small fee will be paid.

The Housekeeper's Dictionary of Facts

THE
30's

The Care of Metal Furniture

METAL furniture is ideal for use in the garden during the summer months, but with the approach of winter it becomes necessary to store away the collection of chairs, tables, stools, etc., in a dry room.

Although stainless steel, nickel, monel metal and other untarnishable alloys are used in the construction of this type of furniture, the fine silvery surface is dulled by constant exposure to damp wintry air. In order to protect the metal from the moist atmosphere and so to ensure the retention of its attractive lustre, it is advisable to give the metal frame a simple protective coating.

First of all dust it well and then smear over its surface a thin coating of vaseline. This is best done by means of a swab of cotton wool soaked in petroleum jelly. In the case of enamelled or lacquered metal, vaseline should not be used, as the metal is already adequately protected.

When desired, the grease may be removed from the frame by means of a dry piece of flannel. The final polishing can be effected without the assistance of any metal polish; a good rub with a chamois leather gives a mirror-like surface to the steel or nickel.

In some cases the upholstery needs attention. Leather cloth may be given an extra spell of attractive life by smearing a little linseed oil over its surface. The cloth will not crack or peel so easily and may be polished up at any time by means of a dry cloth.

Leather should be given a coating of good quality furniture cream which will lubricate the fibres and prolong their life. The grain will take a soft and beautiful polish after this treatment.

To Re-Silver Glass

Mirrors from which the silver has become worn in patches can be repaired as follows: Mix 3 oz. tin, 3 oz. bismuth, and 6 oz. mercury together and warm in a small, clean, iron vessel or a large iron ladle. Paste the edge of the glass to be silvered with a narrow strip of paper to prevent the mixture running off during the process of silvering. Thoroughly clean and warm the glass and pour a small quantity of the hot mixture upon it, tilting it first one way and then the other, until the spot is well covered. Remove the paper, and apply a coat of paint when quite hard.

The Institute's Post-box.

Two years ago, I had an old wash copper taken out and a galvanised iron gas boiler, made by a reputable firm, installed in its place. For the first six months it was entirely satisfactory. Then gradually, each week a kind of scum began to form on the top of the water when it came to the boil and to mark the clothes. I complained through the agent to the makers about it, several times, but can get no satisfaction. They said the fault was not in the boiler, but

LECTURE DEMONSTRATIONS

The following demonstrations will be given at the Good Housekeeping Institute on Wednesday afternoons, commencing at 3 o'clock.

SEPTEMBER 30TH
The Secret of Making Successful Omelettes and Hot and Cold Soufflés.
Savoury Omelette, Sweet Soufflé Omelette, Vanilla Soufflé, Lobster Soufflé, Apricot Soufflé.

OCTOBER 7TH
The Modern Gas Cooker with temperature control will be discussed.
The meal demonstrated will consist of Grapefruit, Roast Duck, Sage and Onion Stuffing, Apple Sauce, Green Peas, and Mashed Potatoes, Caramel Pudding, Meringue Chantilly and Cheese Straws.

OCTOBER 14TH
The Art of Successful Frying. Fried Fillets of Fish with directions for Skinning and Filleting. Ham and Beef Cutlets, Potato Straws, Doughnuts and Pineapple Fritters.

OCTOBER 21ST
The Making and Baking of Afternoon Tea Cakes and Gâteaux.
Pineapple Cake, Ginger Cake, Russian Cake, Jap Cakes, Walnut Cake and Strawberry Layer Cake.

OCTOBER 28TH
Some suggestions for the Nursery Menus.
The Diet of Children of varying ages from two years old upwards will be discussed.
Prune Purée, Junket, Vegetable Soup, Cheese Soup, Liver and Bean Hot Pot, Danish Sponge, Peach Delight, Cranberry and Apple Fluff.

NOVEMBER 4TH
Supper and Savoury Dishes. Blanquette d'Œufs, Cheese Charlotte, Lobster Cutlets, Calves' Liver with Mushrooms, Nut Kromeskies.

For further particulars regarding fees, etc., readers are invited to write to Good Housekeeping Institute, 49 Wellington Street, Strand, W.C.2, enclosing a stamped addressed envelope for the reply

must be due to oil or the soap used and gently insinuated that the boiler was not being kept clean. As a matter of fact, the boiler is scoured every week, being filled with cold water by means of a clean pail, and still there is this trouble every washing-day. I cannot help thinking that it must be caused by something wrong in the galvanised surface. A friend who lives a few doors away got a similar boiler at the same time, uses the same soap and has no trouble at all.

The specimen I am enclosing was scraped off the side of the boiler this morning after the water was baled out.

(W. A., Birmingham.)

In reply to your letter, it is a little difficult to account for the deposit in your boiler, as we believe the water in Birmingham is exceedingly soft. If it had been hard, the scum would no doubt have been due to reaction between the hardness of the water and the soap used. We can only conclude, therefore, that traces of soap and soil from the clothes tend to adhere to the somewhat rough galvanised finish of the boiler, and it is these which are responsible for the scum you notice.

Where the water is of any serious degree of hardness, this trouble is nearly always experienced, especially with a galvanised boiler, but in your case, as already mentioned, it is difficult to give any definite explanation.

We can only suggest that you wipe out the boiler as soon as possible after use, while it is still warm.

We do not know whether you have been using abrasive cleansers, but it is possible that if you have done so, you have roughened the surface, and this may have caused the trouble.

I wonder whether you can help me with the baby's bath screen which I am anxious to make. The frame I have is small and old. Perhaps you can suggest a good material.

(I. A., Liverpool.)

In regard to a suitable material for a baby's screen, we would suggest a nursery cretonne in gay colours, several most attractive designs which are quite inexpensive, costing from about 2s. 3d. a yard. Alternatively you could cover the screen with oil silk, which has the advantage that it can be cleaned by sponging with a damp cloth. This is, however, more expensive than a cretonne and costs 5s. 11d. a yard. Another suitable material is American cloth.

With regard to the making of the screen, if you wish the wooden frame to show, you could have the material gathered at the top to a coiled spring rod, and nailed to the frame. For this, three widths of 31 in. material across would be necessary, so altogether 4 yards, allowing for turnings and heading, would be required.

If you prefer the wooden frame to be hidden, you could have a double cover to slip over it. For this 5½ yards of material would be necessary.

By *Grace Noll Crowell*

SONS

To press my lips
Upon a fair cheek, or a brown,
Of my young sons—
So long I have stooped down;

But suddenly to-day, to my surprise,
I find that I must lift my eyes
To meet their eyes,
That I must stand on toe tips
And reach up
To kiss their lips.
These tall young sons—
Each straight as any pine,
Can they be mine?

Soon I must share them.
Soon I know that they will go,
But oh, I am so glad
That I have had
Small sons to stoop to,
Tall sons to reach to,
Clean sons to give
That other sons may live.

*Illustration
by F. C. Cook*

ASCOT . . . ROYAL ASCOT !

New Ford 24 h.p. Tudor Saloon, £180 at works, Manchester (14.9 h.p. £5 extra).

WORDS suggestive of elegance and luxury, as well as sport. For Ascot, or any other classic social occasion, you must have efficiency in transport, and present conditions point to economy. The New Ford combines efficiency and economy, comfort and compactness, elegance and ease of handling, unequalled by any other car purchasable at the price of the New Ford.

Let the Local Ford Dealer demonstrate the ability of the New Ford to satisfy your every requirement.

FORD MOTOR COMPANY LIMITED,
88 Regent Street, London, W.1. Trafford Park, Manchester

LINCOLN   FORDSON

AIRCRAFT

More Points

from our

ECONOMY COMPETITION LETTERS

Readers found the winning letters that were printed last month so helpful and interesting that we are giving below a selection of hints and opinions taken from other entries

WHEN Mr. Snowden's bombshell fell, the question of economising to meet the extra taxation was forced upon us all. There must have been many, who, like myself, wondered "how can I, who have never been extravagant, economise still further?"

After some considerable thought, I have arrived at the conclusion that economy is not the same thing as "doing without" to cut down expense. If everyone "did without" to any great extent, trade would suffer even worse than it is suffering now. To give one example—if everyone suddenly gave up smoking, shall we say, what would happen to all the millions of people directly and indirectly concerned and employed in the making, manufacturing and selling of tobacco in all its various forms? It would produce chaos—throwing millions of people out of work. It therefore behoves us to find some way of making sixpence go as far as a shilling—or better still, of making use of something that does not cost even sixpence and would otherwise be thrown away.

To take the first instance—that of making sixpence go as far as a shilling. I know of no more astonishing way of doing this than by buying and paying for one's meat, instead of ordering it and running an account. Since I started this habit I have saved quite a third, if not more, of my usual weekly expenditure on meat. I cannot account for this. I merely state it as a fact which everyone who does the same will endorse. Another remarkable economy I have discovered is that marmalade costs 4d. to make against 6d. or 8d. per lb. to buy. Of course, making marmalade takes time and trouble, but I am assuming that the average housewife's time is not money. That being so, and she is endowed with a fair amount of energy, quite considerable savings can be made by canning her surplus fruit. Very few tins of fruit cost less than 1s. per 2 lb. tin, and many are considerably more expensive than that. 2 lb. tins with lids and rubbers complete can be bought for 2s. per dozen, a canning machine can be hired generally from the local Women's Institute for 6d. per day, and in one day two to three dozen cans can be filled and completed, given the fruit to can—and the cans will work out at less than 6d. each, including sugar for syrup, instead of 1s. or more. Here literally 6d. goes further than 1s.

It always goes to my heart to see the amount of waste that goes on in most kitchens in the matter of bread. Crusts are seldom eaten—new loaves are cut before old ones are finished—toast is thrown

THE PERFECT WRINGER
AND THE PERFECT STAND

TWO MILLION HAPPY ACME USERS

THE FASTEST WRINGER & THE EASIEST TO TURN

EVERY WOMAN NEEDS THIS LABOUR SAVER

16 INCH 43/-
14 INCH 39/-
COMPLETE WITH MANGLING BOARD

THE ACME wrings easier, quicker, drier, and cleaner than any other wringer—that is the testimony of two million happy housewives. With 15 easy turns in 27 seconds, the ACME wrings half a pint more water from a large blanket than any other wringer. Clumsy "geared" wringers mean double time and labour—30 turns in 54 seconds. Built of unbreakable rustproofed steel and finished in an attractive blue, the ACME carries a 10 YEARS' FREE REPLACEMENT GUARANTEE, and lasts a lifetime. It is the only wringer that offers FREE CHOICE OF FIXTURES for fixing it to tub, table, sink or bath.

THE NEW ACME TURNOVER STAND No. 25, fitted with 16-inch Acme, centralises all phases of washday—washing, wringing, mangling and ironing. Built like the Acme, of unbreakable steel, the new stand has adjustable rubber-lined feet that never damage linoleum and prevent rocking on any uneven floor. It takes any size of "dolly tub," zinc or enamelled bath, and is provided with a *white porcelain enamelled table top (no extra charge)* and a reversible sliding basket rest. Don't fail to see the new Acme Stand. It is the perfect stand and can be converted in a moment into a splendid everyday table.

WITH WHITE PORCELAIN ENAMELLED TABLE TOP
(NO EXTRA CHARGE)

The ACME
TURNOVER WRINGER STAND No. 25 34/6
WRINGER and STAND COMBINED 77/6

See both wringer and stand at any ironmonger's, hardware or furnishing store. Write for booklet M.49, "IT CLEANS AS IT WRINGS," to ACME WRINGERS LTD., DAVID STREET, GLASGOW, S.E.

THE NEW ACME
ALL BRITISH

THE 30's

 # Gear-changing, ladies? Why, nothing simpler!

4-DOOR SALOON **£285**

(Ex Works, Hendon)

Flush-type weatherproof sliding roof, £10 extra.

Fixed-head Coupé - **£295**

All-weather Saloon and Drop-head Coupé - - **£325**

Special 26-h.p. model for overseas.

● FAULTLESS GEAR - CHANGE

No double declutching, no "feeling" for gears, no stalling, no noise — you never need make a bad gear-change on the Vauxhall Cadet. Synchro-Mesh gears give you a feeling of expert control; the Silent Second makes it pleasant to use your gears as you should. And in performance and appearance the Cadet is all you could wish for. Ask any dealer for a trial run, or write to General Motors Ltd., The Hyde, Hendon, London, N.W.9.

"WHAT do you think Daddy had the cheek to tell me?" inquired Sheila. "He said he got a Vauxhall Cadet this time so that I shouldn't make a row with the gears. I, mind you! When he himself used to make an awful clatter on the old car!"

"Too bad," responded Peter—always the dutiful fiancé. "Still," he added, thoughtfully, "whether he was studying you or himself,

he's picked a winner. I suppose you know this car's got Synchro-Mesh?"

"I didn't—but I'll tell you what I do know. I know that you don't have to double-declutch when you want to change down — you just move the lever, and there you are in second, without making a sound."

"Exactly," chuckled Peter. "That's what Synchro-Mesh does for you—besides giving you a quieter second gear than you've ever known before."

VAUXHALL CADET

(17 H.P. —— SIX CYLINDERS)

It's British

COMPLETE RANGE OF MODELS ON VIEW AT 174-182 GREAT PORTLAND STREET, LONDON, W.1

Economy Competition Letters

away and thick rounds of bread are wasted under vegetables to absorb the water in which no vegetables should be cooked. Let the housewife see to all these distressing extravagances and the bread bill will shrink in a most pleasing way.

One of my pet economies is making newspaper wrappers out of the many large envelopes sent me enclosing advertisements and price lists. This is simply done with a paper knife and a little paste—or the envelopes can be used again as such if required, with or without a luggage label pasted on.

To turn from these small economies to a big one, I would suggest that we should take Italy as our example and import less flour. Mussolini saved some immense sum in Italy by mixing the flour for bread with maize flour. Let us mix our flour with Scotch oatmeal. Not only would we help our budget, but we would help our farmers, improve the flavour and nourishment of our bread, improve our children's teeth and save dentists' bills.

A. R. H., Westmorland.

I HAVE dispensed with the use of firewood by using instead sheets of newspaper folded diagonally and then rolled over to make a long flat strip about 2 in. wide. The strip is then folded to look like the letter "V," but flat. The ends are then crossed one over the other until the whole looks somewhat like a concertina. When ignited, four or five of these burn slowly and soon set the fire going, and I no longer require sixpenny-worth of wood a week. I am more careful than formerly to use up all the cinders. If mixed with coal dust and slightly damped they make a very good and lasting fire.

R. R., Middlesex.

I FOUND that I could do without any domestic help by getting up an hour earlier in the morning, and encouraging the children, who responded very well, to fetch and carry for me, help set meals, help to fill coal scuttles, and do many little odd jobs. Also I found that knitting their suits was a very great saving, and patterns are easy and simple. This I do in the evenings while listening to the wireless.

We have decided to give up smoking, and instituted a " wireless " and " petrol " box, in which we put the money that would otherwise have been spent on cigarettes. We use the car for business purposes, and when we take any pleasure journey endeavour to combine the two.

We have a slow-combustion stove for our hot-water supply and a kitchen range for cooking. But I found that oil is a much cheaper fuel, and a two-burner stove has paid for itself in the course of this last year. We can heat kettles on the boiler, and there again I found that " coalite " is a cheaper and better fuel for our purpose than anthracite, and we can keep the boiler in both day and night with it, burning all our rubbish, even old tins! Small hand oil lamps are cheaper and cleaner than candles.

With regard to food, I use the cheaper kinds of meat occasionally—shin of beef for beef puddings, ribs of beef and necks of mutton. During the summer we use our garden produce to full advantage, and as we buy cheese straight from a Somerset farmer we can do without meat quite largely. Of course, I " put down " eggs (we haven't our own fowls), and bottle fruit and vegetables, making the most of really " free " berries, whortle and blackberries.

PRESERVES

NOW THERE'LL BE NO EXCUSE

For your being unable to keep the family supplied with luscious jams, jellies, pickles, and home-made preserves of all kinds. Our latest guaranteed cookery publication is

Good Housekeeping Sixpenny Series No. 6

PRESERVES

In this, both the theory and practice of jam, jelly, and marmalade-making are made crystal clear, and the recipes, all Institute-tested, are a revelation in new deliciousness. Many of them can be tried out now, before the jam - making season proper begins. Pickles, sauces, and chutneys of many kinds, some never before published, have a section to themselves. Fruit syrups and vinegars for cooling drinks—the full processes of bottling and canning—how to dry fruit and vegetables for keeping—how to seal jars the best way—the growing and preparation of herbs—all these are included in a book which will justify our claim for every number in the Sixpenny Series— " Indispensable for the Kitchen Library."

THE **30**'s

A small matter, but I found that a sacking apron worn by my husband in the garden, saved much darning and mending, for the rub of his arm while digging wore out many pairs of trousers. The boys wore a bathing suit most of the summer (we have a stream at the bottom of the garden) and wear no shoes or stockings in the garden at all. This is a real saving, for shoe leather is a terrible expense.

J. A., Sussex.

AT the beginning of this year, my husband had a brain-wave! Our car is a big roomy saloon, and the seats are like two well-sprung divans. My husband made the back of the front seat to drop back level with the other seat, so that when required it can quite easily be converted into a comfortable bed for two people. For our little boy, he made a hammock composed of a steel frame with strong canvas stretched tightly across it, which, when not in use, straps up flat against the roof of the car and is almost unnoticeable. With a few rugs and an eiderdown, we are able to sleep in the car as comfortably as a hotel. We take a small primus stove for breakfasts, and just what is necessary for washing, etc. We can always get a decent meal if we want one, because we go just where we feel inclined. We have discovered the most delightful spots and felt so free and unrestricted that this kind of holiday has been a revelation, as well as having the additional advantage of not costing much money.

As children need a more settled kind of holiday, I have usually taken our little boy to a quiet seaside place for a few weeks. This has always been irksome to me as I really cannot spare the time. (Amongst my other jobs I do all the bookkeeping in connection with my husband's business.) In addition to neglecting this, it means getting someone to look after things at home when I am away. However, this year I made inquiries, and I found a lady who had been a children's nurse, but who was now a widow living in a small cottage at the seaside. She was quite willing to take charge of our boy at a reasonable sum, and after I had seen the place and felt sure he would be safe and happy there, I arranged to send him for a month. This only cost a fraction of the amount it would have cost had I taken him myself.

D. C., Manchester.

WE bought a tiny oven to stand over a ring on the gas-cooker. It is large enough to bake a pie or cake, apples, potatoes or a custard, or to warm the plates. We use this instead of the big oven whenever possible. If we have to use the big oven for roasting a joint, we take the opportunity of making pastry at the same time, thus using the oven to its fullest capacity all the time the gas is on.

We planned meals so as to make increased use of a three-tier steamer and in this way saved much gas.

We found that the coal fire in the drawing-room burnt much less fuel and threw out a very good heat when a couple of ordinary bricks were placed at the back of the well. (Incidentally a brick or two can often be put in the fire of a kitchen range without impairing its efficiency.)

I found the following a particularly good way of using up meat left-overs, as it is very nutritious, cheap and appetising:

For every pound of cold meat cook half a pound of lentils. Mince the meat, removing gristle but not fat, add the lentils and as much of their liquor as required, season and serve very hot. If necessary, add browning to improve the colour.

When poultry could only very occasion-

...Do you know that GOOD HOUSE-KEEPING INSTITUTE will solve your many household problems for you?

⬥   ⬥   ⬥   ⬥

...Do you know that GOOD HOUSE-KEEPING'S DEPARTMENT of FURNISHINGS and DECORATIONS will completely decorate or rearrange your home under expert direction?

⬥   ⬥   ⬥   ⬥

...Do you know that GOOD HOUSE-KEEPING'S FASHION DEPARTMENT will help you solve your dress problems—showing you: what to wear, how to make, where to buy?

⬥   ⬥   ⬥   ⬥

...Do you know that GOOD HOUSE-KEEPING'S SHOPPING SERVICE will secure you many bargains—and save you much time?

⬥   ⬥   ⬥   ⬥

...Do you know that everything advertised in GOOD HOUSEKEEPING is guaranteed? You can purchase goods advertised with every confidence and without the slightest risk?

Economy Competition Letters

ally be afforded, tripe made a very good substitute. Steamed, passed twice through a fine mincer and delicately flavoured it makes delicious croquettes which even the most confirmed haters of tripe eat with enjoyment.

We bought the cheaper cuts of bacon both for boiling and frying. Best Wiltshire flank is often less than 3d. a pound, and the fact that it is rather fat makes it specially suitable for children.

We made increased use of pulses and cereals and studied the GOOD HOUSEKEEPING cookery books to see how these can be attractively prepared. We gave up peeling potatoes and steamed or baked them in their skins. We made no attempt to curtail our supplies of milk, fruit or vegetables, but merely exercised care to see that there was no waste.

The following were my principles when buying clothes:

To avoid ultra-fashionable styles, bright colours, cheap shoes and any frocks or blouses which would need frequent dry-cleaning instead of washing.

To resist firmly the temptation to buy any other coloured evening frock but black!

To spend little on hats, since it is possible to buy cheap ones which look good.

To have a *good* outdoor outfit in a neutral colour which will last two seasons.

I am very careful to change my outdoor clothes as soon as I come in, and I always save my silk stockings by wearing strong cotton stockings for work in the house and garden and for country walks.

J. B., Sussex.

CHECK the following sources of waste. Condiments left on plates; separate infusions of tea due to unpunctuality of individuals; burst tubes of toothpaste owing to incorrect handling; soap left in water (substitute floating variety for youngsters); extravagant paring of fruit and vegetables; tangled threads in workbox; bills for repairing burst pipes owing to lack of precaution during frosts (case of "nothing for something"!). Avoid breakages of lamp glasses and windows in cold weather by heating former gradually and by wiping both with methylated spirit instead of water. Rubbers on taps lessen crockery breakages.

Buy soap in quantities (at sales), as cut in slices and left to harden it lasts longer. Make all scraps into soap jelly for washing woollens.

W. M. I., Lancs.

I ASKED the maids to co-operate with me in the economy campaign, and they showed great readiness to help. We started on the laundry basket and between us wash everything at home except the household linen and my husband's shirts and pyjamas and "stiff" things. We are handicapped by having no electric iron or gas, which makes the ironing rather heavy, and this is why we cut out shirts and pyjamas. This arrangement saved a considerable sum every week at once. Then I tried the household books. We decided to have two meatless days in the week and to give up meat in the evening entirely, except when we had visitors, and we immediately *halved* our butcher's bill. On the two meatless days we have soup and dumplings once and eggs in various ways once. We now only have a real joint once a week and yet we have plenty of variety. My young cook has really enjoyed "managing" it and inventing vegetable dishes and ways of doing up the left-overs. The milk bill has not been altered as that is one thing the children

must have, but both baker's and grocer's books have been brought down by really careful planning and watching. We never cut new bread, or waste old bread, and our bread book has never been so low as it is now. We have cut out of our grocery order all the unnecessary trimmings and "decorative groceries"—and take extra care to use up the last possible drop in every bottle and packet. We have all given up having early tea (the staff quite voluntarily), and we have only one thing for breakfast instead of a choice, and at tea no scones or muffins and no sandwiches. My husband has not ordered any more whisky, and we have both reduced our smoking considerably. We have practically given up buying expensive fish, or chickens or game, and things like salted almonds and chocolates do not appear at all. For dessert we only have the simplest things—oranges, apples and bananas, and I never buy flowers of course, now. Nanny and I make all the children's clothes, except their tailored coats, and we never send things to be cleaned if they *can* be washed. Also we have no dining-room fire, nor any bedroom fires, but only the nursery and one sitting-room fire going, and a portable oil stove in the dining-room.

B. H., Hants.

I AM attempting to reduce housekeeping expenses by at least £12 per annum. We shall do more washing and cake-making at home; try to substitute cheaper for more expensive articles of food, using less meat and more fish, cheaper cuts of meat, giving the children cod-liver oil instead of cream, using Empire instead of Danish butter, oatmeal instead of prepared cereals, and so on.

Without actually cutting down gifts, I hope to save a little by making as many articles as possible, similarly with clothing. We have reduced newspapers to a minimum and hope to effect a saving on the garden, where we have divided raspberry canes and fruit bushes to fill the space formerly allotted to vegetables (we find fruit growing more profitable), and have taken cuttings, plants and bulbs from the back to fill the front flower-beds, for which we formerly bought fresh plants each season. On such items as these we ought to be able to save £2 more.

M. B., Birmingham.

MY husband has given up his first-class ticket on the railway and travels to business by bus: he prefers this to third-class on the railway. He is also smoking less, which is as good for his health as our pocket. We are all (except baby) wearing rubber soles and heels to our shoes this winter; this is proving a great saving in the shoe repair bill.

E. W. P., London.

MY food economies are very trivial, but the amount saved mounts up.

Meat: I take ½ lb. less on the week-end joint, and instead of the usual Tuesday mince of all meat, add a tablespoonful of rice cooked in boiling water and a beaten-up egg, saving 3d. or 4d.

Instead of fried eggs with bacon, sometimes we have scrambled, but have two eggs between three, making up with fried bread.

For a milk pudding, instead of taking extra, I use what I can spare, making up with water and adding a tablespoonful of shredded suet.

To save fuel: We have a good fire in

Economy Competition Letters

the dining-room for breakfast, which I transfer to the kitchen immediately after, making it up again for dinner in the dining-room. The kitchener keeps me supplied with hot water, the oven is always hot for cooking. I have a stockpot going; also a flat iron handy for pressing or ironing any small article, thus saving gas for cooking and electricity for my iron. Some days I cook double the quantity of potatoes, which are fried up for cold meat the following day. There is usually a pie left over also; this saves the kitchener altogether for that day.

My pet economy—and a surprising one—is that I now send out all my washing, except my own silk underwear and my daughter's school blouses. Owing to ill-health about two months ago, I sent my things to the local "Home Service" wash, and was greatly surprised not only at the way the clothes were done, but by the very moderate charge. Working things out, I found that what I had been paying weekly for soaps, washing powders, starch, etc., plus gas for boiling and electricity for ironing, came to more than the laundry charge, even if I paid extra for special things like blankets and garments that wanted careful ironing. Also I shall probably save a doctor's bill through not catching cold or getting run down. In addition, I have washing and ironing morning free every week. This so far has been devoted to renovations to clothing which would otherwise have been given away.

M. D., Kent.

WE have effected small regular savings, which I suppose is what most of us need to do. We have avoided reducing our gifts to hospitals, churches, charitable societies, and have succeeded in our resolve to add in no way to unemployment. For the housekeeper it involves incessant watchfulness over expenditure and considerable ingenuity in contriving ways and means of avoiding dullness and monotony.

We like to regard this as our small part in a national effort, or even as our own little state department on the smooth running of which depends the welfare of one of the homes of England, and considered thus, it seems worthy of our best.

We have found invaluable help in the columns of your magazine, the advertisements, suggested appliances and your cookery books and articles, whilst the Diary and Account Book have simplified the checking of our weekly expenses.

For this and for the dignity your interest in housekeeping bestows upon us we are most grateful.

M. C., Huntingdon.

INSTEAD of cooking lunch for myself as formerly, I now have grape-nuts (very nourishing) and milk or oatcake and dates or other fruit. I have changed our three-or four-course dinner to a "high tea" at 6.30 p.m.; four days a week we have fish (plaice, haddock or herring instead of sole or turbot), other days rabbit pies, meats, macaroni and cheese or some such dish; always something nourishing, as it is no economy to risk illness through being under-nourished. We have entirely given up expensive sweets and cakes, also the glass of beer or burgundy that we generally had with lunch and dinner, making a glass of milk our drink instead. Instead, too, of our former fairly substantial supper near bed-time, we now have just a glass of milk and perhaps a little fruit, and I really think we are both the better in health for this small self-denial.

E. P., Glasgow.

MY husband and I are now middle-aged; the family have left the home and no longer require much care or help. Most of my friends and acquaintances are similarly situated, and we represent a fairly large part of the community. I have come to the conclusion that the chief waste among the housewives in this section of the community, is *time*.

Most of us probably have some right to rest on our oars at this period of our lives. Our past years have been strenuous: we are now somewhat worn and battered, but I truly believe that many of us are slacking to excess.

Quite a lot of the women I know go out every fine morning "shopping": they attend bridge parties several afternoons a week, and their evenings are spent with their husband, on his return from business, in what is, for him, well-earned rest and ease.

Not much to show for the *woman's* day, is there? Now that we must economise, how about stopping this waste of time, doing more at home, and thus saving part of the running cost?

What was the Mystery of the lonely Mountain-side?

The answer comes in "The Stream," an astonishingly clever story appearing in next month's "GoodHouse-keeping," by the author of "Miss Mole"

E. H. YOUNG

By taking in our own washing (previously sent out) and undertaking the gardening (we had hitherto employed a gardener one day a week at 8s. a day), we have saved a useful and necessary sum each week, with no resultant feeling of irritation or sense of missing anything.

In order to give us time for the gardening and laundry work, we have carried out several happy reforms in the ordinary housework.

The large floor space of old red tiles in kitchen and scullery, tiles with the glaze all worn off, leaving a roughened surface, had to be scrubbed often, and yet never looked clean. A square of carpet or matting, easily kept clean with the vacuum sweeper, now covers the centres of these floors. The surrounding tiles have been given a hard, glossy, beautiful new surface with two coats of a floor preparation, which I found easy to apply. They now require no scrubbing and look very handsome.

The large old kitchen range was, one bit at a time, washed clean of black-lead, and treated with heat-proof black, which now keeps highly polished with an occasional rub over with furniture polish, leaving only

the ribs and hot-plate to be black-leaded.

Twenty-eight brass knobs on doors and cupboards have been painted with liquid porcelain (first slightly roughening the surface), likewise numerous brass taps at sink, bath, gas stove and water softener, thus saving the time and bother of polishing them, and improving their appearance also.

A. B., Warwickshire.

COMING now to food—and here may I say that I have rigidly maintained a well-balanced diet, with ample fruit and vegetables—I abolished the breakfast-dish, and made porridge and toast the foundation for our day's work. Many housewives will, I think, be staggered if they work out the yearly cost of the morning bacon-and-eggs. Tea, in place of coffee, is another useful breakfast-table economy. Of course, familiar items are missed at first, but we all settled down soon to the new régime.

In my household shopping, I find it well worth while to pay cash and split up my orders. Before buying my fruit and vegetables, I look at prices in several windows, and perhaps get my greens in one shop, my potatoes in a second, my apples in a third. Savings of a penny per pound soon mount up, with a household of eight. In the same way, with groceries, although I give a weekly order to a large store in town, I often alter the items, if I find I can buy things more cheaply elsewhere.

As for meat, I have never believed in giving much of it to children; and I have inaugurated meatless dinners twice or thrice a week for us all. When we do have meat, I get it sometimes for half the price I used to pay. The cheaper cuts may look less inviting, but with careful cooking they can be made just as good to eat. My butcher's bill for last month amounted to less than £1, and none of us has suffered in any way.

I have dealt with food costs at some length, because I find our food is the most fruitful field for economy. I add just two more points—that all our jam and marmalade, and cakes and scones, are made at home; and that my husband saves the cost of lunch in town by taking sandwiches to the office.

And now I turn to a brief account of some other economies. We have given up our library subscription, and use the public library instead (incidentally, this gives us the use of four books instead of two). I have most of the laundry done at home, only sending out collars and evening shirts, and sheets; and for these I use one of the cheaper laundry services. I make almost all the children's clothes, and most of my own. By altering, dyeing and mending, I save a lot of expense for new clothing. I hardly ever buy flowers for the house—a real deprivation, this!—and we have done very little stocking of our small garden. We take a penny newspaper instead of a twopenny one; we use the telephone most sparingly; I accumulate my shopping errands for town, and save bus and tube fares by going seldom and only when it is necessary. These small things do count, for the secret of economising really is to "take care of the pence." Of course the constant watching of every penny is irksome at times, when one knows that even the cinema must not be thought of as a relaxation. But the gap in our income is being bridged, and the successful effort brings a real satisfaction which makes it abundantly worth while.

M. K. M., London.

The Housekeeper's Dictionary *of* Facts

Interesting points on all subjects appear monthly on this page

Cleaning Concrete Floors

A VERY simple and successful method of cleaning dirty and oily concrete surfaces has been recently discovered. The method depends on the wonderful grease-removing and cleansing properties of a chemical known as sodium metasilicate and ordinary soap. The former substance is very similar to water glass and is quite cheap. It may be obtained from good-class druggists, who will order it from the large chemical houses if necessary. The proportions of sodium metasilicate and soap are as follows:

95 per cent. of sodium metasilicate.
5 per cent. of common household soap.

Fifteen parts of the above mixture are then dissolved in a hundred parts of boiling water and used for scrubbing or brushing the floor. After this treatment the concrete should be well rinsed with cold water. If desired, the soap and sodium metasilicate can be dissolved in a little boiling water and then diluted to suit requirements.

This method of cleaning will be found particularly useful on a neglected scullery or kitchen floor, or in the garage where the dark and viscid oil from the car engine leaves unsightly patches on the floor.

Uses for Oil Baize

The coloured washable oil baize now supplied by a number of stores has many labour-saving uses. An attractive and practical splash-back for the wash-stand can be made of this material, and fitted by threading picture-cord through a brass rod, leaving a length each end to attach to picture-hooks in the wall. Make a broad hem in the oil baize, and slip the rod through. This type of back looks fresh and clean with a mere fraction of the time required to keep muslin, cretonne, or straw splashers in condition.

This material can also be pasted on to a three-ply board to cover tops of cupboards and wardrobes, and thus simplify their periodical cleaning. In the kitchen a tie-on cushion seat can be given an oil baize cover, the cushion being simply slipped inside it and the cover kept clean with occasional sponging.

A Kitchen Slate

This is a very useful article to have in the kitchen. Costing only about ninepence at a school-

supplies shop and with the addition of a box of white chalks, it is invaluable in several ways. All the menus for the day can be written on one side for the maids' perusal, while on the other side tradesmen's daily and weekly orders, or telephone or other messages received for absent members of the household, can be jotted down. Time usually spent in talking over meals and orders is saved, and it affords a good aid to memory for both mistress and maid. It does not take a minute to wipe the slate clean each morning.

Grow Your Own Parsley

Parsley is a culinary plant which is frequently required in small quantities in the kitchen, and it is not economical to buy too much of it at a time, as it soon loses its freshness. A simple way of having it always at hand is to sow some seeds in an old shallow biscuit tin or any other box that will serve the purpose. It requires no gardening skill to grow it. Make a few holes in the bottom of the tin and fill it with earth, sprinkle in the seeds and cover lightly with soil. The box may be placed on the back window ledge, yard, or other available space. It will grow again as often as it is cut. Thyme may also be grown in the same way.

Economical Cream Cheese

The hard dry cheese just inside the rind of a Stilton can be used to make a delicious " cream cheese," if the pieces are put twice through the mincer, afterwards adding a piece of butter. Pound well together with a wooden spoon until the mixture is well mixed and creamy. Form into dainty little pats and serve with biscuits and celery.

When Cutting Sandwiches

It is possible to make sandwiches quickly and easily, even from new bread. A sharp knife or saw-edged bread knife should be used and the blade dipped into a jug of boiling water. After drying it will be found that the bread can be cut readily and easily without crumbling.

Tomatoes are always a popular ingredient for sandwich fillings. To peel them, drop them into boiling water and leave for a minute or two. Then with the aid of a sharp knife they can be both quickly and thinly peeled.

A Home-made Vanishing Cream

This particular cream has been thoroughly tested over a period of several years.

Pure stearic acid .	10 parts
Soap flakes . .	2 parts
Glycerine .	15 parts
Water . . .	30 parts

The water should be boiled, distilled, or, if preferred, prepared rose water can be used.

Flake up the stearic acid and melt in a small enamel or aluminium pan, add the soap flakes and dissolve slowly with heat. In a separate pan mix the glycerine and water, and heat to a temperature of 60° C. (140° F.). This temperature must be carefully noted, as it is upon this that the production of a successful emulsion depends. Now stir the glycerine and water mixture into the melted fat and soap—add slowly and stir vigorously. It is better to have someone to do the pouring while you whisk up the mixture, using an egg whisk. The more air that can be beaten into the mixture the better, indeed this is the whole secret of a good, soft, easily vanishing cream. When the cream is cool, but while still mixing, add a few drops of essential oil (jasmine or bergamot) or, if preferred, a small quantity of one's favourite perfume. The cream should be immediately filled into stoppered pots or jars, where it will keep indefinitely. Deterioration is only caused through exposure to the air, which results in loss of water and consequent hardening and lumpiness.

The preparation is so cheap that it may be used liberally. The average retail prices of the ingredients are:

Stearic acid .	2d.	per oz.
Soap flakes .	½d.	„
Glycerine .	1½d.	„

Our warm friend MR THERM ---

Not a cold corner in the house — *thanks to* MR THERM

HARRODS

DEBENHAM & FREEBODY

The velvet afternoon dress, a Vionnet model, is a rich deep brown. Full sleeves are gauged on to a low shoulder line and gathered to an elastic cuff which is pushed over the elbow. The neckline stands high in the front and falls in a soft cowl at the back. The buttons are brown spun glass, the skirt sheath-like and plain

A dashing black and white velvet bolero, with the stripes used geometrically, goes over a straight, slim black crêpe frock, but between the two there is a breastplate affair composed of triangles of silver lamé and scarlet, with one small section of the striped velvet. It is bound at the neck with black and buttons at a low waistline at the back

Sheath-like Skirts and Interesting

HARRODS

Winter hats are brief and tilt slightly. All have height in some form or another. A beret in two tones of tucked velvet has a cuff standing well up and is then pulled forward flat as a pancake over the right eye. The cap is in a material called chenille astrakhan, grey and fawn, and looks like tweed

Velvet is the star of the winter millinery collections and is used for the tiny hat below. Here, height is given by an unusual arrangement like a coronet, pulled up from a cap fitting closely to a portion of the head. A fluffy white feather pad is set at an acute angle across the front

Hats must be Brief

and worn

at a dashing tilt

WARING & GILLOW

Necklines

EVERY MEMBER OF THE FAMILY CAN NOW ENJOY **DUNLOP** PROTECTION IN WET WEATHER

★

THE **NEW** DUNLOP SEAMLESS WELLINGTONS FOR ALL THE FAMILY

Made by an entirely new process, direct from Latex, the natural milk of the rubber tree, instead of from sheet rubber, Dunlop Seamless Boots are wonderfully flexible, strong and durable, and at the same time have a fine finish. Guaranteed absolutely waterproof. Get a pair for every member of the family.

Made under British Patents

Women's Fashion Boot (as illustrated)	Men's Utility Boot	Women's Utility Boot	Misses' Utility Boot	Children's Utility Boot
7/11	12/6	6/11	5/11	4/11

—and the famous *"Lightning"* Fastener

"DELATOP" FASHION BOOTS

Made under British Patents

The well-dressed woman's Winter wardrobe is incomplete without a pair of these smartly-cut, perfectly-fitting fashion boots. Fitted in a few seconds by means of the cleverly-concealed "Lightning" fastener, and cosily lined, they offer complete protection from damp and its attendant ills, and a most satisfactory solution to the serious problem of keeping stockings immaculate in bad weather.

Made in full range of fittings in black and tan, with concealed "Lightning" Fasteners **21/-**

All Dunlop Footwear is made from LANCASHIRE COTTON, in the Dunlop specialised Footwear Factory at Liverpool, the largest of its kind in this country.

FROM SHOE SHOPS AND STORES EVERYWHERE

(Prices apply U.K. only.)

Illustrated leaflets on request to :-
DUNLOP RUBBER COMPANY LIMITED (Footwear Division), (Dept. 53), WALTON, LIVERPOOL.
C.F.H.

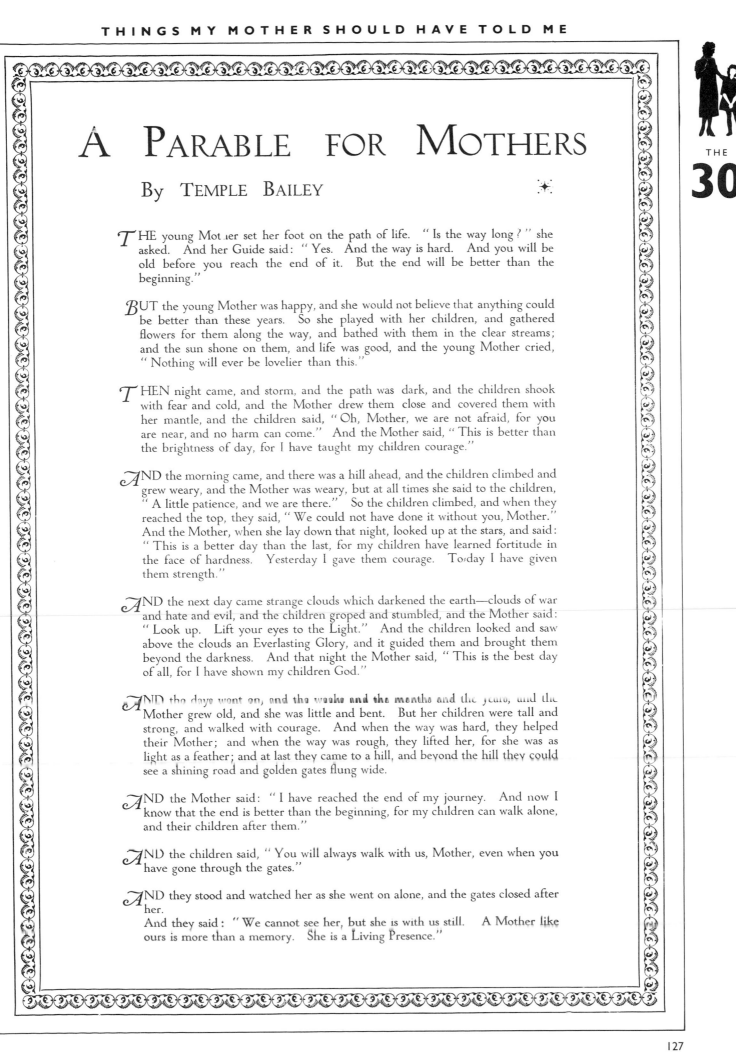

THE 30's

A PARABLE FOR MOTHERS

By TEMPLE BAILEY

THE young Mother set her foot on the path of life. "Is the way long?" she asked. And her Guide said: "Yes. And the way is hard. And you will be old before you reach the end of it. But the end will be better than the beginning."

BUT the young Mother was happy, and she would not believe that anything could be better than these years. So she played with her children, and gathered flowers for them along the way, and bathed with them in the clear streams; and the sun shone on them, and life was good, and the young Mother cried, "Nothing will ever be lovelier than this."

THEN night came, and storm, and the path was dark, and the children shook with fear and cold, and the Mother drew them close and covered them with her mantle, and the children said, "Oh, Mother, we are not afraid, for you are near, and no harm can come." And the Mother said, "This is better than the brightness of day, for I have taught my children courage."

AND the morning came, and there was a hill ahead, and the children climbed and grew weary, and the Mother was weary, but at all times she said to the children, "A little patience, and we are there." So the children climbed, and when they reached the top, they said, "We could not have done it without you, Mother." And the Mother, when she lay down that night, looked up at the stars, and said: "This is a better day than the last, for my children have learned fortitude in the face of hardness. Yesterday I gave them courage. To-day I have given them strength."

AND the next day came strange clouds which darkened the earth—clouds of war and hate and evil, and the children groped and stumbled, and the Mother said: "Look up. Lift your eyes to the Light." And the children looked and saw above the clouds an Everlasting Glory, and it guided them and brought them beyond the darkness. And that night the Mother said, "This is the best day of all, for I have shown my children God."

AND the days went on, and the weeks and the months and the years, and the Mother grew old, and she was little and bent. But her children were tall and strong, and walked with courage. And when the way was hard, they helped their Mother; and when the way was rough, they lifted her, for she was as light as a feather; and at last they came to a hill, and beyond the hill they could see a shining road and golden gates flung wide.

AND the Mother said: "I have reached the end of my journey. And now I know that the end is better than the beginning, for my children can walk alone, and their children after them."

AND the children said, "You will always walk with us, Mother, even when you have gone through the gates."

AND they stood and watched her as she went on alone, and the gates closed after her.
And they said: "We cannot see her, but she is with us still. A Mother like ours is more than a memory. She is a Living Presence."

FINANCIAL INDEPENDENCE

The Technique of Marriage—V

THE claim of women to equal rights with men was inevitable from the moment they learned to read, write and think, however illogically, and equal rights they will get sooner or later.

They have achieved a great deal already. What they have achieved in England is proved by the changes in the common law of the land, especially those that have to do with marriage. Before the Married Women's Property Act was passed, no married woman had the right to own any property whatever. Everything she possessed became her husband's when she married. It was the same in France. Until quite recently no Frenchwoman could sign a cheque on her own bank. She had, in fact, no bank and no bank account, and could draw no money from any bank without her husband's signature.

All that is changed now in the Western world, and if the changes have come slowly it is because most women are half-hearted about the business of their rights. They want freedom and the rights that go with freedom, but they would like to retain the privileges that go with subjection. The life of the harem still has its charm, especially in my own supposedly ultra modern country, and particularly among its most favoured women. For the wife of the American millionaire, in the old America of 1928, was morally very emancipated indeed; she considered herself a powerful and important person, but she belonged intellectually to the slaves and the courtesans of the world. She chose to lead the sheltered existence

of a pampered Queen in a Sultan's palace. She was an idle creature, very fond of luxury, but she took for granted the jewels, the silks and sables the man heaped on her, the money he poured out for her pleasure, the motors and yachts he gave her on her birthdays. She didn't recognise that she owed him anything in return for his generosity. She behaved as if she had a right to these things, and was conferring a favour on her husband in accepting them. He had wanted to marry her and she had consented and her debt was paid. She was now free to do as she pleased.

Her type is a curious mixture of the new and the old, and it is, I believe, disappearing, but there is some of her left in almost all women, even in those who are making a great to-do just now about their rights. Only a few of the most pure-minded fanatics are free of her, and most of those have been freed by necessity. They are the old maids of the world or the embittered and abandoned women. Having no man to depend on, they have been obliged to depend on themselves, and they have made of their independence a religion. But it is not really the men whom they hate, but the slave-woman and the courtesan and the old-fashioned coquette. The clash is really not between men and women at all, but between the new woman and the old, or the new idea in women and the old idea that is still powerful in them to produce a chaos of illogical notions, contradictory longings and confused images. The men are merely the victims of the chaos. Hustled and harried, teased, nagged,

flattered, cursed and openly defied, it is no wonder that they don't understand what is happening or what women really want; and I think it is no wonder that they prefer the old-fashioned woman, no matter how false a Delilah she may be or how heartless a coquette, for she is at any rate a familiar figure, she looks at least like a woman, and she is, or tries to be, pleasing to the eye if only for her own sake. But the woman who smokes cigars, wields a walking stick and talks about her rights, doesn't resemble a woman at all.

The fact is that the process of change has been speeded up to an alarming extent during the last couple of decades; and it has left men completely bewildered, for while the women have changed the men have remained the same.

A whole class of women has been freed recently from a whole set of ideas. All the women between the top and the bottom of the social scale have been affected. Those at the top are free of these ideas already, those at the bottom never can be. The reason is economic. It is a question of money. A great mass of women have got hold of the idea that they can be, and want to be, economically independent. Only the wives of very rich men are uninterested. The Englishwoman of wealth and great social position has too much to do to bother about it. Her husband's wealth has already given her all the freedom and responsibility she can manage; and the working man's wife has no time to waste on such ideas. She thinks it all nonsense. She

The economic outlook of women is changing so rapidly that husbands must learn to adapt themselves to wives who wish to earn salaries or at least to have a settled income

THE
30's

FOR WIVES

By MARY BORDEN

has her work and her husband has his, and the family budget of three pounds a week gives little chance for dispute, unless the man drinks or gambles. In either case she goes for him, and if she can't stop his wasting the money, or if he is unable to get work and doesn't bring in any money, she acts, without being in the least aware of her woman's rights: takes in washing or goes out to scrub other women's floors.

Necessity is the great simplifier of family problems. Poverty has, with a beautiful simplicity, made women the equals of men. To the working woman, the new idea that has taken hold of the middle-class woman is completely devoid of interest, for she knows that she is no more dependent on her husband than he is on her; and she is perfectly satisfied, if he is a decent, hard-working man, with her contract.

Nevertheless, the idea of financial independence is a new idea working in a mass of women, and nothing is more powerful in the world than an idea, and nothing in the world can stop it; not armies of soldiers or massed battalions of husbands. The husbands of England and America may muster their forces in opposition to it, just as the armies of the Allies did against the French Revolution. They will fail to conquer it; their opposition will only fan the flame; they had much better temporise, negotiate, draw up a new treaty between the sexes and sign a new charter of marriage.

I am sorry for the men. Here they are between their old-fashioned and their modern wives, many of them with wives who are half old-fashioned and half new-fangled. They are having a very thin time. It is especially hard on them just now because they are tired to death. They *(Continued overleaf)*

"Women have discovered that their homes don't fall to pieces because they leave them at nine every morning. They have found that their children don't languish, but flourish on a less concentrated diet of mother love"

Illustration by Charles Robinson, R.I.

Financial Independence for Wives

(Continued)

have been getting steadily more tired for the last twenty years, while their women have been growing steadily more vigorous. At present they are struggling with a world depression; before that there was the War. They went off in their millions during 1914–18 to get killed or wounded, and come back, if they did come back, exhausted; and they came back longing for a little peace and quiet, hoping to find their wives sitting at home with their children and their needlework, or busy with pots and pans. But while they were gone their women were having a lovely time, and quite a different sort of lovely time from the usual.

They gave up doing needlework, got out of the habit of sitting at home with their children, took to driving motor lorries, running canteens, nursing in hospitals, or packed the children off to school and took the places of their absent men in shops and factories. And they liked it. Of course the women liked it. Many of them were tasting for the first time the freedom of movement men have always had. It was glorious. Wives, mothers, daughters, went out each morning into the great, bustling, exciting world to earn their living; and at the end of the week they put their own wages or salaries in their own pockets and felt a glow of satisfaction they had never known before.

Most of the wives had to give it all up when the War ended and the men came home. The men demanded back their wives and the jobs their wives had taken. Friction resulted. The wives didn't like giving up their jobs or their freedom. The presence at home of even the most beloved husband seemed to many of them an inadequate compensation, after the first month or two, for the excitement and interest of the world of action.

Many of the women had had time to form new habits, and all had got hold of the new idea, and the idea had changed their whole conception of life, for it had changed their conception of themselves. Home, husband, children, all looked different, because they saw themselves differently in relation to each. They had discovered that their homes didn't fall to pieces because they left them at nine o'clock every morning. They had found out that their children didn't languish, but on the contrary flourished exceedingly, on a less concentrated diet of mother love; and it had occurred to them that it was humiliating to be obliged to ask a husband for pocket money. Women who had never questioned the respectability of being dependent on their husbands for food, clothing, and car fare, now felt that they no longer wanted to be so dependent on any man. They had found out, or thought they had found out, that they were as good as men, and quite as able to battle with the world. They had proved it, if not to the world of men, at any rate to themselves, and they were proud of it. So proud, that to go back to the old system of dress allowances, housekeeping allowances, and allowances for pin money, was too humiliating to be borne.

The man didn't understand at first. He didn't know what was the matter with his wife when she began talking about the humiliation of her position; but when he grasped her idea he found it very unpleasant. He put it to himself that his feelings were hurt. Here he had been working away in his office, too busy earning money for the family, or too worried about not making it, to think about anything else, and now she flung it back at him, said she didn't want him to pay for

her clothes. Why? What had he done? Hadn't he always paid her bills without a murmur? Well, sometimes he had remonstrated, but good heavens! if a man couldn't point out that to run up bills for dresses and hats and shoes—— That wasn't the point. She knew she had been extravagant. Well then, what was the point? The point was that she wanted her own money, wanted to pay for her own clothes, wanted to call her soul her own. When the point was explained to him, he was frightened. He didn't, if he was a nice man, quite know why, but he found his wife's declaration of independence intolerable. The truth was that it threatened his authority as head of the family, and cut across one of his deepest instincts, the instinct of possession. He didn't want her to feel that her soul or her body was her own, for underneath the charming, sensitive skin of this civilised being was primitive man with powerful, ineradicable, primitive instincts.

He wanted to provide for his wife, whether he loved her or not, because he wanted her to be dependent on him in either case, and all the more if she didn't love him. If he loved her and she loved him, it was a pleasure; if they didn't love each other, it was a safeguard. In either case her gesture of independence seemed to him dangerous, for he felt, subconsciously, that if his wife were self-supporting he would no longer have the right to control her activities. She would be really and practically free, and if she were free, she might well do anything. Could a woman be trusted with freedom? Could he be sure of her if she didn't have to depend on him for a roof over her head, and was out from under that roof all day rubbing elbows with a hundred other men? No, he couldn't. If she lived a man's life, she would inevitably acquire a man's point of view, and she might come to think, just as men did, just as he did, that casual infidelity was of no consequence.

An inquiry was held not long ago into the married state of two hundred men and women. A large number of questions were asked of each of these men and women, with the idea of finding out whether their marriage were a success, and if not, why. Subsequently a book was published summing up the conclusions of the investigators. They were not, to my mind, very illuminating or very surprising. The women's continual complaint of housework, running as it did through the entire investigation, was not surprising. What surprised me was that the happiest marriages seemed to be those in which the wife was entirely dependent on her husband: or to put it a little differently, the average chance of marriage happiness was greatest when the woman was financially dependent. It was less when the wife had money of her own. It was least when she went out and earned it.

I puzzled over these facts for some time. My own observation and experience proved to me that active, occupied women made happier wives and mothers than idle ones; that even professional women, such as doctors, whose calling made great demands on their time and energy, were, nevertheless, much appreciated by their husbands. I thought of all the women I knew who spent their time playing bridge or getting into trouble with other men, and I couldn't understand why the marriages of decent, self-respecting, intelligent women who contributed to the family budget should so often go wrong, until it dawned on me that it was the men, not the women,

who were unhappy in such marriages, and they were unhappy, not because they were neglected, but simply because they didn't like the idea of their wives contributing to the support of their homes, and were uncomfortable in houses they didn't pay for entirely themselves.

The whole question is inconceivably complicated, and it bids fair to become even more complicated. The men and the women of the world are out of step. Women are barging ahead, competing with men on their own ground, demanding more and more freedom, and claiming equal rights with men: and the men are digging their toes in, but into what? The economic world is changing so rapidly that already the women of yesterday seem to belong to a bygone age, and the fact stares one in the face that many women can get jobs in the new world when their men cannot.

Personally, I am all on the side of women's economic independence. I think it wrong that any woman should be dependent for her food and clothing and pin money on the pleasure of any man. I think it wrong that any man of property should leave more of that property to his sons than his daughters, and should expect some other men to come along and take his daughters off his hands. But it is useless to disguise the fact that if you are a kept woman, you are one, and you owe something for your keep. Your husband may adore you, that makes no difference. You are in his debt. You are eating his salt every day. He deserves at least the consideration you would show any other friend whose hospitality you accepted. If

you are in a person's debt, you must discharge that debt by services rendered, otherwise you are despicable. If you do not love a man, perhaps have even come to dislike him, yet let him give you everything you need and want, then you are contemptible unless you do your utmost to make his house pleasant to him; and if you do so with a bad grace, or with your tongue in your cheek and let him down on the sly, you are contemptible anyhow.

Men will have to get rid somehow of that old feeling of possession, and even of their old ideas of honour. There is no reason in a man's feeling uncomfortable and humiliated if his wife contributes to the family budget. There is not even any real reason why a man should find it intolerable to be supported by his wife. If he is a slacker, yes. If he sits at home for choice and lets his wife go out to work, yes. But if, as happens nowadays, he can't find a job and she can, why can't they both be glad that one of them is lucky? In a case of necessity any other feeling is nonsensical and all resentment or friction a stupid waste of energy.

Necessity, as I said before, simplifies all things. It will, I believe, settle this question of equality and the rights of wives. A wife has a right to equal responsibility with her husband if she is willing and able to assume it. She is his equal if she contributes equally to their combined needs, and her freedom will be exactly commensurate with her responsibility.

You see as the years roll on, we Grandma's need a Food that is easily digested and enjoyable at all times. We find Benger's a complete Food, fully nourishing and very delicious.

BENGER'S Food
Reg. Trade Mark

Write for the Benger's Food Booklet containing dainty recipes for nourishing light dishes that give digestive rest. Post free from Benger's Food, Ltd. Otter Works Manchester

It's Benger time when you are not so young as you were.

305

The Housekeeper's Dictionary *of* Facts

THE INSTITUTE SUGGESTS MID-DAY MENUS FOR A NURSERY SCHOOL

THIS nursery school is to be opened in a very short time for children from 2-5 years of age. We are to begin with forty children, gradually increasing in number until we reach our full complement of a hundred and twenty.

We are to give them a mid-day meal and each child is to have three-quarters of a pint of milk to drink. The school is in the midst of a slum area and we must endeavour to provide as much nourishment as possible in the one meal. So far no definite charge has been fixed but it will probably be about 2s. a week and we must try to be self-supporting. I should be most grateful if you could give me some idea of suitable and economical menus, with quantities for forty children, also some ideas as to ordering dry foods, meat and vegetables.

I have found a most reliable firm of wholesale grocers and a good butcher, but it is not easy to find a good greengrocer near at hand.

I do hope this will not give you too much trouble and shall be most grateful for your advice.

(Superintendent, Day Nursery School, Manchester.)

It is a little difficult to give you any very helpful advice with regard to catering costs for the nursery school, as you do not tell me whether the 2s. per head is to cover the cost of fuel and labour, or whether this sum is available for food. I conclude that the latter is the case, but

---

Suggested Meals for Children aged from 2-5 years

(Meals to cost 2s. weekly. A glass of milk for each child also provided)

Lentil Soup Wholemeal Bread Stewed Fruit and Junket	Vegetable Soup Bread and Butter Pudding
Puréed Haricot Beans or Green Peas Rice Pudding Baked Apple	Irish Stew (made with a little meat and plenty of bones, potatoes and onions) Milk Pudding
Carrot Milk Soup Mashed Potatoes Prune Purée	Milk and Macaroni Soup Wholemeal Bread Apple Purée
Steamed Fish Potatoes Milk Jelly, Fresh or Stewed Fruit	Minced Meat Cabbage and Potatoes Sago Pudding
Broth and Dumplings Blancmange and Fruit	
Pearl Barley Soup Apple Pudding	Vegetable Stew, with a little meat Suet Pudding
Potato Soup Wholemeal Bread Fresh or Stewed Fruit	Hot Pot Milk Pudding and Fruit

---

here again, I am not sure whether the cost of the milk to be given to each child is included. Further, you do not say whether five or six meals weekly are to be given, but I gather that there will be only five, thus making the daily amount available for each child just under 5d. I am afraid that in any case, for this sum, it will only be possible to provide the very simplest of meals, and I would suggest that roughly half the quantity of milk be used for making either milk soups or puddings, and the remainder given to the children to drink.

I am enclosing some suggestions for nourishing meals which I hope you will find helpful. It is impossible to give the costs very exactly, for prices of foodstuffs, etc., vary a good deal in different parts of the country. You should, however, find that when catering for as many as forty, you are able to buy advantageously.

I think it would probably be a good plan to make a good nourishing soup the basis of the meal, although when you are able to purchase white fish, such as fresh haddock, cod, etc., cheaply, then this could very well be included. At other times, minced meat would help to make a change.

It would also be advisable to let the children have fresh fruit occasionally, and at times when oranges can be purchased inexpensively, at ½d. each, I think it would be a great advantage from the dietetic point of view to provide one for each child. Wholemeal bread would also be an advantage, as this is rich in vitamin B.

COSTS AND QUANTITIES FOR TEN OF THE ABOVE MENUS

	s.	d.
Lentil Soup		
1¼ lb. lentils		4
1 lb. carrots		1
12 pints water		
Bones, dripping		9
1 lb. onions		1
Seasonings		1
Wholemeal Bread (2½ lb.)		6
Stewed Fruit		
10 lb. apples	2	6
2½ lb. Demerara sugar		7½
Junket		
15 pints of milk	3	9
Rennet		3
Milk to drink (15 pints)	3	9
	12	8½
Puréed Haricot Beans with Dripping		
3 lb. beans	1	0
1 lb. spinach		4
Onion		1
Dripping		8
Rice Pudding		
10 pints milk	2	6
20 oz. rice		6
1 lb. Demerara sugar		3
Baked Apples (10 lb.)	2	6
Milk to drink (20 pints)	5	0
	12	10
Carrot Milk Soup		
5 lb. carrots		5
1 onion		1
9 pints milk	2	3
5 pints water		
4 oz. flour		½
10 lb. potatoes		10
8 oz. butter		7
1 pint milk		3
Prune Purée		
10 lb. prunes	5	0
2½ lb. sugar		7½
Milk to drink (20 pints)	5	0
	15	1
Steamed Fish		
20 fillets cod or other cheap fish (10 lb.)	5	0
10 lb. potatoes		10
8 oz. butter		7
1 pint milk		3

	s.	d.
Milk Jelly		
2 pints water		
1 lb. sugar		3
16 pints milk	4	0
8 oz. gelatine	1	0
Flavouring		1
Apples or oranges	2	6
Milk to drink (13 pints)	3	3
	17	9
	s.	d.
Pearl Barley Soup		
2 sheep's heads	1	6
1 lb. onions		1
2 lb. carrots		2
1 lb. turnips		1
1 lb. pearl barley		6
Bunch chopped parsley		1
5 pints milk	1	3
10 pints water		
Seasoning		
Apple Pudding		
10 lb. apples	2	6
3 lb. flour		4½
1 lb. suet		8
Baking powder		2
Boiled Custard		
5 pints milk	1	3
Custard powder		3
3 lb. sugar		9
Milk to drink (20 pints)	5	0
	14	7½
Potato Soup		
2 lb. onions		2
8 lb. potatoes		8
8 pints milk	2	0
8 oz. butter		7
Seasoning		1
10 pints water		
Wholemeal Bread		6
Oranges	3	4
Milk to drink (22 pints)	5	6
	12	10
Vegetable Soup		
1 lb. dried peas		4
6 lb. mixed root vegetables		9
2 lb. spinach and 1 head celery		9

	s.	d.
Bread and Butter Pudding		
1 lb. dried fruits (sultanas)		9
2 lb. bread		3½
½ lb. butter		7
10 pints milk	2	6
10 eggs (when cheap)	1	0
1 lb. sugar		3
Milk to drink (20 pints)	5	0
	12	2½
Irish Stew	s.	d.
10 lb. potatoes		10
3 lb. onions		3
5 lb. neck mutton (middle cut)	3	9
Milk Pudding		
18 oz. sago		6
10 pints milk	2	6
1 lb. sugar		3
Milk to drink (20 pints)	5	0
	13	1
Minced Meat	s.	d.
6 lb. Scotch collops	6	0
7 cabbages	1	6
10 lb. potatoes (mashed)		10
Sago Pudding		
10 pints milk	2	6
1¼ lb. sago		6
1 lb. sugar		6
Milk to drink (20 pints)	5	0
	16	10
Vegetable Stew	s.	d.
3 lb. stewing steak	3	0
4 lb. potatoes (cut very small)		4
6 lb. grated carrots		9
Suet Pudding		
3 lb. flour		4½
3 lb. syrup	1	0
1 lb. suet		8
Milk to drink (30 pints)	7	6
	13	7½
Hot Pot	s.	d.
4 lb. steak or leg of mutton	4	0
6 lb. root vegetables		9

The Housekeeper's Dictionary *of* Facts

*T*HE hood of my car, which is a tourer, has become bleached by exposure to the weather. This hood is of untreated cotton, and I am anxious to dye it black. Could you please recommend any preparation or dye for the purpose?
Middlesex.

With regard to a preparation for treating the hood of your car, I think a good waterproofing paint is what you want. We know of one which costs 9s. 6d. per ¼ gallon and 19s. per ½ gallon. The smaller quantity would be sufficient for a 2-seater car, but you would probably need ½ gallon for a 4-seater. I am afraid I have had no experience of this paint, but it is supplied by a reliable firm, and I have no doubt it is satisfactory.

An alternative suggestion would be to use linseed oil mixed with lamp black. The latter, which is a powder, should be stirred into the linseed oil until the correct shade is obtained, and should then be applied to the hood with a brush. This preparation should render the hood waterproof.

I have just ordered a refrigerator and I should be very grateful if you would tell me whether keeping meat in it for several days is advisable, or whether it destroys any of the beneficial qualities of fresh meat? When fresh meat has been in the refrigerator for, say, four or five days, has it then the properties of cold storage meat or of fresh meat? Has it to be thawed, or in any other way differently treated from fresh meat before cooking? Is it as healthy to feed young children with as ordinary fresh meat? Can it be taken out of the refrigerator first before cooking or would this render it tough and tasteless like some cold-storage meat? In this hot climate it would be a godsend to be able to keep meat for several days in the refrigerator, so long as none of its essential properties were destroyed.

Another query I wish to raise is: does putting milk in a refrigerator destroy all harmful germs? Is it as safe as boiling? Or is it better to boil the milk first before putting it in? Some sterilisation of milk is necessary in this country. Does refrigeration destroy any essential properties of milk for children?

I should also be very grateful if at any time you could let me have recipes for making the following:—
(1) Curd Cheese ⎫ *in small quantities*
(2) Cream Cheese ⎭ *for household use.*
The refrigerator queries, however, are far the most important. I am a regular subscriber to your magazine, and I shall be most grateful for this information.

S. Rhodesia.

I do not think you will find that the chilling of meat in any way destroys its qualities, and I never hesitate to recommend the use of chilled meat, both for children and adults, when for

NEW IDEAS FOR FAMILY MEALS

Why not take a cookery "refresher" course this spring? Housewives will be interested to know that at Good Housekeeping School of Cookery it is possible to obtain instruction for any desired period—from one half-day to a course of a month or more, and a great advantage of the lessons is that they may be commenced at any time convenient to the student. For those who wish to specialise in Domestic Science and later to take posts as lady-cooks in Restaurants, lady-cook house-keepers in Schools, Institutions, etc., a year's combined course in cookery, laundry-work and housecraft can be arranged, while a special course can be taken by those who wish to obtain posts as cake-makers in Tea-rooms, and Home-made Cake Shops. For particulars of fees, etc., apply to the Director, Good Housekeeping Institute, 49, Wellington Street, W.C.2

reasons of economy or to meet other conditions, this is necessary. After taking out of cold storage, such meat should be thawed slowly before being cooked; it then requires to be treated and cooked in the same way as fresh meat. As I think you will appreciate, however, when meat is kept in cold storage, it is maintained at the desired temperature without appreciable variation, but with a household type of refrigerator, which is opened and closed during the day, I am afraid that even when a thermostat is fitted it is not possible to maintain such an even temperature.

The placing of milk in a refrigerator does not actually destroy any of the germs present, although it retards their further development. Keeping it cold, therefore, does not replace the necessity for pasteurising or boiling, if the milk supply is in any way questionable. Unless milk which is equivalent in cleanliness to the British Grade A Certified milk is available, it is advisable either to scald or pasteurise it. This should be done as soon as the milk is received, and afterwards it should be allowed to cool before placing in the refrigerator. Keeping milk cool in a refrigerator does not in any way destroy its essential properties, although, as I think you will appreciate, heating does, and consequently when boiled or pasteurised milk is used, especially in the case of young children, it is also important to give them orange juice, or other fruit juice which is rich in vitamin C.

With regard to the making of Curd and Cream Cheese, I would suggest that you write to the Ministry of Agriculture and Fisheries, 10 Whitehall Place, London, S.W.1, who issue leaflets giving information on this subject. The leaflets you may care to purchase are No. 179—*The Making of Soft and Cream Cheese*—and Advisory Leaflet No. 133, *Small-Holder Cheese.* No charge is made for these, but it is necessary to enclose a stamped, addressed envelope when applying for them.

I should be very grateful for your advice regarding the warming of a small nursery. It is a room roughly nine feet square, with windows facing south about six or seven feet wide. The hot tank served by a boiler, kept in day and night, is on the floor of the airing cupboard eight feet from the wall of the nursery. Could you give me any idea of the cost of installing a radiator? Would this be the cheapest way of keeping the room warm, and would it give sufficient warmth for bathing baby, etc.? There is a gas point in the nursery, but no fireplace. I know that to fix a gas fire or gas radiator would mean a smaller initial outlay, but as my elder son starts boarding school very shortly, the need for economy of running costs is a great consideration.

Perhaps you would also suggest the best place for the radiator, and if it would entail much construction, alteration of walls, etc., in installation.
Isleworth.

I find it a little difficult to advise you with regard to warming the nursery, particularly as I am uncertain whether a flue is available. While hot-water radiators would be very satisfactory for raising the temperature to, say, 50 or 55° F., personally, I would not suggest relying on these entirely. A most healthful way of warming such a room would be to use the radiator only for raising the temperature as mentioned above, to about 50° F., and then installing a gas fire, provided with a flue for removing the products of combustion, or an electric radiator for any further heating required. I conclude, however, that you would not care to go to the trouble and expense of a double installation of this type. Either a gas or electric fire alone would also be suitable, but without knowing the price of current or gas in your district it is impossible to say whether they would prove economical as regards running costs. Another suggestion would be to install a slow-combustion stove, as this is considered ideal for nursery use, and, indeed, for any room which is only used intermittently throughout the day. We have now tested a number of slow-combustion stoves, all of which I have marked on the enclosed list of our Approved Appliances. These are all economical in the consumption of fuel, and they can be kept in day and night. They can also be opened up to give a pleasant fire, when this is desired. During the course of our tests on the above, we have found that the best results are obtained by using a hard Welsh coal, of which I am enclosing details. With this, very little attention is needed, although when an open fire is required it is sometimes advisable to use a little ordinary household coal. This is not, however, essential if a really good red fire is obtained before opening up the stove. An advantage of using this type of fuel is that it is smokeless, and consequently the chimney does not require sweeping.

Guided by the experienced wisdom of

Mrs. 'X' RESOLVES that

1934 • 1934 • 1934 • 1934 • 1934 • 1934 • 1934 • 1934 • 1934

NEW YEAR resolutions may be out of date and in any case, unfortunately, are often made to be broken. It is, however, by no means waste of time for those in charge of a household to " take stock " occasionally and to make any necessary readjustments. Too many women, having organised their housework, finances and other departments some time ago, are now content to let matters take their own course, in spite of the fact that personal and world conditions have altered very considerably during the last fifteen years. There is no better time to take such work in hand than the New Year. Anyone who knows herself rather apt to procrastinate in such perhaps not altogether pleasurable occupations, might do worse than follow the slogan, " Do it now."

We will consider first matters of household and personal finance and would suggest that readers as far as possible resolve to avoid getting behind-hand with their household accounts. All housekeeping bills and accounts should be paid weekly or monthly without fail. If one finds oneself getting behind-hand with these, it obviously means that unless the housekeeping allowance can be increased one is overspending—possibly only very slightly but enough, by the end of six or twelve months, to put one's accounts out completely.

Too much emphasis can hardly be laid on the advisability of setting aside some definite weekly sum for household expenses and keeping within this as rigidly as possible. Looking over last year's accounts will, in many cases, reveal at once where any over-spending has occurred. It may be found that the butcher's bill is out of all proportion to the others, or may be (and this often the case) that expenditure on oddments is surprisingly high. Most cases of over-spending, however, occur where no accounts have been kept, or they have only been kept in a very perfunctory way. There is no doubt that the actual keeping of household accounts is a deterrent against over-spending and does in some inexplicable way very materially help to guard against it. So strongly do we feel at the Institute that simple home accounts should be more commonly kept that for several years past we have published a small home account book. This is combined with a diary and is of a convenient size for carrying in a handbag; therefore all amounts spent can be readily jotted down at the time, and a record kept. The habit of entering up expenditure in this way soon grows, and the average person begins to acquire an interest in keeping figures within bounds and whenever possible showing a small balance week by week—a valuable reserve for times when unexpected expenses crop up.

The following is a typical letter from one of our readers who, if she had budgeted her income carefully, should have had no difficulty in making ends meet. As it is, she is in real difficulties, with an overdraft at the bank and the obligation to pay instalments on various purchases, including a vacuum cleaner and a car. Purchase by instalment is a very convenient and useful arrangement for many people, but in our opinion it should be unnecessary for anyone with an income of over £1,000 a year to need to make such a purchase as a vacuum cleaner in this way. On such an income there should be no difficulty whatever in saving sufficient to make a reserve

1. Plan and rigidly adhere, as far as possible, to her estimated household budget for the year.

2. Make an inventory of household giving particulars of any necessary seem to be required, and which

3. Revise the household routine and if necessary re-plan maids' time-tables to suit new conditions.

4. Read an up-to-date book on food catering in conformity with this, diet a full vitamin ration, adequate

5. Avoid waste of food by watching the larder, and learn attractive ways of réchaufféing " left overs."

the Institute,

she will . . .

1934 • 1934 • 1934 • 1934 • 1934 • 1934 • 1934 • 1934 • 1934 • 1934

BY P. L. GARBUTT, A.I.C.

First Class Diploma King's College of Household and Social Science; late staff Battersea Polytechnic

DEPARTMENT OF HOUSEHOLD ENGINEERING AND HOUSECRAFT

Good Housekeeping Institute, conducted by D. D. Cottington Taylor, Certificate of King's College of Household and Social Science; First Class Diplomas in Cookery, High Class Cookery, Laundrywork, House-wifery, A.R S.I., 49 Wellington Street, Strand, W.C.2

and kitchen stocks. Draw up a list replacements and fresh purchases which can be bought during the coming year.

values and improve the standard of taking special pains to include in the roughage and plenty of mineral salts.

fund for small household and other purchases as and when they are required.

An extract from the letter referred to reads as follows: "My husband has a salary of £1,200 per annum and yet we never seem able to make ends meet. Although we have no expensive amusements and entertain very little, we have at present an over-draft of £55 and as we are moving to the country and shall have additional expenses in setting up a fresh home, we are afraid this must be increased to about £100 within the next month or so. I have very great difficulty in making my housekeeping cheque of £23 10s. monthly meet the demands made on it and very often have to run a small overdraft myself.

"The household consists of myself, husband, baby of 14 months and one maid. We should be very grateful if you could advise us on what you consider to be a fair and reasonable proportionment of our income."

This letter reveals a very unsatisfactory state of affairs which it should have been quite possible to avoid if reasonable care had been taken earlier in budgeting the income wisely.

Food, wages, laundry and dress are the items for which the average woman pays out of her house-keeping and personal allowances. Other expenditure is not of such direct interest to her as she is not as a rule actually responsible for paying rates, rent, gas, electricity, income tax, car expenses, etc.

With care there should be no difficulty in pro-viding adequate and varied menus in the typical middle-class home of five or six persons for from 10s. to 15s. per head upwards. The lower figure mentioned is, of course, only sufficient for the pur-chase of comparatively simple and plain food, but if this is bought advantageously, really healthful and interesting menus can be evolved.

In connection with the question of catering we might remind readers here of the advisability of making a strict resolve to look through the contents of the larder or refrigerator each morning and to plan out, or at any rate adjust, the day's menus with a view to using up any "left overs." Neglect of this very simple item in the daily routine leads to much wastage in countless households.

Further, one might suggest to everyone, particu-larly those with children, the advisability of obtaining and reading some simple but really up-to-date book on food and its relation to health.

The first of a practical series of articles on diet for special cases and ages

IT IS NOT NECESSARY TO BE FAT

By

DR. ELIZABETH SLOAN CHESSER

Some races, some families run to fat. If, for generations, a stock has lived lazily and easily, eaten plentifully and frequently, it becomes "chubby." Contrast the Eastern races with Scottish Highlanders a hundred years back. Butter and beer helped the Germans to increase in girth after twenty-five years of age. In the years following the War there was an extraordinary change for the better amongst German femininity. I was in the Rhineland very frequently after the War. I noticed those young, golden haired, square-figured women slimming in a few short years, owing to two factors. They dieted and they began, in tens of thousands, with the example of the British, to practise physical culture and to take up athletics.

With the exception of what we would call "pathological" cases of obesity (fatness due to disease of internal secretory glands, for example) very few women would get fat if:

(1) They were sufficiently "exercised" in mind and body.

(2) They ceased to be over-clothed and had regular air baths and sun baths.

(3) They gave up that most pernicious vice of civilisation, superalimentation, or in simple language, over-eating.

Obesity is the natural consequence of insufficient output of muscular energy, combined with excessive intake of energy-producing food. This excess of food cannot be oxygenated or burnt up in the body. It is, therefore, deposited as fat. The cells of the tissues are filled with an oily substance which is deposited as thousand and thousands of little cushions, which swell and swell around chest, abdomen and hips, under the chin, and the cheeks till they assume mountainous proportions.

Curious, is it not, that we women fail to see truth in the mirror, fail to realise the significance of the tight belts and bands and fastenings? The human mind has a wonderful faculty of self-deception. Is it lack of interest in one's looks; or is it vanity? Let each woman answer the question for herself. Do not, however, let us forget the medical significance of fat cells permeating, pressing, and pushing into the vital organs, cutting down the expectation of health and life itself. We must not allow ourselves to remain fat or to get fat.

The scales are not necessarily the best estimation of the ideal weight for any individual. The heaviness or slenderness of bones and joints, the strength and breadth of the skeleton, the muscular condition, are all concerned with the number of stones we weigh at twenty-five or fifty years of age. One authority estimates that a healthy person should weigh two pounds to each inch of height. There is neither necessity nor desirability to increase in weight or girth after we reach twenty-five. To keep slim is a matter of wise living and perfect diet. This does not mean underfeeding. It means *restriction* of food in every case of obesity not due to disease.

Here let me emphasise the wisdom and the necessity of every woman who intends to reduce her weight asking her family doctor to examine her and advise her with regard to her fitness for taking exercise, and to recommend what, in his opinion, is desirable in the way of massage, ultra-violet or electrical treatments. In some cases, periods of fasting after judicious purgation are valuable, but, in my opinion, short fasts are preferable.

A Day's Menu for a Person Wishing to Reduce Weight

Breakfast.
Orange or grape-fruit.
Piece of crisp, non-fattening bread.
Pat of butter.
Coffee or tea without sugar or milk.
Luncheon.
White fish or lean ham. (No gravy.)
Salad. One slice of whole-wheat bread.
Cheese and breakfast biscuit. [skim milk.
Black coffee or glass of
Dinner.
Medium serving of lean beef or chop or fowl.
Green vegetables, salad. Thin slice of toast.
Pineapple, apple or orange.

FOODS ALLOWED

Soup. In small quantity. Mutton or chicken broth with parsley.
Eggs. Boiled or poached.
Green vegetables. Cabbage, celery, sprouts, salads (peas and beans sparingly).
Fruits. Currants, raspberries, strawberries, apples, oranges, grape-fruit, water melon, pineapple.
Fish. Sole, whiting, cod, plaice, lobsters, turbot, oysters, haddock, river trout.
Meats. Beef, mutton, rabbit, fowl, game, lean ham.
Sweets. Jellies and a little junket. Stewed fruit without sugar.
Cheese. Small quantities.

FOODS NOT ALLOWED

Soups. Thick, rich varieties.
Eggs. Buttered eggs, omelettes.
Root Vegetables. Beet, carrot, turnip, potatoes.
Fruits. Bananas, figs, dried fruits, peaches, apricots.
Fish. Herring, mackerel, eels, sardines, salmon, halibut.
Meats. Pork, hot-pot, sweetbread, oxtail, sausages, liver, fat bacon, goose.
Sweets. Macaroni, rice, tapioca, and sago puddings, cakes, boiled or steamed puddings, dried fruits, pastries.

Youthful grace is every woman's ideal; attention to diet and exercise will help her to achieve it

THE world-wide fight against obesity is an admirable thing. Nobody should be complacent over getting fat. The woman who has more than a light covering of adipose tissue under her skin, who has lost contour and become lumpy, even slightly lumpy, is in danger. It is a short step to obesity, which, if not a recognised disease, is what physicians call a syndrome, a menace to health and efficiency, not to speak of beauty.

The world of women is fortunately getting thinner. "Slimming," of course, has its dangers. If accomplished by living on a diet which the physiologist calls starvation or famine diet, combined with purgation, the result is emaciation, perhaps serious illness. With the disappearance of supporting fat, signs and symptoms of enteroptosis appear, i.e. dropped colon as well as flabby neck, sunken cheeks, and soft, unhealthy flesh all over the body. The reason is that the disappearance of semi-liquid adipose tissue is not associated with toning-up of muscles and organ supports. In slimming, health is often jeopardised. To feel ill and look unhappy—is it worth while? Better surely to stay fat than to lose weight at all costs. Out of such soliloquy, depression is born.

Let us, therefore, talk constructively. Three factors go to the cure of obesity: first, ill health, especially self-poisoning or auto-intoxication, must be attended to; secondly, exercise must be regulated and increased as the muscles lose fat and flabbiness; thirdly, the right diet should be adopted so that two or three pounds weight per week is lost—and ought not to be regained.

Before discussing the question of diet, let us consider the causes of obesity, which are various, and how best to prevent it, in middle age especially.

In this, as most things about our bodies, the hereditary factor tells.

138

The Housekeeper's Dictionary *of* Facts

LETTERS FROM READERS, WITH THE INSTITUTE'S REPLIES

A Letter from Bromley

*I*N connection with my work as domestic science mistress, I have been asked a number of rather puzzling questions lately, and I would be most grateful if you could answer them for me. I was once a student at the Institute, and turn once again to you for help.

1. Are vitamins destroyed when foods are canned? Does hot fruit juice and sugar have any effect on tin? (a) To destroy the vitamins. (b) To give anyone indigestion.

2. In the ordinary way, if food is turned out of a tin and kept in a cool place, how long should it keep? Why is it that condensed milk seems to keep indefinitely?

3. A cake was made with a marzipan filling containing nuts (walnuts). After a week or ten days, the marzipan filling tasted bitter and rather sour round the nuts. Was this just the result of the nuts going bad, or is there some kind of fermentation caused by the oils and sugar?

With regard to the tinned foods, a certain proportion of the vitamins is probably destroyed, but research seems to indicate that such foods, having been heated and sterilised out of contact with the air, there is smaller destruction than when foods are cooked in an open saucepan, exposed to the atmosphere.

Tin is a metal which is very little acted on by food acids, etc., but I conclude you are probably thinking of tinned iron. If the tin is worn off in any parts, there might be a slight chemical action between an acid fruit juice and the metal, but in any case, any traces of dissolved salts would be harmless.

The question of the destruction of vitamins in the hot fruit juice would depend entirely on the temperature to which the juice is heated and the length of time it is maintained at this temperature, although boiling the fruit juice for any period of time would result in a certain amount of vitamin destruction.

Tinned foods, when properly prepared and sterilised, can be kept indefinitely, but once the tin is opened they should not be kept longer than fresh foods. An open tin of condensed milk certainly keeps very well, and this is largely due to the fact that, on opening the tin, it is completely sterile, whereas the freshest and purest Certified Grade A milk will probably contain a large number of bacteria, amounting to possibly as many as 30,000 per cubic centimetre. If the milk has not been so carefully produced, it may contain millions per c.c. and then, of course, its keeping qualities are likely to be far from good. In the case of sweetened condensed milk, the added sugar is also helpful in aiding its preservation.

It is a little difficult to account definitely for the bitter taste which has developed in your nut cake. Walnuts, of course, normally have a slightly bitter flavour, and if they are not perfectly

---

EARLY ORANGES MAKE EXCELLENT MARMALADES

You can start at once on your 1935 stock of preserves—but first of all you want the best recipes and most up-to-date information on the theory and practice of the subject. All this will be found in the Institute's newest publication, which, besides marmalades of all kinds, contains dozens of new and old recipes for jams and jellies and detailed instructions for canning and fruit bottling. The price is 1s. or 1s. 2d. post free. Send to-day for

JAMS, JELLIES AND FRUIT BOTTLING

edited by D. D. Cottington Taylor

49 Wellington Street, Strand, W.C.2

---

fresh this is increasingly noticeable. Further, the ground almonds, used for the marzipan, may possibly not have been in the freshest condition, and these again tend to become a little bitter with prolonged keeping. I do not think you need fear that the nuts were necessarily bad or that any kind of undesirable fermentation has taken place.

A Letter from Datchet

1. How should a pig-skin case be cleaned which has various travel stains on it?

2. Can washing silk garments that have been redyed be washed as before, or must they be dry cleaned?

3. Has custard made from powder any sort of food value?

4. The water here is very hard and we wondered if it is worth while to instal a softener, or is it best to have a tub for rain-water? If one instals a softener, does one need a separate model for each tap?

1. With regard to the pig-skin bag, it is a little difficult to advise you without knowing the nature of the stains and marks on it. If these are of a greasy nature, they could be rubbed cautiously with a cloth dipped in a little grease solvent, such as carbon tetrachloride. On the other hand, if the bag is just slightly soiled all over, you may find that you are able to improve the appearance by rubbing over with a sparing application of shoe cream.

2. Provided a reliable make of dye has been used, it is, as a rule, possible to wash silk garments satisfactorily after home-dyeing. Care should be taken to avoid using too hot water, and if there is any tendency for the colours to run, it should only be lukewarm.

3. Custard powders, as a rule, consist essentially of starch, often in the

---

form of cornflour; consequently the food value is chiefly due to the carbohydrate present, but as milk is used in preparing the custard, it will have this additional value.

4. As you tell me that the water in your district is very hard, I certainly think it would be worth while installing a water-softener, as the use of softened water will effect considerable saving in soap, soda, etc. It is preferable to have this attached to the main, otherwise you will need a separate softener for each tap.

A Letter from Dublin

Could you give me any enlightenment in the matter of cream machines and their products? I have hesitated to buy a machine to make cream as I find it hard to believe that the resultant emulsion is really cream. I wonder if you have made any tests of this so-called cream, and if so, what is the food value as compared with real cream? My friends say they can make 1s. 6d. worth of cream for 3d., and if this is so, why put the expense of churning to the dairyman's bill? Surely there is a catch somewhere, and I should be most grateful if you could give me some information about the matter. Also, if you have found the manufactured cream satisfactory, which cream-maker do you recommend for ordinary family use?

I do not think you need hesitate to purchase a cream-maker, for the reconstituted cream has identical food value with the fresh dairy product.

Cream, as no doubt you are aware, consists essentially of the fatty constituents of milk, and in using one of the small cream-makers, butter and milk are emulsified together. We find that such cream can be made for about half the price of fresh dairy cream, and provided it is allowed to stand for twenty-four hours in a cold place, preferably in a refrigerator, it can be whipped successfully. The flavour is indistinguishable from fresh cream and it can be used for all cooking and table purposes, the only disadvantage being that it sometimes tends to separate out a little when used in conjunction with hot liquids such as coffee.

As mentioned above, we find the price works out at about half the cost of fresh dairy cream. On the face of it, it would certainly appear as though fresh cream should be cheaper, as its production involves no churning process, but it must be remembered that fresh cream is one of the most perishable of all commodities, especially now that addition of preservatives is prohibited, whereas butter can be kept for a considerably longer period, and therefore sold as the demand arises.

There necessarily being a good deal of waste with exceptionally perishable foods, they are as a rule "costed" to allow for this.

We enclose a list of our Approved Appliances, which contains the names of several cream-making machines which have our fullest recommendation.

You can forget the dinner . . .

It's cooking itself in the NEW WORLD with the 'REGULO' CONTROL

Automatic Cooking—that is one of the advantages you gain by using the "New World" Gas Cooker with its 'Regulo' oven-heat control. Even complete dinners can be cooked simultaneously without any attention, and numerous suitable menus are available.

The "New World" is economical, too, due to its single oven burner and direct bottom-flue-outlet. Cooking also is *better*, the food is more appetizing, more tasty.

And the Gas Match enables you to light the burners without the bother of matches.

"New World" Gas Cookers with their shining porcelain-enamel finish are easily cleaned and keep their attractive appearance. Your Gas Showrooms can give you full particulars. Post the coupon below for Free Recipe Book.

'Regulo'-controlled
NEW WORLD
GAS COOKERS
Radiation LTD.

NEW WORLD
Series 2

Radiation

COUPON FOR FREE RECIPE BOOKLET
To : Radiation Ltd. (Publications Dept. 42 C), 164, Queen Victoria Street, London, E.C.4
Please send your free Recipe Book.

Name_____

Address_____

The Housekeeper's Dictionary *of* Facts

READERS' LETTERS AND OTHER INTERESTING INFORMATION

WILL you tell me if any other than cane sugar can be used for jams, etc.? One reads so much about its being the worst kind of sugar to be dealt with by the digestive organs, I wondered if a better kind could be used with the same results. I use syrup for sweetening puddings for the children. If you can give me any information on the subject I shall be truly grateful.
Plymouth.

I do not think there is any need for you to worry about the effects of cane sugar, for this can be satisfactorily dealt with by the digestive organs of any normal person. It is true that it is one of the more complex of sugars ordinarily found, but this is no reason why it should not be included in the diet, although in certain cases of illness and before exceptionally strenuous and exhaustive exercise a simpler sugar, such as glucose, has the advantage of being more readily absorbed by the human system.

In milk, whether human, cows' or dried milk, the infant finds lactose, a special form of sugar, but by the time he is old enough to be put on to more complex foods, i.e. when about nine months old, the digestion is capable of dealing with small amounts of cane sugar. As the child grows older, more and more of this sugar can be taken. To try entirely to substitute a simpler sugar for cane sugar would be to spare the digestive organs some of their normal functions.

Of course, too much cane sugar is bad for the health and therefore sweets should be given sparingly, though it is not necessary to eliminate them.

If, however, any child shows a digestive intolerance towards cane sugar, it is a different matter, and a doctor should be consulted immediately, as this would indicate some organic trouble. But for any normal, healthy being, after the first few months of life cane sugar is in no way harmful, in fact, by excluding it from the diet definite harm may be done.

A Suggestion for a Nursery Frieze

A reader has sent us the following idea for using the covers of GOOD HOUSEKEEPING, which may appeal to other readers to whom it had not already occurred.

"I have read with great interest your article on nursery friezes and it recalls to me an expedient I used for my own little boy's nursery some six years ago. I wanted to give the child as beautiful a room as possible, but could afford very little outlay. My husband treated the walls with washable distemper in light primrose and I pasted round the room a frieze of silhouettes of children cut from the covers of GOOD HOUSEKEEPING. The result was utterly charming and the figures became real friends to the little boy, who used to

---

THE BEST HOLIDAY ANYONE CAN HAVE

is a complete change from the usual round of one's existence; so there might be some sense in the suggestion that those who do not go to school in term time might do so in the holidays! Good Housekeeping School of Cookery is open all the year round, and one may take long, short or very short courses in any chosen branches of the subject. Write to the Director for full particulars of fees and other details, at Good Housekeeping Institute, 49 Wellington St., London, W.C.2

lie in bed and prattle to them. Placed like that on a plain background, the artistry of the sketches showed to great advantage and the fact that no two figures were alike caused my friends to wonder how I obtained them.

"I feel quite sure that in these days of financial stress this idea might appeal to many, for the beauty and gaiety of these sketches make them just right for nursery use."

Cleaning Old Lace

I am soon to be married and have been lent a short front veil of lace, a hundred years old. Some time ago this veil was sent to be cleaned, and as a result a number of brown marks have been left. If the lace were washed in bran water, would these disappear?
Newcastleton.

Without actually seeing the veil it is difficult to advise you as to how best to treat it. I should imagine, however, that provided the greatest care is exercised it could be washed satisfactorily by squeezing gently in warm soapy water, using a pure soap product.

Care should be taken to keep the lace under the water while it is being cleaned, as if portions are lifted out, a certain amount of strain is liable to be set up. When quite clean, excess moisture should be carefully pressed rather than wrung out, and the veil should be rinsed in two or three fresh waters. After removing excess moisture as before, avoiding any wringing lest this damage the fibres, the veil should be spread out on a flat surface and carefully examined. If any of the brown marks are still there, these could be treated with a diluted solution of hydrogen peroxide. The ordinary solution, as purchased, should be diluted in water 4 or 5 times, and the veil allowed to soak in this for a short while. The hydrogen peroxide should

---

then be rinsed away with plenty of fresh water.

In the case of very delicate old lace, it is sometimes recommended that it be washed in a large bottle with a wide neck, such as those used for fruit bottling. If shaken up in this with warm soap and water, the lace is cleaned with minimum handling and therefore there is less likelihood of strain. Rinsing can be carried out in the same jar.

If you require the veil slightly stiffened, it should be treated with gum water, prepared by dissolving 2 oz. best white gum arabic crystals (acacia or plum tree gum) in ½ pint hot water and adding two or three tablespoonfuls of this to every quart of water used for the final rinse. The lace should then be pinned out carefully into shape on a flat surface and pressed lightly, after removing the pins, with a warm iron when nearly dry. If it requires repairing or mending, I would suggest that you get in touch with the firm whose name I enclose.

Florentines

Will you be so good as to send me a recipe for Florentines? They are a flat nut confection coated on one side with chocolate. I always find your recipes most helpful.
Cambridge.

As requested, I have pleasure in sending you a recipe for Florentines, and I hope that you will find it satisfactory. Prepare equal quantities of walnuts and almonds. Chop the former roughly, blanch, split and brown the latter. Mix together, using sufficient honey to bind. Spread on an oiled tin and bake in a fairly moderate oven until brown and set. When cold, remove from the tin and spread with chocolate previously melted. When doing this, do not allow the chocolate to become hot and liquid. Turn on to a cake wire and leave until the chocolate has set on the underside.

When Curtain Making

If when sewing curtain rings on to heavy material such as velvet, velour, etc., a fine wire is used instead of thread, the wire will hold as long as the curtains last. The wire end can be used as a needle and only a very few stitches will be needed.

Silver and Silverplate

It is sometimes difficult to know where to send articles of silver and silver plate for repairs and alterations with the assurance that they will be executed really neatly and well. Some readers may like to know of a firm of old established craftsmen to whom such work can be safely entrusted. Satisfaction is guaranteed to customers, and special attention is given to repairs of antique goods and also in renovating and repairing ivory carvings and other valuable articles. The name will be sent on application to the Institute.

When Women Borrow

A word to the wise on the "how, when and where" of raising money

By Chandos Bidwell

BORROWED money may be very beneficial to the borrower, or it may cause her only vexation. The reason for the borrowing, the financial position of the borrower at the time, the arrangements she makes to repay and the source from which the loan is obtained are the factors which place it in one category or the other.

To borrow without knowing how the debt is to be repaid is a serious folly. Women who, to satisfy a passing fancy, have borrowed money without having property or securities readily saleable or definite prospects of surplus income with which to repay, have bitterly regretted their action.

From carefully considered borrowing, however, only good can come. It enables the borrower to achieve a desired end or enjoy a comfort when the longing for it is keenest, it satisfies the lender and may be a public benefit by making dormant money work and employ labour.

Whether it is prudent or not to borrow depends on individual circumstances. To women with no capital and no surplus of income over expenditure, borrowing in any form can bring only worry and stress.

To those with ample resources, borrowing to satisfy any reasonable need cannot be imprudent. Many, nevertheless, go in need of some special comfort rather than borrow against the security of those resources, although they can as easily repay the loan out of income as save up till they have the sum required. And all the while they would have the benefit of the object of their need.

No one should create a bank overdraft in order to set up a standard of display beyond her means to maintain. Yet to borrow, when well backed with accepted securities, to buy a house or a car, to travel, to refurnish or electrify a home, or to obtain any one of a score of other comforts, can confer nothing but benefit on a woman and her family. She will take care, of course, to see that the interest to be paid on the loan does not so deplete her income as to endanger the maintenance of her normal standard of living.

Women having only modest resources should give to the matter of borrowing more careful scrutiny. Their holdings of stocks and shares and property may be their only bulwark against misfortune. Inability to repay the loan would result in the loss of a considerable portion of those holdings. They must make sure, therefore, that their borrowing is to satisfy a genuine need—they cannot afford to borrow at the behest of a mere whim. When such a need arises, they will not be unwise to borrow.

A woman who borrows to educate her children is prudent, provided that she borrows only within her means and from the proper sources. Another whose health would benefit by the use of a car in her business or daily round is far-sighted in borrowing. To buy a house no more pretentious than her income justifies, to settle some outstanding bills, to launch a business—these purposes justify borrowing,

when a woman has money so invested that she does not wish to turn it into cash.

Borrowing is often better than realising the most adequate securities, because there is a greater incentive to repay a loan than to repurchase investments.

Some have money only in expectation —future salary cheques and the like. These should only borrow against those expectations when their need is urgent— when medical, surgical or optical treatment is required, or in similar cases.

To all who go a-borrowing, the safety rule is *plan to repay*. Those who create an overdraft to satisfy an ordinary need which they could have supplied by saving up a surplus of income over normal expenditure, should arrange to apply to the repayment of the loan not less than they would have set aside towards the purchase of their requirement.

When a woman borrows to educate children, she must plan to repay as soon as their education is complete. Purchasers of houses, of cars and the like must appropriate a regular part of their income to liquidate the debt. Even borrowers for urgent causes must so readjust their domestic budget as to enable a gradual reduction of their indebtedness.

Those who do not plan to repay would be wiser to sell at once the securities which would have been lodged as backing for their borrowings. If they do not do it now, they will have to do so later.

The sources from which wise borrowers obtain their advances are few. Building Societies, Life Assurance Companies, Banks, and persons with money to invest in mortgages, are the established lenders to all who borrow with deliberation.

It would be impossible to over-emphasise the need to avoid money-lenders. No woman should consider for one instant seeking their help, even in her most stringent need. To eschew borrowing from relations or friends is also a sound maxim, because it so often leads to unpleasant friction.

For ordinary house purchase, a well-established Building Society is generally the best quarter in which to seek assistance. The essential of the customary Building Society loan is prompt and planned repayments of capital. That makes the woman house purchaser's borrowing an act of thrift. Every monthly payment is, in fact, a savings appropriation.

Life Assurance companies will lend to holders of their own life policies. Their rates of interest are generally modest.

For long-term borrowing women owning houses—their own or property occupied by tenants—would do well to consider effecting a mortgage. It might happen that a woman whose father had bequeathed to her a row of houses required money to launch a business. Her solicitor would be able to obtain the money from a client seeking investment. The woman would agree to pay interest on the money and to give the lender the right to reimburse himself by sale of the property, should she fail to repay the loan when required to do so. The rents she received from the houses would pay the interest—probably

WHEN WOMEN BORROW

with something to spare—and the money borrowed would yield profit in her business. There are many other circumstances in which it is beneficial to raise money by means of a mortgage, although this method is only to be adopted when the money is likely to be required for a considerable period. Women should take the advice of their solicitors in the matter, and must, of course, employ them to transact the business.

For most general purposes the Banks are the customary lenders of money. Should she wish to buy a car, or to borrow for travelling or to educate children, if bills are accumulating or if the cost of expensive medical treatment is harassing her, to her Bank manager the woman should go with her request for a loan. If the security offered is sound, and the purpose for which the money is required is reasonable, she will have little difficulty in obtaining what she requires.

Women should approach the banker with a clear idea of what they wish to say to him during the interview. They are satisfied that to borrow will benefit them. They should be able to show that it will benefit the Bank also. When a loan is granted, when interest is duly paid on it, and when it is repaid as arranged, then it *does* benefit the Bank.

As a preparation for the interview, the woman borrower should think out carefully how much money she will want, and for how long. She will be wise to quote a maximum amount and a maximum period. If she never needs to use so much and is able to repay before the expiration of the agreed period, her name will stand higher in the Bank's opinion than if she actually requires more than her original demand and cannot repay within the period suggested by herself.

She must plan, also, her method of repayment. Banks like loan propositions which are to be repaid out of income. Very many loans are repaid by women giving to their Bank manager an instruction to transfer from their current account to their loan account a specified monthly sum until the loan is repaid. This sum they regard as a regular "charge" on their income—just as their rent, their housekeeping withdrawals or a hire-purchase payment. When a woman can reasonably anticipate a surplus of income over expenditure, this is probably the best repayment plan.

There are other equally effective and acceptable plans. A woman may want to anticipate, by borrowing, the maturity of an endowment life assurance policy which will fall due within a year or so. She

may have a sum of money to come in from one of many sources, and can with that liquidate her liability. Not so much the manner of repayment as the fact that definite plans for repayment have been made will impress a Bank manager.

Although the Banks look to customers to repay loans out of income, they must, of course, expect security to be deposited with them to cover the possibility of plans going awry. An anticipated surplus may not be realised, expected income may fail.

Acceptable forms of security include reliable stocks and shares, title deeds to property, life assurance policies and guarantees by persons of good standing.

A woman who owns stocks or shares or property having a value considerably in excess of the amount she wishes to borrow need not fear that her loan request will fail for want of adequate security. Whether or not a life assurance policy will prove acceptable generally depends on how many premiums have been paid on it. A life policy nearing maturity will be readily accepted. The acceptability of other policies depends on their "surrender value," which is the amount which the Life Assurance Company would pay to the assured if she decided to turn the policy into cash at once. This can be ascertained from the assurance company, and will be verified by the Bank.

Women needing advances for which they have no tangible security to offer will have to persuade a relative or friend with means to guarantee to repay the money they borrow should they be unable to do so themselves. This is an acceptable form of security, but resort to it should only be taken when the need for money is urgent, as may be the case if medical or surgical aid is required.

Having obtained her advance, the woman borrower should be careful to fulfil her share of the arrangements. She should never draw cheques in excess of the amount which the Bank has agreed to lend, and, if she finds difficulty in repaying on the date agreed, she should explain her case to the Bank manager. To let the matter drag on until she begins to receive letters about it can only give the Bank manager a wrong impression as to her intentions. She should aim always so to ratify her engagements that the Bank will readily assist her should she need its help again.

Women whose general financial position is sound need have no fear of borrowing. Only to those with no resources is borrowing essentially bad. All borrowers should approach their borrowing thoughtfully and plan to repay.

A YOUNG GIRL—TO THE UNKNOWN SOLDIER

By Elise Betty Kauders

I was only a baby
When you went to war.
I knew nothing
Of the torturing fears
That war can bring,
And yet my heart aches for you—
And for your mother.
To-night, remembering you,
I pray to God.
I beg a puzzled world

To have done with bitterness
And misunderstanding.
I say again and again,
"Do not let my husband and son
Be torn from the tenderness
Of my arms."
It is not a brave way of speaking, no—
But I do not see the tragic splendour
Of your grave.
I see a woman's heart weeping—for you.

Figures IN THE PUBLIC EYE

that keep their lines on Vita-Weat

THE MANNEQUIN

The gorgeous gowns aren't made to fit the girl. *She's* made to fit the gowns ! And Vita-Weat goes to her making. She eats Vita-Weat in place of ordinary bread at every meal. Vita-Weat helps her to keep her slenderness—the envy of all the women watching. Vita-Weat gives her energy for her strenuous hours of dressing and posing. For Vita-Weat contains no unconverted starch to burden the system, to hinder digestion, to form unwanted fat. Vita-Weat is *all* nourishment; all the values and the vitamins of the whole wheat grain are in it.

You too will benefit by making Vita-Weat your daily bread. Your digestion will improve, your system will run regularly and efficiently, your teeth will grow healthier, you will experience a new sense of buoyancy and of youth. And how you will love its "crunchiness" and its ripe-corn flavour !

MADE BY
PEEK FREAN
MAKERS OF FAMOUS BISCUITS

*In cartons 1/6 and 10d.
Packets 6d. and 2d.*

Vita-Weat
REGD.

The British Whole-wheat Crispbread

The Housekeeper's Dictionary *of* Facts

A Letter from an Irish Reader

I WOULD like your advice on the following three questions. (1) Are compressed rubber soles injurious to the health? I have been told by shoemakers they are, and I have been told by salesmen they are not. Who am I to believe? (2) Is margarine better for children than butter? (3) What make of hand-operated washing machine would you advise?

I am answering your enquiries in the order in which you give them:

(1) The great advantage of leather shoe soles is that not only are these more or less flexible, but that leather also allows of a certain amount of ventilation. Rubber or other types of soles are ideal for sports wear, but do not allow the same degree of ventilation when worn for prolonged periods at a time. As a rule, such soles have the benefit of being particularly water-tight, and they are therefore very useful for wet-weather wear.

(2) When butter is available at a reasonable price, such as at the present time, it should as far as possible be given to children and invalids. No doubt you are aware that butter is a valuable food in that it contains a fairly large proportion of vitamins A and D. Margarine and butter have a similar food value chemically, but particularly if made from vegetable oils, the former is apt to be deficient in vitamins, unless an extract is added. With some brands of margarine the food value is enhanced considerably by the addition of such extract.

(3) You do not give me any idea of the size of your household, and it is therefore a little difficult for me to advise you with regard to the choice of a hand-power washer. If, however, yours is a small family of two or three persons, I think you would find one of those I have marked on the enclosed list of Approved Appliances suitable

A Useful Bandage Fastener

A convenient and efficient bandage fastener has recently been used with success in Good Housekeeping Institute. The fastener consists of a short length of elastic, fitted with metal ends and hooks, which grip the bandage. In use, the loose end of the bandage is caught into one end of the fastener, and after stretching the elastic slightly, the hooks at the other end are fixed in the dressing. The makers claim that this fastener can be boiled without detriment, so that it can be sterilised and need not be discarded after using once. It has the great advantage of keeping a bandage taut and firm, and can be adjusted and fixed in position by the patient.

A Bread or Meat Holder

A useful device designed to hold meat or bread while it is being carved or cut has recently been tested at the Institute. To obviate the risk of cutting the hand, this is provided with

---

COME AND LEARN TO COOK

In the light, airy kitchens at Good Housekeeping Institute you may learn all branches of cookery, including cake and sweet making, under the expert tuition of trained teachers. The chief advantage of the instruction is that students are free to commence work at any time convenient to them, as no set courses are arranged and they can, therefore, concentrate on the subjects which interest them. Arrangements can also be made for students to have tuition in electrical or gas cookery or to use an oil or coal range. Lessons in laundry-work and household cleaning and renovating are also given. For further particulars apply to the Director.

Good Housekeeping Institute, 49 Wellington Street, London, W.C.2

---

moderately large prongs which grip the food firmly, as well as a very effective guard. A great advantage is that the bread, etc., is not handled while being cut, and the very thinnest slices can be cut without fear of the knife slipping. Joints of beef and any boneless meat can be easily cut to the last slice.

Some Advantages of Tellurium Lead

Addition of a small quantity of tellurium to lead has been found to be an advantage in imparting an added resistance to corrosion. It also yields a very smooth surface, and imparts greater toughness. This last point is important in connection with household and other lead piping. Greater use of this material in place of ordinary untreated lead should undoubtedly lessen the likelihood of burst pipes occurring after frosty weather, or injury as a result of vibration or bending.

A Reader's Letter from Eastbourne

I am writing to ask if you can help me to elucidate the following mystery. My married daughter, who has had a domestic science training, and is most capable and scrupulously clean, gave me as a present some jam, marmalade— both orange and grapefruit—chutney, and furniture polish, made by herself.

These were packed in a wooden case, in newspaper and straw. When it was unpacked, the colour of the orange marmalade was so strange that I accused my daughter of leaving too much pith in. She said she had not, and we then opened a pot and tasted it. It was perfectly sound but it tasted more like marmalade cream filling for a cake than ordinary marmalade.

I might add that marmalade of the same batch at my daughter's house is perfectly normal, i.e. the change took place while mine was travelling.
A. G. B.

Thank you for your letter. We have now experimented with the sample of marmalade that you sent, and the only fault appears to be that it has crystallised. I think the reason is possible that your daughter did not boil it sufficiently after the addition of the sugar. We certainly advocate only short boiling at this stage, but it should be long enough to invert a certain amount of the sugar, with the formation of some glucose, which helps to prevent crystallisation.

The reason that your samples are unsatisfactory, while your daughter's remain in good condition, is probably due to the fact that yours were jolted about while travelling, and were very likely stored in a cold railway yard for some time. Thus any tendency towards crystallisation would be favoured.

I do not know whether you wish to treat the marmalade, but if so I would suggest that you empty it into a pan, add a little water—about $1\frac{1}{2}$ to 2 tablespoonfuls to each pound jar—bring it to the boil gently, and boil for two minutes. Treated in this way I think you will find the preserve is satisfactory.

When Staining Floors

When floor staining is in prospect, it is useful to know of an inexpensive wood filler which can be used for the gaps between floor boards. Such a filling can be made at little or no cost, by preparing some papier maché from old newspapers. The paper should be torn into small pieces, placed in a pan with boiling water, and allowed to soak thoroughly until of a pulpy consistency. After squeezing out excess moisture, a little glue or paste should be added. The mixture is then ready for pressing well into cracks and crevices.

When quite dry, the surface of the floor should be examined carefully and any necessary levelling done with an old knife or other flat-bladed tool.

A Dressmaking Gadget

For home dressmakers who wish to get the hem of a garment the same distance from the floor all the way round, here is an easily-made gadget which will be welcome. All that is needed is a thin wooden rod about 3 ft. long—the sort that is used to tie up plants—a bulldog paper-clip, and a piece of white chalk. Fasten the piece of chalk firmly to the paper-clip by slipping it through the two round holes in the ends of the clip and securing it there with string. Now grip the paper-clip in the ordinary way on to the rod, and adjust it to the height from the floor that the skirt is required to be. Then, if the wearer stands upright, it is a simple matter for someone to trace a chalk line where the hemline comes, keeping the end of the stick firmly on the ground so that the level of the line does not alter.

If I Had a Daughter

these are the things I would teach her
and expect her to do

Says MARJORY ROYCE

"AUNTIE, I couldn't wear lace!" In a Hampshire bedroom the other day the words were said sharply, decisively. On the green satin bedspread (quilted), the family wedding veil was spread out. It had adorned the dark head of Esmé, the fair hair of the Catherine before her, and before *her,* the flaxen locks of Marianna. Various other relations of all these women had joyously borrowed it, happy to be in the old tradition on their marriage morn.

But Caroline, the bride-to-be, now gazed on it (it had been cleaned, and was white and beautiful, handsome and costly) with cold eyes, quite unmoved.

"I don't like it much," she announced. "No, I shan't need it. I shall have tulle instead. I always said I should have tulle. Thanks just as much, Auntie."

If I had a daughter about to marry, and we had a family wedding veil in our keeping, I should like her to have possessed more family feeling than did this Caroline; more sense of the past stretching behind her, and imagination enough to think out some of the special circumstances that surrounded each bride who had worn it on her great day. To bring this about might not be easy; modern girls do not seem to care for thoughts of their ancestry.

I read over again Lili Wahn's exquisite book on China, *The House of Exile,* and linger over the description of these proud talks on ancestors, delivered to the young admiring descendants by the head of the family in the courtyard of his home, fragrant with the scent of Chinese flowering trees, on summer evenings.

In order to get this sense of the past, I should have to tell my little girl growing up, stories and anecdotes of her relatives; to keep a picture of an old country home of ours on the wall. I would like my girl to study psychology in her later teens; and in order that my Rosamond should have some more understanding of herself, she would have to understand something of the rock from which she was hewn. The right to wear Grannie's wedding veil would be precious to her—lace or tulle. It was Grannie's!

Then I would like her to have great interest in the colour-scheme of a room. Women have always sat in rooms a good deal and always will! Quite recently, in the States, I beheld the joy of a fourteen-year-old in her newly-decorated sanctum. It was buttercup yellow and faint plum colour, little wreaths of violets on the paper, a soft mauvish carpet, stiff taffeta skirts to the dressing-table, of a slightly darker purple; a white corduroy velvet cover to the bed of South American wood, and charming, sophisticated electric lighting with white lamp shades.

I should give my daughter the colouring she liked in her own room fairly early, and show keenness in every detail. I would allow her to be alone in the room a good deal if she liked, without questioning.

Then books! There must be many books about in the home to entice her, and some extravagance should be practised, if possible, over the buying of reviews and papers, as the young are easily attracted by those. She must be a real reader, my Rosamond, for I know that there is no

hobby which provides so much happiness as that (though the number of people who realise this have, strangely, always been few).

It will be very important that she should live in the country a good deal, from the age of eight to fourteen, to make her own acquaintance with hills, and particularly streams. She should not have her time planned for her. Long *empty* holiday hours should be contrived by the skilful mother. The hatless small schoolgirl must be able to go "wooding," primrosing, and especially should she be encouraged to mess about with a boat (see Kenneth Grahame). It is of the highest importance also to give her companionship of the same age.

An early awakening to the sense of loveliness of trees, flowers and water, must, if possible, take place in my Rosamond's life. Sad and wretched the child who never passes through it—eternal the awakening when it once happens. Middle-aged people, and the old folk reading this page, will be able in a moment to think back to the magic period in their own lives when this miracle befell.

In Lady Acland's poignant memories of her little daughter Ellen, we hear of the child running, jumping, walking, exulting in riding and bicycling, with her eyes ever ready to spy out an interesting plant in the woodland. Yet this tomboy, guided by a superb mother, had her small evening dress, worn with pride for parties, covered with bunches of bright flowers.

My daughter should be left alone a good deal. A woman doctor spoke with me the other day of her own childhood out in Jamaica, where her people had migrated, and emphasised the glorious absence of "don'ts" that obtained through her early out-of-door life there. The most successful mother I know (far before her time, as she is now old), made her girls very happy by respecting their opinion directly they were in their responsible teens. "I don't think I quite approve of that, but if *you* feel it is right, pray go!" No sulking, no resentment when the girl followed her own bent. I hope and believe that I should respect my daughter's considered opinions when she was growing into womanhood.

It might be that she had few opinions. It might be that Rosamond had not the priceless gift of natural independence of character—and it is rarer than many suppose. It might be borne in upon me, sadly, that she was going to be one of these girls without a special interest or hobby. What then? I should take action speedily! There is nothing drearier than a girl cut to conventional pattern, merely full of that sentimentality which, as Dame Ethel Smyth has said, is drawn from a tank of "treacle, rose-water and salad oil."

This is to be an age of more leisure, and it seems to me that the only practical way to give people an interest, be they daughters or sons, is to infect them. Get hold of an enthusiastic hobbyist and make your child dwell for a season with him or her, listen to his or her talk, and watch his or her work. I know a schoolmaster who is an authority on moths, butterflies and caravanning. Even at this moment of writing he is probably happily leading a

bevy of small pupils with butterfly nets into the woods. Tents will be pitched on Saturdays. Some of these boys will be infected by his knowledge and enthusiasm, and will themselves begin collections. Others will be bored, perhaps, or will like it for a time, and fall away later. Still, it will have given them more understanding.

If I saw signs in my imaginary Rosamond of that dread disease, love of pleasure; if she were a victim to fits of boredom, she should, if I could possibly arrange it, be forced to pass some time with an enthusiast. And if she didn't show signs of succumbing to his or her influence she would, presently, be quietly thrown in contact with another. But I would not explain what I was deliberately arranging.

A thing I should love to teach my Rosamond is how to listen well—this perhaps could only be suggested by constant remarks about the charm of a good listener. Then she should learn something practical about health and illness, so that when she is ill, she should not be afraid of the word "operation." Again, McDougall says somewhere, that how to bear disappointment bravely is one of the most important things to suggest in a child's education. She might be helped to that at school, and in her personal life, by a stiffening attitude on my part.

Anyhow, I must not watch her too closely, must not idolise her too passionately, must not let her feel she is in the centre of the picture. I must not go into every passing joy and grief too thoroughly with her.

What should I wish for my girl most of all? A little of that quick sympathy of Lady du Maurier. As Muriel Beaumont, freshly engaged to the dashing Gerald, she was desolated because she thought he was in for a cold. And yet I wish for Rosamond some of that control and poise that is so good an armour to wear in a world like this. I hope she may, too, have a firm hold of her religion; gentleness, so strange nowadays that one is startled on meeting it in any young girl; a sense of fun; a saint for a friend, and also a woman of the world; with a love of travel.

Rosamond should have light brown hair; and meditative grey eyes that would survey her mother with most tender indulgence.

Our greatest living woman writer has described her ideal female thus, and my imaginary Rosamond, free and fair and fine, should correspond with the portrait:

"A rosy-flowered fruit tree, laid with leaves and dancing boughs."

A Boon for Every Housewife

Good Housekeeping Diary and Account Book is an annual publication that thousands of women await eagerly, to be their standby in household affairs for the coming year. Full details of the 1936 Diary are on page 212. We advise all readers who so far have never used it to get a copy and then see if they can do without it in the future!

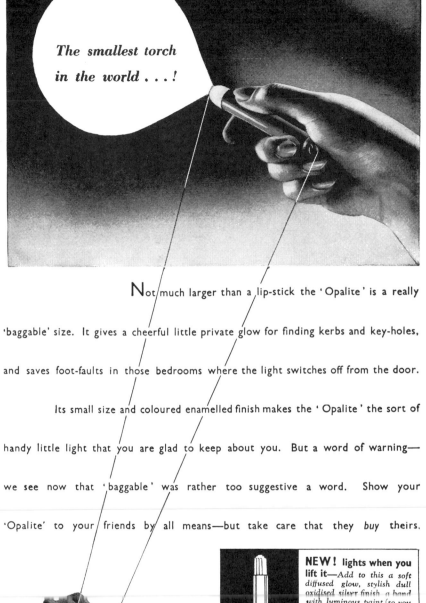

The smallest torch in the world . . .!

Not much larger than a lip-stick the 'Opalite' is a really 'baggable' size. It gives a cheerful little private glow for finding kerbs and key-holes, and saves foot-faults in those bedrooms where the light switches off from the door.

Its small size and coloured enamelled finish makes the 'Opalite' the sort of handy little light that you are glad to keep about you. But a word of warning—we see now that 'baggable' was rather too suggestive a word. Show your 'Opalite' to your friends by all means—but take care that they *buy* theirs.

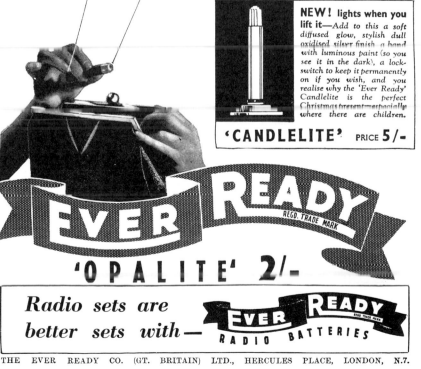

THEY ARE "TELLING ONE ANOTHER"

EACH
5 GNS.

about the **1935** *Jaeger Tennis Coats*

how useful they are—how superbly light and elegant —coats that go with such a swing on the tennis-court, and are so much admired, that one is tempted to wear them on many different occasions during the summer; for always and everywhere they have the same success.

A swagger coat in pale tweed with sloping pockets and welted seams finds much to admire in its waisted wide-revered rival (also in tweed) and both models acknow-ledge the charm of a coat cut on the lines of a masculine ulster with four dashing pockets to complete the effect.

JAEGER HOUSE

204-6 REGENT STREET LONDON W1 MAYFAIR 3144
★ *There are Jaeger Agents in every Town* ★

The Housekeeper's Dictionary of Facts

Do not hesitate to write to the Institute for advice on any household problem

From a Hampstead Reader

I SHALL be most grateful for your advice on several matters. I have recently married and have had no previous experience of housekeeping. (1) What would remove a grease stain on a pink silk bed-spread? I have tried a hot iron and blotting paper but without success. (2) I have got a round zinc clothes boiler to use on my gas stove. It has a percolator in the centre and I wonder if this is necessary as it takes up so much room? (3) What should one do when fruit juice is spilled on the dining-room table-cloth?

1. We think you will find that you are able to remove the grease marks from your pink silk bed-spread by treating with a solvent such as carbon tetrachloride. A clean, soft cloth should be dipped in the solvent and after making a ring well outside the mark, gradually rubbed towards the centre. We should, however, be inclined to suggest that you experiment on an inconspicuous stain first, as you will then be able to judge whether the colour is affected in any way.

2. With regard to your clothes boiler, it would be quite satisfactory to use this without the inner percolator, provided you stir the clothes from time to time while they are boiling, so that there may be no fear of their sticking to the bottom of the boiler and becoming burnt. With the percolator in position there is no necessity for stirring and there is, of course, little or no danger of any damage occurring.

3. With regard to the fruit juice, we would suggest soaking the stained parts of the cloth in a little warm borax and water, as you will probably find this removes the marks satisfactorily. If any small marks still remain, however, the ordinary washing process and boiling will probably remove these.

From a Reader at West Wickham

Could you tell me how to deal with a greenish-brown lumpy scum that comes in my galvanised clothes boiler? Sometimes the deposit settles on the clothes, especially on Turkish towels, and I find it impossible to remove it completely. The water here is very hard and chalky.

The scum is no doubt due to the hardness of the water, a fairly considerable quantity of so-called lime-soap being formed. After using the boiler for laundry work, it should be wiped out at once while still hot, using, if necessary, an abrasive cleanser. Afterwards it is a good plan to rub round with a cloth dipped in a little paraffin or turpentine. Abrasives should not be used unless essential, as they tend to roughen the interior of the boiler and consequently any deposit tends to adhere more readily.

MARMALADES

Now is the time to replenish one's store of marmalade, and our publication, *Jams, Jellies and Fruit Bottling* provides numerous suggestions for thick, syrupy preserves as well as for clear shred and other marmalades. Recipes for orange, tangerine, lemon, grapefruit, and lime marmalade are included, so that the individual tastes of the family, however varied, can be provided for. In all, there are over twenty recipes for marmalade, all of which have been tested in Good Housekeeping Institute, in this book, and a very considerable number of other jams and jellies to be made throughout the year.

Jams, Jellies and Fruit Bottling, as well as other books of the same series—*Cakemaking, Sweets and Candies*, and the latest addition, *Pies and Puddings*—may be obtained, price 1s. 2d., including postage, from Good Housekeeping Institute, 49, Wellington Street, Strand, W.C.2.

A Letter From a Reader Living In New Zealand

I thought perhaps some of your readers might be interested in the way we live in the Antipodes. We do not, on the whole, live so very differently from our English relatives, except that as this is a land of almost perpetual sunshine we live more out of doors. Our homes are in most cases modern wooden structures with every convenience, electric lighting being generally in use even in country districts, as the power is carried long distances through farming lands and therefore made available to those in the vicinity. To many people in rural England it would seem strange to visit farms equipped with electric cooker and lighting; even in the milking sheds there are both milking plants and shearing machines driven by electricity.

In my younger days we had to be content with a coal range and kerosene lamps, but now electricity has revolutionised the countryside. Motor-cars, telephones, electric light, good roads and a daily mail and paper have also played their part in this change. What a difference in a few years from the wearisome journey of five or six miles to the nearest town to post a letter and collect the weekly paper!

I live in a beautiful city which always appeals to our overseas visitors, possibly because of its similarity to an English cathedral town. Like most cities here it is up-to-date in every way, having been built entirely during the last half century.

Our trains, like our buildings, are modern. Our streets well laid out, with plenty of open spaces and a 400-acre park and sports ground in the city proper. Our churches and schools are all well built and airy. Our babies the healthiest in the world. But although most of our homes are replete with every labour-saving device, we housewives do not lead a lazy, self-indulgent life. In the majority of cases we do our own housework, help in the garden, wash, bake, make our own frocks and knit.

We entertain more than our overseas sisters. To take my own case, I am 64 years of age, by no means young, and I have had a hard life, yet frequently I have friends coming in unexpectedly and staying for dinner or tea, all of which I have to prepare myself. There is, however, little ceremony and in most instances one's friends will help with the clearing away and washing up. It would become a burden otherwise, and nowadays when all superfluous articles of furniture are usually scrapped and labour-saving devices reduce work to a minimum, one feels it a pleasure to ask one's friends to stay for a meal.

A Useful Pair of Coal Tongs

An exceptionally neat and useful pair of coal tongs is at present on test in the Institute. These tongs are inexpensive and really effective in use, the serrated edge of the prongs ensuring an extremely good grip, enabling coal and logs to be picked up readily and held firmly.

How often, when groping in a scuttle for just the right sized pieces of coal, one is tempted to "down tools" and use one's hands? With these tongs it is possible to pick and choose to a nicety, and they are so small and inconspicuous that they can be tucked away in any corner of the hearth.

From a Reader at Glasgow

I wonder if you could possibly tell me of anything which would take stains out of a taffeta quilt? The marks are not very conspicuous, but I should like to remove them, if possible, without discolouring the quilt, which is green. One of the stains was, I know, made with beef extract, and none of the marks is greasy.

Without knowing the nature of all the marks on your quilt it is difficult to advise you, as the majority of stains require individual treatment. For the marks due to the spilling of beef extract, however, you will probably find that sponging gently with a little lukewarm salt and water will probably prove effective. After sponging, all traces of salt should be rinsed away with plenty of fresh water.

WHEN UNCLE COMES TO TOWN . . .

There's usually a pleasant little shopping expedition, then lunch at one of the smartest restaurants in town, with perhaps a matinée to follow . . .

A time to be at one's brightest and best, well turned out and with the right perfume—nothing showy or assertive—just the simple, charming fragrance of Yardley Lavender is the ideal.

Sprinkler Bottles 2/6 to 10/6. Larger Sizes up to 2 guineas. Lavender Soap— '*The Luxury Soap of the World*'—2/6 a box of three tablets, Lavender Face Powder 1/9, Compact 2/6, Lipstick 3/-, Bath Salts 2/6 to 10/6, Talc 1/2 and 2/6, Lavendomeal (the new Bath Luxury) 3/-, etc.

Prices do not apply in the Irish Free State.

BY APPOINTMENT
TO HER MAJESTY THE QUEEN

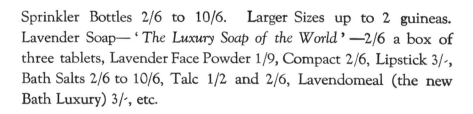

YARDLEY LAVENDER

PREPARING
TO BE AN OLD LADY

THE
30's

" The plaintive lady who never stops complaining "

" Gossiping old women who imagine the worst of everyone "

Drawings
by
Nicolas Bentley

" Elderly women who live only for their food "

Do you realise, Mrs. or Miss Forty-to-Fifty, that already you should be thinking how you'll live when you are Seventy?

BY
LEONORA
MARY ERVINE

THIS article is written for women of forty to fifty years old. I fear that its advice may be too late for many of the after-fifties. I am not suggesting that anyone becomes an old lady until she is well over sixty, but since so many women live to the age of eighty or ninety or even a hundred in health and strength, it is as well to realise that it is easily possible to enjoy being in the seventies. There is no necessity to be a misery to oneself and one's relations.

Let me imagine that you, my reader, are an active forty-two. You dance, you play golf, bridge and tennis. You dress very smartly, and you are thoroughly enjoying life. For, in spite of the patent medicine advertisements, I find that my friends in the forties have never had better health nor enjoyed themselves more than they do at that age. It may be that the War caused an arrest of development in women who are forty and a bittock, and that they are now being compensated for the losses of the War by a prolongation of youth, or it may be that we are all younger for our years than our grandmothers were, although I have a feeling

that, whatever our grandmothers were, our great-grandmothers were minxes: regular post-Napoleonic War girls.

Well now, Mrs. or Miss Forty-two, what about *your* old age? You are coming to it! Have you thought what sort of life you'll lead when you're seventy? Take an hour or so off from bridge and golf, and make a list of the women you know who are between sixty-five and eighty. Which of them do you admire? Is there one of them you would like to imitate? If there are several, you are lucky. Many old ladies yield very easily to displeasing habits, nasty, unlovable traits, which I shall describe quite frankly.

The old lady's worst fault is greed. There are elderly women, who, feeling that all other pleasures have failed them, live only for their food. Some of them are to be seen in expensive hotels at

health resorts. They travel, constantly accompanied by a maid-attendant, and they are a very profitable source of revenue to hotel-keepers. They do not want to leave their money to anyone, and are determined to spend while they can. Some of them eat themselves into bath-chairs, colossally large old ladies who are wheeled into the dining-room, where they sit by themselves and guzzle. They have eyes for nothing but the menu and the side table. They alternately coax and scold the waiters. They generally tip well, and soon get stuffed into the grave—a truly horrible sight. Let us be preserved from that. So now, Forty-two, be careful that love of the table does not grow on you. If you are thinking too much of your meals, pull yourself up. Consider the picture I have just described!

Try to be fastidious about food, and insist on dainty and delicate dishes. Cut down your diet when you can, but do not become a diet bore—one of those terrible women who are not allowed to eat this or that, and are pests in the house. When you pay visits, enjoy your food without over-eating, and give your hostess *(Continued overleaf)*

THE
30's

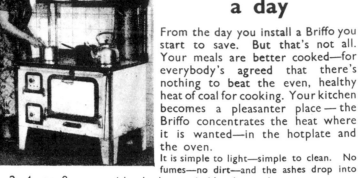

PASSIONATE PEOPLE

The New American Government and its Work. James T. Young. (Macmillan, 15s.)
Revised edition of important text book. Really informative.

Conservatism and the Future. Lord Eustace Percy and Others. (Heinemann, 7s. 6d.)
The Parliamentary Y.M.C.A. speaks its faith.

Travel and Adventure
North to the Rime-ringed Sun. Isobel W. Hutchinson. (Blackie, 12s. 6d.)
This journey through Arctic Alaska in 1933-34 won the writer the Mungo Park Medal. She went to gather flowers for the Herbarium at Kew, but she found numberless adventures and excitements during her exciting ice-bound journey.

Snow People. Taeki Odulok. (Methuen, 5s.)
The first account of the Chudkchee Eskimaux from Northern Siberia written by one of themselves. Primitive life in the Arctic cold—vivid and unexpected.

True Dramas of Wild Life. George Hearn. (Hutchinson, 8s. 6d.)
Stories of partridges, hedgehogs, adders and other English residents told by a naturalist and illustrated by his own camera studies.

Mungo Park and the Niger. Stephen Gwynne. (Lane, 12s. 6d.)
Mr. Gwynne knows Africa, and can tell admirably a tale which would be enthralling even if badly told.

Poetry
Collected Poems. Robert Vansittart. (Lovat Dickson, 6s.)
A wide range of verse written over a period of twenty-five years by a sportsman and traveller with a gift for singing.

American Song. Paul Engle. (Cape, 5s.)
Superbly vital and imaginative young American poet, akin in some ways to Roy Campbell. "America Remembers" is one of the few really fine prize poems of modern years.

PREPARING TO BE AN OLD LADY
(Continued)

the pleasure of seeing you appreciate her hospitality, even if you have to fast afterwards. It is *continual* over-eating that is dangerous.

Then there is another type of old lady I dislike even more than the glutton, the plaintive lady who never stops complaining. She never is *or wants to be* well. She must have a grievance. She must lie about on sofas and fret. No one considers her enough. She says she is forgotten, unloved and ill. She wishes she were dead. So do most of the people around her. She lives for the visits of her sympathetic doctor, and he has to be very sympathetic, for if he tries to brace her up, she dispenses with his attention and looks about for a humbug who will humour her until she dies.

These are probably the two least pleasing types of old ladies, but there are others almost as awful; for example, the selfish mothers who want to accompany their daughters everywhere. These women prey on their sad-faced offspring until they, too, are weary, worn-out old women, but have no daughters to tend them. Then there are the gossiping old women, whose awful tea-parties are hells of evil and scandalous speech. They imagine the worst about everybody. They batten on the least breath of impropriety, and magnify a trifle until it is a monstrosity. Any decent-minded middle-aged or young women would run in horror from such imaginations. Then there are the very horrid old women who go to "shocking" plays in the pretence that they wish to show their disapproval of their juniors when they really want to indulge their unsatisfied lust for nastiness. These are noisome women. Do, Forty-twos, pull yourselves up if you find yourselves enjoying ill-health or liking to harp on the faults of your neighbours.

Consider, lastly, the good-natured, but empty-brained old lady, who must have continual light amusement, who becomes very restless if her juniors want to talk about books and politics, and cries out in agony: "What about our game of bridge?" Be able, by all means, to play an intelligent game of cards, but do not become a card fiend or a gambling maniac. Have you noticed the bejewelled, hard-faced old women in Continental casinos? If so, need I say any more?

Look around your circle, and if you find an old lady of whom everyone is fond, who has plenty of friends, a cheery home and a contented family, do not rest until you have discovered her secret. It is probably in her happy and contented disposition. She loved her associates in her youth and she enjoyed making other people happy. She was a little ashamed of ill-health, especially anything that could be caused by self-neglect or self-indulgence. She was interested in other people. She liked them to tell her what they were doing. She did not have a hundred inhibitions. She did not deny herself unconventional happiness because Mrs. Next-Door-But-One might disapprove. She did what she wanted, within reason, and ignored criticism unless she felt it was deserved. She was never a hypocrite. She never talked of "our class," nor did she regard herself as superior to any intelligent, honest, hardworking man or woman, merely because of her birth or her money. She realised her place in the world and endeavoured to fill it satisfactorily. She was not sloppy or sentimental or unintelligent or censorious. She believed the best of everyone until she had proof that they were unworthy. She cultivated her talents without thrusting them at others. She played the piano and sang because to do so gave her pleasure and cultivated her mind, and not because it gave her opportunities to show off or to bore her friends. She never pretended to appreciate arts that left her cold. My ideal old lady was never a humbug. She was intelligent and honest with herself and other people. She did not lazily decide that she was stupid and therefore nothing mattered but hitting a tennis ball. She said, "I must try and increase my intelligence. I'll learn a foreign language really well. I'll read some history as well as novels. I will try and know quite a lot about some subject, be it cooking, gardening, bringing up children or mysticism. I'll give my mind at least as much attention as I give to my complexion or my manicure. In short, I'll try to be a hundred-per-cent. human being."

Here is a prayer which was found in Chester Cathedral:

Give me a good digestion, Lord,
And also something to digest:
Give me a healthy body, Lord,
With sense to keep it at its best.
Give me a healthy mind, good Lord,
To keep the good and pure in sight:
Which seeing sin is not appalled,
But finds a way to set it right.

Give me a mind that is not bored,
That does not whimper, whine or sigh:
Don't let me worry overmuch
About the fussy thing called "I."
Give me a sense of humour, Lord:
Give me the grace to see a joke:
To get some happiness from life
And pass it on to other folk.

I have never found any better prayer for the middle-aged woman. Have you?

Whichever way you look at it Skippers give you wonderful value. In quantity, nearly four times as many fish as you usually get. In flavour, well, you only have to try these delicious little fish once to discover why they're called the tastiest meal that ever came out of a tin ! In nourishment, too, Skippers take a lot of beating; for the pure olive-oil that goes with them builds up wonderful powers of resistance. Whether you shop for quality or for value—buy Skippers !

'Why does Janet's skin always look so nice ?'

Is there anything more annoying than being compared with another woman ! Dorothy was furious.

'How can you be so *beastly !* ' she said to her husband. 'It's not my fault if I was born with a bad complexion.'

Poor girl ! What a tragic mistake she made ! She was *not* born with that muddy, blotchy skin. It's simply the disastrous result of a long-neglected system. But like so many women, Dorothy didn't realise the truth.

Now, if she'd only take Eno's 'Fruit Salt' every morning, what a change she'd see in her complexion! How gently and thoroughly Eno would banish those poisons which are ruining her looks. How quickly it would purify her blood, and clear away those obstinate blemishes ! In a few weeks her skin would be so clear, so fresh and rosy — she wouldn't know herself for the same woman !

Don't be like Dorothy. Don't be

blind to facts. If you're in the least dissatisfied with your complexion— just remember this : Inner cleansing is far more important than outward cleansing creams. And the wisest, safest way to make sure of it is to take Eno's 'Fruit Salt' every morning.

Eno forms no habit. Contains no harsh aperients to upset you — nothing to encourage fat. Begin the day with a sparkling glass — become radiant and attractive, with a skin like cream and roses.

ENO'S 'FRUIT SALT'

Eno's 'Fruit Salt' is pure, harmless and perfectly natural in its action. It contains no harsh aperients—no sugar to encourage fat. Its work is simply to clear poisons and impurities from your blood — to keep your system in

first-class order and your skin clear and fresh. For over sixty years doctors have approved it. Get a bottle today. Eno costs 1/6 or (double quantity) 2/6. The words Eno and 'Fruit Salt' are registered trade marks.

Have *you* any of these symptoms ?

BAD COMPLEXION
OBESITY
HEADACHES
DEPRESSION
IRRITABILITY
INDIGESTION
SLEEPLESSNESS
CONSTIPATION

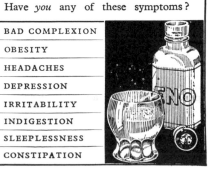

The Housekeeper's Dictionary of Facts

A PAGE OF READERS' QUERIES WITH THE INSTITUTE'S REPLIES

THE
30's

A Question About Fire Extinguishers

AS the provision of domestic chemical fire-extinguishers is expensive, could you give the ingredients of a home-made liquid which could be prepared and stored until required?

Is it possible to eliminate grease marks from matting? I have one such rug which has been spoilt through having liquid paraffin spilt on it. Ammonia and hot water have had little effect—the marks reappearing after a few days.

I am doubtful whether you would find it very practical to store any liquid or other product for extinguishing fire, unless you are also provided with some suitable apparatus for use in connection with this. In many cases the liquid used consists essentially of carbon tetrachloride, but on the other hand there are also extinguishers in which use is made of an acid and carbonate. When using the device, the acid comes in contact with the carbonate, and water highly charged with carbon dioxide gas is ejected.

I think you will find you are able to remove the paraffin marks from your matting by rubbing with a cloth dipped in a little petrol. Use this in the open air.

Removing Acid Stains

I have a coloured silk frock that has been badly stained. We don't know whether the marks were caused by printing ink or by being splashed by contents of a wireless accumulator, and have done nothing to the stains yet by way of removal.

Without knowing the nature of the stain on your frock it is difficult to advise you; but if there is likelihood of this, they are quite possibly due to acid in the accumulator, as acids affect many colours. If so, it will be most important to neutralise the acidity as soon as possible, as otherwise a hole may develop in the fabric. For this I would suggest sponging, or if there are any extensive marks, soaking for a short time in a little ammonia and water.

If, on the other hand, the marks are due to printing ink or any type of duplicating ink, I am afraid you may find that they are extremely difficult, if not impossible, to remove. You could, however, try treating alternately with a dilute solution of potassium permanganate and hydrogen peroxide, after experimenting with an odd piece of material in order to see if the dye is effected by these chemicals.

When Soldered Pans are Unsafe

One of my large pans has recently been repaired by covering part of the

seam with solder. I shall be glad if you will advise me as to whether it is satisfactory to cook jam in a pan mended in this way.

Without actually seeing your pan it is impossible for me to say whether it would be wise to use it for cooking purposes, and in particular for making jam. If, however, the seams have been pressed together and the soldering is entirely on the exterior of the pan, I think you should find it perfectly satisfactory. On the other hand, if the soldering is in the interior, then I would not suggest using it, for solder contains lead in its composition, and this being a cumulative poison, it is very undesirable to consume foods in which traces may be dissolved.

The Care of Pigskin Furniture

I wonder if you could tell me how to clean and care for pigskin leather furniture? Some of the chairs have stains on the leather. I would like also to know how to keep them in a satisfactory condition.

Pigskin furniture should not require cleaning or renovating for at least several years after purchasing, as the grain of this leather is unusually firm and resistant to dirt. In this respect genuine pigskin differs from ordinary sheepskin leathers, which are sometimes sold as pigskin.

If cleaning is absolutely essential, then it should be undertaken with very great care, as it is unfortunately so easy to ruin the appearance of a valuable suite of furniture. The safest and certainly the most efficient dry-cleaning agent is carbon tetrachloride, a non-inflammable spirit obtainable at a reasonable price from the local oil and paint merchant, or chemist. The surface of the leather requires working over with a swab of cotton wool soaked in the spirit. The work should be carried out as rapidly as possible, as the cleaning fluid is extremely volatile. Patchy working should be avoided, and

once a chair is started the entire surface should be treated, although probably parts of the back may need more working than the sides. After treating the furniture with the solvent in the manner described, allow the former to dry.

To complete the cleaning, the leather needs working with a solution made up of milk and water in equal proportions, using a soft rag which is occasionally rubbed with a bar of soap. The rag will require washing out at odd times during the operation. A gentle pressure and a steady circular movement with the rag will achieve the desired result in a very short time, but on no account should the work be rushed. The leather must not be saturated with solution, and it is only necessary to moisten the rag with the milk and water so that easy working is assured.

After cleaning the leather, it should be allowed to dry thoroughly. A good polish with a clean piece of velvet will then bring up a nice, soft sheen, and if desired, the polish may be continued with a little good shoe cream.

It is advisable to avoid the excessive use of furniture cream, as this waxy preparation will darken the leather, and in time give it an unwholesome appearance. Furniture cream in moderation will preserve the leather, but in excess it will clog the pores and darken it.

Keeping Rugs in Place

Will you kindly advise me whether you can recommend some method or article which will prevent rugs and mats slipping about on a polished parquet floor? We have tried a rubberised canvas material which is excellent, but only for a time, as it, too, becomes slippery through daily contact with the polished floor. We have also tried strips of rubber at each end of the rugs and mats, but again without success. I thought you may know of something, or probably be able to find out for me, as you so kindly offer help.

In the Institute we have found the rubberised canvas to which you refer very satisfactory for preventing rugs, etc., from slipping over polished floors. Rubber suction cups stitched to the underside of the mats are also very effective.

Many people do not polish their floors immediately under the mats, or if they do, they apply the polish only very sparingly indeed, rubbing up well afterwards. If this is done, I do not think you should find that the rubber becomes slippery. As, however, you tell me it is now in this condition, I would be inclined to suggest rubbing over the underside of the rubber matting with a cloth dipped in either turpentine or petrol. This would remove the wax polish which has adhered to it, and I think you would then find that the mats grip the floors satisfactorily.

Two ways of dressing a salad

TAKE ONE distracted young housewife, with a thousand and one things to see to because the De Vere s are coming to dinner. Add the difficulty of getting costly, disobedient salad dressing ingredients to mix, too much salt and the lid off the pepper pot. Put in a dash of temper, a flushed face and tears — because the De Vere s have a first-class cook and are such snobs — and serve with humiliation.

OR :

TAKE ONE serene young hostess — who, when she mixes her salad, simply goes to the cupboard and fetches the Heinz Salad Cream. Add the plain truth — that this superb dressing is made with nothing less than new laid eggs, rich English cream, and the clearest, purest olive oil — subtly seasoned and blended velvet smooth by Heinz master chefs. Serve with congratulations.

HEINZ *Salad Cream*

SERIOUSLY, THOUGH, HERE IS A GRAND RECIPE
Lobster Salad. Take some separate salad plates and arrange some crisp lettuce leaves on them. Put a portion of tinned or fresh lobster in the centre of each. Now take alternate slices of tomato, cucumber and orange and make a ring round them. Serve Heinz Salad Cream separately.

57

The Housekeeper's Dictionary of Facts

A WAKEFIELD READER DESCRIBES HER HOUSEHOLD ROUTINE

THE

30's

WHEN my charwoman, who had been with me since my marriage nine years ago, became ill recently and had to give up work she begged me to employ her daughter, aged 15, who had just left school.

I was by no means enamoured of the idea of changing my method of house-keeping, but finally decided to try the girl as a daily help, on the understanding that if after a month the girl and I did not " get on " she would have to go. One of my worries was the probable increased strain on the housekeeping purse although I was prepared to risk that, for during eight years of cooking and catering for two I had learnt that with a few exceptions it would cost very little more to feed three. I therefore decided to give the girl a month's trial, but a question which troubled me was that of training her. Here I must thank you for the help I have received from various articles in GOOD HOUSEKEEPING—actually, when the article entitled " Training a General Maid " appeared in January 1935, my maid asked me if she could keep that volume as she thought it was the most interesting she had ever seen, and expressed gratification that she had been trained on those lines.

The first week was very hard work for us both. I had to teach her how to clear a grate and lay a fire, to insist that only ashes were thrown away, and that we burned every cinder and all our rubbish in the kitchen stove, that the fireback must be swept clear of soot every day and that shovels, coal buckets and firewood were put on the hearth cloth and not on the carpet, and that a dishcloth was not used for washing the hearth. Then when she came to wash up she used about a pint of water, for it took her some time to become accustomed to the idea that an un-limited supply of hot water was available. She had no ideas on the subject of laying tables and trays, or turning out rooms, so it was not difficult to get her into my ways. I quickly dis-covered that she liked working in the house, and altogether I found her very adaptable, so that at the end of her trial month we decided that she should stay.

In the course of a year she has not slacked off at all, but has been anxious to learn new things. She now does the laundrywork—sheets and towels are sent out—and has become a good ironer. I still do most of the everyday cooking, though she bakes cakes and pastry one afternoon a week.

With a maid in for a midday meal and tea we have consumed rather more bread, butter, and bacon, more potatoes and vegetables than before, but the butcher's bills are less. The reason for this is that I now have more time to make attractive and appetising dishes out of the cheaper cuts of meat. I

Summer Courses in Cookery

Lessons of a few hours' duration or a cooking course covering several weeks can be taken at Good Housekeeping Institute. Further details are on page 108, and a prospectus can be had from the Director

Good Housekeeping Institute, 49, Wellington Street, Strand, W.C.2

never buy cakes or pastry now, and this is a great saving. Further, I have had time to make all my year's supply of marmalade, jam and bottled fruit, instead of having to buy half. What perhaps is more important, I have had more free time to devote to my hobbies. I have been less tired when my husband has wanted me to play tennis, and I have had no worry about his meals when I have had to be away from home for a day. We have had to make one big alteration in our style of living. Where-as formerly we had a light lunch, and dinner between 7.30 and 8, now we have a hot meal in the middle of the day, and supper any time between 7.30 and 9.

Here is the time-table we work to. The house is nine years old and the accommo-dation includes washing and keeping cellars, kitchen, lounge, dining-room, three bedrooms, box-room, bathroom and w.c., with entrance hall and porch. Every morning except Sunday I get up at 7.30 and prepare breakfast for 8 o'clock. The table is laid overnight and the porridge prepared. After breakfast I clear away the dishes and at 9 o'clock I make the beds, tidy up bedroom and bathroom for the maid to clean. By this time the maid has lit the fire in the lounge, and I mop and dust it and vacuum all the carpets. By 10 o'clock I go into the kitchen to see about lunch. By 11 I am free until lunch time for shopping, etc., and this finishes my everyday routine.

Maid's Routine

8.30 : Arrive. Rake and make up kitchen stove. Clean shoes. Clean front doorstep. **9 :** Clear lounge grate, lay and light fire. **9.15 :** Wash up supper and breakfast dishes, prepare vegetables for lunch ; tidy kitchen. **10 :** Mop and dust dining-room and bedrooms. Sweep and dust stairs, landing, hall, clean bathroom and w.c. **11 12** or **12.45** (depending on day of week) : Special weekly work. **12 or 12.45 :** Wash, change apron, lay table in dining-room, finish lunch (sauces, gravies, etc.). **12.30** or **1.15 :** Serve and have own lunch. By **2.30 :** Washing up finished, vegetables for supper prepared, kitchen tidy, ashes emptied, coke, coal for the

rest of the day brought into the kitchen. **2.30–3 :** Wash, change uniform, rest for quarter of an hour. **3–3.45 :** Special work for afternoon. **3.45 :** Pre-pare tea. **4.15 :** Take tea on trolley into lounge. **5 :** Wash up tea things, lay table in dining-room for supper and in kitchen for breakfast. **5.30 :** Leave all tidy, change uniform, go home.

Weekly Routine

Monday, **10–12 :** Laundry (I do all housework on Monday) ; **3 :** Ironing. *Tuesday,* **11–12.45 :** Bedrooms cleaned alternately ; **3 :** Bedroom silver, iron-ing finished ; *Wednesday,* **11–12 :** Din-ing-room ; **3 :** Dining-room silver and brasses cleaned. *Thursday,* **11–12.45 :** Lounge. Lounge silver cleaned ; **3 :** Cake and pastry baking. *Friday,* **8.30 :** Clean the cooker ; **11–12 :** Clean bathroom and w.c. Scrub floors. Polish hall and landing. Scrub kitchen floor. After lunch : Kitchen windows are cleaned, kitchen table, stool, etc., are scrubbed. Two kitchen cupboards are turned out. *Saturday,* **11–12.45 :** Outside work. Mop brick forecourt and side entrance, scrub inside cellar steps and keeping cellar. Clean drains. Afternoon free.

Special Arrangement for Sunday

The following is the routine for the maid, but very often we are away for the week-end, and do not require her.

8 : Arrive. Make early cup of tea. Call master and mistress. Lay break-fast table and put electric fire on in dining-room. Light fire in lounge. Prepare breakfast. Dust lounge. **9 :** Breakfast. **9.45 :** Washing up and ordinary housework. **11.30 :** Prepare lunch. **1 :** Lunch. This she has pre-pared and cooked alone. Afternoon free. The maid goes home after she has washed up, and laid the tea trolley and supper table if required.

Some explanations of the foregoing are necessary. Although the maid finishes her work by 5.30 she under-stands that she may be expected to stay any evening to help with a supper or dinner party. She has become quite good at waiting at table, though she is still inclined to breathe heavily through nervousness !

Tuesdays, Thursdays and Saturdays are long mornings, lunch not being until 1.15, therefore the longest jobs are done on those days—bedrooms, lounge and outside work. On Saturdays it is not always possible to do the outside work owing to bad weather, and then other jobs are fitted in, such as sweeping out the garage and cleaning its windows, tidying the box-room or thoroughly dusting the books and book-shelves, of which we have a great quantity.

The times given above may vary slightly from day to day, depending mainly on the amount of washing up, but on the average they work out as given.

Half-Time Home Life

*In this plea for the woman who runs a job as well as a
house, it is the love and thought, rather than the actual
time we put into a place, that makes the home, says*

IRENE STILES

MODERN marriages are more remarkable for their spirit of comradeship than were the marriages
of yesterday. Not that we need pat ourselves on the back about it. Modern conditions make it possible for us to be com-
rades in every sense of the word. Men
and women of to-day meet on more or less
level ground. There is every incentive towards good companionship.

One of the finest comradeships I know
exists between a husband and wife who
share what some of the more critical of
their friends are pleased to call a half-
time home life, a make-shift marriage.
And all because the wife "runs" a job as
well as a home!

"I'm sorry for Peter," these well-mean-
ing critics say, "getting home to an empty
flat" (as he does very rarely), "and
always eating restaurant food" (which is
worse than an exaggeration).

Actually this so-called half-time home is
more efficiently managed and infinitely
more comfortable than many which are run
by whole-time housewives. There is really
no room for criticism or comparison, but
the critics in this case judge not so much
by results as by the amount of time wisely
or unwisely expended in achieving those
results.

Peter's mother, one of the severest
critics, was born of a generation of women
who found all the interest and happiness
they required in the then more various
and complicated aspects of housekeeping
and homekeeping. Her early married life
was a peaceful country affair. As the
wife of a country town solicitor she had
her share of entertaining to do. Butter-
making, extensive preserving and pickling
of orchard and garden produce played
no small part in the household activities.
Naturally enough she found it was as much
as she could manage to be out of kitchens
or garden and into a different frock in
time for dinner at night.

She has to admit when she goes to
Peter's home that everything *looks* all
right and Peter seems well enough. The
food appears to be good; is astonishingly
well cooked and pleasantly served. In
fact the whole atmosphere of Peter's home
is friendly and restful, and everyone, including two growing children, seems very
happy in it. Peter's mother looks on in-
credulously and with a certain half-grudg-
ing admiration, quite convinced that there
is a catch somewhere. She is, so to speak,
always half-expecting to meet some housekeeping skeleton whenever she happens to
go to the linen cupboard or the larder.

She forgets that the old-fashioned house
in which Peter was born was a place of
many stairs and difficulties. She forgets
that those were the days of still rooms
and oil lamps, of obstinate kitchen ranges,
wash-hand stands and constant cold water.
Moreover, families were larger then and
large houses were needed to accommodate
them. It is worse than foolish to compare
her own case with that of Peter's wife
who, in her home life at least, has only
to contend with the conveniences of a

well-equipped, modern, labour-saving flat.

Peter's wife, being a tolerant and good-
humoured woman, suffers her mother-in-
law's unspoken censure and the not unspoken criticisms of her friends with a
smile and the firm conviction that it does
not really matter. Peter, however, takes
it all rather more to heart. Only he,
after all, knows what an essentially good
manager his wife is. For has she not
contrived to be a good worker and earner
outside the home and a good wife and
mother at the same time? Have they not
with their joint savings been able to give
their children a far better education than
would have been possible had there been
only his earnings to draw from?

The busy woman, like the busy man,
finds time for everything. It is invariably
the inefficient housewife who complains
drearily that she has no time to read,
answer her friends' letters or darn her
husband's socks, let alone try to earn
some money in her spare time. Admittedly
a half-time home life needs careful organisation if it is also to be a happy and
comfortable home life. But then, any full
life needs a good deal of organisation,
whether it be the crowded life of a film
star or member of Parliament.

Obviously certain privileges and concessions must be accorded to the woman who
earns her living and runs a home at the
same time. She will, if she can, wisely
suit her home to her present needs. A
good deal must of necessity depend upon
whether she is married or single.

If she is married with a young and
growing family and lack of funds is no
obstacle, she may prefer to live in the
country that lies less than fifty miles from
town. I know one family who do this
very successfully. The family consists of
wife, husband, the wife's brother, who is
in business with the husband, and two
young children not yet ready for the
schoolroom proper.

The original idea was that the small
country house was purchased for the benefit of the children in order that they
could grow up in plenty of space, light
and fresh air. In practice, however, the
grown-ups derive almost as much enjoyment and healthy benefit from the place
as the children do. Long summer evenings away from noise, dust and petrol
fumes, and week-ends in the garden all
the year round prove themselves well worth
working for, and because there are three
bread-winners backing this establishment
in various ways the little extra expenditure
of time and money involved in travelling
to and from town is more than justified.
Health is and should be of first consideration, and change of scene is possibly almost
as important to the mental worker as
change of air.

In this particular household there is a
staff of three: a trained nurse for the
children (who does all the preparing and
cooking of food for the nursery), a cook-
housemaid, and a chauffeur-gardener (who
also does a few odd jobs in the house).
This may seem a large staff for a smallish

HALF-TIME HOME LIFE

house, but a good deal of simple week-end entertaining is done and living out of town would not be practical without a chauffeur.

Many people in similar circumstances prefer a fast train service to a drive to town in the face of increasing traffic difficulties. For the only alternative to keeping a chauffeur waiting about in town all day for the return journey, is to drive oneself, and this is hardly a good preparation for a strenuous day's work. Even if the fast train service is patronised there is the problem of getting to the station, and here the chauffeur-gardener or chauffeur-secretary comes to the rescue. In the case I have quoted the chauffeur-gardener drives the three bread-winners to the station in the morning and fetches them from there at night. In spite of a full, hard-working and incidentally very happy life, the wife and mother in this establishment makes time for quite a number of household and nursery duties, and always does the household accounts and supervises the menus. Most working women, however, are concerned with a flat or small house and possibly one maid, or even, as in my own case, with a small flat and a very little daily help. Here, perhaps, we may start talking about the concessions and privileges!

The half-time housewife, if she is to live in a flat, will naturally prefer one of the labour-saving varieties, complete with central heating, constant hot water and re-frigerating system. If she is already settled in a small house or converted flat without these conveniences, she will choose gas or electric fires for most of her rooms in preference to coal. Should she or her husband prefer a coal fire in one room, she certainly will not feel it her duty to clean her own grate or lay her own fire, for she knows that her earnings warrant her paying someone else to do the rough work.

She will find it very necessary to practise economy in the time as well as the money she spends on her housekeeping, and there is absolutely no need for the home to suffer because of it. Indeed professional women, by very reason of the organisation they must of necessity put into their housekeeping, often become the best and most systematic housekeepers. Unless rigid economy must be observed a telephone cannot be regarded as an extravagance, especially now that rentals have been reduced. The telephone allied to a weekly account with one good "all-in all" store will prove of great assistance. A weekly survey of supplies and accounts and a weekly provisional compiling of menus are great time-savers and will also eliminate too many afterthought telephone orders.

I know one woman (without a telephone) who sends a weekly postcard to her provision merchant with her daily needs written clearly on it. Each day, or every other day as the case may be, her orders are delivered at the time requested. Even with the telephone two or more days' orders may be given in one call. For if you have decided, more or less, what you are going to eat during the week a good deal of ordering may be done at once, and more than one dinner may be prepared and cooked at the same time. Quite apart from one's own inspirations in these matters, there are cooking stoves and cookery books especially designed to meet the needs of busy women.

Where there is no help the chores of the half-time home life should obviously be shared by the family or members of the establishment more or less equally. If the wife should cook and prepare the evening meal, husband and children should

wash up and clear away, but since this is often the mode of procedure in an ordinary household, it is perhaps unnecessary to stress or even suggest this. Obviously again, so far as married people are concerned, the half-time home life would be neither possible nor practicable during the whole of married life. A new baby changes everything and most existing conditions have to be altered because of the newcomer, for the time being at least. Moreover, few mothers will wish to go out and earn a living while small babies need the care which only mothers can give.

When the children are growing up it is a different matter and nowadays, hard and cynical as this may sound, a little extra money may prove far more helpful than a lot of love and care. It is, after all, the old story of a little (practical) help being worth a lot of pity. And once a child is past babyhood it is easy enough for a clever mother to ensure that neither child nor husband suffers in any way because of a half-time home life. Indeed, when we consider that most children are away at school all day and many away for the whole term, it is difficult to see how and where the children of professional women suffer at the expense of their mother's career.

The clever manager of a famous firm of beauty preparation manufacturers could tell you a strange and interesting story if he were writing this article. With his permission I shall tell it instead. Some of his earliest recollections are of being taken to a crèche in New York every morning and being fetched every evening. The pretty creature who took him and fetched him was his mother. Left a widow by the young husband who had taken her to America, she set out to earn her living as best she could. First of all she worked in a hat shop and then at a hair-dressing establishment, which sold its own beauty preparations as a side-line. Working there also was an analytical chemist interested in herbal dyes and remedies. She used to talk to him sometimes about the creams and lotions her own grandmother made from the flowers and fruits of an old Gloucestershire garden. In due course these two, already bound together by the common interest of their work, fell in love and married.

Of this second marriage there were two more children. With each the mother gave up her work until the child could be safely entrusted to the care of others. Apart from these respites that woman continues to be to this day a very successful half-time home maker. Those who criticise her for working when she no longer needs the money receive the very satisfactory explanation that this business which she has helped to build up, not only gives employment to herself, her husband and three grown children, but also to the children of many other mothers and fathers and to the fathers and mothers of many other children!

More interesting than all this, however, are the clever young manager's stories of the small rented room that was once his home. Short as his waking hours with his mother were, the details of that shabby room impressed themselves on his young mind as the details of his later and more comfortable homes did not. It was a poor enough place in which to try to rear a small boy. For him it was a quarter-time rather than a half-time home life, but love and determined cheerfulness in the face of tremendous odds made of it something which he will always remember with tenderness and gratitude. For it is the love and thought, rather than the actual time which we put into a place, that make the home.

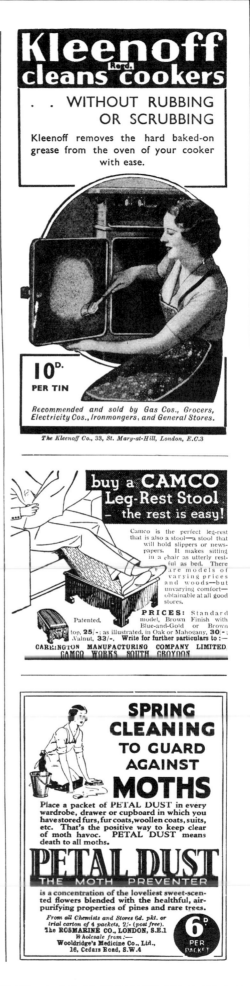

THE **30's**

Women who know are making a dead set at The £100 FORD SALOON

(£6 TAX IN GREAT BRITAIN)

Saloon, £100. Double-Entrance Saloon, £112.10s. Hide upholstery and sliding roof, £10 Extra, when required. All Prices at Works.

As an all-purpose, general-service car, comfortable, amply-powered, completely-equipped and very nicely finished (inside and out), for recreative service, yet lightly handled, compact in overall dimensions for traffic-work and easy parking, during workaday use, shopping, station-work, school-journeys and the like.

Britain's first £100 four-seated saloon, it is an un-challenged value-proposition; but it is also a very nice car, with nothing cheap about it but that figure of £100—*really* completely equipped, let us repeat !

Literature on Request: Dealers Everywhere, All Prepared to Deliver the £100 Ford Saloon, Insured and Taxed, on an Initial Payment of £25.

Come to Dagenham any Monday, Tuesday or Wednesday, to see Ford cars, Fordson vans, trucks, and tractors produced, from iron ore to finished vehicles. The Local Ford Dealer, or Visits Dept., Ford Motor Company Limited, Dagenham, Essex, will gladly arrange your visit, individually or in parties.

FORD CARS, FORDSON VANS AND TRUCKS—PROVED BY THE PAST— IMPROVED FOR THE FUTURE !

FORD MOTOR COMPANY LIMITED, DAGENHAM, ESSEX. LONDON SHOWROOMS: 88 REGENT STREET, W.1

The Housekeeper's Dictionary *of* Facts

THE INSTITUTE CRITICISES HOUSEHOLD ACCOUNTS

My mother, with whom I live, had a breakdown some months ago, since when young servants have carried on as they pleased, and all accounts have steadily increased. I should be obliged if you would make a charge and criticise the accompanying books and accounts for last month. We live in rather a large house, but do not entertain. There is a considerable kitchen garden (about an acre), and a bit outside for potatoes, many fruit trees, and all varieties of vegetables. In family we are two men and two women, all moderate eaters. In the kitchen there are three maids, two of whom are large eaters.

Breakfast : *Grapefruit and eggs and bacon, etc.*

Lunch : *Cold meat, salad, a cold sweet and cheese.*

Tea : *Bread and butter and cake (Men usually out.)*

Supper : *Hot joint or made-up dish, a sweet, and occasionally a savoury.*

A few apples and bananas are usually kept on the sideboard.

I should like to keep groceries at under £2 a week, meat under £1, and fruit at a few shillings. Of the ladies, one is very old and eats little ordinary food: the other is a companion-nurse.

I have looked over the housekeeping books which you enclosed with your letter, and consider that the total for June, which works out at approximately 12s. 6d. per head weekly, indicates careful catering.

The butcher's, greengrocer's and dairy accounts are definitely low, but in proportion the grocer's is still a little high, and I think that with care this could be reduced still more. I notice that orders are sometimes given on consecutive days, and in any case fairly frequently. This shows somewhat careless ordering, and I think it would be far easier to keep a check on matters if you only allowed orders to be given once or twice a week. On looking into details, I find, for example, that 3 lb. of butter were ordered on June 3rd, another 2 lb. on June 6th and a further 1½ lb. apparently on the same day. Tea is also ordered very indiscriminately, and I notice that a very considerable amount of sugar seems to be consumed, quite apart from the small amount of preserving sugar ordered on June 25th.

I think I enclosed in one of my previous letters a list of the average allowances of food per head weekly, and it would be a good plan, at any rate for the time being, if you arranged to give the main order to the grocer once a week, basing the amounts of sugar, tea, butter, etc., on those given on the list. In case you have mislaid the copy, I am enclosing another for reference. You will notice that the average allowance of potatoes is given on this list. I need hardly point out, however, that

---

LECTURE DEMONSTRATIONS
At The Institute

A course of lecture demonstrations on the theory and practice of cookery is now in progress at Good Housekeeping Institute, on the dates given below at 3 p.m. Selections from the dishes mentioned will be made. For further details and tickets (price 2s. 6d. each for a single lecture), apply to The Director, Good Housekeeping Institute, 49 Wellington Street, Strand, W.C.2, enclosing a stamped addressed envelope.

November 4th
The Making of Rich Cakes

Iced Chocolate Cake
Christmas Plum Cake
Caramel Cake

November 11th
Savouries and Cocktail Snacks

Hot and Cold Savouries of various kinds
Cheese Pasty
Celery Creams
Bouchées à la Marquise
Gondoles au Parmesan
Cheese Aigrettes
Prawn Cocktail
Bâtons aux Tomates

November 18th
Bread and Yeast Cakes

Yeast as a Raising Agent
Home-made Bread
Yeast Cakes
Tea Cakes
Plain and Currant Bread
Doughnuts
Milk Rolls
Swiss Buns
Bath Buns
Sally Lunns

November 25th
Sweets, Bon-bons and Almond Icing

Covering Cake with Almond Paste
Fudge
Fondants
Marzipan Sweets
Stuffed Fruits

December 2nd
Icing and Decorating Christmas Cakes and Party Cakes

Transparent and Royal Icing
Designing
Decorating and Piping in Sugar
Flower-making

December 9th
Iced Cakes and Petits Fours

December 16th
Sponge Cake Mixture

December 17th
Cold Sweets for Parties

---

whilst such a list serves as a useful guide, one is bound to find that the quantities require modification to some extent, as while in some households there may be an extravagant consumption of butter, for example, this may be counterbalanced by the fact that consumption of other items is below the average.

I am enclosing on a separate sheet some suggestions for light luncheons for the summer. The recipes for those marked X are all in *Good Housekeeping Menu and Recipe Book* (2s. 9½d., including postage).

Thank you for the detailed information, which is exactly what I require. With it I hope to keep the household accounts within reasonable limits for the future!

Readers' Letters of Thanks

I am in receipt of your letter of the 8th instant, for which I thank you most heartily. I should like also to express my appreciation of the trouble you have taken on my behalf to answer all my questions so fully and comprehensively.

(K. A. W., Kinross.)

Very many thanks for your kind help over my two concrete kitchen floors. The mason has taken up a third of one of the floors, and used a finer cement. The effect is a good deal smoother and better. He has then put on a coating of floor paint, which seems to have dried. The dust, which was appalling, no longer appears. When we have cleaned up the dabs of paint left by the rather untidy workmen, re-painted the woodwork, and also re-colour-washed the walls, the place will look different. Again thank you very much for giving me fresh hope in what was such a discouraging muddle.

(B. K., Isle of Man.)

I must thank you for your letter in reply to my 'phone enquiry of April 18th. Regarding the treatment of polished bathroom walls I followed your advice before painting, and the whole decoration has been entirely satisfactory.

(E. P. P., Mill Hill, N.W.7.)

Please accept my sincere thanks for your courteous, informative reply to my letter. The particulars you send of a mixture for dealing with moth trouble will be most useful.

(W. A. C., Champion Hill.)

Thank you very much indeed for the information *re* a Guide's tie. I must apologise for delay in answering, but wish to thank you for the trouble you have taken now and also at other times when I have written to you.

(N. G., Cardiff.)

It sounds too good to be true!

Incredible—but at last a fact! We here introduce to the world a servant guaranteed to do all the heavy washing and cleaning in your home without ever giving notice! Without ever needing a day off or a night out; mood-proof and even tantrum-proof. This paragon is ATMOS "The Mechanical Housemaid"! At your constant service, to boil clothes (by a *new* and cleaner method), wring them (as easily as turning a mincer), dry them, and provide for the ironing of them; to vacuum clean your home from top to bottom; to do, in short, everything from the week's wash to boiling a kettle!

IT WASHES
CLOTHES

IT BLUES OR
DYES THEM

IT DRIES
THEM

VACUUM
CLEANS

'ATMOS' *The Mechanical Housemaid*

A Clothes Washer; Rinser; Wringer; Drier; Ironer—and a Vacuum Cleaner

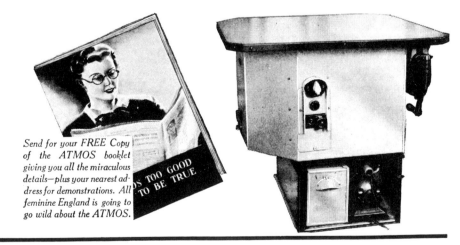

Send for your FREE Copy of the ATMOS booklet giving you all the miraculous details—plus your nearest address for demonstrations. All feminine England is going to go wild about the ATMOS.

BURSLEM'S PATENTS LIMITED, BANK BUILDINGS, 20, KINGSWAY, LONDON, W.C.2

The Housekeeper's Dictionary *of* Facts

ADVICE ON MISCELLANEOUS PROBLEMS

I WONDER *if you can advise me as to the best way to get rid of shiny seams on a coating shantung costume which I was foolish enough to launder myself. I realise now that I should have sent it to be cleaned instead of washing it, and should be glad if you could tell me whether cleaning would now remove the shininess, or whether you think a good steam laundry would solve my problem?*

M. H., Montgomery.

I should imagine that the shiny marks on your shantung costume are due to the fact that it was damp in parts when you ironed it.

Shantung silk is made from a wild variety of silk and is not degummed in the process of manufacture in the same way as other silks, consequently it should be allowed to dry completely after washing and should be ironed with a moderately hot iron, which will soften the natural gum and thus give a smooth finish.

Shantung should on no account be damped down, as greasy-looking marks invariably appear, but the laundering of it presents no difficulty and can therefore be undertaken at home.

Steak with Pineapple

When in Egypt I once had little rounds of steak with a slice of pineapple between them and the toast or bread on which they were served. I am anxious to try this recipe and should like to know whether the pineapple should be cooked or added after the steak has been grilled. I was told the pineapple juice made the steak more tender.

M. C., Chislehurst.

It is not unusual to combine pineapple with steak. The pineapple should, however, for preference be fresh, as the enzyme in the fruit is supposed to aid the digestion of the steak. It is therefore important not to overcook it.

After cooking the steak in butter or half butter and half olive oil, the rounds of fresh pineapple should be put in the pan, and fried very lightly on both sides.

It is quite a good idea to have the pineapple in two sizes, and to have some rounds slightly larger than the fillet of steak, and some smaller. If you adopt this suggestion, you can then dispense with the croûtons of bread, for the steak can be placed on the larger round of pineapple, and the smaller one put on top.

Pineapple is also a good accompaniment to gammon rashers or baked ham.

Thank you so much for your letter. The pineapple with the steak was a great success.
Being a working woman I really have very little time to try my hand at

---

A COURSE OF COOKERY DEMONSTRATIONS

A course of twelve Cookery Demonstrations will be given at Good Housekeeping Institute during the autumn months. These will take place on Wednesday afternoons, commencing on October 7th. A list of the subjects to be demonstrated—which will include the making, icing and decorating of cakes, the making of plain buns and scones and of pastry of all kinds, and deep fat frying—will be published in the October number of GOOD HOUSEKEEPING. Particulars will also be sent on application to the Institute, 49 Wellington Street, Strand, London, W.C.2. Tickets, which may be reserved in advance, will be 2s. 6d. each, or 27s. 6d. for the course of twelve demonstrations.

cookery, but like to experiment sometimes.

M. C., Chislehurst.

Renovating Burnt Leather

I have taken the colour out of a leather-topped writing-table through leaving an iron on what I thought was a very thick pad. Would it be better to treat the whole surface and if so, what would you advise?

I went to a leather shop here, and they gave me a powder stain, but that seems to leave rather a dull gold surface. The colour of the leather is a deep red or maroon.

S. R., Bath.

Without actually seeing your writing-table, it is difficult to advise you. If the leather surface is really burnt, I am afraid that no treatment other than recovering the surface will be effective. If, however, there is only slight discoloration, I should be inclined to suggest applying a reliable make of spirit dye. The directions supplied with the dye should be carefully followed and care must be taken to remove all traces of grease, polish, etc., which may have been left by previous treatment, with a grease solvent.

Removing Tea Stains

Will you please tell me if there is anything that will remove tea stains from a blanket? I have been told that there is nothing.

May I take this opportunity of thanking you for all the helpful information given month by month in your maga-

---

zine. I have been a reader since the first copy was published, and rely on it and the other helpful books and leaflets published by you to solve all my housekeeping problems. I might say that all I know I have learnt from GOOD HOUSEKEEPING, *as I had had no experience of household affairs when I married. Now I do everything, including painting and papering.*

G. D., Grimsby.

Fresh tea stains are usually fairly readily removed from blankets or other articles by soaking in warm water and borax. If, however, the stains have been allowed to remain for some time they are often very resistant, and it is possible that a slight bleaching agent, such as hydrogen peroxide diluted three or four times with water, would give better results. If the stains are old you will probably find a good deal of patience is required to remove them completely.

I am very glad to know how much you appreciate GOOD HOUSEKEEPING.

Installing a Water Softener

I am considering the purchase of a water softening apparatus for my hotel. I am given to understand that:

1. *A water softener will gradually dissolve away the existing scale in the boiler.*
2. *By keeping the boiler free from scale, a softener will materially reduce fuel costs.*
3. *Soft water requires less fuel to heat it than the same quantity of hard water.*

As doubtless you have data in connection with this subject, I should be grateful if you could favour me with your opinion on these points.

L. H. S. London

In reply to your letter, although water softeners have very many advantages, I am afraid you could not expect such an installation to be effective in dissolving away existing scale. Consequently, if the boiler, pipes, etc., are very "furred up," it is advisable to have this attended to before fitting a softener.

It is quite true that if the boiler is kept free from scale, fuel costs are likely to be reduced, but apart from this, the amount of fuel required to heat a certain quantity of water to a definite temperature would not be materially different, whether the water is soft or hard.

A Word of Thanks

My husband, my sister and I visited Good Housekeeping Institute as you suggested, and I should like to thank you for the courtesy extended to us by the member of your staff who showed us round, and for the helpful advice on kitchen equipment.

C. L., Doncaster.

So many of us, on reaching the middle forties, feel that we have accomplished pitifully little, but effort, if it is honest, is never wasted, says this author

Have You FAILED?

I SUPPOSE most of us, however easy or difficult life has been, begin to take stock of ourselves in quiet moments when we get into the middle forties. Sometimes people go on feeling complacent all their lives, but the more imagination one has, the more one feels that there is very little to be complacent about; mistakes come back and sit on one's chest in the night, digging in claws of steel that hurt badly; wasted chances vapour about like ghosts and one is thankful for the twitter of birds and the glimmer of light that mean dawn and the day's small, varied anodynes of duty.

It has been dawning on me for a few years now that I have failed in most of the things I have tried to do. And being a reasonably clear-thinking and honest person, I have tried to find out why. I know now that the only thing I can do really perfectly is cooking—and although I love cooking and am proud of my ability, that isn't enough! I love gardening and tried to run a two-acre garden for six years. For one year it was a great success, when I did it myself with the help of a relative; but that got me into financial difficulties, because I would go out at five in the morning, thinking I would sit down to my typewriter after breakfast. I never did—the garden was altogether too seductive. And although I grew enough vegetables to give away in barrowloads, produced eighty pounds each of strawberries and raspberries, and had

enough flowers to send to friends in huge dress-boxes, I nearly went bankrupt, because during that whole year I couldn't be bothered to write the stories and articles on which I kept up the standard of living I had slipped into. The same with poultry farming and pigs; if I could have spent all my time at poultry and pigs they would have been a success. But they didn't make me enough money, and I was a complete failure as a poultry farmer—although I got more live chicks than anyone else in the district, my eggs were bigger and my table birds fatter than anyone else's. But I couldn't do that and write and run a house and family. So that too was a failure.

I've published fifteen books; some of them have been called works of genius by reviewers whose opinions I respect. But apart from the letters a few hundred people have written to me, telling me that things in these books have been of help to them in facing life, these books have been a failure. I wanted to write literature

—and I haven't done so. For a long time I moaned about this, about lack of recognition for good work. It gave me a bad inferiority complex, made me feel I must be a dud in spite of what reviewers said. It stopped me from writing books for many years.

I got involved in politics some years ago and could have been put up as a candidate for Parliament, which I would have loathed. Often I've had soul struggles about that, thinking that my dread of public appearance and my scorn for political chicanery had let down the people I might conceivably have helped. Altogether, during the past two years, since I realised I was forty-five and never, now, likely to write "great books" nor do the things that women like Miss Jex-Blake, Mrs. Josephine Butler or Mrs. Pankhurst did, I've been thinking that perhaps I was just a conceited idiot who had started out with delusions of grandeur that were not backed up by enough education, enough patience or enough intellect.

Well, that's all true. I'm not educated, as is my daughter, who has been to a university. She can talk of subjects that are Greek to me. The lack of mental discipline, of sheer knowledge, that my scrappy and mostly self-acquired education has given me, have stopped me from ever doing the big work in literature I might have done. I haven't enough patience to do things with the slow, steady, unhasting, unresting courage that means sure foundations. I see rottenness and wickedness and want

Drawing by J. H. Davison

to clear them out as thoroughly as I clear out a room during spring cleaning. And because I'm so impatient I wear out my energy, shout and rage and put people's backs up, which destroys all the effect of one's work. And it is beginning to dawn on me that I'm not actually "clever" enough to do the things I set out to do.

After all, if you are "clever" enough to see a job to be done, whether it is cooking or gardening, farming or running a business, political work or writing, you've got to be much more "clever" than that! You've got to be clever enough to organise your life ruthlessly so that outside things don't interfere. Marriage is a disaster for most women who want to "do things." Marriage means getting involved in other lives—your husband's, your children's, their friends', your employees'. You cannot marry a man and expect him to "stay put." He wants your help in a thousand ways. The very fact of his being there, in your home and your life, is a challenge. He has to be kept comfortable in mind and body, comforted when things get difficult, encouraged and amused. I have managed the comforting, the encouraging, the cooking and so on, but I've never had time to spend with him during his playtimes. He writes—I write. When his writing hours are done my housekeeping hours begin and slop over into his leisure hours. I am usually too tired when we have a holiday to want anything but sleep and a few thrillers and a lazy time. He wants relaxation—and he has to get it away from me, which isn't fair to him, as he prefers my company to anyone else's. Another failure. And the same applies to the children. I have given myself to them as far as caring for their physical needs goes; I have always been there to spur them on in their work, to get them out of muddles they have got into. But now that they are all married and away from me, I realise that I have never played with them. I could never take a holiday when they did, because of journalistic work to be done. I've given

them a great deal, but never my playtimes. Last year, when I spent a fortnight with my married daughter who lives in Italy, she reminded me that it was the first time she had ever been alone with me in her life! That wasn't fair: one's children need more than one's money, or work, or mental stimulus. They want one's companionship. And mine have never had that in any appreciable amount.

Sometimes lately I have felt like creeping away into a decent lethal chamber to get away from this nagging sense of failure. If I had my time to go over again I should not attempt so much. I might be only a wife and mother and do that well; I might be only a social worker and do that well; I might be a writer of important books and do that well. The point was, I didn't know which thing was most important, so I did anything that came along and didn't do any of it extremely well.

Last year this feeling of inadequacy, of time wasted, of opportunities lost, got so badly on top of me that I was ill and even less adequate. I still went on with all the jobs I am doing, still did my journalistic

by LEONORA EYLES

On the left is a photograph of Mrs. Eyles, and right, one of her husband, Mr. D. L. Murray, who is also a journalist and author

" Maybe all that we do here isn't very splendid. . . . Quite a few of us have to go through life without too good an opinion of ourselves, and yet we manage. You'll learn even that some day "

Winifred Holtby

jobs, still fussed and worried over crowds of people in trouble who had to be put right; still managed my home and family, but felt it was all hopeless because I myself was such a dud. Then it dawned on me suddenly that nobody can do more than the instrument with which they work will let them. I've attempted an impossible task with the amount of physical energy and mental vigour I possess. A great doctor of the last century, working on his "*magno sterilisatio*" which should cure every disease, found out by accident a treatment for *one* disease; a psychologist, working on problems of human behaviour, found *one* way through *one* problem. It seems to me that all one can do is to accept failure, not ask for results, not expect to be there when the laurel wreaths of victory are handed out. Most of us, as Winifred Holtby says in the words I have put at the foot of this page, have to discover that we'll go through life without too good an opinion of ourselves. We dig over a bit of waste land and plant things in it; we want to see the former desolations gone, the desert blossoming like a rose. All any of us see is the turned earth, the stick-like plants — and our children or their children see the blossoming.

One of the hardest things we have to accept is the fact that we have hurt others by our blunders, let them down by our failures —and yet still have to go on, managing somehow to make a good thing of the little scraps of success we have had. Effort, if it is honest, if it goes down to the fundamental needs of humanity, is never wasted. Christ was murdered by His generation, and so was Socrates; thousands of other great people have seen their work useless, even if they did not lose their lives for doing it. But their work has lived. Sitting up with sick people, putting hopeless people on their feet now and then have stopped me from writing books, but in the ultimate issue it is possible that this small, humble duty has been valuable.

Now every dinner is a success!!

AS TOLD BY Mᵣˢ LAWSON, WHO RUNS A BOARDING HOUSE

I SHALL BE LEAVING NEXT WEEK Mᵣˢ LAWSON — GOING TO LIVE NEARER THE OFFICE

I'M SORRY TO GO — Mᵣˢ LAWSON'S A DEAR — BUT SHE CAN'T COOK!

Mrs. Lawson ran a boarding house, but no one ever seemed to stop long. Hear her own story of how she turned the tide of ill fortune.

My husband wasn't one to worry about food, so I never thought much about cooking till I had to do it for a dozen people—and then, oh dear! wasn't I in a muddle! They liked everything else, but at meal times . . .

SO THERE I AM JANE. PEOPLE NEVER STAY LONG — I KNOW MY COOKING IS TO BLAME

BUT IT'S SO EASY TO COOK WELL NOW— WHY DON'T YOU TRY SPRY—THE NEW READY-CREAMED COOKING FAT?

I took my troubles along to Jane and straightway she began telling me about this Spry she'd discovered. Spry's an all-vegetable fat that's been ready-creamed so that it never goes too hard or too soft. I was certainly glad to hear of *something* that would make cooking easier.

SPRY'S A MARVEL SO SMOOTH AND LIGHT. IT NEARLY MIXES ITSELF!

After what Jane said about it mixing so quickly and evenly for pastry and cakes, and frying without a single nasty splutter, I *expected* Spry to be good, but upon my word it surprised me! Mixing the steamed pudding with that lovely smooth Spry was like a holiday after the work I used to have. And it was a change to fry without having smoke all over the place the moment you turned your back. And didn't everything taste fine! Nobody leaves anything on their plates now! 'Good old Spry' is what I say from now.

NO ONE DREAMS OF LEAVING NOW

THIS PUDDING IS DELICIOUSLY LIGHT!

YOUR FIGURE'S SAFE WITH THOSE FRIED POTATOES WE HAD— THEY WEREN'T GREASY AT ALL!

WHAT A MARVELLOUS DINNER!

SPRY THE 'ready-creamed' FAT
ONE fat for ALL cooking

★Buy a tin of Spry and judge for yourself. You'll see a fat that's white as snow and smooth as velvet. You'll work with a fat that mixes at a touch, cooks *everything*, pastry, cakes and puddings, and doesn't spark or cause heavy smoke in the frying pan. And afterwards you'll enjoy the delicious natural flavours of Spry-cooked food, the crisp lightness of pastry, the rich and wholesome taste of Spry cakes, the *goodness* of food fried in Spry (nothing greasy or indigestible about Spry-fried food).

Another thing about Spry is that it doesn't go rancid—keep it as long as you like and it will still be pure and fresh when you want to use it.

SPR 44-5

1-lb. size
10d
½-lb. size
5½d

Here's a really valuable recipe book that gives a new angle on cookery. All the most popular recipes and how to make them even nicer and easier to prepare.

FREE COOKERY BOOK

Send off this coupon to-day, with 3d in stamps to cover postage and packing, to the Spry Kitchen (Dept. PP44), R. S. Hudson Ltd., Bebington, Cheshire. *Your envelope should be sealed and bear a 1½d stamp.*

Name ....

Address ....

Town .... County ....
(PLEASE WRITE IN BLOCK LETTERS)

The Housekeeper's Dictionary of Facts

Consult this page every month for information regarding domestic and household problems of all kinds

Preservation of Outdoor Woodwork

GARDEN furniture, rustic work, fences, outhouses, gates, and general decorative and structural woodwork exposed to the elements are all open to attack by fungi and insects, provided certain conditions are present, which in the case of fungi are moisture, air, food and a suitable temperature.

If the enemies of sound timber are allowed to ravage the wood unchecked, the damage may be extensive and repair or replacement long and costly. It is only by adopting precautionary measures when the wood is sound that these destructive pests may be defeated, or at least their attack rendered innocuous.

Trouble due to Fungus Growth

Almost everyone is familiar with the type of fungus that grows on moist wood, and it consists of fine thread-like filaments which penetrate the wood in all directions. Eventually fruiting bodies grow out of the affected wood, and these may be shaped like plates or pancakes, consisting of soft fleshy matter which bears on its surface an enormous number of spores or "seeds" of fungus.

These are blown about by the wind and quickly spread infection. They soon grow in cracks or badly fitting joints if the latter are not well protected by means of preservatives, and thus considerable damage may be done over a wide area by contaminating spores carried by the wind.

Several factors influence fungoid growth, and it has been said on good authority that posts decay more quickly in a gravelly or sandy soil than in heavy clay, and in chalk more quickly than gravel, while a peaty soil has the reputation of imparting a certain amount of durability to timbers which are the least durable in other soils. Woods also vary in their immunity to attack, and it is therefore unwise to use non-durable timbers such as spruce, elm, Scots pine, etc., for important work under conditions where they might be subjected to fungoid attack, e.g. as fence posts.

Insects

A number of insects are liable to attack outside timbers, but the most usual are the powder post beetles, and the common furniture beetles. The presence of these is made known, or can be discovered, by the small holes in the wood, or the tiny piles of finely powdered wood.

The best means of preserving outdoor wood of all kinds against the action of fungoid growth and of insects differ very little in practice, and it may be said that suitable creosote treatment is the best and simplest method available. The

creosote should be purchased from the local gas works or other reliable source, as it is useless applying an inferior preparation or one which has been so diluted that its value is lost. There are a number of excellent creosote compounds on the market which are sold under various well-known proprietary names, and the majority of these are very suitable for the treatment of outdoor furniture, woodwork and fences.

Treatment of Affected Wood

The methods of applying creosote differ considerably according to the kinds of work in hand. Wood not in actual contact with the ground may be well preserved by brushing the surface with a liberal quantity of hot creosote. At least three generous coatings are necessary, and it is recommended to leave an interval of two or three weeks between each coat, so that the preservative sinks right into the heart of the wood. In the case of wood in contact with the ground or actually buried in the soil, the ordinary brush treatment is useless. It is strongly advisable to purchase timber for this purpose which has been previously treated under pressure with hot creosote, or to have one's own wood treated at one of the various wood preserving depots, which are situated throughout the country.

It is a well-known fact that some species of timber absorb creosote very much more rapidly than others, thus larch, oak, sweet chestnut, etc., may be termed refractory, while alder, beech, ash, elm, lime, pines, spruces, and sycamore, etc., are easily treated. In the case of obstinate wood, extra creosote treatment will have to be given, and it is recommended to apply as many as four or five coats to ensure the maximum protection.

Creosote does not deteriorate in the wood or lose its toxic qualities, and providing it has penetrated far enough, excellent protection will be afforded. Examples may be cited where creosoted wood has resisted an attack for over eighty years. Another excellent property of creosoted wood is that it is in no way affected by moisture, and it is therefore safe to employ such wood for flooded areas, or other places where damp conditions are known to prevail.

Probably many readers will be interested to know that there is in existence the British Wood Preserving Association, formed to collect and spread knowledge of all methods of treating timber. Detailed information concerning all branches of wood preservation may be obtained from the Secretary of the above organisation, 48 Dover Street, W.1, or from the Forest Products Research Laboratory, Princes Risborough, Bucks.

Mother Memories

by MARGARET E. SANGSTER

Is to-day's child missing something that yesterday's child holds dear?

★

THE mother memories that are closest to my heart are the small, gentle ones that I have carried over from the days of my childhood. They aren't profound save as loveliness is profound. They aren't dramatic, unless tenderness can be termed drama. But they have stayed with me through my life and I think that, when I am very old, they will still be near.

Small, gentle memories! Of mother mending the favourite doll and drying my tears as she mended it. Of mother kissing the black and blue spots to make them well. Of mother reading aloud from some juvenile book and apparently as interested as I in the unfolding of the simple story. Of mother cutting cakes in the shape of birds and beasts and flowers, and singing as she did the cutting. Of mother listening to the prayers I said as I knelt with my forehead pressed against her knee. Of mother tucking me into bed and turning down the light . . .

These are some of my memories. They have carried me across the world —through fear and disappointment and disillusionment and heartbreak and temptation. They have given my house of life such a firm foundation that it does not rock beneath flood or tempest.

I fancy that my mother memories match the memories of approximately every adult who belongs to my generation. Mothers who lived and loved at the turn of the century were of the type who went in for cuddly things; who stood for spontaneous and unquestioning affection. Who dressed dolls in moments stolen from the family mending, and kept secrets, and did not laugh aloud at confidences.

Sometimes I wonder whether the children of to-day—and the children of to-morrow—will be as fortunate as I? I ask myself, "What sort of a foundation will they possess when they start to build upon their memories? Will they have a certain sensation of tenderness to use as a shield against the hard knocks which the future may hold? Or will the tenderness be a minus quality?" I ask myself these questions and, in all honesty, I have not the wisdom or perception to answer them.

I know many radiant young mothers. Young mothers who fully realise and accept the responsibilities of motherhood. Who are essentially like the mothers of yesterday—like your mother and my mother. Having a baby, even

in this enlightened age, is a serious matter—women have not ceased to go down into the valley of the shadow to bear children. But despite the pain and sacrifice entailed by child-bearing, despite the lack of essential change, the modern means of expressing maternal tenderness is often—modern! Many a mother of to-day seems afraid—or ashamed—to show a Victorian softness when it comes to her relationship with her babies. This is a generation which makes light of many things that are almost sacred; this is a generation of sophistication and wise-cracking.

Just yesterday I was with a young woman who laughed and told her small, sobbing daughter to "be a good sport—nobody ever died of a skinned knee!" She added, "I can't hold you—both my hands are busy!" It was true; there was a cocktail in one hand and a cigarette in the other. I'm not being priggish in recounting this incident—cocktails and cigarettes have to do with the individual taste! But a tiny skinned knee, to my mind, is more important than either—and, in the case of emergency, a glass can be set aside and a cigarette can be snubbed out.

This mother adores her child. I know, for I helped

her during last winter when the child was threatened with mastoid. During a few days the situation was critical—and the mother's face was a tense, wan mask and her eyes were haunted. I think that, in her own idiom, she breathed many a silent prayer. But she shrank from a display of sentiment even then, just as she did yesterday in the matter of the skinned knee. I'm sorry that she did—and does. For her own sake as well as for the sake of her child; and the memories that will be her child's dearest heritage!

Think back over your contacts with the modern young mothers who are your friends. Sane, clever young women for the most part—aren't they? More worldly wise than the mother who kissed away my hurts; far more able to

As I count over my memories to-day, I can see that they have carried me across the world, given my life a firm foundation

endure the conditions of this changing, chaotic period. And yet—and I speak from my own experience (and, of course, with certain reservations!)—it seems to me that they lack something important—extremely important—something that was as much a part of my mother as were her eyes and her dimples and her plump, soft shoulder! They lack the ability to express themselves in the little ways that meant, and still mean, so much to me. They aren't tongue-tied when it comes to a political discussion or a résumé of economic conditions—and my mother was! But they are sometimes tongue-tied when it is evening and the lamps are shaded, and

There is a tenderness that serves as a shield against the troubles of life. I felt it when my mother heard my prayers; I feel it now, remembering her

Illustration by E. M. Jackson

a tiny child begs for a bed-time lullaby.

The modern mother understands the psychology that dictates the actions and the reactions of the young mind, but can she always grasp, as my mother did, the

craving for an affection that is based on a child's unreasonable demands?

The mother of to-day is perhaps more of a pal to her children than was the mother of my generation. She meets her offspring on their own ground and treats them as equals—treats them with clarity and fairness and a sane, understanding regard.

But the modern child is pretty much like yesterday's child—yesterday's child who instinctively craved a judge instead of a pal, and a supreme being instead of an equal. In other words, a mother who was the feminine counterpart of God—save only that she was nearer and warmer!

The Housekeeper's
DICTIONARY OF FACTS
The Institute's Advice on Household Matters

THE
30's

REMOVING STAINS

SOME months ago you gave me very useful advice on how to remove an ice-cream stain from an artificial taffeta dress. I should be very much obliged if you could now tell me the safest way to remove a coffee stain from: (1) a stiff white lace dress, and (2) the white crêpe de Chine underslip. The coffee had milk in it.
P. D., Market Drayton.

We are so glad to know that you were successful in removing the ice-cream stain, and are only too glad to give assistance with regard to the coffee stains.

We think it is probable that you will remove these quite easily by soaking the marks for a short time in a warm solution of borax and water, afterwards rinsing thoroughly. If, however, this fails, when the fabric is dry apply a little glycerine immediately over the marks, allowing this to remain for a short time, and afterwards removing the excess of glycerine by rubbing gently with a cloth dipped in methylated or rectified spirit. Finally, if by any chance a grease mark remains as a result of the milk added to the coffee, this can easily be dealt with, by treatment with a suitable grease solvent such as carbon tetrachloride, using this when the fabric is quite dry.

When treating with a grease solvent, it is advisable to place the affected material over a piece of clean soft material such as a towel, and to apply the solvent in a ring well outside the mark first, gradually rubbing towards the centre of the stain.

CLEANING RUBBER TILES

I have had rubber tiles laid in the bathroom of my new house, and should be very grateful if you could advise me as to the best method of cleaning them.

Also, I should appreciate your opinion about the best method of lining the shelves of kitchen cupboards and larder. I have used American cloth for some years, but find it is inclined to stick to articles placed on it.
A. B., Royston.

The rubber tiles in your bathroom can be washed regularly, or alternatively, and this we are inclined to suggest, polished every two or three weeks with a sparing amount of wax polish. Any reliable make of wax polish can be used, and particular care should be taken to apply this only very sparingly and to rub the floor up well afterwards.

With regard to your kitchen cupboard and larder, for the latter in particular, we recommend covering the shelf or shelves with sheets of enamelled iron. This is obtainable to one's own measurements and is, of course, of lasting

durability and merely requires to be washed over with a damp cloth, to keep it spotless. For any cupboards and shelves for which you require a less expensive treatment, we would suggest

lining with a thin-gauge inlaid linoleum, as this is also very easily kept clean.

VARIED QUERIES

I should be glad if you would very kindly give me your advice on the following questions:

(1) How can I get rid of or prevent flies in my larder? The larder is of the old-fashioned cupboard variety with a sliding door which has a perforated zinc window, and is about 10 in. high. The flies are so tiny that they get through the finest gauge wire meat safe.

(2) What is the best way of cleaning a baby's wicker hamper and its sateen and organdie trimmings? I believe I could detach and wash the linings, but the tray would be very difficult to deal with. If the outside wicker is scrubbed the soapy water will probably penetrate the padding inside.

(3) What is the best way of getting rid of an unpleasant smell inside new furniture? I have a suite of Indian laurel and I think its lining has a very pungent and objectionable smell.

(4) Part of my kitchen ceiling was recently replastered, and the whole ceiling was distempered. The newly plastered area now shows very dark.
E. M., Abernethy.

(1) As you say that the perforated zinc sheet fitted in your larder window is not effective in preventing small flies coming through, you could tack fine muslin closely to the frame, washing it, of course, frequently as it becomes soiled. It will obviously also be important to see that the door of both the larder and meat safe fit closely.

(2) With regard to the wicker hamper, the only satisfactory way of cleaning this thoroughly will be to remove all linings and then scrub it, as you suggest, with warm water. All trimmings and linings should be washed by gently kneading and squeezing and ironing when nearly dry. When quite clean the linings should be replaced, by either stitching or sticking them in position with a suitable adhesive.

(3) With regard to the unpleasant smell you have noticed with your new furniture, we would suggest that you keep it in a well-ventilated room, leaving drawers and cupboards partly opened for a time, when it will probably wear off. Some woods, however, possess a slight smell which is difficult to get rid of completely.

(4) As your kitchen ceiling was replastered and distempered so recently it is surprising that it is already showing signs of darkening. We presume, however, that you keep the kitchen well ventilated so that steam, etc., does not collect unnecessarily. Where ventilation is difficult we consider the use of paint instead of distemper on wall and ceiling surfaces in a kitchen is preferable.

THE
30's

A WOMAN NEEDS A CAR

It keeps her out of a domestic rut and adds much to life

says

GILLIAN MAUD

ANOTHER Motor Show is almost with us. How time flies! Everything on this earth goes in cycles, even cars and horses and other means of personal road transportation. How many of us, I wonder, realise that with the present acceptance of women as responsible motorists—and even the most hard-boiled he-man must admit that women at the wheel have proved themselves the equal of men—we are back to mediæval times? That is not so silly as it sounds. For many a generation we weak, must-be-protected beings have been steered or conveyed with tutelary complaisance by our strong and not-always-so-silent consorts or patriarchs.

One can assume with safety and logic that the average reader of GOOD HOUSE-KEEPING is a woman of means; she is able at least to afford a car of some kind. In mediæval times, women of means were nothing like so numerous in proportion to our population as they are to-day. They travelled as their men folk travelled, astride a horse, on a basis of equality in dexterity, stamina and endurance. With the passing of the centuries, however, things in this particular altered.

This delving into history has much to do with a consideration of motoring in this and the coming year. A wee bit of reflection will help us to comprehend that, having returned, at last, to a position parallel with our husbands and brothers in transport matters, we still have quite a long way to go before we make full use of our emancipation.

Perhaps post-mediæval women became less sturdy and more susceptible to fatigue, perchance their lords and masters (how fatuous that looks in cold print to-day) thought that the time had come to call a halt to their freedom of movement. Be that as it may, the later Middle Ages found the fair sex in "ladies' carriages," contraptions that would have shamed present-day farm carts as regards suspension systems and general comfort. Then followed the "litter," which was nothing more nor less than a glorified, canopied, four-poster bed slung on a pole and carried by man or beast. Even ladies of royal blood were expected to travel in this lumbering, unhealthy way.

Later came stage wagons, private coaches and sedan chairs. Many of us can remember the lighter forms of horse-drawn vehicles that were the vogue down to the days of our grandparents—the dog-carts, the landaus, the cabriolets and the traps, and we can recollect also that precious few women were allowed to take the reins.

In the early days of motoring, the tiller—and later the steering wheel—responded only to the movements of masculine hands. But for the war, when women took over almost every civilian male activity, it is probable that motoring, other than that of passive participation from the passenger seats, would still be a male prerogative. Women, even at the beginning of motoring, were itching to "take over," but I will defy anyone to provide a picture, published prior to the Coronation of King George the Fifth, showing a woman in control of a car. No man would admit that any woman *could* drive. Medical reports show that insanity is decreasing. Probably

It is human to sigh with envy when a super-limousine slinks up and disgorges its opulent freight

this is due to the fact that many people, mostly women, who were considered crazy several years ago are now able to smile and say, "I told you so."

Congested traffic holds no terrors for the women drivers of 1938; on the open road they show a clean pair of heels—or is it bumpers?—to their male counterparts; they compete with success in reliability trials and high speed racing on the tracks of the world. No longer does the family car remain cloistered in its garage until the omnipotent expert returns from his place of business. Only the most timid of matrons refuses to take the wheel of to-day; if there is a car in the family, and the family is a matey one, it is used more by the feminine members than by the head (?) of the house. But . . . there are not enough car-owning families, certainly the number of two-car families is far too small. Thousands of business and professional men who use their cars genuinely for purposes connected with the winning of the daily bread, or selfishly for running merely to and from their offices, can afford a second car yet deny the home team the benefits that one would confer.

If a woman is to live a *full* life to-day she needs a car during the daytime. No longer is a car a luxury. As every woman knows, who has ever had a car to use whenever her whims dictated, it is a definite necessity. It is a far cry from the days of the horseless carriage, when a box of tricks that was nothing more than a landau propelled by an unreliable engine (instead of being pulled by a consistently dependable horse) cost a mint of money. To-day all cars are trustworthy, simple to manage and, according to one's individual tastes, economical to buy and maintain.

It is only human to sigh with envy as some long, lithe, super-limousine slinks silently and majestically up the portico of a luxury hotel or disgorges its opulent freight at a theatre. Some of us *may* be able to afford such creations, but everything is relative, and a car costing, say, £200 can be just as reliable, almost as fast and quite as satisfying in our sphere of life as an expensive giant that is in keeping only with the predilections of a plutocrat.

The modern housewife needs a car of her own if she cannot use the family car during the day. Household equipment, even in these days of inadequate domestic staffs,

In the early days the motor's tiller responded only to masculine hands

has lightened home duties to such an extent that leisure is delightfully increased, and leisure must be used properly if one is to avoid stagnation. A car can mean so much in one's life. Hubby, assuming that he is not the selfish type who considers the train or tube beneath his dignity, can be put on the 8.45 and met off the 6.50. The youngsters can be taken to school (probably a more desirable one than "St. Watisit's," more adjacent, to which they could walk); shopping can be done on the way back, and how much nicer it is to choose one's joint or fruit or vegetables instead of trusting to luck and the telephone!

A visit to the dressmaker can be taken in one's stride, a few sets of tennis or a rubber of bridge encompassed in a day that, carless, would have been impossible. Harriet's birthday can be acknowledged by a heartening call instead of a soulless greeting card; Mary and her new arrival greeted in the nursing home with a bunch of flowers and a smile instead of one of the colourful telegram forms so thoughtfully provided by the postal authorities. A car can help one in a thousand little ways to get and keep out of a domestic rut—and the only differences between a rut and a groove are in the width and depth—not only will it smooth out every day, but enable one to put more into every day without fatigue.

It is very disquieting to read that there was a drop of 7,919 in the number of new cars registered during June compared with June last year. Those were the last official figures published and, to me, they indicate that husbands have gone all economical or wives are not standing up for their rights! Certainly unmarried motorists, men and women, are not holding back in the buying of first or new cars.

There is no dearth of money in Britain for sport or for the average small things of life. It is only when facing possible payments of large single items that our bread-winners announce the need for economy. If hubby does believe that there is something obscure happening called a business recession, the last thing about which he should be parsimonious is the provision of daily enjoyment and ease of getting about for the rest of the family.

If people stop buying cars, the men who make those cars will not be able to buy the things they need for their families; demand will fall for all kinds of things and then there *will* be a recession—or call it by its proper, uncamouflaged name—a slump. Meanwhile more money is being earned and saved than for many a year. Savings banks are overloaded with deposits. Something is wrong somewhere, folks are going slow who need not go slow. The motor industry is one of the greatest and most important in Britain; on its prosperity depends much of the prosperity of the whole country and on its products depend much of the happiness and freedom from inertia of we who run the substantial homes of the country. I repeat, no married woman amongst the readers of GOOD HOUSEKEEPING should be without a car.

A car should be treated as a domestic appliance; to get the best value out of it it should be used, used whenever opportunity permits, and just as we learn how to look after our sweepers, and our radios and our refrigerators and cookers, so should we understand how to treat our cars so that they will give the same trouble-free service. Incidentally, the last person from whom to learn driving is hubby. Either he will assume that you *must* be dull or else he will know that you are wonderful. Either way he will leave too much for granted. You need to know what to do and, just as important, why you do it when learning to take the wheel, control a car and become an expert and confident roadfarer. A good school of motoring gives by far the best tuition.

Your idea of a car's usefulness may be its place in the daily round of pottering about, an aid to social intercourse—a means for whisking a tea hamper and the family away into green fields and God's fresh air for a picnic. Maybe you look upon a car, as did our forefathers with their smart conveyances, as a mark of caste; perhaps you like to let off steam and refresh jaded nerves by an exhilarating dash along arterial roads. Your inclinations may lean towards roomy comfort, smartness of line, speed or economy. There are cars to suit every taste and every purse, some that shine in one particular attribute, some that combine all desires. The best place to see all types of cars together and the only spot where the offerings of all the makers are to be found in one complete gathering is the Motor Exhibition at Earl's Court. It opens on October 13th. It is the only time in the whole year when it is possible to

view such a galaxy of cars, from the "babies" to the juggernauts. I advise every woman who can possibly get there to pay a visit. It is useless looking at everything but, having decided just how much can be squeezed out of the family budget for a new car one can examine and discuss all those that are in the price range (one usually exceeds the agreed figure), and then having narrowed down the choice

If the family is a matey one, the car is used more by the feminine members

to a sensible few, one can arrange for trial runs in one's own locality. That is the way to make the final decision. Whether you go to Earl's Court this year or whether you stay away, remember, that to every woman of moderate means and tastes a car is an absolute necessity if life is to be made to yield all that it offers. There is so much to do to-day that cannot be done without a car that can be available always; and . . . running a car, like running a home, is easy and safe. This may sound elementary and very, very obvious, but the fact remains that thousands of young matrons and eager girls approaching marriageable age are living unnecessarily circumscribed lives because of their inability to keep pace with the times . . . a woman *needs* a car.

The youngsters can be taken to school—a more desirable one than "St. Watisit's" just next door

THEY'RE WORKING FOR A SCHOLARSHIP

This means constant application, mental and bodily strain. Mother would be wise not to neglect . . .

'The Five Food Values'

THE 5 FOOD-VALUES IN SHREDDED WHEAT	
Vitamin 'B'	For Growth
Proteins	For Body-Building
Mineral Salts	For New Tissues
Carbo-Hydrates	For Energy
Bran	For Regularity

THERE'S HEALTH IN EVERY HELPING!

JUST two normal youngsters going through their early struggles. But so much depends upon their power to tackle stepping stones like this. That is why parents should never forget the importance of Shredded Wheat's "Five Food Values".

EVERYTHING FOR SOUND NUTRITION

Study these vital elements carefully. All play a vital part in healthy and progressive child development. And every helping of Shredded Wheat contains them in abundance. Everything that young bodies require for sound nutrition is supplied by this pure whole wheat food in a form that is easily assimilated and rapidly transformed into vigorous strength and energy—giving all that is needed to meet the most exacting demands of strenuous work and play. And this is why in the new national aim for a higher standard of fitness, Shredded Wheat plays such an important part.

ENJOYMENT IN EVERY HELPING

And how much the actual enjoyment of Shredded Wheat means too. Youngsters look forward with eager zest to every delicious helping, and mothers find the adaptability and economy of Shredded Wheat a constant boon. It can be served in so many delightful ways without the need of cooking. Serve Shredded Wheat to every member of the family. Let "The Five Food Values", in their own natural way, safeguard the health and happiness of all.

SHREDDED WHEAT

MADE BY THE SHREDDED WHEAT CO. LTD., WELWYN GARDEN CITY, HERTS.

Pratt's

WEDDED TO BEAUTY

by Ruth Murrin

THE

30's

BEING a mother is a full-time job. So full, it sometimes seems, that there is little time left over for being a wife. You who wake at 2 a.m. and again at 6 to satisfy the infant clamour for another meal don't need to be told. And you who mince the carrot and mash the potato and put beans through a sieve know how hard it is to save a little time to lavish on yourself. It is so easy to be swamped in the routine of feeding, bathing, dressing, training, and the everlasting washing that it is a wonder any girl ever manages to combine the business of being a Parent with that of being a Person.

Yet, if she is to be a successful wife, that is exactly what she must do. She must be well up in vitamins and child training, of course. That is her job. But at the same time she must keep in practice that knack she has of tilting a smart new hat at exactly the right angle on her head. She must keep her mind swept and aired, her conversation bright, and her complexion fresh. In a word, she must somehow be a wise, modern mother and still be the girl her husband fell in love with.

It takes effort and time and money? Of course it does. Everything worth while is costly in one way or another. But the cost of being attractive is minute in comparison with its importance. You owe it to yourself, for when you know you are pleasant to look at, your confidence soars, and everything seems to come your way more easily.

You owe it to your children. I remember a charming woman who told me she seldom used a lipstick until one day her four-year-old son remarked, " Mother, why don't you have red lips and look *new* like other ladies?" Children are keen observers, and from the time they practise their first steps until they are old enough to make their own way in the world, they love to show off a pretty mother.

You owe it to your husband. Though he may seem merely amused at the vagaries of fashion as you adopt them, he is secretly proud of your looks. He, too, likes you to appear new and different even to his familiar eyes. Also it is part of your responsibility as a wife to put your best foot forward, for the world always will judge a man's success, in some measure, by the appearance of his wife.

In these days of excellent cosmetics at small cost, even a skimpy budget can make room for the few necessary ones, and the busiest mother can squeeze in fifteen minutes a day plus a half-hour once a week for face treatments. Odd moments well used with hand lotion, nail cream, emery boards and nail white will do worlds to keep your hands worthy of your nicest parties. Your hair will respond beautifully to brushing if you have only two minutes night and morning to give to it, besides the weekly washing and a really good permanent twice a year. If you find yourself resisting changes in make-up and coiffure, if you have lost your fashion sense, quiz your unmarried friends until you are again up-to-date. They will enjoy advising you; for once they will have a

feeling of superiority over women with husbands and babies and homes of their own.

The hardest thing is to keep from sinking into the easy habit of making excuses for yourself, then gradually becoming blind

to the way you really look. Your skin, for example. How does it compare with the complexion of the girl you were five or ten or fifteen years ago? Even if you have taken pretty good care of it, it is probably drier, not so smooth, not so fresh and luscious, marked by little lines which that young face did not know. Cream used oftener, and a wisely selected powder-base and smart make-up, will do a lot to make it appear young and lovely. But if you have neglected it sadly, and it is now coarse-textured and murky, only the most persistent pampering can bring it back to a semblance of what it once was. It is never possible to undo damage like this in a few weeks or months. I wish I could make every woman understand that every day of neglect must some day be paid for with interest, and since one's skin naturally becomes drier and loses some of its bloom as one grows older, it really should have better and better care as the years pass.

There are still young women who don't take seriously that first thickening of the waist and hip line that makes the difference between a youthful figure and a matronly one. It should send you to the scales immediately to check-up your weight. It should stiffen your will power to say "No, thank you," to rich foods and second helpings. It should make you critical of the way you sit and stand and walk. It should inspire you to do some snappy exercise every day. An easy exercise to fight that broadening is this: Lie on your back on the floor, knees bent and arms outstretched, and flop your legs first to the right and then to the left. You will be thrilled at the prompt way bulges flatten out.

Do you remember how, in the days when you had nothing on your mind but school and clothes and dances, you used to sit in front of a mirror and do your hair endlessly in one fashion after another? You will find it fun even now. First, make a collection of coiffures you like on other people. Clip out the pictures of stage and screen beauties, that new photograph of smart Mrs. Somebody, the illustration you like so much in a current magazine. Then with comb and brush try to get an idea of what each coiffure will do for your face. The process will be good for you if it does nothing more than show you that your hair is chopped off too short at the back or would look sweet with the new upward roll in front.

Don't tell me that your husband does not want you to change—that he forbids you to diet, that he hates cream on your face, that he thinks halo curls are silly, that he regards robin-red nail polish as improper. He may think he thinks so. But, remember, a husband is human. What he really in his heart expects of you is that you should continue to be the leading lady of his life, the heroine of the domestic drama, and that every now and then you should spring on him a new act. In that light, look at the woman you see in the mirror and ask yourself to-day,

"Is she slipping or is she still a star?"

"No need to dust, dear"!

Light and as easy to use as a carpet sweeper. Ready for immediate use anywhere —

THE IDEAL GIFT

Newmaid De Luxe

Send for details of our Special Offer, giving your dealer's name and address, to BURRAGE & BOYDE LTD., (Dept. I), Newmaid Works, Adnitt Road, NORTHAMPTON.

'IT'S *ALL* IN THE BAG *!*'

"It just shows how necessary it is to clean carpets daily by suction. You may say — 'Oh, but I sweep my carpets after every meal!' Perhaps you do, but it isn't the *sweeping* that cleans carpets! Sweeping picks up merely the surface litter and scatters the dust! There's only one way to clean carpets and *trap* the dust — that is by SUCTION.

"NEWMAID your carpets daily and you'll be amazed at the difference. Dusting takes only half the time it did, because NEWMAID cleans by SUCTION. If a sweeper has no bag there's no suction ... no suction — no cleaning. NEWMAID is *the* Suction Sweeper and needs no electricity — there are no trailing wires".

You can see the NEWMAID at any good ironmongers, hardware or furnishing stores. Not sold from door to door.

NEWMAID

PRICES FROM 45/-

Cleans with a smile the carpet pile

★ *Ask to see it in action*

The Housekeeper's
DICTIONARY OF FACTS

MISCELLANEOUS ENQUIRIES

I SHOULD be very grateful if you would give me your valuable help and advice.

(1) I have just purchased three best quality Indian rugs in off-white. These will not have exceptionally heavy wear, but one is placed in front of the fireplace and all the feet in the room seem to rest on it.

Whilst I realise that the rugs must become dirty in time, I am feeling rather upset to think that on their first day of use, someone sat with the backs of his shoes resting on them, leaving a stain due to shoe polish. How can I remove this, how can I keep the rugs fresh and clean, and how can I hasten the process of getting rid of the loose fluff which is floating all over the place? The dealer told me not to use an electric cleaner on the rugs for some months. Is this correct?

(2) My floor is oak strip, the outer border of which has been regularly polished for seven years. Now that the carpet has been removed the floor underneath it is much darker and less pleasing than the polished part. How can I remedy this in the quickest way? I have an electric cleaner with motor-driven polisher.

(3) How can I improve the appearance of a street door of solid oak that is shrinking from lack of feeding? Will the regular application of boiled linseed oil restore this to its original condition?

(4) How can I prevent the inside of a new electric kettle from becoming furred by the hard water of the district?

(5) Can the new glass frying-pans be used on an electric hot-plate?

So many questions, but please forgive me; you have always been so kind in the past that I am sure you will do your best for me this time.

A. T., Ewell.

(1) We are afraid it is inevitable that, in a heavily used room, off-white rugs should become soiled. In most cases, however, the soiling occurs all over the rug and is more or less imperceptible. With regard to the actual mark caused by shoe polish, however, we would suggest rubbing with a cloth dipped in a little turpentine or carbon tetrachloride, which ought to prove effective. When very soiled, however, a reliable carpet soap or liquid cleanser can be used.

With regard to the fluff on the new rugs, we can only suggest that these should be shaken and brushed lightly from time to time in order to remove this as quickly as possible. With new Indian rugs, however, we are afraid that a certain amount of loose fluff is inevitable at first. Many carpet salesmen, we know, consider it wise not to use an electric cleaner until the pile has become more or less set, a matter, generally, of a month or two.

(2) For your oak strip floor, we

INSTITUTE NEWS COLUMN

Summer Cooking Lessons

Good Housekeeping School of Cookery does not close during the summer, except for the August Bank Holiday. This is an excellent opportunity for Teachers and others who are free during July and August to refresh their knowledge and to learn new ideas in cooking. Short courses as well as single days or half-day lessons can be taken, and a prospectus is obtainable from Good Housekeeping Institute, 49 Wellington Street, Strand, London, W.C.2.

Jam Making and Fruit Bottling

This month we are busy making preserves from soft fruits. Good Housekeeping shilling book, *Jams, Jellies and Fruit Bottling* (price 1s. 2d. with postage) contains detailed information on the subject of jam and jelly making, as well as fruit and vegetable bottling. Recipes for the usual, as well as out-of-the-ordinary, preserves are included.

Approved Appliances

The appliances illustrated in the practical section of the magazine have been tested and approved by Good Housekeeping Institute, and can be obtained from Good Housekeeping Centre, 449 Oxford Street, London, W.1.

Employment Bureau

Trained lady cooks and cake-makers requiring posts are invited to write to Good Housekeeping Employment Bureau, 49 Wellington Street, Strand, London, W.C.2.

would suggest rubbing the boards the way of the grain with medium steel wool dipped in a little turpentine or white spirit. This treatment will require a certain amount of patience, but we think you will be pleased with the result. Afterwards, of course, the floor can be polished, using any reliable make of wax polish.

(3) If your front door is at all soiled, the wood could be rubbed the way of the grain with medium steel wool, and afterwards, we would certainly rub in a little boiled linseed oil. It is as well to treat outdoor oak once or twice a year with a little oil in order to feed the wood.

(4) With regard to your kettle, we would suggest a fur collector, either one of the perforated aluminium egg variety or a small "loofah" collector, both of which are satisfactory.

(5) The glass frying-pan is very satisfactory for use over a gas burner, but would not be so suitable over a flat type of electric hot-plate.

A SCHOOLROOM FLOOR

Although I have been a subscriber to GOOD HOUSEKEEPING *since its first issue I do not think I have consulted*

you before. I should be grateful if you could tell me the floor you consider most suitable for a schoolroom. It would have to stand very heavy wear and tear and also the moving of heavy iron desks.

Maple has been suggested, but my experience of it is that it is difficult to polish and very easily gets a greyish dirty look. Pine is delightful to look at, but I do not think it hard enough. I think oak is probably best.

The existing floor is stained deal, very much worn, and I do not think it possible to lay a floor on top of its uneven surface, so I suppose the floor would have to be taken up and a new one laid on the joists. Would 1 in. timber do this and would it need to be tongued and grooved?

Also if you advise oak, would you please say what treatment you advise for it in its early days so that it will acquire a good surface and be easily polished.

I cannot end without a tribute to your splendid magazine, which has been of such help to me on many occasions. I feel sure that if I had my old copies even this problem would be dealt with.

F. H., Donegal.

I have been in touch with the Forest Products Research Laboratory, who tell me there are a large number of woods which are suitable for use for schoolroom flooring, and much depends on whether a light or a dark flooring wood is desirable. They tell me also that " if it is desired to have a wood that will not plainly show the dirt, oak would serve, especially if chosen so as to avoid strips that are either flat sawn or cut on the quarter, showing distinct figures. Another timber, Pyinkado, should also prove satisfactory, both from the point of view of wear and also for not showing dirt quickly. Australian jarrah is a dark reddish wood which gives satisfactory service for flooring.

"It is surprising that you have found maple difficult to polish, as this timber usually takes a good polish and in certain positions becomes too slippery. We would certainly not recommend pine, to which you refer, or any other of the soft woods for use in a schoolroom.

"The existing uneven floor might be planed off sufficiently level to allow the other flooring to be placed satisfactorily on top. If, however, the old floor is lifted, the strips of the new floor should be tongued and grooved and the thickness should be chosen to suit the spacing of the joists. The closer the joists are together, the thinner the floor may be. If the old floor has been stiff enough, that is, not allowing too much spring between joists, an oak floor slightly thinner would suffice, but here again the difference in thickness would be governed by the spacing of the joists and on the species of the new timber selected."

The Housekeeper's
DICTIONARY OF FACTS

★ ★

A READER'S BUDGET

THE following domestic budget was submitted by one of our readers who makes her garden the pivot of her housekeeping:

"I freely admit that the summer work of the garden absorbs many of my hours; but my reward is to gather peas and beans young and luscious, lettuce crisp, fresh and full of vitamins. These products may be cheap at the greengrocer's, but often they are wilted and yellowish.

"We have three-quarters of an acre of garden, of which one-third is given over to kitchen garden and orchard. We grow all the vegetables and salads needed for a liberal twelve-months' self-supporting supply (of course, in the summer months we often give a lot away). The orchard often provides fruit for two to three months.

"In the kitchen garden, peas, beans of several kinds, and lettuce take pride of place. We grow many rows of carrots in succession, as we believe in serving up grated raw carrot (also turnips), mixed with mayonnaise, as well as cooking them. We have two fruit cages, one for strawberries and one for raspberries, which give us a plentiful supply of fresh berries, as well as some for jam. The garden has been planned methodically for easy working. The apple, pear and plum trees are in the orchard, and the fruit cages have a special plot of ground to themselves, leaving the vegetable plot absolutely free from tree-roots, etc.

"Now that the garden is mature, besides being very simply planned, we are able to run it with the aid of only one man, who in winter puts in half a day's work a week, to which must be added Bank Holidays and some summer evenings. When the days are long, he comes from five o'clock till seven or eight and, with our highly efficient little motor-mower, keeps the lawns mown and their edges trimmed. Flower and vegetable seeds cost about £1 annually. We rarely buy plants, as we prefer to raise them from seeds; sprays and lime have to be bought; and we make full use of the oak leaves we sweep up in the autumn, storing them in a pit to rot, and using them in spring as "bottom" to the pea and bean trenches.

"My family consists of my husband and myself, with one daughter aged sixteen, who is still at school. We have no maid, and we planned our house to save labour as much as possible. There is only one open fire, which burns smokeless fuel, while anthracite is used in the slow-combustion stove fitted in the kitchen, which supplies hot water for all purposes, including radiators. We are on the

Lecture-Demonstrations in Cookery

A short course of Cookery Demonstrations will be given at Good Housekeeping Kitchen Theatre, 28-30 Grosvenor Gardens, London, S.W.1, on Wednesday afternoons, commencing at the end of October. Full particulars of these will be published in the October number of Good Housekeeping.

The Institute School of Cookery

Practical instruction in all branches of Cookery is given at Good Housekeeping Institute throughout the year. A prospectus can be obtained from the Institute, 49 Wellington Street, Strand, London, W.C.2.

'all-in' tariff for electricity, and use electric fires. Table and ornamental silver have been practically excluded from the house; instead, we use cut glass and wooden bowls.

"We are small meat-eaters, so I buy the best English lamb, English calves' liver or Scotch beef; and about once in three weeks we have poultry, as I am able to get good, fresh chicken from the country at prices rather below those in the shops.

"As we use a lot of eggs, I preserve about 20 dozen every April. These eggs, which I buy for 10d. or 11d. a dozen when new-laid, are stored for cooking purposes during the winter.

"Good food, like good wine, needs no bush; and no highly seasoned dishes are eaten in our home, nor are condiments used other than the pepper and salt I use in the cooking. We believe in the 'home milk-bar' and regularly enjoy our mid-morning milk, besides using some for evening drinks. My milk bill is high—sometimes we have as many as twenty pints a week. Butter is another item that is not stinted: I allow ½ lb. per head weekly, in addition to a further ½ lb. for cooking purposes, as well as other fats.

"Our fresh fruit bill includes 16 bananas, 2 lb. dessert apples, tomatoes and about a dozen oranges weekly. I have never tried to see how cheaply I could cater, never tried to keep below a given figure per head. But I have insisted that buying should not be slipshod—it must be ample, yet nothing must be thrown away as the result of too much having been bought. To give away home-grown food in prime condition is a joy; but to throw food away savours to me of crime.

"We follow the 'new health' rules, and so the frying-pan is banished. No rashers or fried eggs appear at breakfast. I provide a varied menu, and usually two dishes are sufficient for a meal.

"Breakfast menu: orange or orange juice; porridge in winter or cereal in summer; boiled or scrambled eggs; grilled or cold ham (sometimes); bananas, apples, tomatoes, lettuce. Brown or white bread, butter and home-made marmalade.

"Midday dinner: the usual English type—meat, plenty of vegetables, then light pudding or fruit.

"Schoolgirls can come home very hungry for tea, especially when lessons keep them till nearly five o'clock. There is always bread and butter (or buttered toast), with jam, honey or syrup, and often I serve a savoury dish like cheese with an egg on toast, or some light fish. Home-made cakes are always on the table.

"My domestic and housekeeping budget, exclusive of rent and rates, insurances and such items as doctor and dentist, holidays, etc., is as follows:

	£	s.	d.
Grocer	27	0	0
Butcher	16	0	0
Fishmonger	8	0	0
Dairy	23	0	0
School fees	36	0	0
Clothes for three	65	0	0
Garden expenses	33	0	0
Telephone	8	0	0
Car expenses	49	0	0
Newspapers, stationery, stamps	10	0	0
Solid fuel	9	0	0
Electricity	16	0	0

Total £300 0 0 per annum.

STAINED KNIFE HANDLES

I am wondering whether you can tell me how to whiten my knife handles, which are composition and not ivory. Is there any safe method of dealing with them, as they are somewhat discoloured by use?
G. W., Coventry.

It is possible to whiten composition knife handles very often by rubbing carefully with a cloth dipped in a little benzaldehyde, but as this acts as a solvent, it makes the surface a little sticky at first, and slightly rough when it is dry. It is therefore necessary to rub the handles down afterwards with a cloth dipped in a little moistened pumice powder. We do not know whether you will think it is worth treating the knives in this way, as we are afraid a good deal of patience will be required. You may, however, care to purchase a small amount of the solvent, and experiment with one or two handles.

Mother,

WHY CAN'T YOU LOOK SMART?

THIS is often the thought, even if unexpressed, of many a girl in her teens about her mother. And it isn't that the girls don't love their mothers, but rather because they do, that they want them—as the teen-agers themselves become clothes-conscious—to look well in the eyes of their friends as well as in their own. Lack of interest in clothes and lack of money may sometimes be causes. But we believe that more often the cause is neglect, creeping on unnoticed by the unselfish mothers who give their lives to their families with never a thought of how their appearance affects their sons and daughters.

In their concern for others, and burdened by increasing cares, they unconsciously let time steal a priceless heritage from them long before it should—their youth. For it isn't a matter of money, always, but of time and thought, that keeps a woman lovely as she reaches middle age. She must know the styles, for style *is* all-important. And she must know *herself*: what she can wear, and what she can't; what her good points are and how to make the most of them; what her faults are, and how to overcome or conceal them.

Wanting to help all these women, a fashion expert decided to show what can be done for a typical mother of a growing family. " Mrs. Smedley," the subject of these experiments, is a charming woman who has unconsciously let time add pounds. She said that

A slip, bias-cut at the back, straight in the front, with only one seam at the centre back, does not slide, twist or bulge as you move about

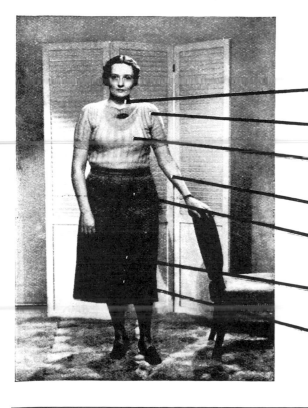

OVERCOMING DEFECTS

1. *A short neck may be overcome by an upswept hair arrangement showing the ears. A V neckline at the front and a low line at the back of the neck are also extremely helpful in overcoming this defect*

2. *Broad, humped shoulders are concealed by keeping them in line with the hips and padding judiciously, if necessary. It is wise always to have a loose armhole, giving a good line but a loose fitting*

3. *A large bust is improved by correct posture and by a foundation corselet designed specially to lift the large bust. Posture is improved by keeping the knees straight and holding in the entire diaphragm*

4. *A long forearm is overcome by the use of various sleeve lengths : for sports dresses wear just to the elbow ; for afternoon dresses, bracelet or three-quarter length ; also overcome by the wearing of bracelets*

5. *Square hips are overcome by a foundation corselet which raises and defines the waistline, gives rounded hips, and controls the thighs. Have the dress skirt made to flare about 10 ins. below the waistline*

6. *Silhouette in general : raise waistline, flare the skirt 10 ins. below the waist, slightly pad shoulders if it is necessary, give loose armhole, avoid tightness, have skirts longer than prevailing fashion*

7. *Avoid materials which are too tweedy, too shiny, too clinging, too knitted, too tight. Don't run to cover with black, but always remember that any age can wear colour, providing it is a becoming one*

THE
30's

These garments are not on sale, being specially designed for the model

" since I felt glamour was no longer my forte I decided I might at least be warm and comfortable, and so I succumbed to woolly jumpers and skirts." This was all wrong for her; but before her clothes problem was tackled, she was sent to a beauty specialist. Exercise, massage and hot baths brought glow to her skin; and a heavy lubricating night cream, which she had not been using, did wonders! The grey-yellow look of her skin was overcome by a powder foundation with a glow, while the rouge was placed high to reduce the sagging lines. Why don't you experiment to determine what powder shades are becoming to your skin and contours; try one shade of powder on one side of your face, a different one on the other, and compare. Mrs. Smedley's pretty brown hair was given a permanent and re-styled. She had been parting it in the middle with the hair combed down; when it was combed up, a widow's peak was revealed! Furthermore, the upsweep gave her needed height, and the combed-up curls at the back gave something she needed even more—length to her neck.

The next step was the fitting of a foundation garment. The one chosen had reinforced uplift to give a younger bustline, a long skirt to control the thighs, and gave a curve at waist and hip.

The corset settled, the fashion expert was free to select a wardrobe for Mrs. Smedley, part of which we illustrate here. A colour scheme of navy blue with old gold, dusty rose and red was chosen, and the lines of the various garments were

There is much to recommend this outfit to anyone with a figure problem. A large bust is miraculously concealed by the cardigan, while large hips are reduced by the same means. Youthfulness and an effect of height are achieved by buttons down the front and a softly flared skirt. The high crown and the quill of the hat give height and thus help to slenderise the silhouette. On the right is a collarless dress of the type that is useful for a variety of occasions. The pleats stitched to 10 ins. below the waist give slimness, and a belt of the dress fabric defines the waist without cutting the figure in two

Wrap-around coats give a square, heavy, droopy look

very carefully studied to emphasise good points and conceal poor ones. Thus hats were chosen to give height and hence slenderness, belts or two-colour effects that cut the figure were avoided.

The result, we think, is a triumph both for the fashion expert and for Mrs. Smedley!

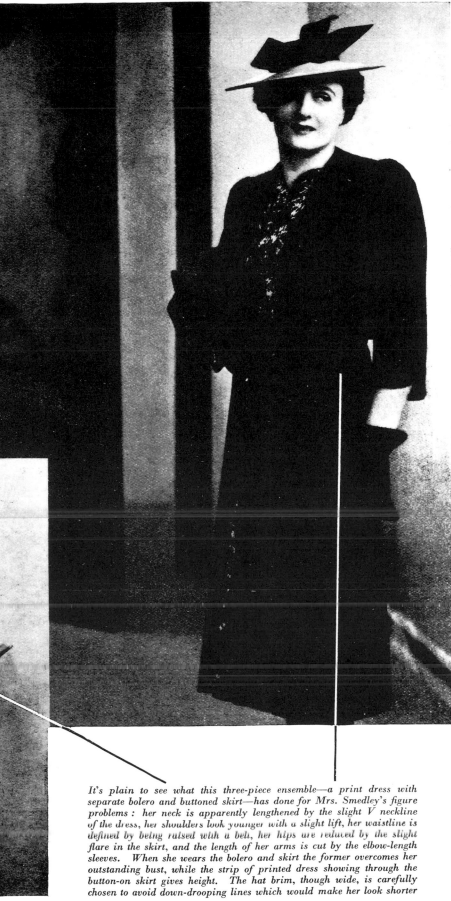

It's plain to see what this three-piece ensemble—a print dress with separate bolero and buttoned skirt—has done for Mrs. Smedley's figure problems : her neck is apparently lengthened by the slight V neckline of the dress, her shoulders look younger with a slight lift, her waistline is defined by being raised with a belt, her hips are reduced by the slight flare in the skirt, and the length of her arms is cut by the elbow-length sleeves. When she wears the bolero and skirt the former overcomes her outstanding bust, while the strip of printed dress showing through the button-on skirt gives height. The hat brim, though wide, is carefully chosen to avoid down-drooping lines which would make her look shorter

Remedies for

by P. L. GARBUTT, A.I.C.

Keep Sinks and Outside Drains Sweet and Clean

AT all times, but particularly in hot weather, pay special attention to sinks and drains. Once a week at least you should swill and brush them thoroughly, to avoid an accumulation of grease. You will find hot, strong soda water a good ally here.

If the sink should become blocked, make up a solution of caustic soda and pour down, but remember that this is very strong, and you must on no account immerse your hands in it. If this is not entirely effective, procure a rubber force cup and try to loosen any obstruction with this. Should your efforts still be unavailing, place a pail under the " U " bend in the piping under the sink, loosen the screw, and clear as far as possible.

Remember the value of a good carbolic disinfectant. Dilute this according to instructions, and swill thoroughly with it from time to time.

Avoid abrasive, scratchy cleaners for the sink, for these will only roughen and spoil it, and result in its staining and becoming extremely difficult to clean. If it should unfortunately become badly stained, a solution of chloride of lime or bleaching powder—about $\frac{1}{2}$ oz. to $\frac{1}{2}$ gallon —will usually whiten it effectively, but if it has been very badly neglected the use of dilute hydrochloric acid, in the proportion of one part acid to five or six of water, may be needed to bleach it. Do not, however, allow the acid to remain in contact with the porcelain any longer than necessary, and rinse away very thoroughly afterwards. Do not forget, too, that hydrochloric acid is very poisonous, and should therefore be used extremely carefully.

An Economy Suggestion for Sweet Dishes

SUMMER-TIME housekeeping calls for the free use of cream. If you are one of those many people who this year, for reasons of economy, have reluctantly cut this out of your menus, why not replace dairy cream by the reconstituted product prepared from salt-free margarine and milk ? This costs next to nothing—in fact, only about 8d. per pint. Your family will not distinguish it from fresh dairy cream when served with fruit, and you will increase the food value of your menus in a very palatable way. Even to-day you can purchase a small cream-maker for 6s. to 7s. Don't imagine that the preparation of the cream will be either tiresome or lengthy.

Before making the cream, run a little boiling water through to ensure that the fine jet is thoroughly clean and free from obstruction. Weigh out $\frac{1}{4}$ lb. of margarine and $\frac{1}{4}$ pint of milk (for double cream). Heat the two together until the margarine is melted, and then pump the mixture through the cream maker. To ensure the best emulsion, it is a good plan to pass the liquid through twice. If possible, also, make the cream the day before it is required, as it will improve and thicken if kept in a cool place overnight.

You will find you are able to make delectable ice-creams and other cold sweets with your home-made product, and at the same time have the satisfaction of knowing that your seemingly extravagant cold dishes are real wartime economies.

If Flies, Ants, or Earwigs are a Menace

LEFT to multiply undisturbed, a single female fly may account for some millions later on in the season, so take active steps against them now.

First and foremost look for possible breeding-places, dark, undisturbed corners and crevices, and spray with a proprietary or home-made preparation. Apart from protecting the larder window, attend also to the kitchen and scullery windows, where food odours may lure in flies, wasps and other insects. Fine net or muslin stretched firmly over the window opening will be found a great help, and a saucer, placed well out of the way of food, containing one teaspoonful of formalin in a little milk, with a small piece of sweet biscuit in the centre, will prove irresistibly attractive—and fatal !

If ants are a trouble, see that all sweet foods are covered and protected. Then, where the insects congregate, sprinkle either borax or a mixture consisting of : 4 oz. calcium phosphate, 2 oz. icing sugar, and 4 oz. sodium fluoride.

Earwigs do not as a rule enter the house in numbers, but if they do, try treatment with paradichlorobenzene. If possible, close up rooms or cupboards in which the insects are congregating, and sprinkle about $1\frac{1}{2}$ lbs. of the crystals in a room measuring 12 ft. square. Solutions of alum, carbolic acid or paraffin will act as a deterrent if painted round the window- and door-frames. If you have creeper on the walls, cut this away where it is close to the windows.

★ **Hot-weather housekeeping is much**

Summer Ills

First Class Diploma King's College of Household and Social Science: late staff Battersea Polytechnic

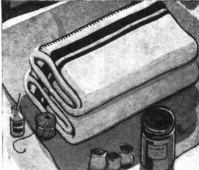

THE
40's

Keep Your House Cool

PULL blinds in sunny rooms early in the day. Plenty of fresh air is to be encouraged, but in really excessively hot weather it is sometimes a help to close windows while the room is still relatively cool. You will thus prevent hot air entering later on. Remember, however, to open the windows again in the cool of the day. If your house is in a sunny position, sun- and door-blinds will also help to protect outdoor paintwork from blistering, so, if there are any indications that this is to be a hot summer, do not consider such fittings a luxury, but rather a wartime economy.

You can help matters further by installing a small exhaust fan in the window of your sitting-room, to draw a current of fresh air through. You will need, however, to cut black-out screens or blinds carefully, so that they fit neatly and exactly round the frame. An air-conditioning plant, whereby the incoming air is purified and can be cooled to the degree required, is the ideal, but such luxuries must be curtailed just now, when all expenditure must be kept down to a minimum. Another year, perhaps !

Cooking smells always create a hot effect, and to prevent their permeating the house, a fan such as that referred to above will be found a great help in drawing out steam and cooking odours. One has been fitted in our new kitchens, and the Institute will gladly help you in making a suitable choice, for efficient models have been carefully tested. Failing a fan, remember to keep the kitchen window open whenever lunch or dinner preparations are in hand, and the door into the house firmly closed.

Your Larder in Warm Weather

SIMPLE precautionary measures should eliminate any anxiety from your summer housekeeping. Your larder, for instance, may be a source of worry to you if you have no refrigerator. You know that disease can be spread if flies have access to food, and that bacteria multiply rapidly when the weather is warm, and cause food to be spoilt and wasted.

Look your pantry over carefully, therefore, and take preventive measures. If your larder unfortunately has a warm aspect, provide a blind, and see that this is pulled before the sun gets round to the window. See also that the window opening is effectively covered with perforated zinc, leaving no loophole for a fly or other stray insect. Don't forget also that flies can enter by the door, so see that this is kept shut. As an extra precaution enclose one section of the larder with perforated zinc. You will find this neater and more effective than a meat safe.

Keep butter in a dish with a porous clay exterior. If it is stood in water, the clay will absorb moisture, and evaporation from the sides will reduce the temperature slightly. The same type of cover is available for milk bottles, or little flannelette jackets can be quickly made. If these are wrung out of water before being placed round the bottle, and the latter is stood in a bowl of water, you will find you are able to reduce the temperature of the milk by about 5 to 7 degrees, according to the rate at which the moisture evaporates.

To Guard Against Moth Trouble

KILL that moth, and don't forget the moth grub, which after all is the real culprit !

The old-time camphor balls are of doubtful value, so don't place too much reliance on them. Paradichlorobenzene is far more efficient. You can purchase it from your local chemist, in the form of the pure crystals or as a prepared repellent.

Before putting away blankets, woollen clothes and furs, first wash them or have them cleaned, for moth grubs are not so partial to clean articles. Then sprinkle with the crystals, or alternatively, fill small muslin bags and spread these among your woollies before making up into air-tight packages. If paper is used, take the precaution of pasting down the seams, and by the way, don't forget to beat furs lightly with a cane and hang them in the sunshine for a few hours before putting away.

If the house is to be shut up for the holiday period, or if the family is evacuated, make arrangements, if possible, to have carpets and upholstery sprayed occasionally with a good insecticide. Keep a sharp look-out for any definite signs of moth, for if they are left to develop undisturbed serious damage may occur, which may put articles beyond the reach of home treatment, or even make it necessary to destroy them. If they are not too far gone, arrange to send them away for expert fumigation without any delay.

easier if you follow these hints ★

I'd like to know

I should be grateful to know the best way of removing ink stains from a fawn rug. The stains occurred a month ago and were rubbed with a duster.

Also, what would you advise for a brick path which is slippery through a mossy growth?

The ink stains should be treated alternately with a solution of potassium permanganate—½ teaspoonful to 1 pint water—and hydrogen peroxide diluted four or five times with water. Apply the permanganate solution to the marks with a fountain-pen filler. Remove excess in a second or two with a damp cloth, and apply the hydrogen peroxide solution to remove the brown stain produced by the permanganate. Rinse with water and repeat the process several times, if necessary, finally rinsing the rug thoroughly free from the chemicals. Patience may be needed, as the stain is old, but do not leave the chemicals on for more than a few seconds at a time.

For the path apply a solution of sodium chlorate, a very efficient weed killer obtainable from most chemists.

There are light oak block floors in our shop, opened six months ago, which seem to show every mark. What is the best way of dealing with them?

My cleaner also finds it difficult to remove rings left by lotion bottles on the natural wood show cases.

When a wood floor is particularly soiled it should be rubbed the way of the grain with medium-grade steel wool dipped in turpentine or white spirit before it is repolished. This treatment should only be applied very occasionally, but the floors need to be regularly polished with a white wax preparation. This helps to retain their light colour, provided clean cloths are used and the floors are swept and dusted before the wax is used.

Presumably the rings on your show cases only occur where opened bottles are stored, and are caused by drops of spilt liquid. Many toilet preparations have a basis of spirit, and are likely to remove stain and polish. Medium steel wool, as suggested for the floor, would remove the marks, and as a protective measure the wood should be polished regularly or covered with glass.

Can you tell me the best way to clean a brick fireplace? My maid has scrubbed it with soap and water, and the bricks now have a smeary white appearance.

Soap and soap powders should never be used for a brick fireplace, for, since bricks are absorbent, thorough rinsing is almost an impossibility, and, as you have discovered, they acquire a white deposit if cleaned in this way.

To remedy this, or to clean a fireplace discoloured by soot, rub the bricks with a cloth dipped in a solution of hydrochloric acid, or spirits of salt, containing 1 part acid to 5 or 6 of water. This acid is extremely poisonous and corrosive, and should only be entrusted to a responsible person, and all trace of it should be rinsed away after use. Precautions must also be taken not to allow it to remain in contact with the cement between the bricks, as it will tend to dissolve it and may loosen them.

Can you tell me how to treat a dressing-table slightly marked by a very weak solution of carbolic disinfectant?

This type of disinfectant is highly alkaline in reaction and would tend to remove polish, etc., from furniture. If the marks are only small you may be able to remedy them by treating in the same way as for heat marks on a polished table. A drop or two (not more) of methylated spirit should be placed on a pad of soft material or cotton-wool. This should be covered by a layer of muslin and the pad so prepared rubbed well over and around the table.

As this method of treatment depends for its effect on removing polish and stain from the undamaged part of the wood to the damaged, it is not likely to be successful if the marks are extensive. In this case rubbing down the whole surface and repolishing would be necessary, and this work is better entrusted to a firm of polishers.

The bath in our rented house has been sadly neglected, and there is a brownish mark at water level, and stains under each tap. What remedy do you suggest?

The brown marks are probably rust caused by iron in the water, and should be easily removed by treating with a hot, strong solution of oxalic acid. Being poisonous, this acid must be used very carefully and rinsed away thoroughly.

If the stains under the taps are caused by the hardness of the water, they can be removed with a weak acid, such as vinegar. If the marks prove very resistant, as is likely if they have been left for some time, use a stronger acid, such as spirits of salt diluted seven or eight times with water. I do not, however, suggest using this if it can be avoided, as there is a possibility of damage to the porcelain. If used, a drop or so only should be applied immediately over each stain, taking care that the acid does not come in contact with the porcelain and rinsing away very quickly and thoroughly afterwards.

Two years ago I laid cork carpet in my hall. This has, however, proved most unpractical, as it shows every mark and never looks clean. Can you advise me as to the best way of treating it?

Cork carpet is one of the most difficult of all floor coverings to keep in good condition. Scrubbing only opens the pores, with the result that it becomes more and more absorbent, and dirt and dust penetrate. Linseed oil is sometimes used to fill up the pores which give cork carpet more or less the characteristics of linoleum. This treatment is rather laborious, as it is necessary to give two or three applications of the oil, allowing an interval of a week or so between them for the oil to oxidise. Finally, after a further interval, wax polish should be applied, and once a good surface has been obtained wax polish, made into a semi-liquid consistency by dilution with turpentine or white spirit, should be rubbed in once a week and the cork well polished twenty or thirty minutes later.

I have unfortunately spilt some lime juice on a dark marble-topped table. Could you tell me how to remove these and other marks?

The acidity of the lime juice has no doubt had a slight solvent action on the marble, but you may find that you are able to mask the marks to some extent by rubbing over with a cloth dipped in a little olive oil.

If this is not effective or if there are a number of resistant stains or marks, the whole surface of the table should be treated with a weak acid, such as vinegar. If this is used it should only be allowed to remain in contact with the marble for a few seconds, and it should be quickly rinsed away with fresh water.

Treatment with vinegar or lemon juice in this way can be applied to a marble mantelpiece, washstand, or other discoloured marble surface. The efficacy of the treatment depending on surface solvent action on the marble, however, quick rinsing afterwards is always imperative.

After using acid the appearance of the marble will be improved by rubbing well with a little oil and polishing with a soft cloth.

How can I clean limed oak furniture? So far I have only dusted it, but the table top, chair legs, etc., are soiled and finger-marked.

My pale green and off-white carpets are spotted and slightly marked, and I should like your advice.

If the furniture is badly soiled it may be necessary to rub it down carefully with very fine sandpaper, but if only slightly soiled rub over with a cloth dipped in petrol or turpentine substitute. Use petrol with the greatest care, as it is highly inflammable. After treating in this way polishing would help to protect the wood, although it might alter the character of the surface slightly.

For marks on the carpet, use a reliable make of carpet soap or liquid cleanser. When removing spots, it is often necessary to go over the whole carpet, as otherwise the result is very patchy. An area about two feet square should be dealt with at a time, and each patch should overlap the next.

Here are useful hints on cleaning problems dealt with in "question and answer" form

by P. L. GARBUTT, A.I.C.

First Class Diploma King's College of Household and Social Science: late staff Battersea Polytechnic

Valstar
BUXTON

Nothing will get through this "Buxton" Trench Raincoat. It is "Jemcoprufed" and guaranteed to withstand the fiercest storm. It is good-looking too—tailored by Valstar from warm wool-union gabardine in serviceable shades and lined with smart check fabric. The front fastens high, there's extra chest protection—in fact, every practical feature of a man's classic stormcoat.

"VALSTAR," 44, St. Paul's Churchyard, London, E.C.4.

NERVES
at tension
NEED
attention

YOU AND YOUR FAMILY NEED
SANATOGEN
NERVE-TONIC FOOD

IN the last war a Cabinet Minister told the House of Commons that "'Sanatogen' is a national necessity for preserving good nerves." In these days the benefits which 'Sanatogen' can bring are even greater than in 1914-1918. Buy a tin for yourself and your family to-day.

Obtainable at all chemists in 19/9 jars (8 weeks' course) and 2/3, 3/3, 5/9 and 10/9 tins.

Have you tried the new COFFEE FLAVOURED 'Sanatogen'?

The Registered Trade Mark 'SANATOGEN' applied to Nerve-Tonic Food, denotes a brand of casein and sodium glycerophosphate chemically combined by Genatosan Limited, the proprietors of the Trade Mark.

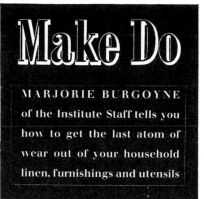

Make Do

MARJORIE BURGOYNE of the Institute Staff tells you how to get the last atom of wear out of your household linen, furnishings and utensils

Bedclothes: Sheets generally wear first down the centre, so slit from top to bottom, and cut out the worn strip. Then turn " sides to middle "— that is to say, seam the two selvedges together, and hem the cut edges, which are now on the outsides of the sheet. If your sheets or tablecloths have small tears elsewhere, remember that the darning attachment provided with many sewing-machines is a great help in making neat repairs. If you have to replace sheets, be sure to buy sufficiently large ones, as this reduces the wear. For durability we recommend an edging of cord stitching rather than hemstitching; this also applies to pillow-cases.

Blankets that have shrunk can still

be used. Extend them on both sides, and at top and bottom, by stitching on a border of sheeting, old linen or even bright-coloured gingham, about two feet deep; this will give the necessary tuck-in, and the warmth of the blanket will be where it is needed. Use up old and thin blankets beneath the sheets. If you have a rubber mattress, try making a blanket pad by sewing together two or three old blankets in the form of a quilt, to put beneath the lower sheet; it will make the bed very cosy. Double blankets worn at the edges can, of course, be cut down for single beds or cots.

A " shampoo " will give your elderdown quite a new look—and it is not difficult to do at home if you choose a windy day and dry out of doors. Prepare plenty of warm soapy water, and wash by kneading and squeezing. The use of a long-handled vacuum washer and a dolly-tub is recommended. After a thorough rinsing down quilts may safely be put through a rubber wringer, and should then be shaken vigorously. Continue to shake frequently during and after drying to separate the down. Thorough airing is essential, during which the quilt should again be shaken in front of the fire. If the cover looks creased, it may be smoothed very lightly with a warm iron before it is quite dry.

Household Linens: Teacloths will last very much longer if they are washed out as soon as soiled. This prevents them from becoming so dirty that harsh agents are needed to clean them. Keep special clearly marked cloths for wiping knives and cutting tools.

Swabs often fray after very little use. To remedy this bind the edges or sew two swabs together. Instead of replacing these, you might consider buying some of the new viscose sponges, which are equally efficient, delightful to handle, and have a very long life.

Turkish towels that have worn in parts can be cut down to make smaller hand towels or face flannels. Two large pieces sewn together make good bath mats. Smaller pieces are useful as cushioning for the top of the bathroom stool. Always keep a special towel in the bathroom for wiping razors.

Household Utensils: Kettles and pots and pans which have small holes can be satisfactorily mended if you buy one of the special pot menders on the market. These consist essentially of two tin discs and a central washer of thin cork. They are screwed into position by means of a small screw and nut.

Holes in pails, dustbins, etc., can also be repaired with cold solder, which is simple enough for any housewife to use. It is squeezed out of the tube in which it is bought in sufficient quantity to cover the hole, and allowed to set. The price is about 6d. a tube.

Cracked earthenware bowls, lavatory basins, etc., can be repaired by working in some fine white cement, allowing it to set, and then strapping on the outside with zinc oxide adhesive plaster tape about an inch wide. Put a strip of the tape along the line of the crack, and then apply short cross strips across the line of the crack at intervals of a few inches.

Soft Furnishings: Lace or net curtains that have been torn can be mended almost invisibly in the following way: place the curtain flat on the table with an ironing blanket or folded cloth underneath the torn part. Take a piece of lace or net curtaining, matching as nearly as possible and large enough to cover the hole, dip it in cold starch, wring out tightly, place it over the hole, and press with a hot iron.

Faded cotton curtains can be bleached or dyed at home to make

them last for another season. Dye shabby, heavier curtains a dark colour and use for black-out linings. Curtains that have shrunk in the wash or that are not long enough for your windows can be lengthened six inches or more by making a deep false hem for the bottom of the curtain in the same or a contrasting material. You can also stitch on an additional piece at the top, where it will be hidden under the pelmet, using for this, if necesssary, another material as near the original colour as possible.

Loose covers will not need washing so frequently nor will they wear out so soon if you make extra " cuffs " for the arms and across the back, where the head rests.

Floor Coverings: Linoleum that has become worn and unsightly can be neatly repaired. First, cut out the worn part with a sharp knife. Place this piece as a pattern on a new cutting of linoleum, taking care to match the design, if there is one. Glue the back of the new piece very carefully and place in the hole, pressing it down well. The patch, if neatly applied, will be hardly noticeable.

Painted linoleum or oilcloth which has become unsightly on account of the pattern having worn in patches may be painted with a hard-wearing floor paint. The floor should first be well scrubbed to remove all trace of wax or oil polish. When thoroughly dry, apply one of the special hard-wearing paints sold for this purpose. If a mat is placed where traffic is concentrated—for example, on the threshold—painted linoleum will wear for a considerable time, especially if it is kept regularly polished with wax.

Carpets that have worn in parts can be repaired by cutting away the worn part and inserting a new piece. First match the pattern where the alteration is to be made. Next, blanket-stitch the raw edges of the carpet on the wrong side, taking the stitches about four threads down, being careful that these stitches do not show on the right side. Now lay the two pieces of the carpet together, right side inside, and, using the over-sewing method, seam them very firmly together, taking the stitches about three threads down. When finished, the join should be very heavily pressed with a hot iron to flatten the seam. Damping the surface to be pressed will give a better result.

Stair carpets can be given a longer lease of life if you move their position slightly every few months. This ensures that the tread comes in a different place, and decreases the wear considerably.

These practical hints will make it easy to—

Be Your Own

IN hundreds of homes now the man of the house is away and it is you, the housewife, who must tackle the small household repairs that formerly lay in his province. In vain you beseech the builder, the plumber, the carpenter or the odd-job man to come to your aid, for they are invariably booked up for weeks ahead, and in any case it is of the utmost importance that the building trade should keep skilled labour on urgent Government work. So for patriotic reasons, as well as for your own convenience, you will have to attend to such matters yourself, even if you can only carry out temporary repairs, until skilled assistance can be obtained.

A Temporary Repair for Broken Windows.—Leave in any glass firmly held by the putty. Give it, and the glazing bars, a coat of gold size inside and out, making sure that the corners, where glass and wood meet, are well covered. Press thick sheets of Cellophane on to the coated glass, both inside and out, pressing them well into the corners. Then, when the gold size is dry—usually after an hour or so—varnish the Cellophane, using a very soft brush and a thin varnish.

If the glazing bars have been blown out you cannot, of course, do this, but you can keep out wind and rain by covering the damaged window with Sisalkraft (a tough, waterproof material). Cut the material to size, allowing 1 in. extra all round. Starting at the top, fold about an inch of the material under, to reinforce the edge, and then fasten with small clout nails. (Don't use tin-tacks for this job; their heads are too small.) Fasten down the sides in the same way, doing about a foot on one side and then the same length on the other and so on, all the way down—it is easy to avoid wrinkles by this means. Fasten the bottom edge last.

If you can obtain laths to nail over the edges, and another for down the centre, so much the better. Use 1-in. french nuts for fastening them.

For metal casement windows obtain a sheet of Steadoglass (a strong waterproof fabric which lets through a good deal of light) about 1 in. larger all round than that part of the window which opens. With the window just ajar slip the fabric between the window and the frame from the outside, cutting nicks in it where the hinges come. Almost close the window, and from inside pull the edges of the glass substitute until all the wrinkles disappear, then shut the window tight. With a sharp knife or old safety-razor blade remove the surplus material to obtain a neat finish. You will not, of course, be able to open the window, but it will, at least, be weatherproof.

To Mend a Leaking Roof.—A flat lead or zinc roof that has been damaged by shell splinters, or has deteriorated from age, is not difficult to repair. Probably your roof has a skylight, so it will be comparatively easy to gain access to the damaged part, but choose a dry day for the

Cover broken window panes with Cellophane. It lets in light and makes them waterproof. It is quite easy to fix

work. First, clean around the hole and paint with pitch and tar in equal parts, previously heated together in an old can. With a piece of slate or glass cover the hole, pressing well down. Then give the patch a thick coat of the mixture. Make sure that the roof is really dry, and that the edges of the patches are well covered.

If a large area is letting in water, but there is no definite hole, clean off all dust and dirt, make sure that the roof is not damp, and give a coat of tar, hot if possible. Then cover the tarred area with Sisalcraft, or even brown paper. Now give another thick coat of tar, especially round the edges.

Electrical Repairs—Flexes and Fuses.—Although in most houses where current is available, there is at least one electrical appliance in use, apart from the lighting system, it is amazing how many women have no idea at all of how to tackle the simple problem of a blown fuse, or how to mend a faulty flex.

When trouble occurs, instead of immediately sending for the electrician, try first to find out just what has happened. If, for instance, your electric iron or vacuum cleaner suddenly refuses to work, although the electric lights switch on quite satisfactorily, you will know that either (1) a fuse has "blown" or (2) your apparatus has a defect. To find out which, it is a good plan to try another piece of apparatus on the same plug, i.e., plug an iron into the point that the vacuum cleaner won't run from, or vice versa. If other appliances work from the plug, then the fuse must be intact and it is the appliance that is at fault—probably a defect in the flex. If, on the other hand, other apparatus won't work from this plug, but will from another one, then the fuse has blown and must be replaced.

A fuse is a sort of safety valve in an electric circuit. It is a piece of

Every woman should know how to mend a flex and carry out simple household electrical repairs without outside help

Odd Job Man

by the Good Housekeeping Institute Engineer

wire that melts much more easily than the rest of the wiring in the house and, having melted, allows no more current to flow.

This wire is held in china holders with a metal clip at each end and screws to fasten the fuse wire in position. The metal clip makes contact with the rest of the wiring in the circuit. Usually the fuses are in a wooden box, a separate one for each floor of the house, and are often to be found in a passage or cupboard, not necessarily near the meter.

When replacing the fuse, first of all—and this is very important—switch off the main switch (always located near the meter). Then pull the fuse wire holders out of the spring clip, one at a time, and examine the wire. If the wire is in a hollow part of the holder, very gently pull the exposed ends with a pin or needle. Any break will then be evident. Two fuses may have blown together, so go through all of them, to make sure.

Having removed the holder with the blown wire, undo the fixing screws and replace the melted wire with a new piece of wire of the correct thickness. This is usually marked on the porcelain holder or on the fuse board, and it is as well to keep a card of wire, obtainable from any electrician's, always in readiness. Be careful to tighten the fixing screws on the wire, and then replace the fuse holder in the box. Then, and then only, switch on the main switch.

When you renew fuses, don't put in fuse wires of capacity greater than that stamped on the fuse-holder. Five-amp. wire is all that you need in a lighting circuit, and 15-amp. wire in circuits feeding portable apparatus.

To Mend a Flex.—If the fuse blows directly you switch on the apparatus again, look for a defect in the flex lead.

Remember the three following simple rules if you attempt to repair a flex:

1. Always remove the plug from the wall socket before you start the repair.

2. Be sure that the wire that goes to the larger pin of the wall socket plug is connected to the bare metal of the appliance. It is called the "earth" wire. Its purpose is to blow the fuse if any defect in the insulation of the appliance should arise. Usually, but not always, it is either white or yellow. Never leave this wire unconnected at either end. If you are using an appliance that has only two wires connected to it you should call in an expert electrician to make sure that it is safe.

3. Don't remove more of the rubber sheathing round each separate wire than is necessary. Don't pull or cut the rubber off level with the end of the outside braid. Half an inch of exposed wire is sufficient. Make sure that the spiral cotton threads are scraped off the wire before clamping it under the contact screws.

It is not difficult to patch a leaking roof, and it will save damage to your rooms by rain till skilled help becomes available

Once you have mastered the art of soldering, there are many small repairs that can be carried out at home, saving money and time

Soldering at Home.—It is going to be increasingly difficult to buy new hardware, but you can easily mend a leaky bath or pail yourself, if you are prepared to take a little trouble.

If you intend to try your hand at soldering, obtain a tin of a reliable make of flux paste and a stick of tinman's solder. Use a soldering iron, not a hot poker. Don't use so-called "cold solders" on pots or pans, or on a flat surface that comes in contact with the floor or sink.

The soldering iron must have a coating of solder on it before you start. If it is a new iron and not coated with solder—"tinned" is the term used—you must first of all tin the iron. Clean the point of the iron with a file or emery paper, dip into the Fluxite or other flux, and make hot— *not red-hot,* just enough to melt the solder when it is rubbed on. Now clean the article to be repaired by rubbing and scraping thoroughly with emery cloth until bright metal appears all round the part to be soldered. Smear on a little flux, momentarily dip the point of the hot soldering iron in flux, and rub it round and round the area to be repaired. When the cleaned surface has an even coating of solder, and not until then, you should melt more solder on to it from the stick.

If two surfaces are to be joined, both must be treated in this way; then with a really hot iron—again not red-hot—melt the solder along the edge of the join; the heat will soon travel to the inner parts. Keep the surfaces well pressed together, and don't release the pressure until the solder is quite set.

If you are mending a small leak, and not joining surfaces, use a cooler iron, and build up a slight mound of solder.

Aluminium cannot be soldered with ordinary solder, and any attempt to do so is foredoomed to failure.

She's always certain OF ROMANCE

"Evening in Paris" Powder gives her skin a soft and youthful finish that is irresistible. "Evening in Paris" Perfume surrounds her with a lingering fragrance which never fails to attract.

You can now get the Perfume in a new 2/6 size, and remember there is a whole range of Beauty Preparations, all delicately perfumed with . . .

Evening in Paris

PERFUME
1/3 to 21/-
POWDER
1/- and 1/9
Hair Cream - 1/6
Brilliantine - 1/6

☆ **BOURJOIS** ☆

Accessory Sense

So many of you nowadays are writing to ask, " What accessories shall I choose to give a fresh look to my last year's clothes ? " that I am going to give a few hints which I trust you will find generally helpful.

Rule 1.

Start with your leather accessories, i.e. shoes and bag. Unless you have a separate set for each outfit, which is rare these days, be sure that you choose your leather accessories in a shade that will go with several ensembles. For instance, do not choose navy shoes to go with a saxe blue suit if you have a black coat, or light brown accessories for your camel coat if they must do duty with your wine dress.

Rule 2.

Choose leather accessories of a type that will go with outfits of various degrees of formality. Very " chunky " shoes of light ice calf with thick crêpe rubber soles will look grand with tweeds, but definitely out of place with a silk afternoon dress. If you have got some smart shoes that you can save up for your dresses, get the heavy brogues for every day, by all means, but if not choose instead leather-soled shoes with medium heels and a less aggressively " country " look, that will appear unobtrusive, if not chic, on all occasions.

Rule 3.

Don't choose bright, hard colours, of which you will easily tire, for accessories that must last a long time. For instance, red is a smart accent to grey or navy, but it is better used for gloves, a scarf, a belt or a hat trimming, than for a complete hat or shoes.

Use this chart as a guide when planning colour schemes

Leather accessories	Costume and coat shades	Etceteras (also frock or sweater)	Hat
Navy	Navy	Yellow, claret or scarlet. Mid blues or green, or navy	Navy (plain or trimmed etcetera colour)
Navy	Grey	Ditto	Grey or navy (plain or trimmed etcetera colour)
Navy	Camel	Bright red, green or navy	Camel or navy

(Costumes and coats of any of the " etcetera " shades mentioned above are also good with navy leather accessories. In such cases hat and etceteras should be of navy, matching the main outfit, or in a paler or darker shade of the same tone.)

Leather accessories	Costume and coat shades	Etceteras (also frock or sweater)	Hat
Black	Black	Any bright or pastel shade and wines, or black (not browns or navies)	Black (plain or trimmed etcetera colour) or matching etcetera
Black	Any bright or pastel shade, and wines, but not browns or navies	Matching, or toning, or contrasting with the costume colour (i.e. mid and lighter blue, with wine; green with beetroot) or black	Matching the costume or etcetera, or black
Wine	Navy or grey	Pastel blue, soft pink, grey, wine or navy	Wine or navy, plain or trimmed with etcetera colour and navy or wine
Wine	Mid blues, dirty pinks	Matching costume, or soft contrast, or wine	Matching costume, or wine (trimmed etcetera shade or wine)
Chestnut brown (or London tan): or ice calf	Chestnut or camel	Any bright or pastel shade except the cyclamen or cerise family or navy	Matching costume and leather accessories, or matching etcetera, plain or trimmed etcetera or costume colour
Chestnut brown	Navy or grey	Navy or chestnut or grey	Navy or chestnut, plain or trimmed reverse shade
Ice calf	Navy	Green, mid blues, camel or navy	Navy or etcetera colour, plain or trimmed reverse

(Costumes or coats of green, mid blues and wines, are also good with ice calf accessories, and green or mid blue with chestnut. Hats and etceteras should match costume or the leather accessories.)

Leather accessories	Costume and coat shades	Etceteras (also frock or sweater)	Hat
Rust and brown	Matching browns or rust	Green, pastel or mid blues, yellows, coral pink, camel	Brown or rust, plain or trimmed etcetera shades
Rust and brown	Green, pastel or mid blues, yellows, coral pink or camel	Matching brown or rust	Brown or rust, plain or trimmed etcetera shades

"When he grows up, I hope . . ."

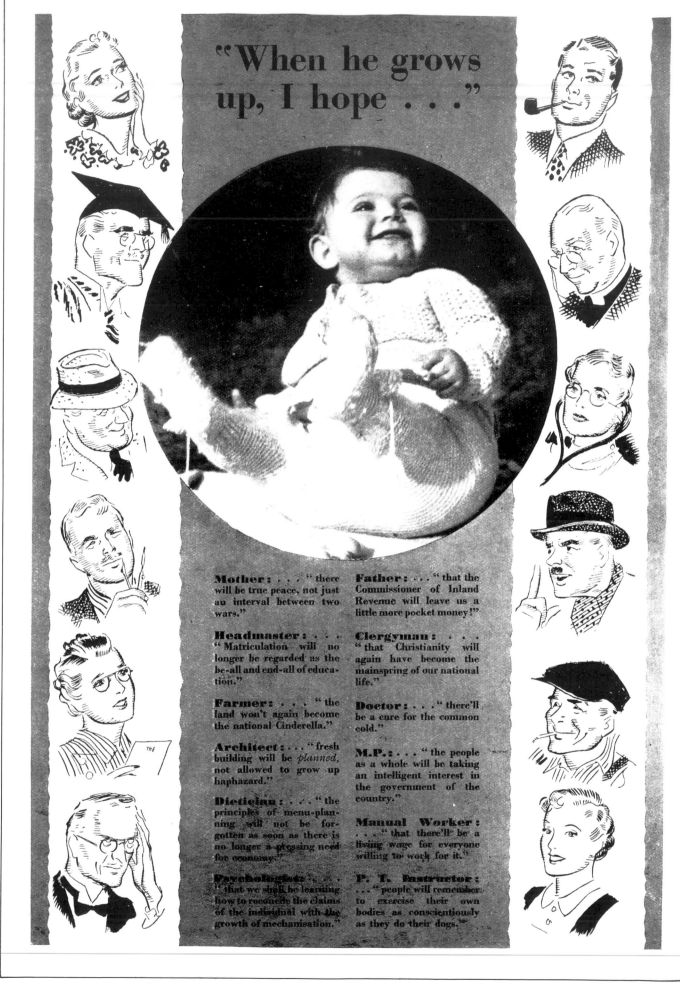

Mother: . . . " there will be true peace, not just an interval between two wars."

Headmaster: . . . "Matriculation will no longer be regarded as the be-all and end-all of education."

Farmer: . . . " the land won't again become the national Cinderella."

Architect: . . . "fresh building will be *planned*, not allowed to grow up haphazard."

Dietician: . . . " the principles of menu-planning will not be forgotten as soon as there is no longer a pressing need for economy."

Psychologist: . . . " that we shall be learning how to reconcile the claims of the individual with the growth of mechanisation."

Father: . . . " that the Commissioner of Inland Revenue will leave us a little more pocket money!"

Clergyman: . . . " that Christianity will again have become the mainspring of our national life."

Doctor: . . . " there'll be a cure for the common cold."

M.P.: . . . " the people as a whole will be taking an intelligent interest in the government of the country."

Manual Worker: . . . " that there'll be a living wage for everyone willing to work for it."

P. T. Instructor: . . . "people will remember to exercise their own bodies as conscientiously as they do their dogs."